Readings in Extraversion-Introversion
1

Theoretical and Methodological Issues

Readings in Extraversion-Introversion

---

1. THEORETICAL AND METHODOLOGICAL ISSUES
2. FIELDS OF APPLICATION
3. BEARINGS ON BASIC PSYCHOLOGICAL PROCESSES

Theoretical and Methodological Issues

Edited by

H. J. EYSENCK
PH.D., D.SC.

Professor of Psychology, University of London

STAPLES PRESS · LONDON

First published 1970 by Staples Press Ltd
3 Upper James Street Golden Square London W1
Printed in Great Britain by
C. Tinling & Co Ltd, Prescot and London

ISBN 0 286 61858 3

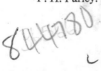

To G. Heymans,
Founder of Modern Personality Theory
and Research

ACKNOWLEDGEMENTS

Grateful acknowledgement for permission to reprint the articles in this volume is made to the following:

The editors of: *Acta Psychologica*, the *American Journal of Orthopsychiatry*, the *Australian Journal of Psychology*, *Behaviour Research and Therapy*, the *British Journal of Educational Psychology*, the *British Journal of Psychology*, the *British Journal of Social and Clinical Psychology*, the *Bulletin de Psychologie*, *Child Development*, *Educational and Psychological Measurement*, the *Educational Review*, the *Journal of Abnormal and Social Psychology*, the *Journal of Applied Psychology*, the *Journal of Clinical Psychology*, the *Journal of Consulting Psychology*, the *Journal of Criminal Law and Criminology*, the *Journal of Educational Psychology*, the *Journal of Personality*, the *Journal of Psychology*, *Life Sciences*, *Multivariate Behavioral Research*, *Psychological Reports*, *Revista de Psicologia*, the *Wiener Zeitschrift für Philosophie, Psychologie und Pädagogik*, the *Zeitschrift für Experimentalle und Angewandte Psychologie*, and to G. Becker, J. Bliss, J. R. Braun, R. B. Cattell, S. Dunn, V. Z. Ehrlich, S. B. G. Eysenck, F. H. Farley, S. V. Farley, G. Forlano, A. Gilliland, B. J. Gomez, R. L. Gorsuch, J. A. Gray, J. P. Guilford, R. B. Guilford, H. J. Hallworth, H. P. Hildebrand, F. Hillinger, J-M. Lemaine, W. McDougall, C. M. Michael, E. Mittenecker, D. P. Morris, D. R. Peterson, J. Ross, M. Siegelman, E. Siipola, E. Soroker, N. H. Sparrow, L. J. Stricker, I. A. Syed and F. T. Vingoe.

A*

CONTENTS

SECTION ONE: HISTORICAL AND THEORETICAL

SECTION TWO: INTERNAL VALIDITY

Contents

Contents

Il n'y a pas de théories fausses et de théories vraies,
il y a des théories fécondes et des théories stériles.

CLAUDE BERNARD

SECTION ONE

Historical and Theoretical

HISTORICAL INTRODUCTION

IN 1947 I published my first book, *Dimensions of Personality* (Ref. 1), and in doing so took under my wing a most unattractive old thing with a caricature of a face—to wit, the concept of extraversion-introversion. In the long story of the development of the notions which finally crystallized into this conception there had never been a time when it had reached a lower point; the war years constituted a nadir from which most psychologists felt it would never rise again. To many, if not most, psychologists interested in personality it seemed as if I had attempted to resurrect a corpse—equivalent, perhaps, to trying to reintroduce into physics the notions of phlogiston, or aether, or a geocentric planetary system. This had many disadvantages, which will be only too obvious; no one wanted to read about extraversion, no one wanted to support research into this field, no one wanted to reconsider problems which were thought to be closed once and for all. But there were also compensating advantages, which may not be so obvious. Research is a rat race in which it is easy to fall behind; when you are the only one in the race you are left in peace to fashion your own theories, carry out your own researches, and reach your own conclusions without having to look over your shoulder constantly to see if others are catching up with you and perhaps overtaking you. If progress was slow, at least it was not forced; other researchers rode off in many other directions, often at much greater speeds, but it seemed possible that perhaps the right direction was more important than the greater speed.

In 1957, with the publication of *The Dynamics of Anxiety and Hysteria* (Ref. 2) the pace began to quicken. In this book I tried to take one step further the purely descriptive, factor analytic work that had formed the basis of my studies until then, and to attempt a theoretical unification of the experimental field in terms of concepts like inhibition and excitation, borrowed from learning theory—in particular, from Pavlov and Hull. Now other workers began to come into the field, and many reports appeared which confirmed—or, more frequently, disconfirmed—the hypotheses which I had worked out. Clearly the theory, while it might be on the right lines, was still quite inadequate to do justice to the known facts, or to make possible unambiguous prediction of facts hitherto unknown. Consequently work was begun on a third model, which saw the light in 1967 under the title of *The Biological Basis of Personality*

3

(Ref. 5); it is believed that this model is more satisfactory than either of the earlier ones, although of course still much in need of improvement, and in due course destined for the scrap-heap when it has served its purpose of stimulating sufficient research to make clearer its imperfections. This third model takes the notions of excitation and inhibition, which were previously used in a purely psychological sense, and attempts to translate them into physiological terms; this effort to link up with recent work on arousal and the reticular formation has made it possible to explain many previously inexplicable findings.

This book of readings was put together to enable readers to find under one cover the most important articles relating to any of the many facets of this topic—pure and applied, psychometric and experimental, theoretical and empirical. A few articles have been included for their historical interest, such as McDougall's famous 1926 paper, but most are recent and represent as it were the growing points of this now rapidly expanding subject. Some degree of order has been imposed on the unwieldy mass of reports spewed forth by the presses every month, and an effort has been made to clarify issues by writing a short introduction to each section; but as always in collections of readings the reader may find the clash of styles and contents, inevitable as it is, less appealing than a single book written by a single person. There are of course advantages in the latter, and possibly my *The Structure of Human Personality* (Ref. 3) may fulfil this role; I am mentioning this book in order to demonstrate that the choice of a set of readings was not due entirely to laziness on my part. A book written by any one author inevitably imposes his own views and prejudices on the material; even the evaluation and abstraction of the articles mentioned by him may be slanted— however unwillingly and unconsciously—in the direction of supporting his own views. A collection of readings presents the original data, as well as their evaluation by the original author, and thus inevitably gives the reader a chance to compare different theories, different intepretations, and different conceptions. The gentle art of persuasion has little to work on in a case like this, and the reader is left to form his own conclusions much more than in the case of a single-author summary of research.

Of course, this presupposes some reasonably objective scheme for selecting the readings; what have been my criteria for inclusion? They have been fairly numerous, and the weighting of different considerations is of course to some degree arbitrary. It seems wise to spell them out in some detail, so that the reader may be alerted to possible prejudices. In the first place, emphasis was laid on experimental adequacy; in this field of personality research standards are well known to be much laxer than in experimental psychology proper, and it seemed desirable to exclude studies not up to the mark in this respect. What remains (excepting those articles included for historical interest as previously mentioned) does, I believe, demonstrate that there is no inherent reason for this unfortunate laxity, and that personality research can be every bit as rigorous as research in other areas of experimental psychology.

In the second place, emphasis was laid on theoretical relevance; again, personality research has often been compared unfavourably with experimental psychology because of the vagueness of its theories, and the lack of rigorous linking of theory and experiment. It seems that in recent years there has been a distinct improvement in this situation, and while still unsatisfactory, it may perhaps be agreed that the most recent articles at least show a striking improvement in the rigour with which theory and experiment have been linked. It seems likely that the next few years will show even more improvement in this respect also.

In the third place, an attempt has been made to cover as wide an area as possible. Perusal of the book will show to what extent this endeavour has been successful; certainly the topics dealt with range over a wide ground. This third aim has at times conflicted with the other two; areas of greatest experimental competence and theoretical relevance would have given rise to too many articles to make inclusion possible, and some of those reprinted from other areas for the sake of wider coverage are clearly inferior with respect to both these primary considerations. There is no way out of this dilemma, other than an all-round improvement of technical competence and theory-directed endeavour; all that can be done at present is to state the dilemma and try to effect the best possible compromise. It would certainly not have been a solution to reprint articles only in the specifically experimental area, and not to include papers from the industrial or educational spheres; a book of readings must be reasonably comprehensive, and show the whole portrait, warts and all—although it may be excused for drawing attention to the warts!

A fourth consideration has led to exclusions, rather than to inclusions. An attempt has been made to exclude papers with negative results, or papers which served merely to contradict some specific theory or other. The reason for this policy is easy to see. In many cases, a good experiment has put paid to a theoretical notion; this is interesting, but if this theoretical notion is now of no importance, then neither is the article which chronicles the slaying of this particular dragon. Consequently it seemed better to leave it out, hard as that may be on the author. In many other cases, the alleged slaying turns out to involve a man of straw; a theory has been misinterpreted, and the experiment does not in fact have much to do with the theory as enunciated. I once put forward the hypothesis that eye-blink conditioning would under certain conditions (e.g. partial reinforcement) favour introverts over extraverts; several psychologists 'tested' and 'disproved' this hypothesis by means of experiments using total (i.e. 100 per cent) reinforcement. There seemed to be little point in reprinting such papers and explaining in detail why the 'disproof' was in fact irrelevant. Rightly or wrongly, concentration has been on papers reporting positive results with a high degree of statistical probability; usually, but not always, these results have been replicated or at least supported by material not reprinted here. In the early stages of growth of a scientific theory, such positive results are to my mind of much greater importance than negative ones unless the latter are in some way crucial; I have discussed this point at some length in *Experiments in Personality* (Ref. 4).

A fifth consideration has been to include a small but carefully selected number of historical papers whose present-day importance is not perhaps too high but which clarify the development of certain conceptions or which have played an important part in this development. Papers written before the Second World War mostly fall into this category, and for them the rigorous standards applied to more recent papers have been lowered. Some readers may not share my interest in the historical development of these concepts, theories and experiments but others, I hope, will find them relevant and important. In any case, I have only included a few because the number of first-rate experimental studies published in recent years obviously had first claim; nevertheless, I did not have the heart to cut them all out.

Altogether, I believe that an adequate understanding of the problems in this field, and the attempted solutions as well, is impossible without some knowledge of the history and the development of the psychological theories of personality. There are roughly speaking twelve periods of development, each associated with an outstanding personality whose work marked a definite advance; it may be useful if these twelve advances are defined in some detail. It is often said that psychology has a long past, but a short history; this is equally true of the study of personality. The moment when intuitive understanding, philosophical speculation and clinical intuition, which constituted the past, gave way to experimental study, psychological theory, and psychometric analysis can be defined more easily here than in most other areas of psychology; the turning point is associated with the extremely original and fundamental work of a man whose very name is probably unknown to most psychologists, even those who are actively working in the field of personality study. This man was the Dutch philosopher and psychologist G. Heymans (1857–1930) who published his views and results in book form in 1929 (Ref. 9) but who had written his fundamental papers (with E. Wiersma and H. Brugmans) some 20 years earlier. To him, appropriately, this book is dedicated; we shall see in a minute just why it is he, rather than others who are more often named and who are better known to psychologists, who may be said to mark the transition point from unscientific past to scientific history.

The story begins—if the human search for an understanding of personality, individual differences, temperamental peculiarities and other deviations from the strictly average sort of behaviour can in any real sense be said to have a 'beginning'—with Galen, a Greek physician who lived in the second century A.D. and who is widely credited with the enunciation of the doctrine of the four temperaments. The melancholic, the choleric, the sanguine and the phlegmatic, shorn of the associated theory of the 'humours' which were believed to cause their striking differences, have passed into every-day language, and the man in the street still uses these phrases in characterizing certain 'types' of behaviour. As we shall see, the theory of extraversion-introversion is intimately connected with this ancient theory, laughable only to those who do not realize that it embodies a large slice of excellent clinical observation, without which it would never have been accepted, or have lasted longer than any other psychological theory. This is not the place to go into the vexed question of Galen's originality in this respect, or to discuss possible prior claims of Hippocrates and others; I am not sufficiently expert to discuss these questions, and for the purposes of this book they are not of too great importance. The reader interested in the early development of these theories may with confidence turn to A. A. Roback's *Psychology of Character* (Ref. 12).

The second chapter of our story opens with the contribution made by the great German philosopher and scientist Immanuel Kant in his book on *Anthropologie* (Ref. 10), which was a kind of text-book of psychology, and in which he brought up-to-date the doctrine of the four temperaments and popularized it and made it acceptable to philosophers, physicians, theologists and other learned men concerned with human personality. Eysenck & Eysenck (Ref. 6) have translated his descriptions of the traits characterizing the four temperaments, and have drawn attention to the close relationship between these descriptions and the results of modern factor-analytic work in this field; they also point out that the main difference between his views and more modern ones lies in his categorical conception of 'types' as being unchangeable and pure. A person belongs to one of these four groups; he cannot change his position, and there are no intermediate degrees. This notion of 'types' has been rightly criticized by modern American writers, but unfortunately they ascribe such views to more recent writers than Kant—writers who in fact do not hold them, like Jung and Kretschmer.

Modern typology parts company with Kant in this respect, and the person who took this important step of translating categorical types into continuous dimensions, and who thus marks our third epoch, was none other than W. Wundt. His contribution is discussed in some detail in one of the papers reprinted in section one of this book, and little need therefore be said here other than that he pointed out that cholerics and sanguinics both shared the characteristic of being *changeable*, while phlegmatics and melancholics were *unchangeable*; substitute 'extravert' and 'introvert' for changeable and unchangeable, and our modern theory (in its descriptive aspects) is born. Add that he considered a second dimension (emotionality—nowadays often labelled neuroticism, or instability) to be formed by the two emotional temperaments, i.e. the choleric and the melancholic, as opposed to the other two, who were considered by him unemotional, and you have a two-dimensional description, continuously variable, of personality, very much as it is given by recent writings of Cattell, Guilford, or the present writer. Wundt, like Heymans, is seldom if ever mentioned by English-speaking writers on personality, in spite of his very important contribution. (Ebbinghaus, too, wrote along rather similar lines.)

The fourth great contribution comes from O. Gross, a Viennese physician who attempted to give a physiological basis to the personality dimension of extraversion-introversion (not then so called, of course; Gross wrote at the beginning of the present century). He conceptualized mental and emotional processes in terms of a primary function, subserving sensation and perception, and a secondary function, which subserved the perseveration of primary processes; individuals differed according to the length of the secondary process—introverts had a long, extraverts a short secondary process. He showed in fascinating detail how this conception (which tied up with the newly proclaimed theories of perseveration of the memory trace, by Müller and Pilzecker) could be used to account for the personality traits of the two types posited. His physiology is of course entirely speculative, as he himself recognized; it is fascinating to see how he (and later on McDougall in a paper reprinted in section one) tried to invent something akin to the Ascending Reticular Activating System, and how both succeeded in describing (by deduction from behaviour) something which at that time was far beyond the ken of physiologists and neurologists. Truly, if the reticular formation had not been discovered, it had certainly been invented by psychologists anticipating later developments!

We come now to the fifth epoch, and to G. Heymans and his colleagues. His contribution is threefold, and in each of his innovations he anticipated a large and important area of research.

(1) *Psychometric.* Heymans was the first to realize the importance of quantifying the implicit relationships between traits which had served earlier writers; where they simply observed and noted subjectively 'what goes with what' (in Spearman's phrase), he suggested the use of correlational methods, and worked out a very crude and elementary, but nevertheless useful, coefficient of association. He also worked out methods of grouping such correlations, thus in essence anticipating factor analysis. He was not a gifted mathematician, and curiously enough rejected product-moment correlation coefficients for quite the wrong reasons, but he did have an intuitive understanding of the logical requirements of mathematical analysis, and pioneered what are now widely used methods.

(2) *Experimental.* He was perhaps the first to realize that observation of every-day behaviour is not sufficient to build a science of personality on, and he carried out experimental studies to measure individual differences in behaviour; these are perhaps the first properly to deserve the name of 'experiments in personality'—Galton's studies, to take but one example that seems to disprove this generalization, were not experimental in the laboratory sense.

(3) *Hypothetico-deductive method.* He realized that science is intimately tied to the use of the hypothetico-deductive method, except perhaps in its first, tentative steps, and he linked the theories of Gross with his psychometric work and his experiments into a nomological network, to use a term which would have been new to him, but the implications of which were apparent in his work. These three major contributions entitle him to be called the father of experimental personality research; unfortunately his writings are widely dispersed and do not lend themselves to reproduction in this volume, but a description, with quota-

tions, of his work has been given in *The Structure of Human Personality* (Ref. 3).

The next claimant for a place in our company of immortals is C. G. Jung, whose contribution to personality study is often misinterpreted. C. Spearman, in his classic *Abilities of Man* (Ref. 12), sums up the work of Heymans, Wiersma and Brugmans by saying:

> So far as scientific status is concerned, this Dutch work stands upon a very high plane. In it mere casual observations—shown over and over again to be grossly misleading—are replaced by most careful and systematic investigations.

He goes on to characterize Jung with equal insight:

> Ideas substantially the same as those mentioned above re-appeared not long afterwards in the work of Jung. But the arduous scientific research of his predecessors . . . now gives way to attractive literary embellishment.

Jung is often credited with giving a long list of other writers who preceded him in delineating his types of extraversion and introversion; it is interesting that although these types are so very similar to Heymans' carefully researched strong and weak secondary function types, yet Heymans is never mentioned—in spite of the fact that much of his work was published in German, and must have been familiar to Jung. If Jung's descriptions are not original, neither is his use of the terms extraversion and introversion; these had been used in European writings for several hundred years before him. His main claim to originality must be his suggestion that extraversion was linked with the hysterical group of neurotic disorders, introversion with the psychasthenic group (dysthymia—anxiety, reactive depression, phobias, obsessive-compulsive disorders). There appears to be some truth in this observation, and while the neurotic typology must be credited to Janet rather than to Jung, nevertheless the identification with normal personality types is important in the historical development of the concept.

Related to Jung in that his main concern was with the abnormal counterparts of normal personality types was E. Kretschmer, but his main contribution did not lie in his identification of extraversion ('cyclothymia') with manic-depressive insanity and introversion ('schizothymia') with schizophrenia (Jung too had thought of schizophrenia as being linked with introversion). The evidence does not suggest that schizophrenia does in fact have such a link; several papers are included in this volume demonstrating that such a generalization would not now be acceptable—although it must of course be realized that the term 'schizophrenia' means many things to many people, and that its use in modern Anglo-American psychiatry may not be identical with its use in German-speaking circles fifty years ago. However that may be, Kretschmer's continuing fame rests on his insistence on the importance of constitutional factors, and on his insight into the relationship between leptomorphic bodybuild and introversion. While again the evidence regarding bodybuild and insanity, on which he insisted so strongly, is at best inconclusive, there seems to be no doubt that in the normal field at least a relationship of the kind postulated by him exists—although much weaker than he (and Sheldon, who took up his system with minor modifications) believed. Correlations of 0·4 or thereabouts are the most that can be expected when the elementary errors in conducting such experiments which disfigure his and even more Sheldon's work are rectified. (Both Kretschmer and Sheldon contaminated their judgement of temperament and of diagnosis by knowledge of bodybuild of the subjects of their studies; this contamination produced unacceptably high correlations often exceeding the reliabilities of the ratings involved! Furthermore, Kretschmer took little trouble to partial out the effects of age; later work has shown this to be essential.) But constitutional factors are important, as we shall see, and Kretschmer was the first to insist on their importance.

The pace now quickens, and our epochs begin to overlap. After Jung, the next great writer to be noted is perhaps C. Spearman, the founder of the London School—a 'school to end schools', as he once put it, in an attempt to crystallize his belief that the method of factor analysis, which he introduced into psychology, was capable of substituting objective, quantitative fact for subjective, intuitive belief. Through his students (Webb, Garnett, Oates) and his collaborators and successors (notably Burt, Stephenson and Cattell) he exerted a profound influence, and while history remembers him more for his work in intelligence measurement, we must note here that he was the first to demonstrate the existence of the two factors, strictly defined and measured, of emotionality-neuroticism ('w' in his terminology) and of extraversion-introversion ('c' in his terminology). He also tried to elaborate experimental tests of perseveration, with which to measure these personality traits; these were unsuccessful, possibly because he and his students were thinking in terms of psychometric group tests, not in terms of experimental laboratory examinations, given to one person at a time. Whatever the defects of his work, viewed from the vantage point of hindsight, his contribution, substantive and methodological, was crucial in transplanting the Dutch work to English soil.

The contribution of our ninth great figure, J. P. Guilford, can best be understood in terms of the problem which he set out to solve. Briefly, the situation may be summarized by saying that the success of the Woodworth Neuroticism questionnaire, and the appearance of the English translation of Jung's book, inspired many psychologists in the U.S.A. to produce questionnaires of neuroticism and introversion respectively. The essentially subjective method used of picking out items and combining them in an essentially arbitrary fashion guaranteed that these 'measuring instruments' measured nothing in particular, and when it was found that neuroticism inventories intercorrelated only about 0·3, while neuroticism and introversion inventories showed correlations of equal size, it was concluded that this whole approach had been a failure. The bitter taste of this failure survived for a long time, without realization that it was not due to any faults in theoretical conceptualization or in the principle of questionnaire construction but rather to inadequacies in the make-up of these particular questionnaires. It is easy to see this now but at the time many psychologists vowed never again to use personality inventories and never again to think in terms of introversion-extraversion; in many cases this vow survived the Second World War and is only slowly losing its compulsive force. Guilford's great contribution was the realization that the intercorrelations between inventory items, and the factor analysis of these intercorrelations, constitute indispensable steps in the isolation of stable personality factors and the construction of suitable questionnaires; his pioneering work is suitably recognized by the inclusion in this book of one of his early papers. Guilford also contributed experimental studies which at the time were outstanding examples of the laboratory approach to personality study. If the findings were largely negative this was perhaps inevitable at the particular stage of development reached at that time by both personality theory and experimental psychology.

Our tenth author is the Russian writer B. M. Teplov, who has taken up the Pavlovian teaching with respect to the 'strong' and 'weak' nervous system, and has built upon this an impressive series of experimental studies of individual differences, ably recounted in English by J. Gray (Ref. 8). It has always seemed to me that Teplov's 'weak nervous system' is analogous to the introverted type, his ' strong nervous system' to the extraverted type; hence his inclusion in this list. A lengthy discussion of the points of similarity and difference between the two typologies by J. Gray is included in volume one of this book, so no more needs to be said on this point. It may be worth while, however, to point out the novelty and interest of many of the techniques pioneered by the Russian workers. The stereotyped choice by Western psychologists of such obviously poor measuring instruments as the Rorschach or the M.M.P.I. when called upon to investigate personality traits is put to shame by the inventive genius of the Moscow group. Perhaps only Cattell escapes this censure on our side of the fence, because he, too, has attempted (with considerable success) to break out of the bear-hug of tradition. The Russian work, too, has its weaknesses, of course, and these may loom larger to psychometric readers than its strengths but Teplov's successors are taking great strides to eliminate these weaknesses and the immediate future may benefit greatly from cross-fertilization.

We are now nearing the present day, and the work of our next exponent is still very much in progress. (Guilford, too, is of course still active at this writing, but his interest has shifted to the study of cognitive dimensions and originality.) R. B. Cattell has transferred the traditions of the London School to American soil, and has combined exceptional mastery of statistical techniques of multiple factor analysis with large-scale empirical studies employing ratings and self-ratings, and objective, experimental and physiological measurements of the most varied groups. This work goes well beyond the confines of our interests here but it should be noted that in all his groups the two factors (usually extracted as higher-order factors derived from the intercorrelations between oblique primary factors) of extraversion-introversion and neuroticism (called 'anxiety' by him) emerge more clearly and strongly than any others. As undoubtedly the foremost living exponent of the factor-analytic approach, this constant verification of the fundamental descriptive hypothesis on which much of the material in this book is based is most valuable and welcome, and the large area of factual agreement between him, Guilford, and the present writer on this point has been factually documented in great detail (Ref. 7).

Last, least, and only after much hesitation the writer would place his own contribution. In essence, what he has tried to do has been a continuation of the three-fold approach of the Dutch school, as adapted by Spearman and made by him a characteristic of the London school. Our psychometric work has been summarized extensively, with much new material, in *The Description and Measurement of Personality* (Ref. 6). Our experimental work has been similarly summarized in *The*

Dynamics of Anxiety and Hysteria (Ref. 2) and later papers and writings. Our hypothetico-deductive approach can best be studied in *The Biological Basis of Personality* (Ref. 5), in which an attempt is made to deduce extravert-introvert differences in behaviour, both social and in the laboratory, in terms of differences in cortical arousal, mediated by the reticular formation. The success of these efforts is still too doubtful, and the work itself too recent, to comment on it in any detail; the reader will be able to judge for himself after perusal of the relevant articles reprinted in this volume.

Thirty years of work in this neck of the woods, and careful reading of documents straddling 2,000 years of historical development, have given rise to some general impressions which may be useful to newcomers to this field. In the first place, there is a strong feeling of historical continuity. Galen's and Kant's observations do not strike the modern observer as ridiculous and outmoded; our own work may be more extensive, better controlled and statistically more defensible, but it is recognizably a development of ideas mooted all these centuries ago. Gross's and Heymans' speculations about physiological mechanism have little factual substratum, but they are not out of line with what we now know about the structure of the cortico-reticular arousal loop, and its functioning. Spearman's and Guilford's early factorial studies are now very out-dated, but modern methods, aided by computers, do not give results essentially different from theirs. In fact, what we recognize throughout this historical development is the usual scientific progress, slow, step by step, brick by brick, until finally we arrive, almost by stealth, at a splendid, well-built usable structure. So many hands have made their contribution that it becomes difficult to say: *he* built it. All those who contributed have built it, although some have made a bigger contribution than others.

In the second place, there is a feeling that for a long time contributions were made by single people, or at best small groups; others were slow to take up the contributions made. Heymans' work has been followed up in Holland, and later in South Africa, but is hardly known elsewhere; even the recent work of Cattell is carried out mostly by his students and fellow-workers, not by the general body of research students. This position is slowly changing; gradually a more general approach is being elaborated in which theories are being tested in different laboratories all over the world.

A third point which may be important is that personality study is beginning to cease to be the prerogative of a small set of psychologists who happen to be interested in individual differences, while the great body of experimental and theoretical psychologists goes its own way, profoundly unmoved by whatever may be going on in this small corner. If extraverts and introverts differ in their habitual arousal level, as well as in their sensory thresholds, orienting reactions, adaptation rates, E.E.G., E.M.G. and G.S.R. response patterns, rates of conditioning, perceptual after-effects, and a thousand and one psychological and physiological measures, then it ceases to be practical for the experimentalist to proclaim his disinterest in 'personality' and relegate individual differences to the error term in his analysis of variance; interaction terms, embodying personality in the form of extravert-introvert differences, become extremely important and should be extracted from any well-planned study, even when personality differences are not the main point of interest. I have discussed this point at some length elsewhere (Ref. 8) and will not insist on it here to any greater length. It is my impression that the lesson is gradually being learned, and that more and more hard-bitten experimentalists are taking individual differences into account.

It is unfortunate in this connection that the terms extraversion and introversion are in many people's minds linked so closely with the putative father of this personality typology, C. G. Jung. From the point of view of scientific study, his contribution has been largely a negative one; by allowing his mystical notions to overshadow the empirical, observational data he has done his best to remove the concept of personality type from the realm of scientific discourse. His extremely complex system, involving four 'functions' arranged in contrasting pairs, all of which can be extraverted or introverted, and which compensate each other in a complex manner in which conscious extraversion may be linked with unconscious introversion, has not found much favour with even his more devoted followers; as he once pointed out when questioned on whether a given person was extraverted or introverted: 'In the last analysis I decide who is an extravert and who is an introvert!' This splendid assertion of faith mirrors Goering's famous statement when someone pointed that his personal favourite, *Luftwaffe* General Milch, was in fact Jewish: 'I decide who is a Jew!', but it will prove somewhat less attractive to scientists who attempt to construct a universal, objective science of personality structure and measurement. Psychologists will have to learn the plain historical fact that the personality types of extraversion and introversion owe very little to Jung, and the sooner this message reaches psychological textbooks, the better.

Publication of this book comes at a moment when the river of publications on extraversion-introversion differences, which until recently was little more than a trickle, is beginning to swell and grow. Even a year or two ago I had little difficulty in keeping track of all the experimental and statistical publications in this field, and indeed to remember them without reference to my index or file. At the moment more new material is being added each year than the total amount of material available a few years ago, and this new material comes from sources one would not have looked to previously—Japan, say, or Austria, or Russia, or Hungary. In ten years' time it will be very difficult for one person to edit such a book with any degree of reassurance that he had in fact examined practically all the worth-while claimants for a place. Until that happy day, this book of readings may serve to give a reasonable impression of the position of extraversion-introversion research, as of the end of 1967.

H.J.E.

REFERENCES

1. EYSENCK, H. J., *Dimensions of Personality*. London: Routledge & Kegan Paul, 1947.
2. ——, *The Dynamics of Anxiety and Hysteria*. London: Routledge & Kegan Paul, 1957.
3. ——, *The Structure of Human Personality*. London: Methuen, 1970 (3rd Edition).
4. —— (ed.), *Experiments in Personality*. London: Routledge & Kegan Paul, 1960.
5. ——, *The Biological Basis of Personality*. Springfield, Ill.: Charles C. Thomas, 1967.
6. ——, and EYSENCK, S. B. G., *The Description and Measurement of Personality*. London: Routledge & Kegan Paul, 1969.
7. —— ,and EYSENCK, S. B. G., On the unitary nature of extraversion, *Acta Psychol.*, 26, 383–390, 1967.
8. GRAY, J. A., *Pavlov's Typology*, Oxford: Pergamon Press, 1964.
9. HEYMANS, G., *Inleiding Tot de Speciale Psychologie*. Harlem: Bohn, 1929.
10. KANT, I., Anthropologie in pragmatischer hinsicht, in *Werke*, Vol. IV. Berlin: Bruno Cassirer, 1912–1918.
11. ROBACK, A. A., *The Psychology of Character*. London: Kegan Paul, 1927.
12. SPEARMAN, C., *The Abilities of Man*. London: Macmillan, 1927.

1

The Chemical Theory of Temperament Applied to Introversion and Extraversion

WILLIAM MCDOUGALL

First published in
Journal of Abnormal and Social Psychology, **24**, 293–309, 1929

WE CAN hardly hope to make progress in the understanding of the differences between one personality and another until we shall have achieved some agreement as to the main classes of constituent factors of personality and some consistency in the terminology we employ in discussing them. We have seen in recent years a number of interesting attempts to distinguish types of personality from the psychiatric point of view. These have, I think, thrown some light on the problems of genesis, especially of psychogenesis, and on the problems of treatment. But all the efforts in this direction with which I am acquainted seem to me to suffer from neglect to distinguish clearly between the main classes of factors that enter into the make-up of personality. They seem to assume that certain types of personality of significance for psychiatry may be distinguished and defined on a single basis, without any prior analysis of the chief classes of constituent factors. In so far all the theories of types seem to me to be at fault.

Personality is extremely complex; it comprises factors of many distinguishable classes. It seems very improbable that individual differences in respect to any one class of factors should be of such overwhelming influence as to swamp the influence of factors of other classes and to render possible a useful scheme of types drawn up on the basis of that one class alone.

I suggest[1] that, if we are to avoid confusion and many cross divisions of types, at least five great classes of factors of personality must be distinguished. For these five classes seem to be, in great measure, though not entirely, independent variables in the make-up of personality; that is to say, the factors of any one of these five classes may be combined

[1] In accordance with the scheme which I have long used in teaching and which is indicated in my *Outline of Psychology* (Ref. 4).

in any one personality with any combination of factors of the other four classes. These five classes are:

(1) The factors of intellect (under which head I include intelligence and knowledge and such peculiarities as retentiveness of memory, types of imagery, etc.).

(2) The factors of disposition (which I conceive to be the array of innately conative or affective tendencies varying widely in their relative strengths from one individual to another).

(3) The factors of temper. These are the least recognized and the most woefully confused and obscured of all by our present chaotic psychological terminology and theory. Yet they are of prime importance in the make-up of personality. I conceive them as general peculiarities of the mode of working of all the conative tendencies or 'drives'[1]; such peculiarities as persistency, urgency or intensity, high affectability by success and failure, and the opposites of these.

(4) Factors of temperament. These may be broadly defined as the influences, direct or indirect, of bodily metabolism (more especially of the endocrine secretions) upon the psycho-physical processes of the nervous system.

(5) Factors of character. These are matters of acquired organization of the affective tendencies in sentiments and complexes, which in turn are organized in great systems or (in well developed character) in one hierarchical system.

These five classes of factors of personality are, it seems to me, largely independent of one another; thus any type of intellect may go with any type of temper, temperament, disposition, or character; and so of each of the others; hence, in order to characterize a personality, we must state its type of intellect, of disposition, of temper, of temperament, and of character. When it is attempted to set up types of personality, as so many have done, without first distinguishing these five main classes of factors, the result inevitably is a mass of false generalizations, exceptions to which are at least as easy to find as conforming instances.

Such inevitable confusion is well illustrated, I suggest, by the efforts of Dr C. G. Jung to define two types called by him the introvert and the extravert types. That Jung is attempting by the use of these terms to point to some deep-lying and very important peculiarities of personality I have no doubt. I have found the distinction between introversion and

---

[1] I am driven to use this unsatisfactory word because it is the only one which will serve to indicate to many possible readers what I am driving at.

extraversion extremely useful, both in theory and in the practical handling of cases of neurotic disorder, and also in understanding normal personalities. And many other workers in the field of abnormal psychology seem to have accepted the distinction and made much use of the terms. Yet I feel sure that Jung has attempted to give too rich a content to the terms. He seems to regard the peculiarities which he seeks to define as temperamental; yet, in describing the two types, he assigns to them peculiarities which are peculiarities of intellect, of disposition, of temper, and of character, as well as of temperament proper.

Jung, accepting William James' famous classification of thinkers as tender minded and tough minded, identifies his introverts with the former and his extraverts with the latter. He thus commits himself to the view that introverts are rationalists and system-makers, who care little for facts and forcibly fit data into their ideal constructions in accordance with their a priori premises; that the extravert, on the other hand, cannot construct a system, is interested not at all in the inner life of man, but only in objective facts, is positivist, determinist, fatalist, irreligious and a sceptic. Jung further identifies his introverts with the 'classics' of Ostwald and his extraverts with Ostwald's 'romantics'; and thus adds to the characteristics of the former as follows: 'They produce with much difficulty, are little capable of teaching or of exercising direct personal influence, and, lacking enthusiasm, are paralysed by their own severe criticism, living apart and absorbed in themselves, making scarcely any disciples, but producing works of finished perfection.'

Jung then chooses as illustrative examples of his two types, Dr Sigmund Freud and Dr Alfred Adler, seeking to explain the peculiarities of their psychological teachings as expressions of extraversion and introversion respectively. Could anything be more unfortunate? Freud, with his lifelong intense interest in the inner life of man and his highly elaborated system, is classed with those who are not interested in the inner life and cannot make a system. Adler, who has a large popular following and whose voluminous writings are peculiarly lacking in system and order, with those who cannot exert personal influence and who are paralysed by their severe self-criticism and who produce works of finished perfection.

While the extravert is said by Jung to be interested only in the outer world, the introvert is said to shrink from it; 'the objective world suffers a sort of depreciation, or want of consideration, for the sake of the exaltation of the individual himself, who then, monopolizing all the interest, grows to believe no one but himself worthy of consideration'.

And in many other passages Jung insists on the introvert's lack of interest in the world of sense-perception. It is further implied that the introvert is but little given to bodily exertion and little interested in physical activities. Let us see how this fits with the facts in the case of a great writer of whom we have very full accounts; I mean the late Count Tolstoy. Tolstoy's vivid interest in the inner life of men and especially his own, his seclusiveness, his difficulty in 'getting on' with other men, his prolonged internal conflicts and perpetual self-examination, all these traits mark him unmistakably as strongly introverted; yet the author of a recent study (Ref. 1) insists that 'his purely sensory life was unusually vivid and clearly defined. . . . Any description in Tolstoy's work is apt to be striking for the minuteness and accuracy of the detail; his powers of simple observation are probably unrivalled in literature'. Again we are told: 'He was very fond of eating and drinking, of hunting, riding, walking and outdoor sports of all kinds, of dancing, carousing and gambling'. We see here very clearly how the interests and intellectual traits refuse to conform to Jung's demands and to exhibit the alleged correlation with the temperamental trait of introversion. Many other such instances may easily be found.

In one passage Jung ascribes to the extrovert a high degree of docility or suggestibility, a peculiarity which seems to me to be one of disposition rather than of temperament, and one perfectly compatible with marked introversion; and one might ask whether his chosen example of extraversion, Dr Freud, exhibits high suggestibility. In another passage he ascribes to the extravert as a distinctive trait great sensitiveness to the regards of other men, a peculiarity which, I submit, belongs to character rather than to temperament.

If we inquire how Jung conceives his introvert and extravert traits to be founded in the structure of personality, the answer is very unsatisfactory. Although he speaks of the distinction as one of temperament, he cannot regard it as founded in any general chemical influence affecting the nervous system; for he asserts that the conscious and the unconscious parts of the personality are always opposites in this respect, that where the conscious is introverted, the unconscious in extraverted, and vice versa. He falls back upon the common but extremely unsatisfactory expedient of postulating two mechanisms, an introverting and an extraverting mechanism possessed by all subjects, the one predominating in the conscious life of the introvert, the other in his unconscious (and vice versa for the extravert).

There is in all Jung's discussions of this topic only one statement that seems to me at once illuminating and altogether acceptable, if we are to define introversion and extraversion as pure temperamental peculiarities. This is the passage in which he writes that 'hysteria is characterized by a centrifugal tendency of the libido, whilst in dementia praecox its tendency is centripetal'. (Ref. 2)

I suggest that, accepting the cue given in this passage, we can single out of the complexities of the traits to which Jung applies the terms extraversion and introversion, a simple personality factor which is purely one of temperament in the proper or strict sense, the possession of which in various degrees of intensity is an important constitutional factor in every personality. I suggest that all personalities can be ranged in a single linear scale according to the degree to which this factor is present in their constitutions. Those who stand near one end of the scale are the marked extraverts; those near the other are the well-marked introverts; and the greater part of mankind, possessing this factor in moderate degree, stand in the middle region of the scale.[1]

Such a distribution of a temperamental trait is most naturally explained by the influence of some one chemical factor generated in the body and exerting a specific influence upon all the nervous system in proportion to the quantity that is produced and liberated into the blood stream.

Let me illustrate by reference to the internal secretion of the thyroid gland. Each of us seems to have a natural or normal rate of thyroid secretion which plays an important rôle in determining his position in the scale of rapidity of general metabolism. In morbid conditions the rate may be gravely increased or diminished. At or near the one end of the scale stands the sufferer from Graves' disease; at or near the other the victim of myxoedema or thyroid insufficiency. In this case we know that the one end of the scale represents excess of an endocrine, the other end a defect of the same secretion. In the case of the extraversion-introversion scale we have no such clear indication as to which end of the scale represents excess, which defect, of the postulated chemical substance (presumably an endocrine secretion of some one gland, or possibly a more widely secreted product of the metabolism of various tissues). But I suggest that in all probability extraversion is the positive state, introversion the negative; that is to say, extreme introversion represents a defect, a minimal quantity or minimum rate of secretion of the postulated substance—(let us call it X); and extraversion in its various degrees is the consequence of correspondingly large quantities

[1] It seems probable that the distribution of degrees of this factor may follow a normal curve; but this is a matter for future research.

or rapid rates of secretion of X. My ground for preferring this view will be stated in a later paragraph.

Let me first try to define the difference between what I take to be simple extraversion and simple introversion, the pure temperamental traits as I conceive them. And since introversion is the simpler state, while extraversion (according to the view I am putting forward) is the consequence of the additional constitutional factor X, or of its presence in larger quantity, I begin with introversion.

The marked introvert is the man in whom the inhibition normally exerted by activity of the cerebral cortex on all lower nervous functions is manifested in high degree. We are most familiar with this inhibitory influence of cortical activity in the case of the spinal reflexes. We know that cortical activity depresses or inhibits the spinal reflexes, and that destruction or impairment or arrest of cortical function releases the cord from this inhibitory influence. We do not know how this inhibitory influence is exerted; though it is, I believe, capable of explanation in terms of the drainage hypothesis. Yet the fact is well established in the case of the spinal reflexes; and we have similar though less abundant evidence that the activity of the cortex depresses or partially inhibits in a similar way the functions of the thalamus or of the mid-brain structures in general. I refer here chiefly to the observations of Dr Henry Head, which show that the protopathic functions of the thalamus are intensified as a consequence of certain lesions of the cortex or of the cortico-thalamic paths.

We may, I think, go further and point to evidence that the cortical regions of highest function (the so-called silent areas) exert similar inhibition upon the cortical areas of lower function, the sensori-motor areas. I refer to the fact, first pointed out by Francis Galton, that children and primitives seem to use imagery in their thinking more freely and copiously than do civilized adults; and that, with the development of powers of reflective and abstract thinking, the use of imagery seems to decline, to become less free, less abundant, less vivid.

The introvert, then, is the man in whom the lower levels of the nervous system are constantly subject to a high degree of inhibition by the higher cortical activities; and of these lower inhibited functions the most important are the affective or emotional-conative functions of the thalamic region. I have long accepted and taught in my books[1] the view that the emotional functions have their principal seat in the thalamus, and Professor W. B. Cannon has recently adduced evidence which seems

[1] E.g. in my *Social Psychology* (Ref. 3).

to put this view beyond doubt. We may confine our attention to them. Now if my view of inhibition is correct (namely, that it is effected by drainage of the energy liberated in one system of neurones into some other system more actively functioning), inhibition of the affective centres of the thalamus by the cortex does not mean that their excitation is prevented. It means only that the energies liberated in the affective centres is diverted from its normal channels of expression, from all those efferent channels which directly lead to the bodily expressions of emotion; it is diverted or long-circuited to and through the cortex, where it co-operates in substaining the activities of reflective thinking, a process which results in the simultaneous excitation of various affective tendencies which partially check or neutralize one another so far as external expression is concerned.

Thus the introvert, by reason of the free dominant activity of his cortex and in virtue of its restraining or inhibitory effect on the outflow of thalamic excitation in its normal or direct channels of emotional expression, is a man in whom thought seems to flourish at the expense of emotion. It is not that he is incapable of emotion or strong affects; but his affects do not readily find outward expression; they are absorbed in and disguised by the supervenient cortical activities and the consequent arousal of conflicting tendencies. He seems relatively cold and expressionless; he cannot easily let himself go; his emotional expressions, in word or gesture or other bodily forms, are very moderate and restrained even when he is strongly moved. He tends to be over self-conscious and introspective; and that adds to his general inhibitedness.

Introversion seems then to be the natural consequence of the great development and free activity of the cortex. Hence children in general grow more introverted as they grow up, i.e., as the cortex assumes its full rôle, and primitives on the whole are less introverted than the civilized. The grown dog is more introverted than the puppy; and if we deprive him of his cortex in part or whole by surgical interference, we remove in part this restraining influence on the thalamic levels, he becomes emotional and restless, perpetually on the move so long as he is awake; he regresses to puppyhood.

As the cortex developed its enormous proportions in the human species, there was danger of excessive introversion; danger that the life of phantasy, of reflection, of deliberation, should render men unfit for the life of action and unfit for social intercourse, for maintaining that sympathetic rapport with their fellows which is the basis of all social life and is rendered possible only by a certain freedom of emotional expression. Man's increasing capacity for thinking threatened to diminish unduly his capacity for action and for social life.

Hence nature has provided an antidote against such increasing and excessive introversion. It has generated in the tissues, or in some tissue unknown, an extraverting hormone or endocrine substance X, the function of which is to prevent, to diminish in some measure, this inhibiting paralysing influence of the cortex upon the more primitive lower-level functions of the nervous system. And the man who is constitutionally provided with a large amount of this antidote to cortical inhibition is the extravert.

The extravert, then, is the man who, though he may possess, and commonly does possess, a cortex developed just as highly as that of the introvert, nevertheless does not suffer in the same degree the inhibition of all emotional expressions that characterizes the introvert. Every affect, every emotional-conative excitement, readily flows out from the subcortical levels into outward expression instead of being largely drained off to and absorbed into the cortex. His emotional stirrings find immediate expression in action, save only on the occasions when some real difficulty or problem compels him to stop to think, or when he makes a voluntary effort to deliberate before action.

Individuals certainly differ widely in respect to this freedom of out-flow of affective excitement into action and expression, and I suggest that we shall do well to restrict the terms introversion and extraversion to denote the various degrees of this one simple temperamental peculiarity. For these degrees seem to be the most essential feature of the highly complex traits to which Jung and others have applied these names.

How, then, may we conceive the postulated internal secretion X to work upon the brain to maintain various degrees of extraversion, to antagonize and moderate the inhibiting influence of the cortex? I suggest that we may find the clue to a simple, intelligible and adequate hypothesis in consideration of the influence of alcohol upon the brain functions (and of ether and chloroform), and that the phenomena of alcoholic intoxication go very far to justify the hypothesis.

I have observed in a number of cases that the markedly extraverted personality is very susceptible to the influence of alcohol. A very small dose deprives him of normal self-restraint and control and brings on the symptoms of intoxication, all of which are essentially expressions of diminished cortical control over the lower brain-levels. The introvert on the other hand is much more resistant to alcohol. He can take a considerable dose without other effect than that he becomes extroverted;

that is to say, the predominance of his higher cortical processes over those of lower levels is diminished; he becomes less inhibited in action and expression; he enjoys for the time being the advantages of the extravert; he talks freely and expresses his emotions in action, gesture, tears and laughter. Alcohol, in short, seems to be an extraverting drug pure and simple so far as its influence on the nervous system is concerned. What exactly, then, is the mode of action of alcohol on the nervous system? In an article first published as long ago as 1898 (Ref. 6) I suggested that alcohol acts directly upon the synapses of the brain to increase their resistances to the passage of the nervous current. In a later publication (Ref. 5) I have elaborated this view, showing that we have only to conceive that alcohol acts upon the synapses of the various brain-levels, increasing their resistances in the order from above downwards (in the inverse order of their fixity of organization) in order to have a simple and perfectly adequate explanation of all the stages of intoxication. Since this scheme met with the approval of the several eminent physiologists and pharmacologists with whom I co-operated in writing that little book, it may be said to be pretty well founded.[1]

In order to explain extraversion, I make, then, the simple assumption that in the extravert some tissue (or tissues) normally and constantly secretes the extraverting substance X, a substance whose action upon the nervous system is very similar to that of alcohol (ether and chloroform); that is to say, I assume that the extraverting internal secretion X acts directly upon all synapses raising their resistance to the passage of the nervous current or discharge from neurone to neurone. I make also the highly probable assumption that the synapses of the various levels of the nervous system are in the main solidly and stably organized in proportion to the phylogenetic and ontogenetic age of the levels in which they occur. In other words, I assume that the synapses of the higher levels are the less solidly organized, have higher resting resistances and are less stable, more subject to variation of their resistances by a variety of influences, including the chemical influences of strychnine, alcohol, and the postulated substance X.

According to this view, then, the marked extravert is he whose metabolism constantly or normally furnishes and throws into the bloodstream enough of the substance X to keep the subject in a state of mild

---

[1] I have further supported this view by showing (by the aid of a special and very delicate laboratory procedure) that alcohol and ether are precise antagonists of strychnine in its influence upon cerebral process; and the probability is great that strychnine works upon synapses to diminish their resistances.

B*

or incipient intoxication. And the position of each individual in the introvert-extravert scale is a direct and simple function of the amount of X normally secreted by his tissues; the extreme introvert being the man with a well developed cortex and a minimum of X.

I find support for this view in the relation of introversion and extraversion to the incidence of nervous and mental disorder. Jung has expressed the opinion that the introvert is the more liable to neurasthenia and schizophrenia, the extravert to hysterical and manic-depressive disorder. My own small experience leads me to accept this view. And I would add insomnia to the list of characteristic introvert troubles. The introvert mind or brain does not easily come to rest. The introvert in many cases finds the need of a night-cap in the shape of a stiff peg of whisky in order to pass quickly into sleep. Further, he cannot easily be hypnotized.

To the list of extravert peculiarities I would add susceptibility to hypnosis, to crystal visions, trances and automatic actions of all kinds. All these differences seem to mean the greater liability of the extravert to suffer dissociative effects in the nervous system whether local, as in local functional paralyses and anesthesia, or general, as in general amnesia, trance, hypnosis and sleep. And this is to be expected; for, just as alcohol is a dissociating drug which acts first and most intensely upon those most delicately organized synapses that are involved in the latest acquired and highest-level processes of the cortex subserving self-conscious control and self-criticism, and involving the reciprocal play of one cortical system of highest level neurones upon another; so also the extraverting substance X may be supposed to affect most markedly these higher level synapses, maintaining during waking life an incipient state of dissociation and rendering easier the onset of all more pronounced states of cerebral dissociation, from normal sleep and alcoholic intoxication to hypnosis and functional paralyses and amnesias. In short, the introvert is the more liable to disorders of continuing conflict, because conflict cannot readily be obviated by dissociation; while the extravert readily finds relief from internal conflict through the onset of some complete dissociation between conflicting systems and tendencies.

A last point in support of this view may be made by contrasting the British[1] and the American people in respect to introversion-extra-

---

[1] British introversion is well illustrated by a recent advertisement labelled 'Chatterboxes'. Two Britishers foregather for a friendly chat, both smoking a famous brand of tobacco in their pipes. One says: 'Good stuff this!' After a silence of five minutes the other replies: 'Yes, not bad!'

version. It seems beyond question that position in the scale is in the main determined by hereditary constitution, and varies from race to race; some races, like the Negro, being predominantly extravert, others, like the red men of this country, predominantly introvert. If this is so, how explain the notorious fact that, by and large, Americans are decidedly more extraverted than the British? I do not suggest that all Americans are extravert. The typical Yankee is perhaps hardly on the extravert side of the scale. Yet the difference is on the whole considerable. The difference may be perhaps in part explained by the more expansive surroundings of the American. But it seems likely that in the main it is due to the influence of a climate on our metabolism. On coming to America we all notice a marked difference of climate which renders it easy to keep running about maintaining social contacts of all sorts. And the Britisher hardly feels the need of the alcohol to which he is accustomed to resort for the relief of his extraversion. I suggest that the essence of this climatic effect is the stimulation of the tissue that produces the extraverting substance X, and a more rapid secretion of it into the blood.[1]

According to the usage I propose, the words extraversion and introversion would imply solely the two opposite and extremer degrees of a purely temperamental peculiarity, one that is simple, fully intelligible in terms of our knowledge of the nervous functions, and profoundly important from the points of view of education, psychiatry and mental hygiene.

I conclude by drawing attention to the fact that Pavlov describes very clearly two types of temperament in the dogs that served in his experiments on the conditioned reflex.[2] His descriptions of the two types might well serve as definitions of the human introvert and extravert. If, then, introversion and extraversion are well marked in dogs, the fact indicates that they are based on some relatively simple physiological factor such as is here postulated.

[1] The observations reported by Dr C. A. Neymann (at the Atlanta meeting of the American Psychiatric Association, May, 1929) to the effect that active tubercular disease seems to conduce to increase of extraversion, fits very well with this simplified view of the nature of introversion and extraversion and with the chemical theory here maintained.

[2] Compare my condensed account of these observations (Ref. 7).

REFERENCES

1. DAVIS, H. E., *Tolstoy and Nietzsche*. New York: New Republic, 1929.
2. JUNG, C. G., *Collected Papers on Analytical Psychology*. London: Ballière, Tindall & Cox, 1917.
3. McDOUGALL, W., *An Introduction to Social Psychology*. London: Methuen, 1908.
4. McDOUGALL, W., *An Outline of Psychology*. London: Methuen, 1923.
5. McDOUGALL, W., *Alcohol and its Effects on Human Organisms*. London: H.M.S.O., 1924.
6. McDOUGALL, W., Contributions towards an improvement in psychological method, *Body and Mind*. London: Methuen, 1928.
7. McDOUGALL, W., The bearing of Professor Pavlov's work on the problem of inhibition. *J. gen. Psychol*, 1929.

2

What do Introversion-Extraversion Tests Measure?

A. R. GILLILAND

First published in
Journal of Abnormal and Social Psychology, **28**, 407–412, 1934

SINCE JUNG first used the terms introversion and extraversion these words have had extensive usage in psychology. They have been used in many connections and with many different meanings. Conklin (Ref. 3), Freyd (Ref. 5), Guilford & Braly (Ref. 7), and others have carefully summarized these various meanings. The last named writers illustrate the diversity of these definitions by showing that sometimes the distinction between introversion and extraversion has been made on the basis of interest, at other times on the basis of adaptation to social environment, and at still other times on the basis of overt and covert behaviour. To this list might well be added a fourth major distinction which Kempf (Ref. 11) and Marston (Ref. 15) make on the basis of the autonomic nervous system and the emotions versus the central system and skeletal activity.

Other attempts at distinguishing between introversion and extraversion have been made on the basis of performance under controlled experimental conditions. Travis (Ref. 17) and Schanck (Ref. 18) studied the difference in sensory threshold between introverts during reverie. Introverts, they found, had a distinctly higher threshold during reverie than extraverts. Guilford & Hunt (Refs. 8 & 9) following a suggestion of McDougall found that extraverts had a much slower fluctuation of reversals in the wheatstone cube than introverts and normals. Darrow (Ref. 4) at first found some relation between certain psychogalvanic changes and test scores for introversion-extraversion, but later study did not verify this finding.

Another method of distinguishing between introversion and extraversion is by means of pencil and paper tests. Here even greater diversity of assumptions and methods is to be found than with the physical tests. Freyd (Ref. 5) and Laird (Refs. 13 & 14) using techniques based upon the Woodworth Personality Inventory have constructed well known tests. Heidbreder (Ref. 10) reorganized the Freyd questionnaire for use on University of Minnesota students. Conklin (Ref. 3) constructed a test for introversion based upon the interests of students. Neymann & Kohlstadt (Ref. 16) revised a test constructed by Kohlstadt (Ref. 12) and used as the basis for a Master's thesis at Northwestern University. Marston (Ref. 15) constructed a test for use either in self-rating or in rating others. Bernreuter (Ref. 1) has recently published a test which may be scored in four different ways. One of these is for introversion-extraversion. The Northwestern University Introversion-Extraversion Test has been described in a recent article (Ref. 6). It is based upon differences between the responses of manic patients as extraverts and dementia praecox patients as introverts. As yet the test has not been printed for general distribution.

The following table gives a brief summary of the principal introversion-extraversion tests.

TABLE 1

Name of author or of test	No. of questions or items	Reported reliability	Approximate time required in test
Laird C2	48	0·79 to 0·85	15–20 min.
Freyd	54		
Heidbreder	54	0·40 to 0·55	30 min.
Conklin	40	0·92 (300)	20–30 min.
Marston	20	0·83 to 0·98	15 min.
Neymann-Kohlstedt	50	Not given	12–15 min.
Bernreuter	125	0·89 to 0·85	20–25 min.
Northwestern University	120	0·87	20 min.

While the preceding survey gives the background for the study to be reported here, the particular problem of this paper is a study of the degree of agreement or disagreement in the results of some of the various pencil and paper tests now available. In other words, how much consistency in test results is to be expected if one or another of the tests now in common use is employed in the measurement of introversion-extraversion. Guthrie made a study of this kind several years ago. He used four different tests, including in the group the Colgate Personal Inventory C2. His correlations on these four tests ranged from −0·18 to +0·12. In other words, these tests, whatever they were measuring, were not measuring the same thing. Conklin (Ref. 3), in one of his studies, found a correlation of 0·37 between his own test and the Colgate C2 test. Guilford & Hunt (Refs. 8 & 9) correlated the Colgate Personal Inventory C2 with the Marston Rating Scale and the Neymann-

What do Introversion-Extraversion Tests Measure? 31

Kohlstadt test and found all correlations 'very small, some positive and some negative'.

In the study here to be reported a class of 172 students in general psychology were given four different introversion-extraversion tests on approximately alternate Fridays. The tests used were (1) the Colgate Mental Hygiene Inventory C2, (2) the Bernreuter Personality Inventory test, scored for introversion-extraversion, (3) the Marston Personality Rating Scale, and (4) the Northwestern University Introversion-Extraversion Test. These tests were correlated with each other and each was correlated with intelligence test scores. The results are presented in the accompanying table.

TABLE 2

SHOWING CORRELATIONS BETWEEN DIFFERENT INTROVERSION-EXTRAVERSION TESTS

	Bernreuter	Colgate	Marston	Northwestern	Intelligence Test Scores
Bernreuter	·80±·02*	·47±·04	·37±·05	—·09±·05	·08±·05
Colgate	·47±·04	·55±·04*	·30±·05	·10±·05	·08±·05
Marston	·37±·05	·30±·05	·84±·02*	·25±·05	·07±·05
Northwestern	—·09±·05	·10±·05	·25±·05	·62±·03*	·07±·05

* These figures represent reliability coefficients. Scores corrected by the Spearman-Brown formula.

From these results it is apparent that if any one of these tests measures introversion-extraversion satisfactorily, with one possible exception, none of the others measures the same thing. The only correlation that approaches fifty is between the Bernreuter and Colgate tests and Bernreuter used this method for validating his test. By so doing he obtained a correlation from 0·92 to 0·99. In one case 40 subjects were used and in the other case, 20 students. In our study with a much larger group the correlation is 0·47. Of course, there is no proof from these results that any of these tests measures introversion-extraversion. One thing is certain: none of these tests measure intelligence.

How may these low correlations be explained? Several possible causes might be listed: (1) the tests themselves may not be reliable, (2) the authors may not mean the same things by the terms introversion-extraversion, (3) because of different notions about introversion-extraversion the questions of which the tests are composed may be greatly dissimilar, and (4) the test items may be scored differently. The low correlations between the tests may be accounted for by one or the other or a combination of two or more of these factors. Let us briefly consider each of these possibilities.

It might be argued that the variation is due to the fact that these tests do not have a high reliability. However, the published reliabilities of these tests are all fairly high: Colgate C2, split-half method, 0·79; by repetition, 0·85; Bernreuter, split-half method, 0·89 and 0·85; Marston, one-half of test with the other half, boys 0·95 and girls, 0·91: and the Northwestern Test, 0·87.

It is interesting to note that the reliability coefficients given in the above table are consistently not as high as those reported by the authors of the tests. Why this is true is hard to explain. However, it is not un-common for others to obtain lower validity and reliability coefficients than those obtained when a test is standardized.

Another possible cause for the low correlations between tests of introversion-extraversion is a difference in what is meant by these terms by the different authors. Laird following Jung describes introverts as characterized by their emotional outlets being expressed largely within themselves (Ref. 13). The extravert in contrast expresses his emotions in action and associating with others. Bernreuter seemingly has not published anything about his test except what is contained in the manual. In this he says that introverts are imaginative and tend to live within themselves. Extraverts rarely worry, seldom suffer emotional upsets, and rarely daydream. Marston (Ref. 15), after quoting Jung with approval, defines introversion and extraversion in terms of feeling. Introversion is the dissipation of emotionally aroused energy within the organism rather than the adequate discharge of this energy through skeletal channels upon the environment, while extraversion is a normal skeletal expression of emotions. Introversion, therefore, for Marston is abnormal. The authors of the Northwestern University test of intro-version-extraversion describe introversion as that tendency to withdraw from the real world which when it leads to abnormalities is charac-terized as dementia praecox and extraversion as an interest in people and things outside one's self which when it becomes abnormal is characterized as manic depressive insanity.

From a study of these definitions it is apparent that despite general external differences there is considerable in common in them.

If we examine the tests themselves, considerable similarity will be found between them. The questions centre about such problems as self-consciousness, daydreaming, getting along with people, emotionality, impulsiveness, and sex relations. The tests vary in the form of the questions and the number of test items varies; but there is probably more uniformity in the topics upon which the questions are based than any other fact about the tests.

The methods of scoring vary. Laird scores all those items of his test in which the answers are in the lower quarter of the distribution for that question. This gives a score for introversion. The higher the score the greater the degree of introversion. Bernreuter has a weighted method of scores. The method of weighting is not described, other than it was on the basis of the extent to which each question differentiated between the criterion groups composed of extreme individuals. Marston used a weighted scoring. This was accomplished by means of a five-point scale for each item of the test, the degree of the possession of the item being designated by the rater in appropriate checking. The Northwestern test is also weighted. The weighting was determined for each item of the test on the basis of the per cent of 'yes' answers to the item by dementia praecox and manic insane patients.

It is probable that the difference found between the tests in this study is due to a combination of the differences in meaning of the terms introversion and extraversion, a difference in the items included in the tests, and a difference in the method of scoring the tests.

Whatever the cause or causes, the differences in scores are so great that the various authors of tests should come to some agreement of what is meant by the terms; call their tests measure of alpha, beta, abilities or something having no implications; or produce a better test of the trait before foisting any more tests at so much per on the all too gullible public. The author, who is now using the eighth revision of an unpublished introversion-extraversion test which is in the course of its development and who has given the test to about two hundred insane patients and a thousand college students, believes that much more care must be exercised in the construction of tests. Until widespread publication is suppressed and care exercised in construction, so-called personality tests cannot hope to gain the general respect of psychologists and administrators or others in positions of responsibility.

REFERENCES

1. BERNREUTER, ROBERT G., *The Personality Inventory: Manual of Instruction.* Stanford: Stanford University Press, 1935.

34   *Theoretical and Methodological Issues*

2. CONKLIN, E. S., The definition of introversion, extraversion and allied concepts. *J. abnorm. soc. Psychol.*, **17**, 367–383, 1923.
3. CONKLIN, E. S., The determination of normal extravert-introvert interest differences. *Ped. Sem.*, **34**, 27–37, 1926.
4. DARROW, C. W., *Studies in the Dynamics of Behavior*. Chicago: University of Chicago Press.
5. FREYD, M., Introverts and extraverts. *Psychol. Rev.*, **31**, 74–87, 1924.
6. GILLILAND, A. R., & MORGAN, J. J. B., An objective measure of introversion-extraversion. *J. abnorm. soc. Psychol.*, **26**, 296–303, 1932.
7. GUILFORD, J. P., & BRALY, K. W., An experimental test of McDougall's theory of extraversion-introversion. *J. abnorm. soc. Psychol.*, **25**, 382–389, 1931.
8. GUILFORD, J. P., & HUNT, J. M., Some further tests of McDougall's theory of introversion and extraversion. *J. abnorm. soc. Psychol.*, **26**, 1931.
9. ——, Fluctuations of an ambiguous figure in Dementia Praecox and in manic depressive patients. *J. abnorm. soc. Psychol.*, **27**, 443–452, 1933.
10. HEIDBREDER, E., Measuring introversion and extraversion. *J. abnorm. soc. Psychol.*, **21**, 120–134, 1926.
11. KEMPF, E. J., *The Autonomic Functions and the Personality*. Washington: Nervous and Mental Dis. Pub. Co., 1921.
12. KOHLSTEDT, K. D., Unpublished Master's thesis in Northwestern University Library.
13. LAIRD, D, A., Detecting abnormal behaviour. *J. abnorm. soc. Psychol.*, **20**, 128–141, 1925.
14. ——. How personalities are found in industry. *Indus. Psychol.*, **1**, 1926.
15. MARSTON, L. R., The emotions of young children. *Iowa Studies in Child Welfare*, No. **3**, 1925.
16. NEYMANN, C. A., & KOHLSTADT, K. D., A new diagnostic test for introversion-extraversion. *J. abnorm. soc. Psychol.* **23**, 482–487, 1929.
17. TRAVIS, L. E., Suggestibility and negativism as measured by the auditory threshold during reverie. *J. abnorm. soc. Psychol.*, **18**, 350–368, 1924.
18. SCHANCK, RICHARD L., Changes in auditory threshold during abstraction. Unpublished M.A. thesis, Northwestern University Library.

3

Principles and Methods of Personality Description, Classification and Diagnosis

H. J. EYSENCK

First published in *British Journal of Psychology*, **55**, 284–294, 1964

CLASSIFICATION is an absolutely fundamental part of the scientific study of human personality; a satisfactory typology is as necessary in psychology as was Mendeleev's table of the elements in physics (Ref. 17). This has, of course, always been recognized, and almost everyone is acquainted with the famous typological classification into melancholics, cholerics, sanguines and phlegmatics dating back to Galen and even earlier. As this system still has much to teach us, I shall present it as Fig. 1; the outer ring in this figure shows the results of a large number of factor analytic studies of questionnaires and ratings (Ref. 23). As is customary in these diagrams, the correlation between any two traits is equal to their scalar product, that is to say, in this case, the cosine of their angle of separation.

Fig. 1 immediately confronts us with some of the main problems of classification. The first of these may be phrased in terms of the question: 'Categorical or dimensional?' Kant, to whom this system owes much of its popularity during the last two hundred years, was quite specific in maintaining the categorical point of view, i.e. the notion that every person could be assigned to a particular category; he was a melancholic, or a phlegmatic, or a sanguine or a choleric, but any mixtures or admixtures were inadmissible. This notion of categories is, of course, similar to the psychiatric notion of disease entities and their corresponding diagnoses; hysteria, anxiety state, paranoia, obsessional illness, and so on, are often treated as categorical entities in this sense.

Opposed to this notion we have the view that any particular position in this two-dimensional framework is due to a combination of quantitative variations along the two continua labelled 'introversion-extraversion' and 'stable-unstable'. Wundt (Ref. 51), who is the most notable proponent of Galen's system in modern times, favours the dimensional view; he labelled the one axis 'slow-quick' instead of

Figure 1. Diagram showing relation between the classical four temperaments and results of modern factor analytic methods of personality
description.

'introversion-extraversion', and the other 'strong-weak' instead of
unstable and stable.

It may be interesting to quote Wundt's very modern-sounding discussion:

The ancient differentiation into four temperaments ... arose from
acute psychological observations of individual differences between
people. ... The fourfold division can be justified if we agree to postulate two principles in the individual reactivity of the affects: one of
these refers to the strength, the other to the speed of change of a
person's feelings. Cholerics and melancholics are inclined to strong
affects, while sanguinics and phlegmatics are characterized by weak

ones. A high rate of change is found in sanguinics and cholerics, a slow rate in melancholics and phlegmatics.

It is well known that the strong temperaments . . . are predestined towards the *Unluststimmungen*, while the weak ones show a happier ability to enjoy life. . . . The two quickly changeable temperaments . . . are more susceptible to the impressions of the present; their mobility makes them respond to each new idea. The two slower temperaments, on the other hand, are more concerned with the future; failing to respond to each chance impression, they take time to pursue their own ideas (pp. 637, 638).

There is no reason to believe that the notion of a typology presupposes a categorical system; both Jung and Kretschmer, who were probably the best known typologists of the inter-war period, postulated a dimensional rather than the categorical system. The widespread notion that typologists imply discontinuities, bimodal distributions, and the like, does not accurately represent the writings and views of modern typologists.

Most writers on the subject of personality come down in favour of either the categorical or the dimensional point of view without basing themselves on any experimental demonstration. I have always felt that this is unwise and that it should not be impossible to devise experimental and statistical means for verifying the one and falsifying the other hypothesis. I have tried to do this in terms of the method of criterion analysis, which relies on separate factor analyses of intercorrelations between tests administered to two or more criterion groups (say normals and psychotics), and the comparison of the factors emerging with a criterion column derived by serial correlation between the tests and the criterion (Ref. 10). The results of this method have in every instance supported the doctrine of continuity, and failed to support the doctrine of categorization, even when the latter seemed most firmly entrenched, as in the case of psychosis (Ref. 12).

Assuming for the moment, therefore, the doctrine of dimensionality, we are required to build up on an experimental and statistical basis a quantitative system of personality description (Ref. 36). The most widely used tool for this purpose is, of course, factor analysis, and the main results of the application of this tool are shown in Fig. 1. It is notable that for many years factor analysis has been criticized because, so it was said, there was no agreement between factor analysts. Whatever may have been true twenty or thirty years ago, there can be no doubt that nowadays there is comparatively little disagreement between investigators in this field. Cattell's most recent book (Ref. 3) shows him in firm agreement with the system I first put forward in 1947 (Ref. 9), and Guilford, too, now appears to recognize the existence of these two main factors in personality description which I have used as the major axes in Fig. 1. Vernon (Ref. 49, p. 13) also puts forward a similar scheme. Equally we are all agreed that each of these factors is what Thurstone called a 'second-order factor', i.e. is extracted from the intercorrelations between 'first-order factors' or traits. It is with respect to these traits that much research is still needed before any final agreement is reached. Nevertheless, the major outlines of the picture are certainly beginning to appear, and it is notable that this agreement has been reached between workers using different premises, different factor analytic methods, different subjects, different tests and questionnaires, and different methods of rotation.

If we accept the principle of continuity, then we should be able to find a place for the major psychiatric classification of neurotic disorders within our Fig. 1. The theory has been put forward that neurotics suffering from anxiety, reactive depression, obsessions, phobias, and so on, would be found in the 'melancholic' quadrant, while hysterics and psychopaths would be found in the 'choleric' quadrant; psychotics would lie on an axis orthogonal to both E and N (Ref. 11). Descriptively there seems little doubt about the truth of this hypothesis at least as regards the neurotic groups; it is only necessary to look at the traits characterizing people in these two quadrants to realize that they might almost have been quoted from a psychiatric text-book, rather than being the result of factor analytic studies of normal people. Nevertheless, more experimental support would seem to be required. Such support, in so far as it is based purely on descriptive measures, does not remove us from some of the difficulties implied in the use of the factor analytic method. It has often been shown, as for instance in the literature deriving from the Maudsley Personality Inventory (Ref. 41), that hysterics, psychopaths and various dysthymic groups are in fact all high on neuroticism or emotionality, but are differentiated very significantly with respect to extraversion and introversion.

However, on a more fundamental level we may still be bothered by what is in fact the second major problem posed by our Fig. 1. This problem relates to the exact position of the axes. Mathematicians and statisticians would agree that it is perfectly legitimate to use scalar products to indicate the relative position of two traits in the dimensional space indicated in Fig. 1, and they would also agree that the position of the traits can be legitimately referred to any two arbitrary axes drawn at right-angles in the plane. They would not, however, agree with the claim sometimes made that the position of these axes can be determined in any but an arbitrary or trivial sense by statistical or mathematical considerations alone, as is suggested by many psychologists, particularly in the United States. I have always agreed with this criticism and have tried to argue that by retaining purely statistical criteria of axes psychologists have got themselves separated off from the main body of experimental psychology, and have remained cocooned within a small tail-chasing system incapable of generating hypotheses that could be falsified (Refs. 13, 14, 15 & 19). What then is the answer to this problem?

My suggestion would be that a purely descriptive system in science inevitably must carry the burden of subjectivity, and that it is because they have only been interested in description that factor analysts have failed to make a major impact on psychology. What is required, so I would maintain, is a set of theories linking the major aspects of the descriptive system to causal theories which would be capable of falsification (Ref. 21). As an example of what I have in mind I may perhaps mention the set of theories relating introversion to heightened cortical excitation and lowered cortical inhibition. This enables us to make large numbers of predictions of an experimental nature which are unlikely to be verified unless both the descriptive and the causal systems, and the relations specified to exist between them, are in fact in some degree related to reality. Many such predictions have in fact been made, and the great majority have been verified; I may refer in this connection to hypotheses such as that extraverts, as compared with introverts, would be more difficult to condition, have larger reminiscence scores, have greater pain tolerance but less tolerance for sensory deprivation, are more subject to satiation, have lower sedation thresholds, have greater alpha frequency and amplitude on the EEG, more involuntary rest pauses during massed practice, have poorer vigilance, have greater speed/accuracy ratios, shorter after-images, and so forth.

This differentiation between descriptive and causal is of course related to that between phenotypic and genotypic, first made in the personality field by Pavlov on the basis of some of his animal experiments. (For a discussion of Pavlov's views and their development, Teplov's very interesting account may be consulted with advantage; it is available in English together with a detailed evaluation of recent Russian work in the personality field (Ref. 39).) I have tried to indicate the difference, from the point of view of personality structure, in Fig. 2; a detailed discussion of this point is given elsewhere (Ref. 24). In this diagram, the subscripts 'C' and 'B' refer to constitution and behaviour respectively; 'E' refers to environmental influences. It will be seen that at the most fundamental

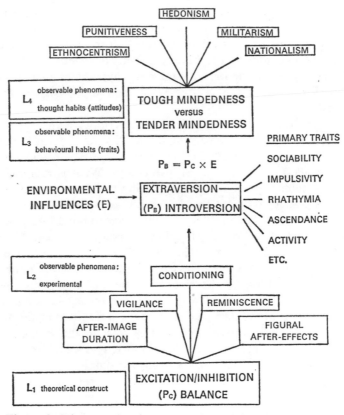

Figure 2. Diagram showing genotypic and phenotypic aspects of personality.

level we have the constitutional concept of the excitation/inhibition balance, which may be tilted in one direction or the other to give rise to constitutional, genotypic differences in extraversion-introversion; these may with some degree of accuracy be measured in terms of condition-ability, vigilance, figural after-effects and other laboratory phenomena. Observable behaviour is a function of these constitutional differences in interaction with the environment; this interaction gives rise to descriptive, phenotypic differences in extraversion-introversion, which can best be measured in terms of questionnaires such as the M.P.I.[1]

We can now make deductions from these various postulates which enable us to perform critical experiments taking us out of the narrow circle of factor analysis altogether, and which make possible the use of the much more powerful techniques of multiple discriminant function analysis. Consider the following experiment in which sixteen normal subjects, sixteen dysthymics and sixteen hysterics were given a battery of six tests, selected on the basis of the causal theory outlined above (Ref. 33). We can predict, of course, how each group shall score as compared with the others, but we can go further than that. Our theory predicts that, if we carry out a discriminant function analysis, this should give us two significant latent roots; it can further be predicted that if we derive variate scores for the forty-eight subjects of our experiment, they should be situated in a prescribed manner in a two-dimensional plane generated by the two significant variates. To put this prediction in its simplest form we may say that the mean variate scores for the three groups should lie at the corners of an equilateral triangle.

Fig. 3 shows the outcome of the experiment. It will be seen that the prediction is verified, and that the first variate discriminates completely between the dysthymics and the hysterics. The second variate, with only slight overlap, discriminates between the normal group on the one hand and the two neurotic groups on the other.

Even where a causal hypothesis is not available it is often possible to use discriminant function analysis to decide between two hypotheses regarding the description of personality. Consider two hypotheses very frequently advanced regarding the neurotic and psychotic disorders (Ref. 18). Psychoanalysts often advocate the one-dimensional hypothesis; most psychiatrists, however, nowadays favour a two-dimensional hypothesis. A crucial test can, therefore, be devised involving the

[1] It seems reasonable to suppose that genotypic differences will ultimately be linked up with observable structural differences by physiologists and neurologists: an attempt to frame certain hypotheses of a testable character along these lines has been made by Eysenck (Ref. 30), who suggests that different parts of the ascending reticular formation may be implicated in the precise balance of the excitation/inhibition system. The effects of stimulant and depressant drugs on personality (Ref. 31) can also be brought into line by the assumption that the ascending reticular formation is concerned most intimately with the psychological constructs of excitation and inhibition.

dimensionality of the performance of the three groups on a battery of tests selected on the basis of some hypothesis regarding their relevance to neurotic and psychotic disorder (Ref. 18). In the actual experiment 20 normal controls, 20 neurotics and 20 psychotics were tested on four objective laboratory tests. Multiple discriminant function analysis disclosed two significant latent roots, thus rendering impossible the

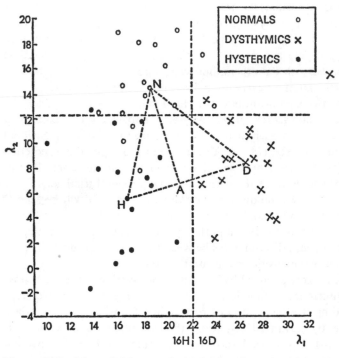

Figure 3, Position of 16 normal, 16 dysthymic and 16 hysteric subjects in two-dimensional space generated by multiple discriminant function analysis.

assumption that one dimension was sufficient to incorporate the results. Fig. 4 shows the actual positions of the members of the three groups; the correlation ratio between the three groups and the two variates was 0·84, which indicates a refreshingly high validity for the tests used in predicting these psychiatric criteria. That this figure is not higher is probably due to lack of reliability of the criteria; it will be seen in Fig. 4 that two of the neurotics, labelled A and B, were grouped with the psychotics by the tests. Both were readmitted later and diagnosed as psychotic.[1]

There are other ways in which theories of this type can be tested. One of these is the genetic method. If it is true that psychotic and neurotic disorders are orthogonal to each other, then we would expect that the children of psychotic parents should not show any greater degree of neuroticism than would the children of normal parents. This very

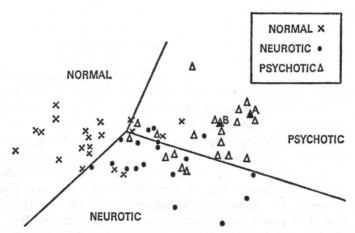

Figure 4. Diagram showing position of 20 normal, 20 neurotic and 20 psychotic subjects in two-dimensional space generated by multiple discriminant function analysis.

interesting hypothesis was tested by Cowie (Ref. 7) and her results leave no doubt that the genetic implication of neuroticism in the children of psychotic parents is non-existent; if anything they tended to be less neurotic! This finding may also serve as a warning to those who would overstress the importance of environment in giving rise to neurotic disorders; it is difficult to imagine a more severe stress to a child than having psychotic parents. In line with a generally hereditary view of the main dimensions of personality are also the results of a recent study of identical twins brought up in separation; in this work Shields (Ref. 46) found high correlations between the two twins for both extraversion and

[1] It is interesting that cultural differences do not seem to affect the applicability of method or conclusion to any considerable extent. Devadasan (Ref. 8) has duplicated many of the details of S. B. G. Eysenck's (Ref. 35) study in this field on an Indian population in Kerala (Trivandrum) with almost identical results.

neuroticism; he also found that these correlations were, if anything, higher than corresponding ones for identical twins brought up together! This type of proof which agrees well with previous studies by Eysenck & Prell (Ref. 34), Wilde (Ref. 50), Lienert & Reisse (Ref. 43) and many others, is relevant for the following reason. If we locate our axes in a random fashion, or according to some erroneous hypothesis, then we would not expect measures based on these placements to achieve any kind of biological reality. However, it has been amply demonstrated that extraversion, neuroticism and psychoticism show a powerful independent hereditary determination; it would seem to follow that the location of our axes cannot be random but must be at least to some degree in the right direction.

The last type of argument and proof, which I would suggest as appropriate, relates to the working out of aetiological models, and the design of methods of treatment related to these. It is a basic principle of behaviour therapy that neurotic disorders are simply maladaptive habits, acquired through a process of conditioning; or alternatively socially desirable habits which have failed to be acquired (Refs. 25 and 32). This hypothesis has led to much work relating dysthymic disorders to over-quick conditionability of patients, and hysteric and psychopathic disorders to chronic underconditionability of patients. (It will be remembered that overconditionability and underconditionability, respectively, are related to introversion and extraversion.) Support has already been brought forward to sustain these hypotheses, but I would be the last to claim that the case has, in any definitive sense, been proven; many points remain to be clarified and settled. The theory has, nevertheless, succeeded in giving rise to a method of treatment—behaviour therapy—which has been outstandingly successful as compared with previous methods. Again I will not claim too much for these new methods, and I will not go into the large and growing literature in any great detail, except to point out that success of treatment, if this is based on a definite theory, must to some degree strengthen the claim of that theory to be taken seriously. I would suggest, therefore, that aetiology and treatment must be taken into account in arriving at a final view of the adequacy of any principles of psychiatric classification claiming to be taken seriously.

The main points to emerge from this discussion are perhaps these. Factor analysis, principal component analysis, or some such technique, is necessary but not sufficient for the elaboration of a proper system of personality classification. The results achieved are inevitably subject to a large degree of subjectivity, and it is in principle impossible to avoid this subjectivity by statistical or mathematical manipulations. The descriptive results of factor analysis require to be integrated with causal theories relating to the factors tentatively established or indicated. It is only when these causal theories are tested and verified that the descriptive scheme can be accepted as forming part of the large body of data which make up experimental psychology.

There are, of course, many types of causal hypotheses which can be put forward in different situations, and there are many different types of deductions which can be made. It has been our task in this paper to touch in passing on several such causal hypotheses and deductions, and to show that the resulting picture is a reasonably congruent one which integrates observations, data, theories and experiments from a great variety of sources. There is, of course, no single proof of a theory such as the one here advocated, and no possibility of a crucial experiment; the burden of proof must lie in the general strength of the nomological network, linking together all these factors. It is believed that in this way psychiatric classification can be made much more reliable, valid and useful than it has been in the past when it relied exclusively on subjective observation, non-quantitative argument and non-experimental demonstration. Obviously the procedure of making our typologies more scientific has only just begun, and still has a long way to go before we can hope to achieve a satisfactory level of accuracy, reliability and validity; nevertheless, the success which has attended our first faltering steps does suggest that the method followed is the correct one and will in due course lead to a better understanding as well as to a better description of human behaviour and personality.

REFERENCES

1. BROWN, F. W., Heredity in the psychoneuroses. *Proc. R. Soc. Med.* **35**, 785–90, 1942.
2. CATTELL, R. B., *Factor Analysis*. New York: Harper, 1952.
3. —— & SCHEIER, I. H., *The Meaning and Measurement of Neuroticism and Anxiety*. New York: Ronald, 1961.
4. CLARIDGE, G. S., The excitation-inhibition balance in neurotics. In *Experiments in Personality*, vol. II, ed. H. J. Eysenck. London: Routledge & Kegan Paul, 1960.

46 *Theoretical and Methodological Issues*

5. ——, Arousal and inhibition as determinants of the performance of neurotics. *Brit. J. Psychol.*, **52,** 53–63, 1961.
6. —— & HERRINGTON, R. N., Sedation threshold, personality and the theory of neurosis. *J. ment. Sci.*, **106,** 1568–1583, 1960.
7. COWIE, V., The incidence of neurosis in the children of psychotics. *Acta Psychiat. Scand.*, **37,** 37–87, 1961.
8. DEVADASAN, K., Personality dimensions: a critical study. Ph.D. Thesis. University of Kerala, India, 1963.
9. EYSENCK, H. J., *Dimensions of Personality.* London: Routledge & Kegan Paul, 1947.
10. ——, Criterion analysis—an application of the hypothetico-deductive method to factor analysis. *Psychol. Rev.*, **57,** 38–53, 1950.
11. ——, *The Scientific Study of Personality.* London: Routledge & Kegan Paul, 1952.
12. ——, Schizothymia-cyclothymia as a dimension of personality. II: Experimental, *J. Pers.*, **20,** 345–384, 1952.
13. ——, Uses and abuses of factor analysis. *Appl. Statistics,* **1,** 45–49, 1952.
14. ——, The logical basis of factor analysis. *Amer. Psychologist,* **8,** 105–114, 1953.
15. ——, A psychological approach to the problem of non-uniqueness in multi-variate solutions. *Proc. Conference on Multi-Dimensional Analysis,* 24–27. Ann Arbor: Univ. of Michigan Press, 1954.
16. ——, Zur Theorie der Personlichkeitsmessung. *Z. diag. Psychol. Personlichkeitsf.*, **2,** 87–101, 171–187, 1954.
17. ——, Abord statistique et experimental du problème typologique dans la personalité neurotique, psychotique et normale. *L'Évolution psychiatrique,* **3,** 377–404, 1954.
18. ——, Psychiatric diagnosis as a psychological and statistical problem. *Psychol. Rep.*, **1,** 3–17, 1955.
19. ——, L'analyse factorielle et le problème de la validité. *Colloques int. Cent. nat. Rech. sci.*, Paris, **58,** 237–252, 1956.
20. ——, The questionnaire measurement of neuroticism and extra-version. *Riv. Psicol.*, **50,** 113–140, 1956.
21. ——, *The Dynamics of Anxiety and Hysteria.* London: Routledge & Kegan Paul, 1957.
22. ——, *Manual of the Maudsley Personality Inventory.* London: Univ. of London Press, 1959.
23. ——, *The Structure of Human Personality.* London: Methuen, 1960.

24. ——, Levels of personality, constitutional factors and social influences: an experimental approach. *Int. J. soc. Psychiat.*, **6,** 12–24, 1960.

25. ——, *Behaviour Therapy and the Neuroses.* Oxford: Pergamon Press, 1960.

26. ——, *Experiments in Personality*, ed. H. J. Eysenck. London: Routledge & Kegan Paul, 1960.

27. ——, Classification and the problem of diagnosis. In *Handbook of Abnormal Psychology*, ed. H. J. Eysenck. London: Pitman Medical, 1960.

28. ——, Personality and social attitudes. *J. Soc. Psychol.*, **53,** 243–248, 1961.

29. ——, Correspondence. *Brit. J. Psychol.*, **53,** 455–456, 1962.

30. ——, Biological basis of personality. *Nature*, **199,** 1031–1034, 1963.

31. ——, *Experiments with Drugs*, ed. H. J. Eysenck. Oxford: Pergamon Press, 1963.

32. ——, *Experiments in Behaviour Therapy*, ed. H. J. Eysenck. Oxford: Pergamon Press, 1963.

33. —— & CLARIDGE, G., The position of hysterics and dysthymics in a two-dimensional framework of personality description. *J. abnorm. soc. Psychol.*, **69,** 46–55, 1962.

34. —— & PRELL, P., The inheritance of neuroticism: an experimental study. *J. ment. Sci.*, **97,** 441–465, 1951.

35. EYSENCK, S. B. G., Neurosis and psychosis: an experimental analysis. *J. ment. Sci.*, **102,** 517–529, 1956.

36. ——, EYSENCK, H. J. & CLARIDGE, G., Dimensional personality, psychiatric syndromes and mathematical models. *J. ment. Sci.*, **106,** 581–589, 1960.

37. FOULDS, G. A., The logical impossibility of using hysterics and dysthymics as criterion groups in the study of introversion and extraversion. *Brit. J. Psychol.*, **52,** 385–387, 1961.

38. FRANKS, C. M., SOUIEFF, M. I. & MAXWELL, A. E., A factorial study of certain scales from the MMPI and the STDCR. *Acta Psychol.*, **17,** 407–416, 1960.

39. GRAY, J. A., *Pavlov's Typology: Recent Theoretic and Experimental Works from the Laboratory of B. M. Teplov*, ed. J. A. Gray. Oxford: Pergamon Press, 1964.

40. HILDEBRAND, H. P., A factorial study of introversion-extraversion. *Brit. J. Psychol.*, **49,** 1–11, 1958.

48   *Theoretical and Methodological Issues*

41. KNAPP, R. R., *The Maudsley Personality Inventory Manual.* San Diego, California: Educational and Industrial Testing Service, 1962.
42. LAWLEY, D. N. & MAXWELL, A. E., Factor analysis as a statistical method. *The Statistician,* **12,** 209–229, 1962.
43. LIENERT, G. & REISSE, H., Ein korrelativer-analytischer Beitrag zur genetischen Determination des Neurotismus. *Psychol. Beiträge,* **7,** 121–130, 1961.
44. McGUIRE, R. J., MOWBRAY, R. M. & VALLANCE, R. C., The Maudsley Personality Inventory used with psychiatric inpatients. *Brit. J. Psychol.,* **54,** 157–166, 1963.
45. SHAGASS, C. & NAIMAN, J., The sedation threshold as an objective index of manifest anxiety in psychoneurosis. *J. psychosom. Res.,* **1,** 49–57, 1956.
46. SHIELDS, J., Monozygotic twins brought up apart and brought up together. *An Investigation into the Genetic and Environmental Causes of Variation in Personality.* London: Oxford Univ. Press, 1962.
47. THOMSON, G. H., *The Factorial Analysis of Human Ability,* 5th ed. Univ. of London Press, 1951.
48. THURSTONE, L. L., *Multiple Factor Analysis.* Chicago: Univ. Press, 1947.
49. VERNON, P. E., *Personality Tests and Assessments.* London: Methuen, 1953.
50. WILDE, G. J. S., *Neurotische Labiliteit gemeten volgens de Vrangenlijstmethode.* Amsterdam: Uitg. F. van Rossen, 1962.
51. WUNDT, W., *Grundzüge der physiologischen Psychologie.* 5th ed., vol. 3. Leipzig: W. Engelmann, 1903.

4

Strength of the Nervous System, Introversion-Extraversion Conditionability and Arousal[1]

JEFFREY A. GRAY

First published in *Behaviour Research and Therapy*, **5**, 151–170, 1967

THE SOVIET work on the dimensions of personality known as *Strength of the Nervous System* and *Equilibrium in Dynamism* is compared with the Western work on introversion-extraversion, in the light of the suggestions that have been made that each of these three dimensions is related to level of arousal. Two particular hypotheses are discussed in relation to existing data: (1) that introversion-extraversion is identical to strength of the nervous system; (2) that introversion-extraversion is identical to equilibrium in dynamism. Some general theoretical implications of these two hypotheses are considered.

In the last decade a group of workers under the direction of the late Professor Teplov in Moscow have made considerable progress in the development of Pavlov's theory of the physiological basis of personality so that it may be applied to Man. The Pavlovian background is reviewed in exhaustive detail by Teplov (Ref. 64). In addition, I have reviewed elsewhere (Ref. 27) the work done by Teplov's group in applying to Man one particular aspect of Pavlov's theory, namely that dealing with a dimension of personality termed 'strength of the excitatory process' or 'strength of the nervous system'. Table 1 lists some of the major differences which have been found to exist between individuals who are at the extreme 'strong' or extreme 'weak' ends of this continuum; though it should be emphasized that it is only by consulting the full review that the reader will be able to discover the experimental procedures (which are in some cases extremely complex) associated with these findings as well as their theoretical significance. In general, I have summarized the difference between the strong and weak nervous systems (taking these

[1] My thanks are due to H. J. Eysenck, with whom I had the benefit of discussing many of the issues mentioned in this paper, and to S. Rachmann for his comments on the manuscript.

Theoretical and Methodological Issues

terms to refer to the two extremes of a continuum, not to two different types of nervous system) as follows:

> The weak nervous system is more sensitive than the strong: it begins to respond at stimulus intensities which are ineffective for the strong nervous system; throughout the stimulus-intensity continuum its responses are closer to its maximum level of responding than the responses of the strong nervous system; and it displays its maximum response, or the response decrement which follows this maximum, at lower stimulus intensities than the strong nervous system.
>
> These same differences may be expressed by saying that the strong nervous system is more stable than the weak—it is better able to withstand extreme intensities of stimulation, better able to continue responding appropriately and without decrement at high stimulus intensities. (Ref. 27, p. 281.)

In an attempt to put these findings of the Moscow group in a theoretical context which would be less unfamiliar than the strictly Pavlovian framework used in Teplov's laboratory, I have suggested (Ref. 28) that it is possible to reinterpret the data on strength of the nervous system as showing that this dimension of personality is a dimension of levels of arousal or 'arousability'. In other words, it is suggested that the individual with a weak nervous system is more highly aroused than a strong individual when both are exposed to objectively identical physical stimulation. This reinterpretation may be taken on a purely behavioural level, using the kind of theoretical framework developed by such workers as Duffy (Ref. 13) and Freeman (Ref. 22). Alternatively, we may give the notion of arousal level a physiological substrate by supposing that it is dependent on the degree to which the cerebral cortex is bombarded by impulses from the non-specific reticular activating system (RAS) discovered by Moruzzi and Magoun (Ref. 40) and linked with notions of arousal in the psychological sense by a number of writers (Lindsley, Ref. 36; Hebb, Ref. 33; Malmo, Ref. 38; Berlyne, Ref. 3; Samuels, Ref. 54). In either case, the hypothesis that weak and strong individuals differ from one another in arousability remains to a large degree a re-interpretation of the Pavlovian theory, rather than a rival theory. For, as pointed out elsewhere (Ref. 28, pp. 296–300), the key concept in the Pavlovian theory used by Teplov's group—'the intensity of the excitatory process' (which, under most conditions, is said to be higher, the weaker the nervous system)—bears very considerable similarities to the Western concept of arousal.

TABLE 1

DIFFERENCES BETWEEN STRONG AND WEAK NERVOUS SYSTEMS (GRAY, Ref. 27)

	Strong nervous system	Weak nervous system
Response decrement due to 'extinction with reinforcement' (transmarginal inhibition')	Low	High
Absolute sensory thresholds	High	Low
Reaction time at low stimulus intensities	Slow	Fast
Threshold of 'concentration of excitation' as tested by the 'induction method' (p. 183 et seq.)	Low	High
Threshold of 'irradiation of excitation' in the 'induction method'	High	Low
Critical frequency of flashing phosphene (see footnote on p. 196)	Low	High
Change in absolute sensory threshold due to heteromodal stimulation	Lowered	Raised
Susceptibility to effects of stimulant drugs (caffeine)	Low	High
Dependence of EEG photodriving effect on stimulus intensity (Nebylitsyn, Ref. 45)	Low	High

If there is any merit in the hypothesis that strength of the nervous system is a dimension of arousability, one obvious and important line of experimental advance would be to compare measures of strength of the nervous system with measures of the various Western dimensions of personality which are believed to have some connection with level of arousel. When I wrote my review of the work of Teplov's group, it seemed that the most obvious candidates for this role were the dimensions of neuroticism (Ref. 14) or manifest anxiety (Refs. 61 and 62). However, in the last few years there have been a number of suggestions (Refs. 10, 7, 8 and 15) that the dimension of introversion-extraversion (Ref. 14) may be, in part or in its entirety, dependent on differences in arousability. This view is dealt with most thoroughly by Eysenck (Ref. 19), who makes out a strong case for it, while not abandoning the belief that other physiological differences also underline this dimension of personality. Since there are sufficient data to hand to make it worth taking this view seriously, the present paper will be devoted to a consideration of the hypothesis (Hypothesis 1) that the dimensions of strength of the nervous system and introversion-extraversion are identical, with the weak nervous system corresponding to the introvert. We shall not consider here the possibility of identifying neuroticism with strength of the nervous system, largely because there are few data relevant to this hypothesis but also because such data as do exist run counter to it at one key point;

it is not the case that neurotics have lower sensory thresholds (see below) than normals (Ref. 25). We shall, however, consider a second alternative hypothesis, namely, that introversion-extraversion corresponds to the dimension described by the Moscow group as 'equilibrium in dynamism' (Ref. 45).

Since there is no account in English of the work of the Moscow group on 'dynamism', it will be necessary to indicate the salient features of this work. The account that follows is largely based on the writings of V. D. Nebylitsyn (Refs. 42, 44, 45, 65 and 66), an outstanding young Soviet psychologist who succeeded to Teplov's chair after the latter's untimely death in 1965.

The concept of 'dynamism' ('dinamichnost' in the Russian) is very close to the notion of 'conditionability', as this term is used in Western writings, with the exception that in the work of the Moscow school it is thought that there are two independent forms of dynamism: dynamism of the excitatory process (roughly, the ability to form positive conditioned reflexes rapidly) and dynamism of the inhibitory process (the ability to form inhibitory conditioned reflexes rapidly). The term 'dynamism' was introduced by Nebylitsyn (Ref. 42) after he had shown in a historical and theoretical review that the Soviet literature contained a serious ambiguity[1] in its use of the notion of 'equilibrium of the nervous processes'. This ambiguity took the following form.

It has been customary to measure 'equilibrium' in Soviet work on typology by comparing the speed of formation of positive and negative conditioned reflexes. At the same time, it has been usual to describe 'equilibrium' as 'equilibrium in the strength of the nervous processes'. Yet, as the reader will see from Table 1, the more basic dimension of strength of the excitatory process is not measured by the speed of formation of positive conditioned reflexes, nor is the dimension of strength of the inhibitory process measured by the speed of formation of inhibitory conditioned reflexes. (Indeed, work from Teplov's laboratory suggests that, contrary to the views expressed by earlier Soviet workers, there are no differences in speed of conditioning between individuals of different degrees of strength of the excitatory process [see Gray (Ref. 28, p. 299). This is a point to which we return below.] In that case, Nebylitsyn rather naturally asks, what is the equilibrium that is measured by

---

[1] This ambiguity probably has its origin in the gradual change in Pavlov's theory of types from a system based on the notion of equilibrium to one in which the concept of strength of the nervous system played the leading role. (Ref. 64, pp. 5–27 for a detailed account of this change.)

the relative speed of formation of positive and negative conditioned reflexes equilibrium between? As he shows, there is no reason to suppose that speed of formation of conditioned reflexes depends on either of the two basic Pavlovian dimensions—strength and mobility of the nervous processes (Ref. 49, p. 313; Ref. 64)—and from this he concludes that there must be some other basic property of nervous functioning of which the dimension of 'equilibrium', as this has traditionally been understood in the Soviet literature, is a derivative. It is this basic property which he proposes to call 'dynamism'.

Another important conclusion which flows from Nebylitsyn's analysis (Ref. 42) is that, since the equilibrium usually measured in Soviet laboratories is not equilibrium in strength of the opposing processes of excitation and inhibition, there should also be a dimension of equilibrium in strength which it is possible to measure. In fact, he proposes that, in general, a complete description of an individual's type, in the sense of his position along a number of independently varying dimensions of personality, should involve the determination of a value on any given dimension separately for the processes of excitation and inhibition, followed by the calculation of a derived value for equilibrium between the two processes with respect to that dimension (see Table 2).

TABLE 2

GENERAL METHOD FOR CLASSIFICATION OF PROPERTIES OF THE NERVOUS SYSTEM AND FOR EVALUATING EQUILIBRIUM (FROM NEBYLITSYN, Ref. 42)

	Strength	Dynamism	Mobility
Excitation	2	4	3
Inhibition	2	1	5
Equilibrium	0	−3	−2

In this connection, it should be pointed out that the dimension of strength of the nervous system discussed in this paper and reviewed elsewhere (Ref. 27) is, strictly speaking, a dimension of strength of the excitatory process only. As discussed by Teplov (Ref. 64, pp. 95–97), it is also possible to measure, in principle, a dimension of strength of the inhibitory process and, consequently, equilibrium with respect to strength of the nervous processes. Efforts are being made by the Moscow group to develop methods of measuring the strength of the inhibitory process (Refs. 51 and 45, pp. 201-205), notably by increasing the duration or frequency of presentation of an inhibitory conditioned stimulus and observing any consequent disruption of the inhibitory conditioned reflex. However, it is too early to say whether these efforts are likely to bear fruit. Concerning the remaining Pavlovian dimension, 'mobility' of the nervous processes (Ref. 64, pp. 73–94), Pavlov himself pointed out at a 'Wednesday' meeting in 1935 (Ref. 45, p. 24) that it is necessary to test the degree of mobility of both the excitatory process and the inhibitory process separately in each experimental subject.

'Dynamism of the excitatory process', then, refers to that property of the nervous system which underlies the ability to form positive conditioned reflexes with more or less rapidity; while 'dynamism of the inhibitory process' refers to that property of the nervous system which underlies the ability to form inhibitory conditioned reflexes with more or less rapidity. Furthermore, there is, in the Russian view, a third, derived, dimension of nervous functioning, namely, 'equilibrium in dynamism'. This is the property of the nervous system which underlies the relative superiority in speed of conditioning which is shown, in a given individual, by either positive or negative conditioned reflexes: where positive conditioned reflexes are formed relatively more rapidly, we speak of a 'predominance of excitation with respect to dynamism'; where inhibitory conditioned reflexes are formed with relatively greater rapidity, we speak of a 'predominance of the inhibitory process with respect to dynamism'.

Now there are rather obvious similarities between the concept of equilibrium in dynamism and Eysenck's view of the excitation-inhibition balance (Ref. 14) which he believes to underlie the personality dimension of introversion-extraversion. Indeed, Eysenck has explicitly connected this dimension with conditionability, introverts being supposed to develop positive conditioned reflexes more rapidly than extraverts. There is, however, one important difference between Eysenck's approach and that of the Moscow group which should be brought out. As Nebylitsyn (Ref. 45, pp. 308–309) points out, once it is admitted that for any given property of nervous functioning, it is necessary to investigate the excitatory process and the inhibitory process separately, it follows that there are, in principle, three possible forms of relation between variation in the resulting two dimensions. These may be totally unrelated to one another; they may be related positively, in the sense that high values along the dimension relating to the excitatory process are accompanied by high values along the corresponding dimension relating to the inhibitory process; or they may be negatively related, in the sense that high values on the one dimension correspond to low values on the other.[1] The latter relationship is assumed in Eysenck's hypothesis as to the physiological substrate of introversion-extraversion: introverts are said to generate excitatory potentials more easily and inhibitory potentials less easily than extraverts (Ref. 14). Yet, it is clearly an empirical question whether this is indeed the correct relationship to assume. Nebylitsyn (Ref. 45, pp. 314–323) discusses the data obtained in his laboratory relevant to the relationship between dynamism in excitation and inhibition and concludes that no final decision is yet possible. He appears, however, to incline to the view that there is a great deal of independence between the two dimensions. My own view of the data he adduces is that they leave open a strong possibility that the relation between the two forms of dynamism, or speed of conditioning, is in fact of the kind postulated by Eysenck. If we assume that this is the case, it makes it easier to compare the Soviet work on dynamism with Eysenck's work on introversion-extraversion, and we shall therefore do so. However, the empirical and theoretical issues involved in this question of the general relationship between measures of positive conditioning and of inhibitory conditioning are clearly of very great importance, and it is to be hoped that they will receive more explicit experimental attention in the future than has been the case to date.[2]

The general similarity between the Russian concept of equilibrium in dynamism and Eysenck's view of the excitation-inhibition balance is reinforced by the fact that, just as Eysenck (Ref. 19) has proposed that this balance is critically dependent on the activity of the reticular activating system, so Nebylitsyn (Ref. 44) has proposed that dynamism in excitation is dependent on activity in this same system. On the assumption that dynamism in excitation and dynamism in inhibition[3] are negatively related to one another, it follows that Nebylitsyn's proposal amounts to the suggestion that a high level of activity in the reticular activating system is conducive to a predominance of excitation in dynamism. There are therefore grounds for proposing, as an alternative way of linking the work of the Moscow group with the dimension of introversion-extraversion, a second hypothesis—Hypothesis 2: the

---

[1] Similar arguments are advanced by Claridge (Ref. 8).

[2] See Appendix, where some of Nebylitsyn's data are briefly presented and this general problem is considered further.

[3] Nebylitsyn (Ref. 44) also suggests that dynamism in inhibition depends on 'regulating cortical influences'. There is not space here to consider the implications of this part of his theory.

dimensions of introversion-extraversion and equilibrium in dynamism are identical, the introvert corresponding to the individual with a predominance of excitation in dynamism. For the reader to be able to evaluate this hypothesis it is necessary for him to have some idea of the way in which individuals at the extreme poles of the 'equilibrium in dynamism' dimension have been shown to differ from one another. The most important findings made by the Moscow group are set out in Table 3.

TABLE 3

DIFFERENCES BETWEEN INDIVIDUALS WITH A PREDOMINANCE OF EXCITATION
AND THOSE WITH A PREDOMINANCE OF INHIBITION IN DYNAMISM[1]

	Predominance of excitation	Predominance of inhibition
Speed of conditioning (EEG)	High	Low
Duration of a-depression to novel stimulus, whether auditory or visual	Long	Short
Duration of conditioned a-depression	Long	Short
Speed of habituation of a-depression to novel stimulus	Slow	Fast
Speed of extinction of conditioned a-depression	Slow	Fast
Speed of formation of differentiation in EEG conditioning	Slow	Fast
Amount of a-depression during presentation of CS for delayed CR (EEG)	High	Low
Speed of formation of delayed CR (EEG)	Slow	Fast
a-index	Low	High
a-amplitude	Low	High
a-frequency	High	Low
B-index	Low	High
B-amplitude	Low	High
B-frequency	Low	High
O-frequency	Low	High
EEG photo-driving effect	Small	Large

Before we turn to a consideration of the data relevant to our two hypotheses, one general point must be made. We have two hypotheses (introversion = weakness of the nervous system, and introversion = predominance of excitation in dynamism) only because of the data from Teplov's laboratory suggesting that the dimension of equilibrium in

[1] Based on data—all obtained from EEG experiments—from Nebylitsyn (Refs. 42, 43 and 45).

dynamism is orthogonal to the dimension of strength of the nervous system. These data were obtained from carefully conducted factor-analytic studies, one of which is reviewed by Gray (Ref. 27, pp. 267–274); see also Nebylitsyn (Ref. 42) and Nebylitsyn *et al.* (Ref. 46). However, only the last of these studies has simultaneously used a fairly large number of tests of strength of dynamism, as well as further tests unrelated to these dimensions. It remains possible that a really large-scale study of this kind might show that strength of the nervous system and equilibrium in dynamism are not so completely unrelated as it is at present believed. It might turn out, for example, that, although to some degree distinct from one another, they constitute two subfactors both related to a single major factor, perhaps the factor uncovered in Western studies as that of introversion-extraversion, or the factor described by Claridge (Ref. 8) as 'dysthymia-hysteria'. This is a possibility which should be borne in mind in what follows.

Now the obvious way to settle the issues raised by our two hypotheses is by experiment. What is needed, of course, is a large-scale study in which a group of subjects is tested on the Western measures of introversion-extraversion and on the Russian tests of strength and dynamism. Not only has no such experiment yet been conducted but the fact that the situations used by the Russians are very different from most of the procedures used in the work on introversion-extraversion makes it difficult to bring data to bear on our two hypotheses in any but the most general way. This situation, however, has one big advantage: the difference in procedures means that, if future research does show that one of the Russian dimensions can be identified with one of the Western ones, we would be justified in putting much more confidence in its reality. The purpose of this article is to suggest the lines of research in this field which, in the light of existing data, are likely to prove most fruitful.

To these data we now turn. We shall consider first those points which are in favour of the introversion weakness of the nervous system hypothesis; and then those points which are in favour of the alternative hypothesis and therefore offer some difficulty for the identification of introversion with weakness.

Sensory thresholds

One of the most important findings of Teplov's group is that individuals with a weak nervous system have low absolute sensory thresholds in both the visual and auditory modalities (Ref. 27, pp. 207–230). It is therefore of considerable significance that it has also been shown in

c*

recent experiments that introverts have lower auditory (Ref. 58) and pain (Ref. 32) thresholds than extraverts. The possible connection between lowered sensory thresholds and heightened arousal has been discussed by Gray (Ref. 28, pp. 308–314).

The effects of distraction

Yermolayeva-Tomina (Ref. 70; see Ref. 27, pp. 248–260) has shown that sensory thresholds are lowered in the strong nervous system but raised in the weak by the simultaneous presentation of a distracting heteromodal stimulus. Elsewhere (Ref. 28, pp. 330–332) it has been suggested that this result is due to the effect of the additional stimulation on level of arousal, this being taken closer to the optimum for this particular task in the less highly aroused (strong) individual but beyond the optimum in the more highly aroused (weak) individual. A number of similar findings have been reported for the effects of distraction on introverts and extraverts. Bakan, Belton & Toth (Ref. 2) and Colquhoun & Corcoran (Ref. 9), using vigilance-like tasks, found that introverts perform more efficiently in isolation, extraverts in a group. Claridge (Ref. 7), also using a vigilance task, found the same result when he introduced the simultaneous performance of a second task as the additional source of stimulation. Furthermore, Corcoran (Ref. 12) has presented data to support the view that these effects of additional stimulation are due to the fact that introverts start off with a chronically higher level of arousal than extraverts.

Stimulus intensity and transmarginal inhibition

Both weak individuals (Ref. 27) and introverts (Ref. 19) have been conceived as, relative to their opposite numbers, amplifying stimulation. (The connection between this view and notions of arousability will be obvious.) Thus it is expected that any change in performance which can be produced by increasing stimulus intensity will be reached at a lower stimulus intensity in the more highly aroused (weak, introvert) than in the less highly aroused (strong, extravert) individual. I have reviewed the data on strength of the nervous system from this point of view elsewhere (Ref. 27). In the case of introversion-extraversion, the evidence for this hypothesis is not yet so firm, but there are nevertheless some interesting pointers. Thus Corcoran (Ref. 11) found that unconditioned salivation to an acid stimulus was higher in introverts than in extraverts, as it is, of course, if the acidity is increased. Furthermore, Eysenck & Eysenck (Refs. 20 and 21) have reported that, if the stimulus (lemon juice) is made extremely strong by getting the subjects to swallow it, this relation may be reversed, introverts now salivating significantly less than extraverts, though both show an increase relative to the situation in which the lemon juice is not swallowed. This may be an example of transmarginal inhibition, that is, a performance decrement which occurs when stimulus intensity is raised to a very high level. If further studies support this view, we would have an extremely important piece of evidence in favour of the introversion-weakness hypothesis; for the greater susceptibility of the weak nervous system to transmarginal inhibition is the cornerstone of the theory of strength of the nervous system (Ref. 27).

From the hypothesis that introverts amplify stimulation it may also be deduced that introverts will prefer lower levels of stimulation than extraverts (Ref. 19). In accordance with this deduction Weisen (Ref. 69) found that extraverts (psychopaths) would work to turn stimulation of high intensity on, introverts (anxiety neurotics) to turn it off. Other studies have shown greater tolerance for pain in the extravert (Refs. 37 and 50). Finally, Eysenck (Ref. 19) discusses a number of experiments which suggest that introverts have greater tolerance for sensory deprivation than extraverts.

Flicker phenomena

There is a very confused situation at present in the Russian work on flicker phenomena as a function of personality. A curious discrepancy exists between the arguments that are applied to the critical frequency of flashing phosphene[1] (CFP) and the critical frequency of flicker-fusion (CFF). The former is taken as a measure of strength of the nervous system (Refs. 41 and 27, pp. 242–248), the weak individual having a higher CFP than the strong. This is because CFP varies positively with stimulus intensity and the dependence of this measure on strength of the nervous system fits the familiar pattern of weak individuals reacting as though to a higher intensity stimulus than strong individuals. Furthermore, it has been shown that, over a critical range of voltages, CFP does indeed correlate with other measures of strength (Ref. 41, p. 244). CFF, on the other hand, which varies in the same way with stimulus intensity (Ref. 26) has never been used in experiments on strength of the nervous system. Instead, it is taken to be a measure of

---

[1] When the frequency of an electric current, which is passed through the eye so as to produce the visual sensation known as a 'phosphene', is increased, a threshold is reached beyond which no further visual sensation is produced: this is the 'critical frequency of flashing phosphene'.

'lability of the nervous processes' (Ref. 45 and 64, pp. 73–94).[1] However, the logical parallels between CFP and CFF are reinforced by a
number of experimental findings proceeding from Teplov's group
(Refs. 4, 67 and 24) which suggest that high lability and high weakness
are intimately connected with one another. It seems possible, therefore,
that the weak individual, relative to the strong, is characterized by high
thresholds both of CFP and CFF. Elsewhere (Ref. 28, pp. 314–318) I
have discussed the possibility that, in general, the ability to resolve a
train of high-frequency stimuli into its discrete components will be
facilitated by a high level of arousal.

The importance of these findings in our present context is that there is
evidence from a number of studies (Ref. 57) that CFF is higher in
introverts than in extraverts. Thus, if CFF is higher in the weak nervous
system, as is CFP, we have another piece of evidence favouring the
identification, introversion-weakness.

Drug effects

There is a striking similarity between the role played by caffeine in
the theory of strength (Ref. 27) and the role played by stimulant drugs in
the theory of introversion propounded by Eysenck (Refs. 15 and 19):
caffeine moves people towards the weak end of the dimension of
strength and stimulant drugs are said to have an introverting effect.
(There is no reason to suppose that the effects attributed to caffeine in the
Russian work would not equally be expected of other representatives of
the class of stimulant drugs.) Another important similarity is that in
both cases stimulant drugs appear to have a relatively greater effect in
the more aroused (introverted, weak) individual (Ref. 27, p. 279 and
passim; Ref. 19). The data supporting these statements are reviewed in
the articles by Gray and Eysenck cited above. It is clear that the parallel
treatments accorded to stimulant drugs in the two bodies of work is a
powerful argument in favour of the identification, introversion-weakness,
as well as being in good agreement with the view that both these dimensions are functions of arousal level.

[1] Recent work from the Moscow laboratory (Ref. 45) shows clearly the complex
nature of the functions described by Teplov (Ref. 64) under the heading 'mobility
of the nervous processes'. One group of these functions is now regarded as separate
from the others and is collectively described as 'lability'. Among the tests being tried
out as measures of 'lability' are—apart from CFF—the adequate optic chronaxie
and the relation between the ascending and descending psychophysical thresholds.
However, it is too soon to say whether a genuinely unitary function is being measured
by these tests.

In the Western work on introversion-extraversion an important role is also played by depressant drugs, which are supposed to have an extra-verting effect (Refs. 15 and 19). This view has been supported empirically, notably by the work on the sedation threshold pioneered by Shagass and his colleagues (e.g. Ref. 56; see Ref. 19 for review). It would be of great value to obtain similar data for the effects of depressant drugs on individuals varying in strength of the nervous system.

Susceptibility to fatigue

One of the interesting things about the work on fatigue as a function of personality is that, in this instance (in the absence of any linkage with notions of arousal), the theory of strength and the theory of introversion, which usually make their predictions in somewhat similar ways, come up with different predictions. On the basis of the notion that the weak nervous system is one with a low 'working capacity' (a term which is defined by Teplov (Ref. 63) as 'the capacity to endure stimulation which is extreme in its duration or intensity') it is predicted that weak indi-viduals will show a decline over time in their efficiency of performance which is greater than the comparable decline shown by strong indi-viduals. On the basis of the notion that extraverts are more susceptible to reactive inhibition than introverts, it can be predicted from Eysenck's theory that it is the former who will show a greater decline in efficiency as a result of fatigue. In other words, contrary to the general form of the identification we are examining, this time extraverts are expected to behave in the same way as the weak nervous system. In some ways, then, the relation between these two personality dimensions, on the one hand, and susceptibility to fatigue, on the other, makes a particularly good test both of the identification of weakness with introversion and of the hypothesis that each of these dimensions of personality is a function of arousal level.

Before turning to the relevant data, let us consider what changes we would make in our predictions if we based ourselves on an arousal view of the two personality dimensions. Clearly, our prediction will depend on whether continuation at the particular task leads to a gradually decreasing or a gradually increasing level of arousal.[1] In the former case,

---

[1] This is probably the same distinction as that made by Rozhdestvenskaya (Ref. 52, p. 371) between conditions leading to 'exhaustion of the nerve cells' (trans-marginal inhibition or high arousal) and those leading to 'the onset of a hypnotic state' (low arousal). The introduction to Rozhdestvenskaya's paper contains interest-ing data obtained in classical conditioning experiments relevant to this distinction.

we would predict that the individual high on arousal (weak, introvert) would show less of a decline in efficiency than the individual low on arousal (strong, extravert). In the latter case, however, we would predict that the individual low on arousal (strong, extravert) would be more resistant to fatigue. In other words, both the Teplovian and the Eysenckian prediction would be made, but under different conditions. Furthermore, since continuation at the same task must involve some degree of monotonous stimulation, it is likely that a gradual decrease in arousal level over the duration of the experiment will more often be encountered in work on fatigue than the converse; thus we would expect it to be more difficult to arrange conditions so as to make the Teplovian observation than to make the Eysenckian observation.[1]

What, then, are the facts? Data supporting Eysenck's prediction that the extravert is more susceptible to fatigue have been presented by Broadbent (Ref. 5), by Bakan, Belton & Toth (Ref. 2) and by Halcomb & Kirk (Ref. 31), all using vigilance tasks, in which overall stimulus intensity is relatively low and monotony great—conditions which should lead to a decreasing level of arousal. Early data from Teplov's laboratory (Ref. 71; see Ref. 27, pp. 260–262) also seemed to support the Teplovian prediction, that the weak nervous system would be more highly susceptible to fatigue. Here the task used was a mental arithmetic task, in which it is extremely difficult to estimate what is likely to be happening to arousal level; but there is certainly no obvious reason to suppose it should be increasing to any great extent. However, recent work conducted by Rozhdestvenskaya & Yermolayeva-Tomina (Ref. 53) failed to confirm these results and indeed, found that individuals with a strong nervous system showed greater physiological signs of fatigue in a vigilance-like situation. Thus, in the only case where both Russian and Western work has used the same type of situation (a vigilance task) the results support the identification of introversion with weakness—results which are particularly convincing inasmuch as the expectation of the experimenters was exactly the opposite of what was obtained.

It should not be thought, however, that it is always the highly aroused subject (weak, introvert) who is more susceptible to fatigue; and of course our analysis in terms of arousal does not lead us to expect that this will be the case. As well as the Yermolayeva-Tomina finding (Ref. 71) referred to above, there are also indications in the literature on introversion-extraversion that there are conditions in which the greater

[1] It has been suggested to me by S. Rachmann that it might be possible to use a gradually increasing administration of a stimulant drug for this experiment.

susceptibility to fatigue of the introvert can be abolished or even reversed (e.g. Refs. 7, 12 and 9). It is clear that much more detailed findings are needed, especially from experiments in which overall level of stimulus intensity is deliberately varied. Nevertheless, it seems possible that our analysis in terms of level of arousal is not too far from the truth, and if this could be established, it would be a strong argument in favour of the view that both introversion and weakness are consequences of high arousability.

Reactive inhibition

Hull's (Ref. 34) concept of 'reactive inhibition' has played a considerable role in Eysenck's treatment of introversion-extraversion (Ref. 14). However, in the last decade or so the difficulties involved in this concept have become increasingly clear (e.g. Ref. 23). At the same time, more and more of the data once explained in terms of reactive inhibition have been dealt with in other ways. We have just seen an example of this, in the alternative account proposed for susceptibility to fatigue in terms of changing levels of arousal. Other examples are the treatment of extinction of instrumental behaviour in terms of a theory based on 'frustration' (Refs. 1 and 58), or the revised account of certain aspects of the 'reminiscence' phenomenon in terms of consolidation proposed by Eysenck (Ref. 17). Again, it would seem relatively easy to deal with the disruptive effects of massed practice on learning in terms of a lowered level of arousal due to the greater monotony of stimulation produced by this procedure; though obviously this hypothesis stands in need of experimental test.

The question therefore arises whether there is still any need, either in general learning theory or in the theory of introversion-extraversion, for the concept of reactive inhibition. This question is of particular relevance in the present context because there is considerable similarity between 'reactive inhibition' and 'transmarginal inhibition' as the latter is used in the Russian theory of strength of the nervous system. For example, the phenomenon of extinction with reinforcement is attributed to reactive inhibition in the Western literature (Ref. 35) and to transmarginal inhibition in the Russian literature (Ref. 27). Again, both massing of trials and increased stimulus intensity (which leads to increased response magnitude) are thought to lead to a growth in both forms of inhibition. Yet in Eysenck's theory (Ref. 14) it is the extravert who is most susceptible in reactive inhibition, while in the theory of strength of the nervous system (Ref. 27) it is the weak individual who is more susceptible to transmarginal inhibition. This would lead to an identification of the weak individual with the extravert, the reverse of the identification which we have considered throughout this paper.

This dilemma is, of course, the general form of which the problem of susceptibility to fatigue in the two theories of personality, considered in the preceding section, is a special case. A tentative resolution of the dilemma was reached there by re-analysing the problem in terms of level of arousal. Is it possible to extend this solution to all the situations in which Eysenckian theory predicts greater susceptibility to reactive inhibition in the extravert?

An analysis of the general Hullian treatment of reactive inhibition suggests that there are two separate ideas mixed up in this concept. One is a tendency to cease making a specific response which has just been made; this is the way in which the term is formally defined by Hull (Ref. 34) and we can call it 'reactive inhibition proper'. The other is a general fall (i.e. not specific to any particular response) in the organism's level of functioning; it is this that corresponds to 'de-arousal', and although never so defined, it is often this that is meant by 'reactive inhibition'.[1] Now, if there were no evidence for a process corresponding to reactive inhibition proper, we could abandon the concept of reactive inhibition entirely and substitute for it that of de-arousal. At the time that Hull introduced the concept, there was indeed very little evidence for the existence of such a process. It was introduced, rather, as a theoretical postulate which, it was hoped, would account for the phenomena which Pavlov had subsumed under the heading 'internal inhibition'. (In fact, as Gleitman, Nachmias & Neisser (Ref. 23) have shown, it does not do this job at all well.) Recently, however, good evidence has been obtained in Eysenck's laboratory (Refs. 59 and 16) that there is indeed an empirical phenomenon which corresponds very closely to reactive inhibition proper. This evidence was obtained from a simple tapping task in which it was possible to measure the number and duration of involuntary rest pauses, the assumption being that such pauses are produced by the accumulation of reactive inhibition proper. Furthermore—and this is the important point for our present purpose—extraverted subjects were considerably more susceptible to reactive inhibition measured in this way, in accordance with the prediction from Eysenck's theory (Ref. 14).

It appears, then, that it is not possible entirely to abandon the concept of reactive inhibition in favour of a concept of de-arousal. It remains unclear how significant reactive inhibition proper is, and how the

[1] See Appendix at end of chapter.

extravert's greater susceptibility to it relates to his lower arousal level. It is also difficult to see what structure or process in the central nervous system is likely to be responsible for the phenomenon. Furthermore, the relations between 'reactive inhibition proper' and 'transmarginal inhibition', assuming that both these terms correspond to real processes, remain to be worked out. It is clear that, if the general identification of weakness of the nervous system with introversion is correct, these two forms of inhibition cannot be the same. In that case, it is going to require considerable experimental ingenuity to distinguish clearly between them. With regard to our general theme—the relation between strength of the nervous system and introversion-extraversion—it is obviously very important to find out whether individuals classified by the Russian tests as 'strong' show a greater susceptibility to reactive inhibition proper, as measured by the Speilmann tapping test for involuntary rest pauses. There are at present no data available on this point.

EEG Measures

We come now to the most serious difficulty for the identification of weakness with introversion and at the same time evidence for the identification of introversion with predominance of excitation in dynamism. Both Savage (Ref. 55) and Marton & Urban (Ref. 39) have reported lower indices of a-activity in introverts as compared to extraverts. Claridge (Ref. 8) reports similar findings in a population mainly composed of diagnosed neurotics. On the other hand, Nebylitsyn (Ref. 43) found that predominance of excitation in dynamism was correlated with low a-index, low a-amplitude and high a-frequency and that none of these measures related to strength of the nervous system. Moreover, Marton & Urban reported that introverts showed slower EEG habituation than extraverts, as was the case for Nebylitsyn's subjects with predominance of excitation in dynamism. If it can be confirmed both that introverts have lower a-indices than extraverts and that there is no relation between a-activity and strength of the nervous system, it would be impossible to maintain that the dimensions of introversion-extraversion and strength of the nervous system are identical.

Speed of conditioning

One of the most important elements in Eysenck's theory of introversion-extraversion (Ref. 14) has been the supposition that introverts condition better than extraverts. It is clear that this places the dimension of introversion-extraversion very close to the dimension of equilibrium in dynamism, since this dimension is actually defined in terms of speed of conditioning. Furthermore, there is no evidence to date of any systematic differences in speed of conditioning between weak and strong individuals (see Ref. 28, p. 299). On the face of it, then, this offers another serious difficulty for the identification of introversion with weakness of the nervous system. However, Eysenck's more recent statements on the relation between introversion-extraversion and speed of conditioning (Ref. 18) show that his general theoretical system predicts that introverts will condition better than extraverts only under certain conditions. Furthermore, empirical data obtained by Eysenck & Levey from studies of the conditioned eyelid response in introverts and extraverts (Ref. 18) suggest that the most important of these conditions would probably also favour individuals with a weak nervous system as compared to those with a strong nervous system: namely, a weak UCS (given the established difference in sensory thresholds between weak and strong individuals) and a short CS-UCS interval (given the established difference in reaction time between weak and strong individuals). Thus, although much more work clearly remains to be done in this important field, the evidence from speed of conditioning for the hypothesis is not as negative as it at first appears. Nevertheless, it remains true, that, if introversion is indeed equivalent to weakness and if the Moscow group is correct in supposing that it is possible to define a dimension of conditionability which is orthogonal to that of strength of the nervous system, then the effect of degree of extraversion on speed of conditioning must be a comparatively minor one, occurring only under special conditions.

It will be clear that no final conclusion as to the merits of the various hypotheses discussed in this paper is possible. Indeed, we have raised far more questions than we have offered answers. Nevertheless, there appears to be sufficient evidence for it to be worth devoting serious attention to the hypothesis that the dimensions of strength of the nervous system and introversion-extraversion are identical, both being based upon level of arousal.

REFERENCES
References marked * are in Russian

1. AMSEL, A., Frustrative nonreward in partial reinforcement and discrimination learning: some recent history and a theoretical extension. *Psychol. Rev.*, **69**, 306–328, 1962.
2. BAKAN, P., BELTON, J. A. & TOTH, J. C., Extraversion-introversion and decrement in an auditory vigilance task. In *Vigilance: a Symposium.* (eds. Buckner, D. N. & McGrath, J. J.). New York: McGraw-Hill, 1963.
3. BERLYNE, D. E., *Conflict, Arousal and Curiosity.* New York: McGraw-Hill, 1960.
4. *BORISOVA, M. N., GUREVICH, K. M., YERMOLAYEVA-TOMINA, L. B., KOLODNAYA, A. Ya., RAVICH-SHCHERBO, I. V. & SHVARTS, L. A., A comparative study of different indices of mobility of the nervous system in man. In *Typological Features of Higher Nervous Activity in Man.* (ed. Teplov, B. M.), pp. 180–201. Moscow: Akad. pedagog. Nauk RSFSR, 1963.
5. BROADBENT, D. E., *Perception and Communication.* Oxford: Pergamon Press, 1958.
6. BROADHURST, P. L., Applications of biometrical genetics to the inheritance of behaviour. In *Experiments in Personality.* Vol. 1 Psychogenetics and Psychopharmacology, (ed. Eysenck, H. J.), pp. 3–102. London: Routledge & Kegan Paul, 1960.
7. CLARIDGE, G. S., The excitation-inhibition balance in neurotics. In *Experiments in Personality.* Vol. 3 (ed. Eysenck, H. J.), New York: Praeger, 1960.
8. ——, *Personality and Arousal.* Oxford: Pergamon Press, 1967.
9. COLQUHOUN, W. P. & CORCORAN, D. W. J., The effects of time of day and social isolation on the relationship between temperament and performance. *Brit. J. soc. clin. Psychol.*, **3**, 226–231, 1964.
10. CORCORAN, D. W. J., Individual differences in performance after loss of sleep. Unpublished Doctoral dissertation, Univ. of Cambridge, 1961.
11. ——, The relation between introversion and salivation *Amer. J. Psychol.*, **77**, 298–300, 1964.
12. ——, Personality and the inverted-U relation. *Brit. J. Psychol.*, **56**, 267–274, 1965.
13. DUFFY, E., *Activation and Behavior.* New York: John Wiley, 1962.

14. EYSENCK, H. J., *The Dynamics of Anxiety and Hysteria*. New York: Praeger, 1957.
15. ——, *Experiments with Drugs*. Oxford: Pergamon Press, 1963.
16. ——, Involuntary rest pauses in tapping as a function of drive and personality. *Percept. mot. Skills*, **18**, 173–174, 1964.
17. ——, A three-factor theory of reminiscence. *Brit. J. Psychol.*, **56**, 163–181, 1965.
18. ——, Conditioning, introversion-extraversion and the strength of the nervous system. *Proc. Eighteenth Int. Congr. exp. Psychol.* Moscow. Ninth Symposium, pp. 33–44, 1966.
19. ——, *The Biological Basic of Personality*. Springfield, Ill: Charles C. Thomas, 1967.
20. EYSENCK, S. B. G. & EYSENCK, H. J., Salivary response to lemon juice as a measure of introversion. *Percept. mot. Skills*, **24**, 1047–53. 1967.
21. —— & ——, Physiological reactivity to sensory stimulation as a measure of personality. *Psych. Rep.*, **20**, 45–6, 1967.
22. FREEMAN, A. L., *The Energetics of Human Behaviour*. Ithaca: Cornell Univ. Press, 1948.
23. GLEITMAN, H., NACHMIAS, J. & NEISSER, U., The S-R reinforcement theory of excitation. *Psychol. Rev.*, **61**, 23–33, 1954.
24. GOLUBEVA, E. A., Photo-driving brain potentials and typological characteristics of the nervous system. *Proc. Eighteenth int. Congr. exp. Psychol.* Moscow. Ninth Symposium, pp. 127–132, 1966.
25. GRANGER, G. W., Night vision and psychiatric disorders. *J. ment. Sci.*, **103**, 48–79, 1957.
26. ——, Abnormalities of sensory perception. In *Handbook of Abnormal Psychology*. (ed. Eysenck, H. J.), pp. 108–166. London: Pitman Medical, 1960.
27. GRAY, J. A., Strength of the nervous system as a dimension of personality in man: a review of work from the laboratory of B. M. Teplov. In *Pavlov's Typology*. (ed. Gray, J. A.), pp. 157–287. Oxford: Pergamon Press, 1964.
28. ——, Strength of the nervous system and levels of arousal: a reinterpretation. In *Pavlov's Typology*. (ed. Gray, J. A.), pp. 289–364. Oxford: Pergamon Press, 1964.
29. ——, Disappointment and drugs in the rat. *The Advancement of Science*, **23**, 595-605, 1967.
30. —— & SMITH, P., An arousal-decision model for partial reinforcement and discrimination learning. Paper delivered to the Sym-

posium on Discrimination/Learning, Experimental Analysis of Behaviour Group, Brighton, April 5–6, 1967.

31. HALCOMB, C. G. & KIRK, R. E., Organismic variables as predictors of vigilance behaviour. *Percept. mot. Skills*, **21**, 547–552, 1965.

32. HASLAM, D. R., Individual differences in pain threshold and the concept of arousal. Unpublished Ph.D. thesis, Bristol University, 1966.

33. HEBB, D. O., Drives and the cns (conceptual nervous system). *Psychol. Rev.*, **62**, 243–254, 1955.

34. HULL, C. L., *Principles of Behavior*. New York: Appleton-Century, 1943.

35. KENDRICK, D. C., Inhibition with reinforcement (conditioned inhibition). *J. exp. Psychol.*, **56**, 313–318, 1958.

36. LINDSLEY, D. B., The reticular system and perceptual discrimination. In *Reticular Formation of the Brain*. (eds. Jasper, H. H. *et al.*), *Henry Ford Hospital International Symposium*, pp. 513–534. London: Churchill, 1957.

37. LYNN, R. & EYSENCK, H. J., Tolerance for pain, extraversion and neuroticism. *Percept. mot. Skills*, **12**, 161–162, 1961.

38. MALMO, R. B., Activation: a neuropsychological dimension. *Psychol. Rev.*, **66**, 367–386, 1959.

39. MARTON, M. & URBAN, YA, An electroencephalographic investigation of individual differences in the processes of conditioning. *Proc. Eighteenth int. Cong. exp. Psychol.* Moscow: Ninth Symposium, pp. 106–109, 1966.

40. MORUZZI, G. & MAGOUN, H. W., Brain stem reticular formation and activation of the EEG. *Electroenceph. clin. Neurophysiol*, **1**, 455–473, 1949.

41.*NEBYLITSYN, V. D., The correlation between certain indices of the electrical excitability of the eye and strength of the nervous system. *Dokl. Akad. pedagog. Nauk RSFSR*, **2**, 99–102, 1960.

42.*——, The structure of the fundamental properties of the nervous system. *Vopr. Psikhol.*, **4**, 21–34, 1963.

43.*——, An electroencephalographic investigation of the properties of strength of the nervous system and equilibrium of the nervous processes in man using factor analysis. In *Typological Features of Higher Nervous Activity in Man*. (ed. Teplov, B. M.), vol. 3, pp. 47–80. Moscow: Akad. pedagog. Nauk RSFSR, 1963.

44.*——, Cortico-reticular relations and their place in the structure of the properties of the nervous system. *Vopr. Psikhol.*, **1**, 3–24, 1964.

70   Theoretical and Methodological Issues

45.*——, *Fundamental Properties of the Human Nervous System.* Moscow: Akad. pedagog. Nauk RSFSR, 1966.

46.*——, GOLUBEVA, E. A., RAVICH-SHCHERBO, I. V. & YERMOLAYEVA-TOMINA, L. B., A comparative study of rapid methods for determining the basic properties of the nervous system in man. In *Typological Features of Higher Nervous Activity in Man.* (*ed.* Teplov, B. M.), vol. 4, pp. 60–83. Moscow: Akad. pedagog. Nauk RSFSR, 1965.

47. OSGOOD, C. E., *Method and Theory in Experimental Psychology.* New York: Oxford University Press, 1953.

48. PAVLOV, I. P., *Lectures on Conditioned Reflexes: Twenty-five Years of Objective Study of the Higher Nervous Activity (Behavior) of Animals.* Vol. 1 (Trans. and ed. Gantt, W. H.). New York: International Publishers, 1928.

49. ——, *Selected Works.* (Trans. Belsky, S.). Moscow: Foreign Languages Publishing House, 1955.

50. PETRIE, A., COLLINS, W. & SOLOMON, P., The tolerance for pain and for sensory deprivation. *Amer. J. Psychol.,* **123,** 80–90, 1960.

51.*ROZHDESTVENSKAYA, V. I., The determination of strength of the inhibitory process in man by extending the duration of action of a differential stimulus. In *Typological Features of Higher Nervous Activity in Man.* (ed. Teplov, B. M.), vol. 3, pp. 108–116. Moscow: Akad. pedagog. Nauk RSFSR, 1963.

52. ——, The strength of the nervous system as shown in the ability of nerve-cells to endure protracted concentrated excitation. In *Pavlov's Typology.* (ed. Gray, J. A.), pp. 367–378. Oxford: Pergamon Press, 1964.

53. —— & YERMOLAYEVA-TOMINA, L. B., A study of mental capacity for work in relation to typological characteristics of the nervous system. *Proc. Eighteenth int. Congr. exp. Psychol.* Moscow: Ninth symposium, pp. 51–59, 1966.

54. SAMUELS, INA, Reticular mechanisms and behavior. *Psychol. Bull.,* **56,** 1–25, 1959.

55. SAVAGE, R. D., Electro-cerebral activity, extraversion and neuroticism. *Brit. J. Psychiat.,* **110,** 98–100, 1964.

56. SHAGASS, C. & JONES, A. L., A neurophysiological test for psychiatric diagnosis: results in 750 patients. *Amer. J. Psychiat.,* **114,** 1002–1009, 1958.

57. SIMONSON, E. & BROEŽK, J., Flicker fusion frequency: background and application. *Physiol. Rev.,* **32,** 349–378, 1952.

58. SMITH, S. L., The effect of personality and drugs on auditory threshold when risk-taking factors are controlled. Submitted to *Psychom. Med.*, 1967.
59. SPIELMAN, J., The relation between personality and the frequency and duration of involuntary rest pauses during massed practice. Unpublished Ph.D. thesis, University of London, 1963.
60. STEIN, L., Reciprocal action of reward and punishment mechanisms. In *The Role of Pleasure in Behavior*, (ed. Heath, R. G.), pp. 113–119. New York: Harper & Row, 1964.
61. TAYLOR, JANET A., A personality scale of manifest anxiety. *J. abnorm. soc. Psychol.*, **48**, 285–290, 1953.
62. ——, Drive theory and manifest anxiety. *Psychol. Bull.*, **53**, 303–320, 1956.
63.*TEPLOV, B. M., Some results of the study of strength of the nervous system in man. In *Typological Features of Higher Nervous Activity in Man*. Vol. 2. Moscow: Akad. pedagog. Nauk RSFSR, 1959.
64.*——, Problems in the study of general types of higher nervous activity in man and animals. In *Pavlov's Typology*. (ed. Gray, J. A.), pp. 3–153. Oxford: Pergamon Press, 1964.
65.*—— & NEBYLITSYN, V. D., The study of the basic properties of the nervous system and their significance for the psychology of individual differences. *Vopr. Psikhol.*, **5**, 38–47, 1963.
66.*—— & NEBYLITSYN, V. D., The experimental study of the properties of the nervous system in man. *Zh. vȳssh. nervn. Deyat.*, **13**, 789–797, 1963.
67.*TUROVSKAYA, Z. G., The relation between some indices of strength and of mobility of the nervous system in man. In *Typological Features of Higher Nervous Activity in Man*. (ed. Teplov, B. M.), vol. 3, pp. 248–261. Moscow: Akad. pedagog. Nauk RSFSR, 1963.
68. WAGNER, A. R., Frustration and punishment. In: *Current Research on Motivation*. (ed. Haber, R. N.). New York: Holt, Rinehart & Winston, 1966.
69. WEISEN, A., Differential reinforcing effects of onset and offset of stimulation on the operant behaviour of normals, neurotics and psychopaths. Unpublished Ph.D. thesis, University of Florida, 1965.
70. YERMOLAYEVA-TOMINA, L. B., Concentration of attention and strength of the nervous system. Translated in *Pavlov's Typology*. (ed. Gray, J. A., 1964), pp. 446–464. Oxford: Pergamon Press, 1959.
71.*——, Individual differences in the ability to concentrate attention and strength of the nervous system. *Vopr. Psikhol.*, **2**, 184–195, 1960.

Appendix

Inhibition and Excitation

It seems worth commenting at a little more length on certain general issues which were touched upon in the body of this paper. These issues arise out of the problem posed by the relationship between measures of positive and of inhibitory conditioning—that is, the problem described by Nebylitsyn (Ref. 45) as the relationship between dynamism in excitation and dynamism in inhibition. Before considering these issues themselves, we must be clear about the sense in which 'inhibition' is meant in the phrase 'dynamism in inhibition'. A general examination of the most important ways in which the term 'inhibition' has been used in Pavlov's and Hull's theories of learning may also clarify some of the problems which, as we have seen, are involved in the Hullian construct of 'reactive inhibition'. We begin, then, with a general examination of this kind.

In general it is possible to distinguish three main kinds of phenomenon which have been subsumed under various inhibitory constructs. First, there is a specific response decrement which occurs when the contingencies of reinforcement are changed in such a way that a particular response is no longer followed by the consequences which used to follow it; this is the kind of response decrement which Pavlov regarded as being due to 'internal' inhibition. Second, there is a specific response decrement which is due to causes other than changes in the contingencies of reinforcement; examples of this are various phenomena which Pavlov attributed to 'transmarginal' inhibition and Hull to 'reactive' inhibition. Third, there is a non-specific response decrement, i.e. a response decrement which affects all forms of the organism's functioning simultaneously; in modern theories this might well be called 'de-arousal'.[1]

Now, in both Pavlov and Hull, concepts of inhibition which are of one of the first two kinds (i.e. specific to a particular response) are apt to change, often unnoticed, into concepts of the third kind. This occurs most explicitly in Pavlov's paper *Inhibition and Sleep—One and the Same Process* (Ref. 48, p. 305). Pavlov justifies the change on the grounds that the repeated presentation of an inhibitory CS leads often to sleep.

---

[1] Claridge (Ref. 18) uses the term inhibition in yet another way—as the process which underlies suppression of response to certain stimuli during selective attention to others.

However, he does not consider the possibility that the causes of internal inhibition and of sleep, even though these are both observed in the same experiment, might be different—namely, the omission of reinforcement in the first case and the monotonous conditions of stimulation which result from the omission of reinforcement in the second case.

In Hull, the transition from inhibition as specific response decrement to inhibition as non-specific fall in level of functioning is more insidious. Perhaps the most revealing case is his application of the concept of inhibition to serial learning phenomena (see Ref. 47, p. 502 et seq.). Hull attempts to use this concept to account both for the typical bow-shaped curve of errors obtained in serial learning experiments and for the fact that the number of errors is increased under conditions of massed practice. To cope with the shape of the error curve, it is pointed out that each item in the series can be considered at once as stimulus for every item that follows it and response for every item that precedes it. It is then proposed that each of the resulting S-R bonds (except the one which, at any particular point in the series, is correct) will be under inhibition of delay and that the greatest number of responses inhibited in this way will be in the middle of the list. So far, the analysis is logical enough, and it will be observed that it depends on a form of inhibition which is specific to a particular response and to a particular stimulus. However, in order to link the shape of the error curve with the effects of distribution of practice, it is said that the inhibition generated during a trial dissipates with time during the inter-trial interval, thus producing the superiority of spaced practice. It is here that the transition to a non-specific kind of inhibition takes place. It is clear that 'inhibition of delay' cannot dissipate in time, for the whole function of such an inhibitory process is to adjust the time of response so that it coincides with the arrival of the reinforcing stimulus. Thus, at the end of a trial in a serial learning experiment, there can be no inhibition of delay remaining to be dissipated. Evidently, Hull is now thinking rather of some general fall in the organism's level of functioning which can be reversed by a rest pause or by a change of stimulation.

It is hoped that these general comments on the uses—and abuses—of 'inhibition' by Pavlov and Hull will help unravel some of the tangles we discovered in our attempt to survey the possible relations between strength of the nervous system and introversion-extraversion. In the case of reactive inhibition—which plays such an important role in Eysenck's treatment of extraversion—it would seem that the process of 'de-arousal' could equally well account for many of the phenomena which have often been attributed to reactive inhibition. As we have seen, vigilance decrement is one case in point. 'Reactive inhibition proper', however—that is, a response decrement contingent upon making a response and specific to the response made—is clearly beyond the scope of the concept of de-arousal. Finally, the inhibition involved in 'dynamism in inhibition', or 'inhibitory conditionability', is obviously inhibition in the first sense distinguished above—that process which underlies response decrement due to the omission of reinforcement.

With this preamble, we turn to the problem of how 'dynamism in excitation' and 'dynamism in inhibition' relate to each other. There are in fact a number of different but interlocked issues in this problem.

First, there is the question whether the same relationship will be found to hold in both classical and instrumental conditioning. In other words, suppose it is the case that individual differences in speed of formation of classical positive conditioned reflexes relate in one of the three ways distinguished by Nebylitsyn (positively, inversely, or not at all) to individual differences in speed of formation of classical inhibitory conditioned reflexes; will individual differences in speed of acquisition of rewarded instrumental behaviour relate in the same way to individual differences in speed of extinction of unrewarded instrumental behaviour?

Secondly, at the instrumental level, it is possible that the problem of the relationship between individual differences in the speed of acquisition and the speed of extinction of rewarded behaviour is the same as the problem of the relationship between sensitivity to reward and sensitivity to punishment; for there is evidence that the same physiological mechanism is involved in the extinction of positively reinforced behaviour and the acquisition of negatively reinforced behaviour (Refs. 68 and 29). The extent of our ignorance in this field may be shown by the following example. The Maudsley Reactive and Non-reactive strains of rats (Ref. 6) have been selectively bred to be, respectively, highly sensitive and highly insensitive to the effects of punishment. Much is known about the behaviour patterns of these two strains; yet there are no grounds to predict whether there will be any differences in their sensitivity to reward and, assuming such differences do exist, whether they will take the form of the Reactive strain being more or less sensitive to reward than the Non-reactive strain.

Thirdly, if it is generally true that the response decrement which occurs when reinforcement is discontinued is due to the operation of a punishment system, then the similarity which sometimes appears to exist between concepts of 'inhibition' and of 'de-arousal' (see Ref. 48,

p. 305 et seq.; or Ref. 7, pp. 136–137) can be misleading; for the operation of the punishment system will often lead to an increase in arousal (Ref. 30).

Finally, there is the extremely important question of the role played by drug effects in Eysenck's treatment of introversion-extraversion (Ref. 15). He regards stimulant drugs, such as amphetamine, as having an introverting effect and depressant drugs, such as sodium amylobarbitone, as having an extraverting effect. If introversion-extraversion is linked with level of arousal, these drugs are seen as having, respectively, an arousing and de-arousing effect. But there is an alternative possibility. There is evidence that, in instrumental conditioning situations amylobarbitone reduces the effects of both punishment and frustrative nonreward (Ref. 29) and also evidence that amphetamine increases sensitivity to reward (Ref. 60). It is possible, therefore, that introverts are relatively more sensitive to the effects of both reward and punishment: the use of amphetamine would then mimic introversion by increasing sensitivity to reward, amylobarbitone would mimic extraversion by decreasing sensitivity to punishment and the arousing and de-arousing effects of

TABLE 4

CORRELATION MATRIX OF EEG MEASURES OF DYNAMISM

Measures	1	2	3	4	5	6	7
1. Duration of a-depression to first presentation of auditory stimulus		493*	334	447*	437	709‡	440
2. No. of stimulations to extinction of a-depression to auditory stimulus			665†	700‡	363	358	600†
3. Duration of a-depression to first presentation of visual stimulus				855‡	531*	334	622†
4. Mean duration of a-depression to ten presentations of visual stimulus					561†	449*	697‡
5. Mean duration of a-depression to 25 joint presentations of auditory CS and visual UCS						509*	513*
6. Mean conditioned a-depression to isolated presentation of auditory stimulus							411
7. No. of stimulations to extinction of a-depression							

Zeros and decimal points omitted.
* $P < 0.05$; † $P < 0.001$; Data from twenty Ss reported by Nebylitsyn (Ref. 45, p. 318).

TABLE 5

FACTOR ANALYSIS OF EEG MEASURES OF DYNAMISM

Measures	Centroid analysis							Bifactorial analysis			
	Factors						h^2	g	c_1	c_2	h^2
	Centroid			After rotation							
	I	II	III	A	B	C					
1. Duration of a-depression to first presentation of auditory stimulus	685	−430	−240	**823**	190	075	72	583		608	71
2. Number of stimulations to extinction of a-depression to auditory stimulus	745	261	−285	397	**731**	094	70	485	682		70
3. Duration of a-depression to first presentation of visual stimulus	806	394	218	193	**693**	**573**	85	709	593		85
4. Mean duration of a-depression to ten presentations of visual stimulus	875	309	149	318	**700**	**536**	88	749	542		85
5. Mean duration of a-depression to 25 joint presentations of auditory CS and visual UCS	667	−151	248	469	206	**515**	53	749			56
6. Mean conditioned a-depression to isolated presentation of auditory stimulus	668	−516	026	**789**	026	278	71	680		497	71
7. Number of stimulations to extinction of conditioned a-depression	761	151	−076	398	**574**	345	61	684	479		70

Zeros and decimal points omitted. Factor-loadings higher than 0·05 are in bold type. Data from twenty Ss reported by Nebylitsyn (Ref. 45, p. 319).

these drugs would be a secondary phenomenon, due to increased input from the reward system or decreased input from the punishment system, respectively, to the arousal system (Ref. 30). In that case, it should be noted, we would be treating introversion-extraversion, to put the matter in the Russian terminology, as a dimension of dynamism in which high values of both excitation and inhibition coincide at the introverted pole. All these possibilities remain open, awaiting experimental attack.

So that the reader may judge for himself the correctness of Nebylitsyn's conclusion that dynamism in excitation and dynamism in inhibition are relatively independent of each other (Ref. 45) (contrary to the Eysenckian assumption that they are inversely related to each other), Tables 4 and 5 show some of the data upon which he bases this conclusion. In Table 5 are shown two alternative factor-analytic solutions to the matrix of correlations between various EEG measures (presumed to be related to dynamism) shown in Table 4. On the left of Table 5 is shown the centroid solution; Nebylitsyn interprets Factor A as 'dynamism of the excitatory process' and Factor B as 'dynamism of the inhibitory process'. (Factor C, interpreted as 'a-reactivity', is of no importance in the present context.) On the right is shown a solution involving a general factor (g) perhaps a general factor of equilibrium in dynamism—and two group factors (c_1 and c_2) which correspond, respectively, to Factors B and A in the centroid analysis.

Internal Validity

Editor's Introduction

The articles in this section deal with problems of internal validity, i.e. the factorial unity of the scales proposed for the measurement of extraversion-introversion, the nature of the first-order factors which go to make up the second-order factor in question and other similar questions. The literature in this field is so vast and often so technical, that the choice was extremely difficult; it is believed that the papers reprinted raise important questions and are worthy of study, even though it is not implied that other papers not reprinted might not be equally worthy of study.

The papers chosen illustrate the growth of the idea that extraversion is not a primary factor, like for instance impulsiveness, or sociability, or activity, but rather a second-order based upon the observed correlations between different primary factors. We deal with four levels of description. At the lowest level we simply describe specific responses, such as 'goes to a party on Wednesday'. If such specific responses occur with some regularity we reach the level of habitual responses—'goes to a party once or twice a week'. If this sociable habit can be shown to be related to other sociable habits—likes to talk to people, has many friends, doesn't like solitude—then we reach the trait level; it now becomes possible to talk about a trait of sociability. And if we observe that people who are sociable are also impulsive, active, lively and excitable, then we may postulate a descriptive concept of extraversion.

Many of the earlier authors confused the trait and type levels and argued that because there was less than perfect congruity between the traits which go to make up extraversion, therefore this type concept had no meaning—which would only be true if these trait factors were absolutely independent and did not in fact show substantial correlations. Even now this argument is often heard, but perhaps with decreasing vigour; it rests on a misunderstanding of what the theory maintains and is not relevant to the facts of the situation.

Another argument is often advanced, relating to the importance (practical and theoretical) of primary as opposed to second-order factors. According to some psychologists, description by means of a dozen or so primary 'trait' factors, even though these be correlated, is better (more inclusive, more detailed) than description by means of a single, or a pair, or second-order 'type' concepts. American authors tend

D

to accept this argument, British ones to reject it. The position seems to be that in principle the Americans are right; by using only 'type' concepts we throw away some useful variance which is specific to the 'traits'. But this assumes that there is universal agreement on the existence and nature of these traits; this is not the case. Guilford's primary factors bear little if any relation to Cattell's, or to Eysenck's either. Within each author's system, factors demonstrable for men are not identical with those demonstrable for women. Across ages, too, as Peterson has shown in a paper included in this section, there is little agreement for primary factors. Until these problems are settled, it seems likely that the British view is better adapted to the prevailing circumstances, even though inferior in theory. Eventually, no doubt, reliance on second-order factors exclusively will be replaced by a more balanced regard for both primary and second-order factors, but at the moment the latter are far more firmly established and the evidence regarding them is much more conclusive, than that regarding the former.

H.J.E.

5

Personality Factors S, E and M and Their Measurement

J. P. GUILFORD & RUTH B. GUILFORD[1]

First printed in *Journal of Psychology*, **2**, 109–127, 1936

THREE years ago the writers reported what was perhaps the first attempt to apply the new factor analysis methods to a personality questionnaire in order to determine what common variables of personality might be represented therein (Ref. 2). A typical set of 36 questions such as had been traditionally used to diagnose tendencies towards introversion or extraversion was prepared and administered to 930 students. The responses to every item were tabulated and intercorrelations were computed between each item and every other item. The Spearman-Dodd test was applied to the intercorrelations in order to determine whether a two-factor pattern of Spearman's type would apply. The results indicated that there was no universal 'g' factor extending throughout all the test items and that a number of common factors had to be assumed to account for the obtained intercorrelations. Thurstone's method of factor analysis, then in its earliest stages of development, was adapted to the problem. Four common factors so indicated were considered of sufficient importance to mention. They were tentatively identified as (a) social introversion-extraversion, (b) emotional sensitiveness, (c) impulsiveness and (d) interest in self.

Since this preliminary study appeared, Thurstone (Ref. 4) has brought his factor theory and his computational methods of factor analysis to a higher degree of refinement. We therefore thought it worth while to apply his improved methods to our original data in order to determine more precisely the number of common factors which are of consequence in the set of questions and to compute their factor loadings. We also recomputed the intercorrelations, this time finding tetrachoric coefficients. In the previous study we found coefficients of contingency from

[1] This study is a third that was made possible in part by the generosity of the Social Science Research Council. We wish to express here our gratitude to the Council.

which were estimated equivalent Pearson coefficients. On the whole the new coefficients differed very little from the former ones, although they averaged nearly two per cent greater. The correlation between the 630 old and new r's was 0·940. The range of the new tetrachoric coefficients was from −0·600 to +0·689. The tetrachoric r's are probably better material to which to apply factor analysis.

Although the list of questions has been published by the writers before, we present it again here because the exact wording of the items is very important when we attempt to identify the common factors in them. The 36 questions are:

1. Do you express yourself better in speech than in writing?
2. Are you inclined to limit your acquaintances to a select few?
3. Do you generally prefer to take the lead in group activities?
4. Do you prefer to read about a thing rather than experience it?
5. Do you like work which requires considerable attention to detail?
6. Are you generally very particular about your dress and personal property?
7. Are you inclined to be considerate of other people's feelings?
8. Are you inclined to act on the spur of the moment without thinking things over?
9. Have you ever kept a personal diary of your own accord?
10. Do you work much better when you are praised?
11. Do you like to change from one type of work to another frequently?
12. Are you inclined to study the motives of others?
13. Do you daydream frequently?
14. Do you prefer to work with others rather than alone?
15. Are you inclined to worry over possible misfortunes?
16. Are you frequently somewhat absent-minded?
17. Do you like to persuade others to your point of view?
18. Are you inclined to keep in the background on social occasions?
19. Are you more interested in athletics than in intellectual things?
20. Do you usually dislike to change opinions you have already formed?
21. Do you like to speak in public?
22. Do you prefer to work things out on your own hook rather than accept suggestions from others?
23. Do you have frequent ups and downs in mood, either with or without apparent cause?
24. Are you inclined to be slow and deliberate in movement?
25. Are your feelings rather easily hurt?

26. Do you enjoy getting acquainted with most people?
27. Are you inclined to keep quiet when out in company?
28. Do you adapt yourself easily to new conditions?
29. Do you like to confide in others?
30. Do you express such emotions as delight, sorrow, anger, etc., readily?
31. Are you inclined to think about yourself much of the time?
32. Do you like to have people watch you when you are working?
33. Do you frequently rewrite social letters before mailing them?
34. Do you like to sell things?
35. Do you get rattled easily in exciting situations?
36. Are you a male?

The technique of factor analysis was carried out in the manner described by one of the writers (Ref. 1). The original factor loadings obtained in terms of the centroid axes as reference vectors are not given here. They may be had from the writers upon request. Suffice it to say that the analysis was carried on until the average residual was 0·055 and the standard error of the typical original r (r = 0·20) was 0·051. Five factors seemed sufficient to account for the intercorrelations, with insignificant residuals. We next proceeded to rotate the centroid axes, attempting to maximize some of the factor loadings which were already large in certain test items and at the same time to maximize the number of zero factor loadings for all the factors. It so happened that those items with the greatest communalities, which means the items most heavily saturated with one or more of the five common factors, including in particular items 6, 7, 15, 18, 19, 23, 25, 26, 27 and 36, occupied positions on vectors almost exactly at right angles to one another. The only notable exceptions to this rule were items 6 and 19, which retained significant loadings in two independent factors to the end. It was therefore reasonable to assume orthogonal axes which means complete independence of the five fundamental dimensions involved in the test. Eleven rotations, in one plane at a time, were required to bring about satisfactory positions for the five reference axes to best fit the configuration of points. The final factor loadings with reference to the rotated axes are presented in Table 1. The communalities are given in the column headed by h^2, h^2 being the sum of the squares of the five factor loadings in an item. It represents the total variance of an item that can be attributed to the five common factors.

In order to make some further estimates concerning the variance of an item, we need to know the coefficient of reliability of the item.

TABLE 1

THE FACTOR LOADINGS OF THE THIRTY-SIX ITEMS AFTER ROTATION OF THE CENTROID AXES; THE COMMUNALITIES, ESTIMATED RELIABILITIES, SPECIFICITIES AND THE VARIANCES ATTRIBUTABLE TO UNIQUENESS AND TO SAMPLING ERRORS

Item	I	II	III	IV	V	h^2	S	E	U	r_{aa}
1	−0·350	0·133	0·145	0·060	0·095	0·174	0·642	0·184	0·826	0·816
2	0·494	0·279	−0·030	−0·067	−0·057	0·330	0·403	0·267	0·670	0·733
3	−0·495	−0·007	0·286	−0·110	−0·500	0·589	0·330	0·081	0·411	0·919
4	−0·431	0·123	−0·159	−0·040	−0·032	0·229	0·491	0·280	0·771	0·720
5	0·104	−0·120	−0·030	0·184	−0·098	0·070	0·766	0·164	0·930	0·836
6	0·142	−0·032	−0·085	0·640	0·330	0·547	0·305	0·148	0·453	0·852
7	−0·060	−0·024	−0·115	0·765	−0·015	0·603	0·267	0·130	0·397	0·870
8	−0·227	−0·334	−0·245	−0·225	−0·135	0·292	0·512	0·196	0·708	0·804
9	−0·086	0·062	−0·416	−0·113	−0·217	0·244	0·756	0·000	0·756	1·000
10	−0·074	0·275	−0·247	0·034	−0·076	0·149	0·651	0·200	0·851	0·800
11	−0·130	−0·197	−0·010	−0·176	−0·084	0·094	0·674	0·232	0·906	0·768
12	−0·144	−0·008	0·058	−0·130	−0·417	0·215	0·593	0·192	0·785	0·808
13	0·084	−0·420	0·079	−0·060	−0·016	0·288	0·476	0·236	0·712	0·764
14	−0·239	0·010	0·208	0·060	0·437	0·295	0·585	0·120	0·705	0·880
15	0·087	0·541	−0·093	0·241	−0·022	0·368	0·396	0·236	0·632	0·764
16	0·042	0·200	−0·466	−0·091	0·066	0·272	0·506	0·222	0·728	0·778
17	−0·328	0·210	0·224	−0·102	0·040	0·214	0·683	0·103	0·786	0·897
18	−0·658	−0·013	−0·023	−0·001	0·052	0·436	0·318	0·246	0·564	0·754
19	0·013	0·065	−0·412	−0·070	−0·690	0·655	0·145	0·200	0·345	0·800
20	−0·086	0·216	−0·031	−0·087	−0·140	0·082	0·432	0·486	0·918	0·514
21	−0·390	−0·109	0·281	−0·072	−0·329	0·356	0·572	0·172	0·644	0·928
22	−0·123	−0·238	0·094	−0·117	−0·335	0·206	0·447	0·347	0·794	0·653
23	0·051	0·572	0·094	−0·108	−0·133	0·368	0·428	0·204	0·632	0·796
24	−0·414	−0·047	0·140	0·246	−0·105	0·265	0·675	0·060	0·735	0·940
25	−0·028	0·560	−0·125	0·001	−0·106	0·341	0·502	0·157	0·659	0·843
26	−0·649	−0·028	−0·051	0·222	−0·239	0·531	0·362	0·107	0·469	0·893
27	−0·720	−0·009	−0·037	−0·050	0·112	0·535	0·337	0·128	0·465	0·872
28	−0·414	−0·250	0·132	−0·100	0·245	0·316	0·492	0·192	0·684	0·808
29	−0·303	−0·234	−0·038	−0·100	0·189	0·194	0·551	0·255	0·806	0·745
30	−0·365	−0·423	−0·162	−0·019	0·104	0·350	0·363	0·287	0·650	0·713
31	−0·078	0·353	−0·078	−0·266	−0·231	0·261	0·348	0·391	0·739	0·609
32	−0·250	−0·151	0·341	−0·056	−0·049	0·207	0·500	0·293	0·793	0·707
33	−0·012	0·268	−0·018	0·183	−0·096	0·115	0·785	0·100	0·885	0·900
34	−0·285	0·083	0·436	0·087	−0·033	0·287	0·621	0·092	0·713	0·908
35	0·161	0·393	−0·383	−0·065	−0·124	0·347	0·453	0·200	0·653	0·800
36	0·047	−0·013	0·830	−0·012	−0·047	0·694	0·306	0·000	0·306	1·000

As is well known, the estimate of the reliability of a test or of an item varies according to the method by which it is obtained. There is no direct way of computing the split-half reliability of a single item. Our short questionnaire had been administered to 277 subjects two different times, the time interval being one month. Three objections can be raised against this procedure in this project. In the first place, in a month's time a subject's personality may have undergone some minor changes, or at least his mood and set at the two times may differ considerably, so the coefficients of self-correlation would accordingly be lowered. On the other hand, even after a month's time a subject may remember how he has answered certain items before and the motive to be self-consistent might determine similar rather than dissimilar answers. This would tend to raise the estimate of reliability. In this particular problem the inter-correlations are based upon 930 subjects and the reliability estimates upon only 277. There may be discrepancies due to this fact. However, we present in the last column of Table 1 the list of self-correlations of the items as obtained by the methods described above for what they are worth. From a superficial examination of the list, the variability in r_{aa} would seem to be reasonable when we consider the nature of the corresponding questions. Remembering that any values of r_{aa} are merely estimates, we shall use them here as rough indicators. The use of three decimal places does not indicate any belief on our part of three decimal place accuracy in the values of r_{aa} or in any of the constants which are derived from them. We are merely making them consistent with the rest of the table, which probably bears some claim to three place accuracy.

In the column headed S are given the specificities of the test items. These are found by the relation $r_{aa}-h^2$. The specificity of an item is that part of its variance attributable to factors belonging to that item alone; these factors do not appear in any other items of this set of 36, although they may be held in common with this item by items outside the list. The column headed E contains the error variance. The determiners of this variance differ not only from item to item but from time to time in the same item. The letter U stands for uniqueness. It is equal to $S+E$, or to $1-h^2$. It is the sum of all the variance produced by factors other than the five common ones in this test, or all variance that is due to the specific and the error factors combined. The total variance, which is equal to $1\cdot000$, is the sum of h^2+U, or the sum of h^2+S+E, or the sum of $r_{aa}+E$. The first row of Table 1, which has to do with question 1 (Do you express yourself better in speech than in writing?), is to be read as follows. It has a negative factor loading of $-0\cdot350$ with factor I.

This means that those who possess a great amount of the positive aspect of factor I are inclined to respond by saying 'No'; they do not express themselves better in speech than in writing. This same item has small and perhaps negligible loadings with factors II, III, IV. The total variance in this item is about 17·4 per cent ($h^2 = 0·174$) due to the five common factors, about 64·2 per cent ($S = 0·642$) due to constant factors other than the five and about 18·4 per cent ($E = 0·184$) to variable factors or to the so-called errors of measurement. In the same way all the other items are to be interpreted from the data given in Table 1.

Before we attempt to identify and name the five common factors, let us observe some general facts about Table 1. In the first place, it is hard to find in the whole list of 36 questions, each one of which has been very commonly used as an indicator of introversion-extraversion, a pure, unambiguous question. By an unambiguous question we mean that a response to it is indicative of one fundamental dimension of personality and one alone. The question that comes nearest to this ideal is 36, 'Are you a male?' The answer to this question indicates factor III to the extent of 0·694 or 69·4 per cent. Since its reliability is perfect, 30·6 per cent of the response is indicative of other factors still unknown. Item 18 is perhaps the next in greatest purity. Its variance in factor I is 0·436, but it still has an unknown variance of 0·318. Item 27 is also relatively pure for factor I so far as this test is concerned, but is still an unknown quantity to the extent of 0·337. Item 7 is very pure with factor IV as its chief determiner (60·7 per cent) but its determination is still 26·7 per cent unknown, if we are to judge from the data of Table 1. It can now be seen that since most of the items are ambiguous and that the responses to them are multiply determined, when they are used in a battery to measure individual differences on any one dimension of personality great care must be taken in their selection and combination. It would be highly desirable, naturally, to know the full variance of any item that can be attributed to common factors, that is, all except the error variance. When the full common factor variance is unknown, the use of a very large number of impure items might still give valid results, if the loadings with the irrelevant factors exist in a hit and miss fashion in the various items and hence behave like errors of measurement. However, this hardly excuses us from attempting to determine with as much accuracy as we have at our command the probable types of variance in every question that goes into our inventories.

IDENTIFICATION OF THE FACTORS

Let us now attempt to identify and name the five independent factors indicated by the analysis. We list first, in order of importance, the items significantly loaded with factor I. The factor loading is given, without algebraic sign, and a descriptive phrase is attached. The algebraic sign of the loading as seen in Table 1 is taken into account in stating the description.

FACTOR I

Item No.	Factor Loading	
27	0·720	Inclined to keep quiet when out in a social group
18	0·658	Inclined to keep in the background on social occasions
26	0·649	Does not enjoy getting acquainted with most people
3	0·495	Generally prefers not to take the lead in group activities
2	0·494	Inclined to limit acquaintances to a select few
4	0·431	Prefers to read about a thing rather than to experience it
24	0·414	Inclined to be slow and deliberate in movement
28	0·414	Does not adapt readily to new conditions, situations, etc.
21	0·390	Does not like to speak in public
30	0·365	Does not express his emotions readily
1	0·350	Expresses self better in writing than in speech
17	0·328	Does not like to persuade others to his point of view
29	0·303	Does not like to confide in others
34	0·285	Does not like to sell things
32	0·250	Does not like to be watched while working

FACTOR II

23	0·572	Has frequent ups and downs in mood
25	0·560	Feelings are rather easily hurt
15	0·541	Inclined to worry over possible misfortunes
30	0·423	Expresses his emotions readily
13	0·420	Daydreams frequently
35	0·393	Gets rattled easily in exciting situations
31	0·353	Inclined to think about himself much of the time
8	0·334	Inclined to act on the spur of the moment

D*

2	0·279	Inclined to limit acquaintances to a select few
10	0·275	Works much better when he is praised
33	0·268	Frequently rewrites social letters before mailing them
28	0·250	Does not adapt readily to new conditions, etc.
29	0·234	Likes to confide in others

Factor III

36	0·830	Is a male
16	0·466	Is not frequently absent-minded
34	0·436	Likes to sell things
9	0·416	Has not kept a personal diary of his own accord
19	0·412	More interested in athletics than in intellectual things
35	0·383	Does not get rattled easily in exciting situations
32	0·341	Likes to have people watch him while at work
3	0·286	Generally prefers to lead in group activities
21	0·281	Likes to speak in public
10	0·247	Does not work much better when he is praised
8	0·245	Not inclined to act on the spur of the moment
17	0·224	Likes to persuade others to his own point of view

Factor IV

7	0·765	Inclined to be considerate of other people's feelings
6	0·640	Very particular about his dress and personal property
13	0·314	Does not daydream frequently
31	0·266	Not inclined to think about self much of the time
24	0·246	Inclined to be slow and deliberate in movement
15	0·241	Inclined to worry over possible misfortunes
8	0·225	Not inclined to act on the spur of the moment
26	0·222	Enjoys getting acquainted with most people

Factor V

19	0·690	Not more interested in athletics than in intellectual things
3	0·500	Generally prefers to lead in group activities
14	0·437	Prefers to work alone rather than with others
12	0·417	Inclined to study the motives of others
22	0·335	Prefers to work things out in his own way
6	0·330	Not very particular about his dress or personal property
21	0·329	Likes to speak in public
28	0·245	Does not adapt readily to new conditions, etc.

26   0·239   Does not enjoy getting acquainted with most people
31   0·231   Inclined to think about himself much of the time

In attempting to interpret these factors and to name them, it is necessary to keep in mind the nature of the original data. We must constantly remember that the response of a subject may not represent exactly what the question implies in its most obvious meaning. Subjects respond to a question as at the moment they think they are, with perhaps a lack of insight in many cases as to their real position on the question. They also respond as they would like themselves to be and as they would like others to think them to be and as they wish the examiner to think them to be. They also respond with some regard to self-consistency among their own answers. Whether these determining factors are sufficiently constant to set up individual differences which are uniform in character and so constitute common factors in themselves is difficult to say. Should any one of them be so pervasive it should introduce an additional vector in the factor analysis. With the possible exception of factor III, there were no constellations of consistently socially desirable characteristics to give the appearance of such a variable.

On the whole we should be willing to believe that the responses represent the cooperative efforts of the subjects to give fair appraisals of their own likes and of their behaviour as they know it. We are willing to let their answers, taken by and large, signify just what the intercorrelations demand that they mean when those intercorrelations are referred to the smallest number of reference axes that the data will permit. Whether our five factors correspond to real dimensions of personality or whether they would coincide in definition with dimensions found from the factor analysis of objective measurements of personality we do not know. This question can be subjected to experimental verification and we propose to do this later. The most parsimonious interpretation that can be given to the data is that we have applied 36 stimuli to 930 students who are rather homogeneous as to age, intelligence and education and who by common instruction and in a common classroom situation have reacted to those stimuli in one of two ways. The intercorrelations between items then represent indicators of similar reactions to pairs of stimuli. The factors to which the responses can be referred are indicated by the statistical analysis of the factor methods. For at least three of the resulting factors we believe that the striking consistency that is shown by the clusters of characteristics will be convincing of the validity of the whole technique. This same consistency will furthermore be a satisfactory test of the ability of Thurstone's factor method to give meaningful results.

Some students of personality may object that our constellations of items are due to similarity of meaning of the terms employed in them. These possible critics are also likely to maintain that there are no dimensions of personality and perhaps not even any consistent traits. An individual's tendency to act consistently in different situations, they maintain, is due to specific habits. The 'different' situations are similar enough, or have identical or equivalent elements which give them the power to call forth the same or similar responses from the same individual. Subjects would accordingly react similarly to questions containing similar language or suggesting logically similar situations. We believe that the mere identity or similarity of language in different items can be dismissed as a trivial cause when intelligent subjects are used. The question of logical similarity is more serious. The logical similarity may be attributed in large measure to the existence of real dimensions of personality and to the power of the average intelligent individual to sense those dimensions, however vaguely. There will be those who will say at this point, 'Yes, the factors you will find by factor analysis are unitary traits merely because they have become recognized as such in our culture pattern'. As if the act of assigning any new concept to our 'culture pattern' thereby disproves any claim to reality on the part of the concept. Such an argument makes the concepts of 'atom', 'electron', 'gene' and 'intelligence', likewise merely social conveniences. We believe that our culture pattern, at least that part of it which can be attributed to scientific endeavour, has a closer correspondence with reality than is implied in the remarks cited above. In so far as the task of our subject is one of self-rating and in so far as his responses to the questions are controlled by his desire, conscious or unconscious, to seem self-consistent, we shall have to agree that to that extent the resulting factors are definable as logically independent ideas or concepts in the minds of the raters. However, in the original preparation of the set of questions an effort was made not only to include questions which most writers on introversion most frequently mention, but also to avoid as far as possible too much overlapping of situations suggested by them. Certainly such items are those referring to 'keeping a personal diary', 'inclined to worry', 'disliking to change one's opinions' and 'being absent-minded' are remote from one another in terms of language and in terms of type of situation. Logic would not carry one far in predicting the correlations among such disparate items. It should be pointed out, also, that in view of the many significant negative factor loadings occurring in a somewhat random fashion in Table 1, any two items may be weighted with similar algebraic signs in one factor but with opposite signs in another factor. This means that logical consistency might require that two items should be answered in the same way when one factor is considered but in opposite ways when another factor determines the logic of the situation. Because of the general ambiguity of the items and the actual wealth of logical subtleties involved, we hesitate to believe that even very intelligent subjects could contrive to give the intricate factor pattern which comes out of the analysis even if that were their primary goal. Many a subject remarks after taking such a questionnaire that he made some seemingly glaringly illogical responses. This may show concern on the part of some subjects for logical consistency, but at the same time it shows the impossibility, due to the complexity of the items, of letting that motive dominate the replies. It also shows a fixed belief in the regularity and lawfulness of behaviour without which there could be no science of psychology.

The first factor is undoubtedly of a social character. At one end of the scale the individual seeks to withdraw, to remove himself from social contacts and social responsibilities; at the other end of the scale he seeks social contacts and depends upon them for his satisfactions. One might name this dimension social introversion-extraversion, sociability, shyness, or other similar designations. There are some characteristics in the list, however, that do not suggest directly anything social. For example, 'inclined to be slow and deliberate in movement' and 'does not express his emotions readily' imply nothing on the surface that is of a social character, although these qualities might make social adaptations difficult. Until a more exact definition of this dimension is established we prefer to label it simply as factor S.

The second factor gives a rather neat picture. It is undoubtedly an emotional factor. But to use simply the term 'emotionality' is not sufficiently definitive. The use of the concept of emotional introversion-extraversion is probably one of place, for traits such as 'expresses his emotions readily' and 'his feelings are rather easily hurt', the one traditionally regarded as an extravert characteristic and the other an introvert characteristic, both have positive weights. So, also, do such traits as 'daydreams frequently' and 'inclined to act on the spur of the moment'. Running throughout the list of characteristics is a thread of emotional immaturity or emotional dependency. The individual having those traits would seem to lack self-sufficiency and at the same time to lack cortical control over the emotional centres. We shall call this dimension factor E, until a better concept can be applied and we shall define it in terms of the list of characteristics which is given above.

The third factor is definable in terms of a list of twelve traits. Heading the list is 'being a male' with a factor loading of 0·830. This suggests in itself the dimension of masculinity-femininity. The remaining characteristics, however, have additional suggestions to make. There is an element of aggressiveness in some of the items; this might be the oft mentioned trait of dominance or of ascendance-submission. There is a strong hint of some idealized characteristics, except, perhaps for the confession of the individual who stands high in this factor that he 'likes to have people watch him while he is at work'. One might name the factor the 'masculine-ideal'. However, for the present we shall name it with the more non-committal letter M.

Factor IV is a difficult one to define. Two items, 6 and 7, must carry the greater part of that responsibility. An individual ranking high in this factor is 'inclined to be considerate of other people's feelings' and to be 'very particular about his dress and personal property'. These two traits suggest extreme care and caution, if not conscientiousness and meticulousness. The trait of 'not daydreaming frequently' adds a rather practical disposition. The remaining picture is that of a slow, methodical, deliberate person who is slightly inclined to depression. The opposite picture may help. This is the individual who is careless about his dress and personal property and about the feelings of others, who daydreams but is impulsive and perhaps relatively free from worry. This gayer side suggests a carefreeness and perhaps even a happy-go-lucky disposition. With this possibility in mind the writers have prepared a new set of questions similar in content to those having loadings with factor IV and stressing more than has been emphasized already the contrast between carefreeness and depression. This questionnaire has been administered to over a thousand subjects and a new factor analysis will soon be made in the hope of describing factor IV more explicitly. We have tentatively identified this variable as factor R, the letter R standing for a word coined from the Greek 'rhathymia' which means freedom from care.

As regards the fifth factor we are in much the same position as with factor IV. There are more items having significant factor loadings here, however, so the picture is a little clearer. The pattern includes 'interest in intellectual things', 'prefers to lead in group activities', 'inclined to study the motives of others', 'prefers to work things out in his own way' and also 'prefers to work alone rather than with others'. At first thought, the picture is one that the authors were looking for in the previous analysis, namely 'thinking introversion'. The positive qualities of liking to lead and the dislike to be led and the liking to speak in public present new angles to the picture, however. The descriptive term might rather be 'intellectual leadership'. New questions designed to bring out more sharply this dimension have been used in the same new questionnaire referred to in connection with factor IV. The aspect emphasized is the liking for thinking and tackling problems requiring thought, versus a liking for prompt, overt action. We shall refer to this factor temporarily as factor T.

THE MEASUREMENT OF S, E AND M

Having isolated the factors in our questionnaire, we next sought to develop in questionnaire form the means of evaluating individuals on at least three of the factors. Factors S, E and M seemed sufficiently well defined for us to set about the practical task of measuring them. We recognized that although the short questionnaire had served its purpose quite satisfactorily for the analysis and identification of these three dimensions, there were an insufficient number of items to make a reliable scale of measurement for any factor. The reliabilities of scores based upon our same short questionnaire of 36 items had previously been found to vary between 0·80 and 0·85. This is hardly satisfactory for measuring individual differences. If a questionnaire, like a test of ability, increases in reliability according to the Spearman-Brown prophecy formula, by tripling the length we should obtain a reliability of 0·92 to 0·95. With this hope in mind, we devised and selected a sufficient number of additional items like those most heavily loaded with factors S and E especially, to bring the number to 123. Some of the items were reversed in meaning; others were recorded so as to indicate stronger or weaker degrees of a characteristic for the same reply. Many entirely new questions were added, some of which have been included in the customary lists touching on introversion-extraversion. This longer questionnaire was applied to 815 new subjects, including 382 men and 433 women. The plan was to separate these subjects into highest and lowest quartiles for factors S, E and M separately and from the three pairs of criterion groups to validate every test item and to derive a scoring weight for it in one or more of the factors.

In order to obtain the extreme criterion groups it was necessary to set up a preliminary scoring scale for the short test. We did this by assigning weights to the responses in rough agreement with their loadings.[1] A scoring weight, to be sure, should not be identical with a factor loading, for there are intercorrelations among the items. But for the preliminary separation of extreme groups this procedure is defensible. The correlations between the sets of scoring weights for factors S, E and M were zero except for a correlation of $r = -0.208$ between the weights for factors E and M. The absence of correlations is important here, since we wish finally to obtain scores in uncorrelated variables. In order to know whether the preliminary scoring scales introduced significant correlations in the scores for the three factors, we obtained the coefficients $r_{se} = 0.175$, $r_{sm} = 0.092$ and $r_{em} = -0.242$. There was more correlation here than that found between the scoring weights themselves, but not enough to destroy the high degree of independence among the factors measured. The correlations among the scoring weights, for comparison, were $r_{se} = -0.018$, $r_{sm} = 0.017$ and $r_{em} = -0.208$.

The division of the subjects into two extreme quartiles for factor M is worthy of comment. Even after allowing a weight of eight points for being a male there was considerable overlapping between the two sexes. Twelve of the men were in the lowest quartile and sixteen of the women in the highest quartile, the total range of scores being from 60 to 114, Q_1 being at 82 and Q_3 at 95. We might have arbitrarily put all men in one criterion group for 'masculinity' and all women in another. But not being sure that factor M is precisely and purely a sex difference in responding to the questionnaire, we retained the quartiles which depended upon the preliminary scoring. In fact, this extensive overlapping of the sexes in the M factor strongly indicates that it is not simply a sex-difference factor or masculinity-femininity as was at first thought.

Another fact of interest connected with the M factor is its significant relationship to the strength of hand grip. With 40 subjects (25 men and 15 women) the correlation was $+0.646$ with a PE of 0.064. When the item 'Are you a male?' is eliminated from the scoring of the M factor the correlation is still significant, being $+0.477 \pm 0.082$. For the 25 men taken alone the correlation is $+0.316 \pm 0.122$.[2] Whatever the M factor is, it is correlated with muscular strength even when sex is held constant; it may in truth be the dominance or ascendance variable.

In order to derive scoring weights for all 123 items, including the original 36, we resorted to Strong's technique which he has employed in

---

[1] These factor loadings were derived from an earlier factor analysis and they do not coincide with those given in Table 8, but are comparable with them.

[2] We are indebted to Mr Tom Andrews for these correlations.

finding scoring weights for occupations in his Vocational Interest Inventory.[1] This involves finding the difference in the proportions of subjects in the two criterion groups who react in a similar manner (Ref. 3). In our lengthened test we included the intermediate category of '?'. For example, in the case of item 1, (Do you express yourself more easily in speech than in writing?)[2] the numbers in the high criterion group (socially withdrawn) responding 'Yes', '?' and 'No' respectively, were 61, 6 and 133. The corresponding numbers in the low group were 142, 8 and 50. The differences between the high and low groups were, therefore, −81, −2 and 83. Strong found that the scoring weights are approximately proportional to these differences. Arbitrarily setting a range of weights extending from −4 to +4, on this basis, the weights to be assigned to item 1 for factor S were −2, 0 and +2 for responses 'Yes', '?' and 'No' respectively. In order to eliminate all negative weights we arbitrarily added a constant of 4 to all the weights. Of the 123 items, 101 were found to have significant scoring weights for one or more of the three factors and so were retained in the test which we have called 'The Nebraska Personality Inventory'.

With the scoring weights thus obtained, fairly satisfactory results have been secured, at least for two of the factors. For the S factor a range of scores from 225 to 450 has been found; for the E factor a range of 240 to 440; but for the M factor the range is only from 200 to 295. The reliabilities which we expected to be raised above 0·90 are still probably short of the mark. With 100 test papers selected at random the reliabilities were 0·93, 0·89 and 0·65 for factors S, E and M, respectively. In the case of the S factor, at least, it seemed that the Spearman-Brown prophecy was fulfilled. But when 665 papers were selected in order to make a more accurate check upon the reliability, the reliability coefficients were 0·85, 0·86 and 0·75, respectively. These coefficients are all based upon the split-half method, correlating first and last halves of the questionnaire. Since the original 36 items appear in the first half and the last half is composed entirely of new items, we have probably given the inventory its most rigid test of reliability.

The question of the independence of the three factors as scored in the long scales is of interest in view of the fact that there were some small intercorrelations between two factors as scored in the short scale. The long scale of 101 selected items has been given to a large number of new

[1] Published by the Stanford University Press.
[2] The reader will note the slight change in wording in this item as compared with the original.

subjects. From these we selected at random 200 test papers, scored them for factors S, E and M and computed intercorrelations. The results were somewhat disheartening in view of the fact that practical independence had been wanted. The correlation r_{se} was $+0\cdot463$; r_{sm} was $+0\cdot402$ and r_{em} was $-0\cdot010$. This amount of correlation between S and E on the one hand and between S and M on the other hand was hardly to be expected from the relatively low corresponding correlations with the short scales. The result is probably an example of the difficulty one has to contend with in attempting to score the very same items two or more ways when most of the items are impure or ambiguous and when their raw intercorrelations are not taken into account. This same difficulty is patent in the Bernreuter inventory. In the Bernreuter inventory, however, the extremely high intercorrelations are due in part to the lack of independence of the four variables upon which the original criterion groups were based.

We have now begun the task of deriving new scoring weights, this time separating the extremes of the criterion groups on the basis of items that are practically pure for each factor. The items used to discriminate extremes on the S factor are numbers 1, 4, 18, 24, 26 and 27; items relatively pure for factor E are 13, 15, 23, 25 and 31; for the M factor, 9, 16, 28, 34 and 36. Items with a factor loading greater than $0\cdot500$ were doubly weighted in determining the extremes in each factor. Care will be taken to avoid intercorrelations between factors in the selection of the three pairs of criterion groups. New scoring weights will be determined again on the basis of Strong's method. We must exercise caution in making too many items do double or triple duty lest the scoring scales become correlated. Relatively pure measuring scales for factors S, E and M should then be obtained. Factor M needs further study and the addition of more items to the inventory in order to assure ourselves of its real nature and to make a reliable scale. This is a problem for future work.

SUMMARY

A short questionnaire of 36 items reputedly diagnostic of introversion-extraversion was subjected to a new factor analysis using Thurstone's centroid method including the rotation of axes. The results show that five independent dimensions of personality as revealed by the responses of subjects to questions about their own likes and behaviour can account for the obtained intercorrelations between the items. These are tentatively identified as S (social introversion), E (an emotionality factor), M (perhaps masculinity-feminity, or possibly a dominance or ascendance-submission factor, O) R (a rhathymia, or happy-go-lucky or carefree factor) and T (a thinking introversion or an intellectual leadership factor). Further work is being done to determine more exactly the nature of the factors R and T and to develop an inventory for their measurement.

A long inventory intended to measure factors S, E and M more reliably was devised. Items were validated and scoring weights were empirically determined by the correlation of items with extreme criterion groups as established by means of the short inventory. Significant correlations between factors that are by definition independent indicate that greater care must be taken in developing scoring weights for this type of inventory. The reliability of the long questionnaire is probably higher than that for the short one, but the Spearman-Brown predictive formula was apparently not valid in this connection. The preparation of three new sets of scoring weights is now under way by a procedure which should guarantee independence in the scales measuring factors S, E and M.

REFERENCES

1. GUILFORD, J. P., *Psychometric Methods*. New York: McGraw-Hill, 1936.
2. —— & GUILFORD, RUTH B. An analysis of the factors in a typical test of introversion-extraversion. *J. abnorm. soc. Psychol.*, **28**, 377–399, 1934.
3. STRONG, E. K., Jr. The interest test for personnel managers. *J. Pers. Res.*, **5**, 194–203, 1927.
4. THURSTONE, L. L. *The Vectors of Mind*. Chicago: Univ. of Chicago Press, 1935.

6

The Questionnaire Measurement of Neuroticism and Extraversion

H. J. EYSENCK

First published in *Revista de Psicologia*, **50**, 113–140, 1956

Introduction

A considerable degree of interest in the possibility of measuring personality by means of questionnaires was aroused at the time of the First World War, when Woodworth was commissioned to produce his Personal Data Sheet, the first neuroticism inventory ever to be produced. Many other psychologists imitated his procedure and constructed questionnaires for the measurement of neuroticism by ransacking psychiatric text books and rephrasing the neurotic symptoms described there in the form of questions.

Later on, when Jung's theory of extraversion-introversion became popular, questionnaires were constructed to measure this personality dimension also. The writer has shown elsewhere (Ref. 5) how these efforts ran into difficulties, due in part to lack of statistical sophistication in their construction and partly to lack of psychological insight and acumen on the part of the test constructors. The situation was changed when J. P. & R. B. Guilford (Refs. 12, 13, 14 and 15) published a series of factor analytic investigations of the intercorrelations between question- naire items. They discovered a large number of factors such as social shy- ness (S), depression (D), nervousness (N) and so forth; these were finally published in the form of the Guilford S.T.D.C.R. and G.A.M.I.N. scales.

These scales are not entirely independent of each other, but correlate together, sometimes to an appreciable extent. It seemed desirable to discover by means of factor analysis just what are the second-order factors which emerge from the intercorrelations of these Guilford scales. From his previous work in the personality field (Refs. 2 and 3), the writer hypothesized that the two main dimensions to emerge would be neuroti- cism and extraversion-introversion and, as has been shown elsewhere (Ref. 5), this hypothesis is indeed borne out. The scales characterizing the neuroticism factor are primarily the C scale, followed by the

D.I.O., Ag and N scales. The scales characterizing the extraversion factor are primarily the R scale, followed by G and A. These factorial studies have in their interpretation been considerably strengthened by the fact that studies employing outside criteria have shown the scales to act in predictable ways.[1] Thus, hysterics and psychopaths who, according to theory, are extraverted neurotics, have been found to give high scores on the R scale as compared with dysthymics (anxiety states, reactive depressions, obsessive compulsive patients), who, in terms of the theory, are introverted neurotics. Both groups have high scores on the C and D scales as compared with normals (Ref. 16).

Other predictions have been made in terms of the author's dynamic theory of hysteria and anxiety (Ref. 6), all of which have been verified. Thus, subjects with high R scores have been found to be less easily conditionable (Ref. 10), to have stronger kinaesthetic figural after effects than subjects with low R scores (Refs. 7 and 18) and to have high scores on the extraversion factor derived from a large battery of objective tests (Ref. 16). Consequently, there is ample evidence to support the view that the R scale is a promising measure of extraversion, whereas the C scale is a promising measure of neuroticism.

However, there are certain weaknesses in these scales which make them less useful than they might otherwise be for the measurement of these two dimensions or second-order factors. In the first place, the scales are long and repetitive. This, no doubt, increases split-half reliability but may not increase validity correspondingly. It also tends to put off intelligent subjects, who dislike being asked the same question in different guise and it prolongs the time which can be allocated to the questionnaire part of an experiment unduly.

[1] Guilford himself has argued that factor analyses or correlations between his scales are not, properly speaking, permissible (Ref. 11). While the writer agrees with him in this he would point out two things. In the first place, if factor analyses are not admissible, neither is it permissible to use correlations between the different scales, a practice Guilford himself has encouraged. In the second place, as long as results from such factor analyses are interpreted in broad outline rather than in fine detail, they do serve a valuable function in orienting the research worker with respect to the observable relationships. Guilford's main reason for rejecting factor analysis is because the same items are scored for different factors. It would certainly have been better if Guilford had not in his scales used the same items as part of many different scales. However, having constructed his scales in this unsatisfactory manner he can hardly refuse responsibility of indicating just how the relationships between these scales should be established if it is not to be done by means of correlation coefficients and factor analysis. This whole argument is not vital to our demonstration as the scales developed here draw upon quite different sources of evidence.

In the second place, little attention had been paid in the derivation of the scales to the possible importance of sex differences, i.e. to the possibility that an item which is a good predictor of a high score on the C or the R scale for men may not be a good predictor for women. We have observed considerable sex differences of this kind in our studies and it seemed desirable to submit these accidental findings to a more definitive type of examination.

In the third place, it was our impression that some of the items included in the R scale correlated very little if at all with the total score on R, whereas items from other scales correlate quite highly with the total R score. Similarly, some C items did not appear to be correlated with C at all, whereas items from other scales actually had higher correlations with the C score than the majority of C items. It seemed desirable therefore to improve the validity of the R and C scales as possible measures of extraversion and neuroticsm by carrying out an item analysis which would enable us to throw out poor items and include items from scales other than R and C, provided that these items showed high relationships with either the R or the C score. (In all this, of course, a paramount consideration was that the zero correlations between the R and C scales, which had been empirically observed by several writers, should be preserved.)

In the fourth place, the scales are presented by Guilford as measures of unitary factors. Empirically it appeared that this hypothesis was not in fact always borne out, particularly in the case of the S (social shyness) scale. It appeared that some items were measures of an introverted type of social shyness, whereas others were measures of a neurotic type of social shyness, the total scale thus breaking up into two relatively un-related parts. Again, a more definitive study of this point seemed desirable.

The studies reported in this paper constitute an attempt to construct on the firm basis of Guilford's own empirical work improved scales for the measurement of neuroticism and extraversion. This was done by means of item analyses and factor analyses. It was also intended to throw light on certain subsidiary but important problems such as the influence of sex on questionnaire responses and the unitary or dual nature of sociability. Among the features we expected to find in our final questionnaire were the following:

1. A reasonably small number of items
2. A reasonably high reliability

3. Independence statistically of the two scales
4. Lack of sex differences
5. A reasonably high correlation between the new neuroticism scale and C
6. A reasonably high correlation between the new extraversion scale and R

The Experiment

A questionnaire was prepared containing 261 items in all. Included in this were all the items from the Guilford scale S.D.C.R.G. and A. Also included were the items of the writer's Maudsley Medical Questionnaire, a neuroticism inventory which has been used very widely in England (Refs. 2 and 3) and Germany (Ref. 4). This was included in order to obtain evidence on the relationship between neuroticism, as measured by this scale and Guilford's C scale.[1] It would have been desirable to have included items from other Guilford scales, but British subjects are very much less docile in their reactions to demands on the part of psychologists than are American students and it proved very difficult indeed to find sufficient subjects to fill in even the relatively short questionnaire constructed in this fashion.

Our subjects were 200 men and 200 women, all British born, white and over 18 years of age. The majority were in the 20–35 year age range and most of them were upper middle, lower middle and skilled working class. Nearly all of them were urban, as testing was carried out only in London, Manchester, Bristol, Exeter and other towns of similar size. Approximately half the subjects had had some kind of University education. The sample thus is by no means representative although

---

[1] In using both these scales, high correlations of between ·80 and ·95 were usually obtained with different populations. It also became apparent, however, that the Maudsley Medical Questionnaire gave a slightly better discrimination between normals and neurotics, while the C scale correlated more highly with neuroticism in normal groups. Two hypotheses were elaborated to account for these findings: (1) Many of the items in the Maudsley Medical Questionnaire are only endorsed very rarely in normal populations; such items, therefore, do not contribute much to the measurement of neuroticism in such populations; (2) The Maudsley Medical Questionnaire contains items measuring extraversion rather than neuroticism, and thus scores are weighted slightly by introversion as well as by neuroticism. As most random samples of neurotics contain more dysthymics than hysterics, this would aid in clinical differentiation but would make the measurement of neuroticism as such less univocal. As will be shown later, some evidence was found in favour of both these hypotheses.

certain points may be mentioned in connection with this. In the first place, our sample is probably more representative than samples on which questionnaires are usually standardized. In the second place, it is for practical purposes difficult to administer the same questionnaire to unskilled working-class groups and to University students. Groups with low education fail to understand many of the questions in the Guilford scales and if these are reworded in the kind of language spoken by lower working-class subjects, they are not acceptable to highly educated middle-class subjects. As this questionnaire is more likely to be employed with subjects having at least an average amount of education it seemed desirable to retain the original wording (except for one or two American terms which had to be changed as they would not be generally intelligible in Great Britain). Lastly, in our experience the Guilford factors do not correlate appreciably with intelligence, education, age (up to 50), or sex, so that a refined method of sampling taking these variables into account would, at the present stage of development, seem supererogatory.

Administration of the questionnaires was anonymous, but subjects were offered a chance to receive a detailed personality profile if they wanted this. The great majority did express a desire to have a personality profile and, indeed, expressed a considerable degree of interest in the project and in the profile in particular. It is impossible to prove that the questionnaires were answered truthfully, but the combination of anonymity and the subjects' interest in finding out about themselves seems as potent a way of achieving relative sincerity as can be found at the present stage of development of psychological testing. Some time was spent with a few individuals who signed their names and these interviews suggested strongly that no conscious efforts were made by these subjects to fake their scores.

TABLE 1

MEANS AND STANDARD DEVIATIONS FOR SIX GUILFORD
SCALES FOR MEN AND WOMEN SEPARATELY

	Men	Women
R	37·13±11·86	37·83±11·00
G	10·37± 4·94	10·72± 5·10
A	16·42± 6·72	14·75± 6·26
D	19·08±10·97	20·86±10·54
C	21·90±12·72	24·09±11·91
S	20·77± 9·93	21·32± 9·14

When sufficient questionnaires had been collected, scores were obtained on the individual scales. These scores are given in Table 1. They cannot be compared directly with Guilford's norms as these are given in terms of centile scores. However, certain points may be noted. On the R scale both men and women are just at the bottom of Guilford's 60th centile for adults and at the top of the 40th centile for University students. Combining these two American standardization groups there seem to be no marked national differences. On the G scale both men and women are at about the 35th percentile, whereas on the A scale they are at the 30th percentile. Taking scores on the R, G and A scales as measures of extraversion, then, we might conclude that our group is somewhat less extraverted than Guilford's standardization groups. This is in line with the popular stereotype of the American as being extraverted, but in view of the many differences in sampling in the two studies little value can be placed on this conclusion.

With respect to the C scale our subjects appeared to be less neurotic than Guilford's students or adults and the same is true of the D scale. Regarding the S scale, our subjects would seem to be roughly similar to the American samples. By and large, then, it might be said that the differences found are relatively small and not very impressive, particularly when the relatively poor sampling in both researches is taken into account.

With respect to the intercorrelations of the various factors, we were particularly interested in two points. The first was the relationship between the three extraversion factors, i.e., R, G and A. Table 2 shows separately the correlations between these three for males and females in our sample; given below the leading diagonal are the comparative values obtained by Guilford; these are put in brackets to indicate that they are taken from mixed sex groups. By and large, the figures are all similar enough to suggest that the conclusions drawn from the American work are applicable to British populations also.

TABLE 2

INTERCORRELATIONS OF R, G AND A SCALES FOR MEN AND WOMEN SEPARATELY. IN BRACKETS GUILFORD'S OWN VALUES

		Males			Females	
	R	G	A	R	G	A
R	—	0·404	0·423	—	0·452	0·482
G	(0·56)	—	0·369	(0·56)	—	0·549
A	(0·52)	(0·44)	—	(0·52)	(0·44)	—

The correlations of these three variables with C is of some interest. Guilford has reported a correlation of 0·02 between C and R, a correlation of −0·19 between C and G and one of 0·31 between C and A. We summed scores on the R, G, and A factors and correlated this sum of the three extraversion scores with C. The resulting coefficients were −0·024 for the men and +0·072 for the women; both of these are quite insignificant. It thus appears that here also our results are essentially similar to Guilford's.

Our next step was to carry out an item analysis of all the 261 questions and their relationships with the C and R scores. This was done by taking the 100 men and 100 women with the highest C scores and comparing their replies on each question with those of the 100 men and 100 women having the lowest C scores. Similarly, the 100 men and 100 women having the highest R scores were compared with the 100 men and 100 women having the lowest R scores. The two sexes were kept separate throughout so that we have eight groups: high C males, high C females, low C males, low C females, high R males, high R females, low R males, and low R females.

The statistic used to assess the relationship of answers to each of the questions with the R and C scales was chi². It would have been more usual to have chosen some form of correlation such as phi, biserial, or tetrachoric, but there seemed to be little point in such a transformation. Our main interest lay in the significance of observed relationships, which can best be tested by means of chi² in any case and as numbers of subjects are identical in the various groups, different values of chi² can be compared directly without being transformed into some semblance of a correlation.

We therefore end up with four series of figures, giving us the chi² for all our 261 items with our two scales (R and C) for men and women separately. It is these figures on which we shall draw for most of the comparative studies made in the course of this paper.

Significance values of chi² with the number of cases used here are 3·841 for the 5 per cent level, 5·412 for the 2 per cent level, and 6·635 for the 1 per cent level. Quite arbitrarily we have chosen as a standard of significance a chi² value of 10 which is well in excess of the 0·1 per cent level of significance. Our reason for this choice was as follows. For each of our four groups (C male, C female, R male, R female) we have over 250 items, making a total of over 1000 chi² values. By chance alone, 10 of these would be significant at the 1 per cent level (this is not quite accurate, of course, as the items are not independent, but it will serve to illustrate the point we are making). If we, therefore, use the 1 per cent level of significance we would be wrong in a sufficiently large number of cases to make our results less reliable than they ought to be. By taking a p value well in excess of the 0·1 per cent level we ensure as far as possible that of all the conclusions presented as reaching the level of significance none, or at most one, are at all likely to be reduced to insignificance on repetition of this study. Psychologists have traditionally accepted low levels of significance in most of their work, but the choice of a level of significance is arbitrary, and in the present type of work a higher level seems desirable. Fisher's distinction between errors of type one and errors of type two should be borne in mind in this connection. (Another point should be borne in mind, although it does not affect our results to any considerable extent. Items in the R scale, because they contribute part of the total score, must be expected to have very slightly higher chi^2 than all other items with the R scale. Similarly, items in the C scale must be expected to have slightly higher chi^2 than all other items with the C scale. In view of the large number of items involved, the influence of this factor is probably negligible).

The Dual Nature of Sociability

In questionnaire construction sociability has always played an important role. In questionnaires of neuroticism, items indicative of social shyness have always been scored as prognostic of neuroticism. In questionnaires of extraversion-introversion, items indicative of social shyness have always been scored as prognostic of introversion. As items of this kind tended to make up a high proportion of all the items in both types of questionnaires, it was soon found that questionnaires of introversion correlated just about as highly with questionnaires of neuroticism, as did questionnaires of introversion with each other, or questionnaires of neuroticism with each other (Ref. 20).

This situation was profoundly changed through the work of Guilford, who demonstrated the existence of the unitary factor, which he labelled S or social shyness (Refs. 12 and 13). This factor entered into several further factorial analyses, such as those by Lovell (Ref. 17), North (Ref. 9) and others, and has also formed part of experimental studies, such as that of Hildebrand (Ref. 16). The evidence has been reviewed in detail by the present writer and leaves little doubt that the S factor is highly correlated, both with introversion and neuroticism (Ref. 5).

While this fact appears to be beyond dispute, there are certain alternative possibilities which deserve further investigation. One of these two possibilities is based on the factorial derivation of the S factor. If the items contributing to the total score in Guilford's S questionnaire are indeed univocal, as they should be in view of the fact that S is presented to us as a unitary trait, then not only should the total S score have high correlations with both introversion and neuroticism, but so should each single item in the scale, depending only on its factor saturation. In other words, if we plotted the correlations of all the items in the S scale against a good measure of introversion, such as the R scale and a good measure of neuroticism, such as the C scale, then we would expect the items to be strung out in the form of an oval in the centre of the space generated by these two orthogonal factors or tests. This would seem to follow from the theory of factor analysis and from the method of test construction used by Guilford.

An alternative view, however, is indicated by a detailed study of social behaviour of people of known degrees of neuroticism and introversion. Such observation suggests that introverted social shyness is different in many ways from neurotic social shyness. To put the hypothesis suggested here in a nutshell, we might say that the introvert does not care for people, would rather be alone, but if need be can effectively take part in social situations, whereas the neurotic is anxious and afraid when confronted with social situations, seeks to avoid them in order to escape from this negative feeling, but frequently wishes that he could be more sociable. In other words, the introvert does not care to be with other people; the neurotic is afraid of being with other people. If this hypothesis were true it seems likely that different items in the S scale would be chosen by introverts and neurotics respectively to express their non-sociable attitude. In the extreme case, i.e., where every item was indicative either of the neurotic or of the introvertive type of social shyness, but none of both, we would expect one set of items to have high correlations with a good measure of introversion, such as the R scale, but none with a good measure of neuroticism, such as the C scale, while another set of items would have high correlations with the C scale, but no, or very low, correlations with the R scale. We thus see that the factorial, and what we may perhaps call the clinical hypothesis, generate quite different expectations and it will be of interest to see which of the two hypotheses is borne out in fact.

All items of the S scale on which members of either sex produced a significant chi^2 with either the R or the C scale were tabulated (cf. Table 3). Even a casual look at the Tables will show that the clinical hypothesis is borne out and the factorial hypothesis refuted. For the men it is found that none of the items showing a significant relation with R shows a significant relation with C. Similarly, not one of the items showing a significant relation with C shows a significant relation with R. With the exception of one item the same is true for the women. It therefore appears that in the central part of the diagram where, according to the factorial theory, we would have expected all the items to lie, not a single item is found for the men and only one item out of over 50 for the women. This fact appears to furnish strong evidence against the factorial view and to support our hypothesis of the dual nature of sociability.

TABLE 3A

ITEMS FROM THE S SCALE SIGNIFICANTLY RELATED TO THE R SCALE

	R		C	
	M	F	M	F
Are you inclined to be quick and sure in your actions?	45	24	1	0
Can you usually let yourself go and have a hilariously good time at a gay party?	44	43	1	5
Do you like to mix socially with people?	40	22	0	0
Are you inclined to take life too seriously?	40	12	10	0
Would you rate yourself as a lively individual?	54	35	0	0
Are you usually a 'good mixer'?	32	31	4	0
Are you inclined to keep in the background on social occasions?	52	30	0	0
Do you usually take the initiative in making new friends?	26	28	1	0
Would you rather spend an evening reading at home than attend a large party?	8	26	0	0
Do you like to have social engagements?	25	52	9	0
Does it embarrass you a great deal to say or do the wrong thing in a social group?	23	8	6	6
Do you adapt yourself easily to new conditions, that is, new places, situations, surroundings, etc.?	24	13	0	4
Is it easy for you to act naturally at a party?	22	22	7	2
Are you inclined to keep quiet when out in a social group?	22	18	0	0
Do you often 'have the time of your life' at social affairs?	52	5	2	9
Are you inclined to limit your acquaintances to a select few?	18	17	5	0
Do you generally prefer to take the lead in group activities?	19	8	1	2
In social conversations, are you usually a listener rather than a talker?	7	19	1	0

Chi^2 appears as the column group heading above R and C.

Theoretical and Methodological Issues

TABLE 3A *continued*

ITEMS FROM THE S SCALE SIGNIFICANTLY RELATED TO THE R SCALE

				Chi^2	
		R		C	
		M	F	M	F
Do you find it easy, as a rule, to make new acquaintances?		17	17	1	0
Do you have difficulty in making new friends?		17	17	4	0
Do you shrink from speaking in public?		4	17	3	0
Were you ever the 'life of the party'?		5	16	5	8
Do you generally feel uncomfortable when you are the centre of attention on a social occasion?		12	15	6	0
Would you be very unhappy if you were prevented from making numerous social contacts?		14	15	1	2
Do you nearly always have a 'ready answer' for remarks directed at you?		14	9	1	0
Do you usually prefer to let someone else take the lead on social occasion?		13	8	0	1
Do you enjoy getting acquainted with most people?		14	7	2	2
Are you often hesitant about meeting important people?		13	9	6	7
Do you enjoy entertaining people?		13	7	0	4
Are you inclined to be shy in the presence of the opposite sex?		12	10	0	0
Is it usually difficult for you to make decisions?		10	5	7	6
Do you like to speak in public?		6	10	6	1
Are you troubled with feelings of inferiority?		2	17	14	28

A glance at Tables 3A, B will indicate to what extent our hypothesis regarding the precise nature of the difference between introvertive and neurotic sociability is borne out. The sociable extravert lets himself go and has a hilarious time, likes to mix socially, is a lively individual who does not take life seriously, is a good mixer who does not stay in the background on social occasions, who takes the initiative in making friends, has many social engagements, acts naturally at parties, adapts easily and so forth. In other words, he is a person who enjoys social intercourse with people as opposed to the introvert who does not enjoy social intercourse with people. When we return to the items indicative of neurotic social shyness we find the shy person troubled about being self-conscious, experiencing periods of loneliness, troubled with feelings of inferiority and self-conscious with superiors, worrying over humiliating experiences and about being shy, ill at ease with other people and not well poised in social contacts. In other words, we meet a kind of person

TABLE 3B

ITEMS FROM THE S SCALE SIGNIFICANTLY RELATED TO THE C SCALE

	Chi²			
	R		C	
	M	F	M	F
Do you often experience periods of loneliness?	2	6	10	38
Do you 'get rattled' easily at critical moments?	3	0	32	16
Are you troubled about being self-conscious?	7	7	32	23
Are you troubled with feelings of inferiority?	2	17	14	28
Are you self-conscious in the presence of your superiors?	5	5	23	10
After a critical moment is over, do you usually think of something you should have done but failed to do?	0	3	14	23
Are there times when your mind seems to work very slowly and other times when it works very rapidly?	0	0	23	16
Do you feel that the world is distant and unreal to you?	0	0	16	24
Do you worry over humiliating experiences longer than the average person?	17	9	4	19
Do you think there is a great deal more happiness in the world than misery?	3	0	15	10
Are you usually well-poised in your social contacts?	3	5	12	2
Are you worried about being shy?	3	2	7	12
Do you often feel ill at ease with other people?	2	7	19	12

who is troubled and worried over his social contacts and would like to be more adequate in his dealings with other people, but whose emotional reactions seem to interfere with his social adjustment. The reader must judge for himself the adequacy of our theory regarding the nature of these two entirely separate aspects of social shyness. Our data are not sufficient to prove this hypothesis to be correct, of course, but merely furnish some preliminary support.

There are several hypotheses which may account for the difference of our results and those expected on the basis of Guilford's work. In the first place, Guilford's original work was done with American College students, our own work done with a more representative and older sample of British subjects; thus, age, education and nationality in the two studies were markedly different. The fact that in our experiments norms on the Guilford scales for British groups of the kind used here are rather similar to those obtained by Guilford in the United States suggests, but does not prove, that this difference is unlikely to have been a decisive one.

Another possibility is that only some of the items of the S scale form part of the original factorial study; others were added later by Guilford to make the scale longer and more reliable. (Guilford has confirmed this point in a private communication.) It is possible that these additions, which were made on the basis of item analyses are responsible for the non-unitary nature of the resulting scale. This seems to the present writer a feasible hypothesis and if true it suggests that all the Guilford scales would have to be investigated in order to weed out items added to the original pool of factorially pure questions in order to make the scales longer and more reliable. Such an undertaking with respect to the R and C scales is reported in the next section.

Item Analysis of the R and C Scales and of the
    Maudsley Medical Inventory

An analysis similar to that reported in the preceding section was carried out on the items comprising the R and C scales, as well as on those comprising the Maudsley Medical Questionnaire. The results will not be presented in detail as they are of technical interest rather than being of general psychological importance, like the dual nature of sociability. We will first deal with results from the R and C scales.

In the first place, let us consider items scored for both R and C. Some of these items show significant relationships to both R and C, others to R but not to C, others yet to C but not to R, while yet a fourth group show no significant relationships to either R or C.

In the second place, items scored only for C mostly show significant relationships with C. Some also show significant relationships with R, some items show significant relationships with R only, but not with C and several items show no significant relationship with either C or R.

In the third place, items scored only for R mostly show significant relationships with R. Some also show significant relationships with C, some items show significant relationships with C only, but not with R and several items show no significant relationship with either R or C.

These findings re-enforce our belief that purification of the R and C scales by item analysis is desirable and that a certain number of items in these scales are merely dead wood and may in fact detract from the validity of the scales for which they are scored.

Similar findings were made in connection with the Maudsley Medical Questionnaire. One out of 40 items showed relationships only to the R but not to the C scale and a number of items showed very low relationships with the C scale. As had been suspected (see footnote, p. 176), the items showing such low relationships tended to have very few endorsements. Of 80 chi^2 values (40 items for each sex), 35 were found in respect to items endorsed by over 20 per cent of subjects and 45 in items endorsed by fewer than 20 per cent of subjects. Of the former items 25 had high chi^2 values and 10 had low ones, whereas of the latter only 14 had high chi^2 values and 31 low ones. It would appear, therefore, that in part at least the unsatisfactory validity of the Maudsley Medical Questionnaire with normal groups may be due to the gross divergences from a 50/50 distribution of answers.

Sex Differences

Twenty-nine items out of the 261 showed large differences in the number of 'Yes' answers between the two sexes, a large difference being arbitrarily defined as one of 30 or more points. The actual items involved and the number of men and women respectively answering 'Yes' to each are given in Table 4.

TABLE 4

ITEMS SHOWING LARGE SEX DIFFERENCES IN ENDORSEMENT

	Per cent Endorsement:	
	M	F
Do you generally prefer to take the lead in group activities?	79	46
Are you inclined to be slow and deliberate in movement?	64	33
Do you enjoy getting acquainted with most people?	149	180
Do you shrink from speaking in public?	91	141
Are you inclined to be overconscientious?	127	87
Do you often crave excitement?	49	118
Do you ever feel 'just miserable' for no good reason at all?	45	86
Are you inclined to stop and think things over before acting?	166	128
Would you rate yourself as a lively individual?	72	111
Do you sometimes feel happy, sometimes depressed, without any apparent reason?	57	95
Are you inclined to take life too seriously?	94	130
In social conversations, are you usually a listener rather than a talker?	76	116
Do you like to have time to be alone with your thoughts?	148	185
Do you find it difficult to go to sleep at night because experiences of the day keep 'running through your head'?	30	77
Are you inclined to keep your opinions to yourself during group discussions?	62	105
Are you frequently bored with people?	75	33
Do you ever have to fight against bashfulness?	56	93
Do you enjoy entertaining people?	130	170
Is your own mood very easily influenced by people around you, that is, by happy people or sad people?	56	100
Does it embarrass you a great deal to say or do the wrong thing in a social group?	104	141

E

TABLE 4 *continued*

When climbing stairs do you often take the steps two at a time?	169	118
Do you find it difficult to get rid of a salesman to whom you do not care to listen or give your time?	47	91
Have you ever, on your own initiative, organized a club or group of any kind?	120	82
Would you rather work for a good boss than for yourself?	77	139
Do you (or would you) like to take on new and important responsibilities such as organizing a new business enterprise?	120	79
Do you usually speak out in a meeting to oppose someone who you feel sure is wrong?	126	82
Do other people regard you as a lively individual?	71	115
Do you seek to avoid all troublesome situations?	134	104

From these answers a fairly conventional and stereotyped picture of the two sexes emerges. According to their answer pattern men like to take the lead in group activities, are slow and deliberate in movement, overconscientious, inclined to stop and think things over before acting, frequently bored with people, tend to organize things on their own initiative, like to take on new and important responsibilities, speak out at meetings in order to oppose someone they think wrong, seek to avoid troublesome situations and often take two steps at a time when climbing stairs.

Women are opposite to men on all these points; in addition they enjoy getting acquainted with most people, shrink from speaking in public, crave excitement, often feel 'just miserable' for no good reason at all, consider themselves as lively individuals and are regarded as such by other people, sometimes feel happy and sometimes depressed without any apparent reason, tend to take life too seriously, be listeners rather than talkers in social conversation (!), like to have time to be alone with their thoughts, find it difficult to go to sleep at night because experiences of the day keep running through their head, keep their opinions to themselves during group discussions, have to fight against bashfulness, enjoy entertaining people and are easily influenced in their mood by people around them. It embarrasses them a great deal to do or say the wrong thing in a social group. They find it difficult to get rid of salesmen, and lastly, they would rather work for a good boss than for themselves.

The pattern, as one might have expected, is a highly conventionalized one. The men see themselves as leaders and organizers and quite generally as not being afraid of responsibility and of standing up for themselves. They are conscientious and act rationally rather than on impulse. They are more interested in work than in social life and like to be physically active. Women, on the other hand, are mercurial, interested in social things and excitement rather than in work and responsibility. They are more dependent on the opinion of their immediate social group and also are more emotional than men. To put the results in a nutshell, we might say that women are more neurotic and more extraverted than men, who are more introverted and more stable. Putting it more concisely still, one might simply say that women as compared to men tend to be more hysterical, a view which can hardly be said to be sparkling with originality as it tends to mirror the writings of many people on this subject for the past 2000 years and has indeed found expression in the etymological derivation of the very term 'hysteria'.

It would be fascinating, though pointless, to discuss to what extent what our subjects say about themselves is in fact true. The fact that the women say that they prefer listening to talking may not be a reliable guide to objective fact and altogether answers from both sexes may be to an unknown degree influenced by stereotypes and preconceptions. Our experiment was not designed to throw light on this point. Nor are we concerned with the eternal problem of causation, i.e., the question of whether observed differences are in any sense innate or are merely due to social pressure and the roles which society expects men and women to play. Our results are exclusively concerned with self reports, i.e., the way men and women in our society see themselves when answering questionnaires. Quite a different type of research would be required to answer the other questions raised in this context.

If the conceptions men and women have of themselves in relation to extraversion and neuroticism differ as much as is indicated in the figures presented above, then we should expect that considerable differences might also be found in the degree to which individual items measure extraversion and introversion for the two sexes respectively. This is a very important point because unless it is taken into account, this difference between the sexes will make the selection of items very much more difficult. Little appears to be known on this point and a perusal of the literature does not suggest that sufficient attention has been paid to this problem.

Our first step in investigating this question consisted in determining the correlation between the chi^2 values of the 261 items between men and women. This correlation amounted to 0·803 for the C scale and 0·643 for the R scale. Both values are significant; both are significantly different from unity; and additionally they are significantly different

116   *Theoretical and Methodological Issues*

from each other. It appears, then, that the meaning of our questions when regarded as measures of neuroticism or extraversion differs from sex to sex; that these differences are much more pronounced when we are concerned with the measurement of extraversion; and that in both cases positive steps have to be taken in the construction of a questionnaire to take these differences into account. This can be done in two ways. Either we can construct separate questionnaires for the two sexes, or we can use the same set of questions for both sexes, but take care in selecting the items to choose only those in which discrepancies are small or non-existent. If feasible, the second alternative is preferable, but enough items may not always be available and in that case recourse must be had to the device of constructing separate questionnaires for men and women. Failure to use one or the other of these methods must seriously invalidate questionnaires constructed for the purpose of measuring extraversion or neuroticism, or indeed any personality trait in which sex differences of the kind discussed here can be demonstrated.

It may be of interest to have a look at the discordant items, i.e., items with large differences in the chi^2 values obtained by men and women respectively. Defining a large difference quite arbitrarily as one of 30 points, we find 14 such discordant items with respect to the C scale and 12 such items with respect to the R scale. One item is common to both sides. Table 5 below lists the items concerned and the chi^2 values for men and women respectively.

TABLE 5A

SEX DIFFERENCES ON R ITEMS

	Chi^2 M	F
Are you ordinarily a carefree individual?	46	18
Are you inclined to keep in the background on social occasions?	52	29
Would you rate yourself as an impulsive person?	4	46
Are you much depressed when others criticize you?	32	10
Are you inclined to take life too seriously?	40	12
Are you inclined to be quick and sure in your actions?	45	24
Do you like to have many social engagements?	25	52
Do you dislike to stop and analyse your own thoughts and feelings?	34	3
Are you rather good at bluffing when you find yourself in difficulty?	0	26
Do you usually start to work on a new project with a great deal of enthusiasm?	5	34
Do you like to bear responsibility alone?	24	2
Do you often feel reluctant to meet the most important person at a party or reception?	28	8

TABLE 5B

SEX DIFFERENCES ON C ITEMS

	Chi²	
	M	F
Are you inclined to worry over possible misfortunes?	49	14
Do you have frequent ups and downs in mood, either with or without apparent cause?	77	54
Would you rate yourself as an impulsive person?	39	10
Do you often experience periods of loneliness?	10	38
Are you much depressed when others criticize you?	48	22
Are you inclined to 'jump at conclusions'?	46	23
Do you often feel disgruntled?	48	16
Did you often get 'stage fright' in your life?	38	10
Are there times when you seek to be alone and you cannot bear the company of anyone?	24	48
When failing to have your own way, do you often resort to resentful thinking?	55	24
Do you usually keep in fairly uniform spirits?	42	20
Do you become angry very quickly and also recover very quickly?	35	9
Do you like to indulge in a reverie (daydreaming)?	44	15
Do you usually shrink from meeting a crisis or emergency?	29	4

Bearing in mind that the fact of a particular item having a higher chi² for men than for women means that this item has more serious diagnostic implications for men than for women, we find that out of the 14 discordant C items, 12 have higher chi² values for men and only 2 have higher chi² values for women. Apparently, having periods of loneliness and seeking to be alone are both more diagnostic of neuroticism in women than in men. Conversely, worrying over possible misfortunes, having ups and downs in mood, being impulsive, being depressed when criticized, jumping at conclusions, being disgruntled, having stage fright, being given to resentful thinking, not being in uniform spirits, being angry very quickly, daydreaming and shrinking from meeting crises are much more indicative of emotional instability in men than in women. It almost appears as if to women, as long as they are extraverted enough, a certain amount of latitude is given in their display of emotionality. It is only when they show introvertive traits (periods of loneliness, seeking to be alone) that the prognosis becomes poor. One might think that where the stereotypes of male and female conduct differ, the fact that women come closer to the more neurotic stereotype of their own sex is in some sense taken as an ameliorative feature. If this hypothesis were correct we would expect a greater number of 'Yes' answers by men for those items in which women have a higher chi² and a great number of 'Yes' answers by women on items on which the men have higher chi². This, however, is by no means true. There are a few large differences in endorsement. The differences that are found are equal in both directions and on both items in which women have higher chi² they also have a large number of 'Yes' answers. We cannot, therefore, account for the observed differences along these lines.

The same is true of the discordant R items. Apparently the following items are much more diagnostic of extraversion for men than for women: Being a carefree individual, not tending to keep in the background on social occasions, not being depressed when criticized, not taking life too seriously, being quick and sure in action, disliking to stop and analyse one's feelings, not liking to bear responsibilities alone and not being reluctant to meet important people. Conversely, the answers to the following items are more significant of extraversion in women: Being impulsive, liking many social engagements, being good at bluffing when in difficulty and starting new jobs with enthusiasm. The facts are there but they do not suggest any obvious hypothesis to the present writer.

Construction of the Maudsley Personality Inventory

On the basis of the considerations discussed in the preceding sections and the factual results of the item analysis, two questionnaires were prepared in the hope that these might prove to be improved measures of extraversion-introversion and neuroticism, as compared with the R and C scales. 24 items were selected to form the new neuroticism scale (to be called the N scale henceforth) and 24 items were selected to form the new extraversion-introversion scale (to be called the E scale henceforth). Five spare items were added to the N scale and seven spare items to the E scale in case one or the other of the chosen items might prove unsuitable, or in case it might later be desirable to lengthen the scales. For the purpose of computing split-half reliabilities each scale was divided into two parts: N_1, N_2 and E_1 and E_2, each consisting of twelve questions.

The principles governing the selection of questions were as follows: All items in the N scale should have significant relations with the C scale for both men and women and insignificant relations with the R scale for both men and women. Items in the E scale, conversely, were chosen in such a way that all had significant relations with the R scale for both men and women, but not for the C scale. The actual chi² values, as well as the items selected and the scoring key, are given in Table 6 and it will be seen that the requirements are adequately met by these questions.

TABLE 6A

NEUROTICISM SCALE

	Key:	R_M	R_F	Chi² C_M	C_F
N_1:					
1. Are you inclined to be moody?	Y	5	1	54	44
2. Are your daydreams frequently about things that can never come true?	Y	0	1	29	18
3. Are you inclined to ponder over your past?	Y	1	1	28	37
4. Do you ever feel 'just miserable' for no good reason at all?	Y	1	1	35	51
5. Do you often find that you have made up your mind too late?	Y	1	0	30	27
6. Have you often lost sleep over your worries?	Y	0	0	19	13
7. Do you sometimes feel happy, sometimes depressed, without any apparent reason?	Y	0	0	64	61
8. Are you often troubled about feelings of guilt?	Y	3	0	25	25
9. Are your feelings rather easily hurt?	Y	2	2	27	20
10. Would you rate yourself as a tense or 'high strung' individual?	Y	0	1	25	13
11. Does your mind often wander while you are trying to concentrate?	Y	0	0	39	34
12. Do you often experience periods of loneliness?	Y	2	0	10	38
N_2:					
13. Do you have frequent ups and downs in mood, either with or without apparent cause?	Y	0	0	77	54
14. Do you like to indulge in a reverie (daydreaming)?	Y	0	2	44	15
15. Do you spend much time in thinking over good times you have had in the past?	Y	1	1	18	25
16. Have you often felt listless and tired for no good reason?	Y	0	0	31	38
17. After a critical moment is over, do you usually think of something you should have done but failed to do?	Y	0	3	14	23
18. Do ideas run through your head so that you can not sleep?	Y	0	0	42	30
19. Are you sometimes bubbling over with energy and sometimes very sluggish?	Y	0	2	48	59
20. Have you ever been bothered by having a useless thought come into your mind repeatedly?	Y	1	0	16	25
21. Are you touchy on various subjects?	Y	0	1	25	24
22. Do you often feel disgruntled?	Y	0	2	48	17
23. Are you frequently 'lost in thought' even when supposed to be taking part in a conversation?	Y	0	2	30	39
24. Do you have periods of such great restlessness that you cannot sit long in a chair?	Y	0	5	11	28

TABLE 6B

EXTRAVERSION SCALE

	Key:	R_M	R_F	C_M	C_F
				Chi^2	
E_1:					
25. Are you inclined to keep in the background on social occasions?	N	52	29	0	0
26. Is it difficult to 'lose yourself' even at a lively party?	N	28	20	1	0
27. Are you inclined to be overconscientious?	N	23	9	2	0
28. Do you like to mix socially with people?	Y	40	22	0	0
29. Are you inclined to limit your acquaintances to a select few?	N	18	17	5	0
30. Are you inclined to be quick and sure in your actions?	Y	45	24	1	0
31. Do you ever take your work as if it were a matter of life or death?	N	12	31	2	5
32. Do you like to have many social engagements?	Y	25	52	9	0
33. Do you generally prefer to take the lead in group activities?	Y	19	8	1	2
34. Are you inclined to be shy in the presence of the opposite sex?	N	12	10	1	1
35. Do you nearly always have a 'ready answer' for remarks directed at you?	Y	14	9	1	0
36. Would you rate yourself as a happy-go-lucky individual?	Y	52	37	0	5
E_2:					
37. Are you inclined to keep quiet when out in a social group?	N	22	18	0	0
38. Can you usually let yourself go and have a hilariously good time at a gay party?	Y	45	43	1	4
39. Do you like work that requires considerable attention?	N	13	6	1	0
40. Would you rate yourself as a lively individual?	Y	54	35	1	1
41. Would you be very unhappy if you were prevented from making numerous social contacts?	Y	14	15	1	2
42. Are you happiest when you get involved in some project that calls for rapid action?	Y	10	24	4	3
43. Are you inclined to take your work casually, that is, as a matter of course?	Y	18	14	1	4
44. Do other people regard you as a lively individual?	Y	29	32	0	7
45. Do you usually take the initiative in making new friends?	Y	26	28	1	0
46. Would you rate yourself a talkative individual?	Y	39	24	1	1
47. Do you like to play pranks upon others?	Y	28	17	2	4
48. Do you prefer action to planning for action?	Y	21	16	0	5

TABLE 6C

NEUROTICISM SCALE

N Spares:	Key:	Chi² R_M	R_F	C_M	C_F
Do you ever change from happiness to sadness, or vice versa, without good reason?	Y	0	0	47	35
Do you usually feel disappointments so keenly that you cannot get them out of your mind?	Y	2	6	44	29
Are there times when you seek to be alone and you cannot bear the company of anyone?	Y	4	0	24	48
Do you usually keep in fairly uniform spirits?	Y	1	2	42	20
Do you ever have a queer feeling that you are not your old self?	Y	0	0	27	11

EXTRAVERSION SCALE

E Spares:					
Are you ordinarily a carefree individual?	Y	46	18	7	2
Do you have difficulty in making new friends?	N	17	17	4	0
Do you find it easy, as a rule, to make acquaintances?	Y	17	17	1	0
Are you usually a 'good mixer'?	Y	32	31	4	0
Do you often 'have the time of your life' at social affairs?	Y	52	52	2	9
Do you enjoy participating in a showing of 'Rah Rah enthusiasm'?	Y	17	10	0	3
Do you derive more real satisfaction from social activities than from anything else?	Y	12	14	2	1

Various other requirements were also borne in mind. Thus, an attempt was made to select only items where chi² values for men and women were not too dissimilar; where differences between the sexes were observed on one item another item was selected in such a way as to balance the disproportion. In this way it was hoped to obtain scales which could be used for both sexes equally. Another requirement was that items should not be mere duplicates of each other, slightly changed in wording, but should cover different aspects of neuroticism or of extraversion-introversion. Judgments here are, of course, subjective, although there is a partial check on their accuracy in the results of the correlational analysis to be described below.

Scoring and Results

The scoring of the two questionnaires is as follows: Any 'yes' answer on the neuroticism scale is counted two points; any 'no' answer is counted 0 points; any '?' is counted one point. Similarly, on the extraversion scale, answers in conformity with the key are scored two points; answers contrary to the key are scored 0 points; '?' answers are scored one point. The highest possible score on either scale therefore is 48 points, the lowest is 0 points. The actual scores obtained by our 200 males and 200 female subjects are as follows: On the neuroticism scale the men have a mean score of 17·810 with a standard deviation of 11·321. The women have a mean score of 19·445±11·018. Men and women together have a mean score of 18·628±11·186. On the extraversion scale the mean for the men is 24·620±10·037 and the mean score for the women is 25·165±9·331. The total score for both sexes is 24·892±9·673. There are no significant differences between the sexes on either scale.

Split-half reliability correlations, corrected for length, are as follows. On the neuroticism scale, r = 0·9013 for men, 0·8658 for women and 0·8839 for the two groups combined. On the extraversion scale, r = 0·8468 for the men, 0·8173 for the women, and 0·8313 for the total sample. As regards the correlation between these two scales r = −0·1476 for the men, −0·0364 for the women and −0·0924 for the two sexes combined.

In view of the importance attaching to the independence of the two scales and bearing in mind that cross validation is always desirable in analyses of this kind, the two scales were given to another male group of 200 subjects altogether. The mean scores of this group for neuroticism and extraversion respectively were 23·23±11·27 and 25·26±8·84. The correlation between the scales was −0·07. We thus end up with two scales which are virtually independent of each other, the very small negative correlation between them being equivalent to only about ½ per cent of the total variance. It will be seen that all the desiderata listed at the end of the introduction for the construction of a set of scales have been accomplished.

Factor Analysis

As a check on the adequacy of the item analyses on which the selection of items was based a factor analysis was performed. The 48 items in the N and E scales were intercorrelated separately for men and women, using tetrachoric coefficients and the resulting tables analysed by means of Thurstone's centroid method. Two factors were extracted from each of the two matrices, the residuals remaining after the extraction of these two factors being too small to warrant further analysis. Rotation was carried out according to the dictates of simple structure which, in this case, was relatively easy as the analysis disclosed two groups of items clustering closely around centroids which were orthogonal to each other. The results of the analysis are shown in Table 7.

TABLE 7

FACTOR SATURATION OF MEN AND WOMEN SEPARATELY
FOR THE 48 ITEMS OF THE N AND E SCALES

	Women:		Men:		
	I	II	I	II	h^2
1.	0·04	0·69	−0·04	0·75	0·5618
2.	0·03	0·72	−0·01	0·81	0·6625
3.	−0·12	0·59	−0·05	0·58	0·3449
4.	0·26	0·52	0·12	0·44	0·2122
5.	−0·03	0·49	0·10	0·59	0·3625
6.	−0·02	0·61	0·00	0·63	0·3973
7.	−0·05	0·72	−0·10	0·79	0·6425
8.	0·12	0·59	−0·04	0·67	0·4513
9.	0·05	0·71	−0·10	0·52	0·2788
10.	−0·08	0·65	−0·15	0·67	0·4736
11.	0·00	0·50	−0·13	0·57	0·3460
12.	−0·02	0·57	0·03	0·65	0·4181
13.	0·08	0·58	0·03	0·82	0·6673
14.	0·06	0·56	0·01	0·67	0·4537
15.	0·12	0·64	0·01	0·70	0·4925
16.	0·02	0·74	−0·06	0·83	0·6964
17.	−0·08	0·53	−0·01	0·54	0·2969
18.	0·08	0·65	0·11	0·45	0·2165
19.	0·17	0·43	0·23	0·55	0·3536
20.	0·08	0·58	−0·04	0·46	0·2180
21.	0·20	0·71	0·00	0·61	0·3706
22.	−0·09	0·65	−0·13	0·67	0·4597
23.	−0·03	0·59	−0·06	0·67	0·4517
24.	0·11	0·39	0·01	0·66	0·4349
25.	0·45	−0·30	0·51	−0·33	0·3681
26.	0·53	0·08	0·47	−0·10	0·2340
27.	0·22	0·07	0·29	−0·08	0·0925
28.	0·69	−0·15	0·80	−0·06	0·6370
29.	0·53	−0·16	0·70	−0·07	0·5013
30.	0·51	−0·04	0·58	−0·09	0·3425
31.	0·48	−0·29	0·38	−0·26	0·2152
32.	0·19	−0·09	0·38	−0·13	0·1521
33.	0·41	−0·06	0·41	−0·06	0·1754
34.	0·75	0·01	0·72	−0·02	0·5234
35.	0·45	0·17	0·57	0·11	0·3434
36.	0·23	0·00	0·31	−0·03	0·0986

TABLE 7 *continued*

37.	0·64	−0·09	0·40	−0·18	0·1933
38.	0·57	−0·01	0·63	−0·21	0·4450
39.	0·18	−0·37	0·29	−0·19	0·1181
40.	0·65	−0·16	0·87	−0·05	0·7540
41.	0·58	−0·08	0·67	0·03	0·4513
42.	0·66	0·10	0·59	0·12	0·3697
43.	0·78	−0·07	0·62	0·24	0·4381
44.	0·44	0·19	0·37	0·07	0·1429
45.	0·66	0·14	0·72	−0·15	0·5466
46.	0·48	0·29	0·47	0·12	0·2329
47.	0·66	0·08	0·57	0·24	0·3812
48.	0·73	0·03	0·70	−0·09	0·4964

It will be seen that our expectations are fulfilled. The neuroticism items cluster together; the extraversion items cluster together; and there appears to be no relationship between the two clusters. The cluster of neuroticism items is clearly more compact than the cluster of extraversion items; this fact, presumably, accounts for our observation of greater split-half reliability for the N scale than for the E scale. Some of the items are relatively poor measures of their respective factors, e.g. items 32 and 27 on the female side and items 39 and 27 and 36 on the male side. Some items, such as 25 for both men and women and 46 for the women, have rather high loadings on the factor which they are not supposed to be measuring; as those loadings, however, appear to balance out on the whole it did not seem wise to disturb the balance of the test. In any case, it should be remembered that the correlations on which the analysis is based have standard errors of approximately 0·15, so that in a group of 2×48 items some considerable departures from the true values may be expected. On the whole the items selected emerge from the factor analysis reasonably well.

DISCUSSION

No discussion appears necessary with respect to the procedures adopted in the analysis reported in this paper. They are all quite orthodox in character and raise no essential problems. A word may, however, be said with respect to the problem of validity. There is no evidence in this paper with respect to the ability of the neuroticism scale to differentiate between normal and neurotic subjects, or the ability of the E scale to discriminate between extraverts and introverts, or between hysterics and dysthymics. Such evidence will be reported in a later paper.[1]

There are, however, solid grounds for regarding these scales as possessing considerable validity. Evidence has been quoted earlier in this paper showing that the C and R scales with all their imperfections nevertheless have a considerable degree of validity. The purification of these scales, involving as it does the throwing out of items not themselves correlated with the scales, should have the effect of improving the validity of the scales; it is difficult to see how such purification could result in a lowering of validity. This argument is not presented in order to obviate the necessity of further empirical work; it is merely advanced to indicate that there is considerable theoretical reason for expecting such empirical studies to give favourable results.

Two studies have quite recently been completed [Franks (Ref. 9) and Eysenck (Ref. 8)] in which the new scales were used as criterion measures to test certain predictions made by the writer with respect to conditioning and reminiscence. It was predicted from the writer's general theory (Ref. 6) that extraverts would be more difficult to condition than introverts, but that there would be no relationship between conditionability and neuroticism. It was also predicted that extraverts would show greater reminiscence phenomena than introverts and that the degree of reminiscence would be positively correlated with degree of neuroticism. These predictions have recently been tested using the eye-blink as a conditioned response for the conditioning experiment and using pursuit rotor learning in connection with the reminiscence phenomenon. All predictions were verified at acceptable levels of significance.

This type of validation may appear somewhat unusual, but it is in good accord with the principles of 'construct validity' advanced by Cronbach & Meehl (Ref. 1) in a recent paper. As they point out 'construct validation takes place when an investigator believes that his instrument reflects a particular construct, to which are attached certain meanings. The proposed interpretation generates specific testable hypotheses, which are a means of confirming or disconfirming the claim.' This interlocking system of laws which constitute a theory, they call a nomological network and it is in terms of such a network that our evidence in favour of the

---

[1] On small groups of neurotics tested incidentally in our clinical work, we found scores on the N scale approximately one S. D. above the normal mean, i.e. 33 ± 12 for N = 95. 10 Hysterics and 10 Dysthymics had scores on the E scale of 28 and 18 respectively. The correlation between N and C is ·92 for our sample of 400, that between E and R is ·79.

validity of our scales rests. It is realized, of course, that this evidence is far from complete, but even so, a case could be made out that at least as far as the extraversion-introversion scale goes, few other scales have as good a claim to consideration as the one presented here.

SUMMARY

The scales here reported for the measurement of neuroticism and extraversion-introversion are based on the Guilford C and R scales which had previously been found to be reasonably valid and reliable measures of these two dimensions of personality. In this work it had also become apparent, however, that not all the items in these scales could be regarded as well-selected and that items from other scales, if included, might lend additional validity to the C and R scales as measures of neuroticism and extraversion-introversion. Item analyses were therefore performed on several of the Guilford scales, as well as on items from the Maudsley Medical Questionnaire, to establish their relationships with R and C. A preliminary set of items for the new scales to be constructed was selected and submitted to a factor analysis. The results of this analysis confirmed the view that selection had in fact succeeded in obtaining two clusters of items which were independent of each other. The split-half reliabilities of the two scales were found satisfactory and the relationship between them to be insignificant. Preliminary experimental studies gave independent evidence of validity. The two scales are therefore put forward as promising and useful measures of neuroticism and extraversion-introversion respectively.

REFERENCES

1. CRONBACH, L. J. & MEEHL, P. E., Construct validity in psychological tests. *Psychol. Bull.*, **52**, 281–302, 1955.
2. EYSENCK, H. J., *Dimensions of Personality*. London: Routledge & Kegan Paul, 1947.
3. ——, *The Scientific Study of Personality*. London: Routledge & Kegan Paul, 1952.
4. ——, Fragebogen als Messmittel der Persönlichkeit. *Z. exp. angew. Psychologie*, **1**, 291–335, 1953.
5. ——, *The Structure of Human Personality*. London: Methuen, 1953.

6. ——, A dynamic theory of anxiety and hysteria. *J. ment. Sci.*, **101**, 28–51, 1955.
7. ——, Cortical inhibition, figural aftereffect and the theory of personality. *J. abnorm. soc. Psychol.*, **51**, 94–106, 1955.
8. ——, Reminiscence, drive, and personality theory. *J. abnorm. soc. Psychol.*, **53**, 328–33, 1965.
9. FRANKS, C. M., Personality factors and the rate of conditioning. *Brit. J. Psychol.*, **78**, 119–26, 1957, to appear.
10. ——, Conditioning and personality: a study of normal and neurotic subjects. *J. abnorm. soc. Psychol.*, **52**, 143–150, 1956.
11. GUILFORD, J. P., When not to factor analyse. *Psychol. Bull.*, **49**, 26–37, 1952.
12. —— & GUILFORD, R. B., An analysis of the factors in a typical test of introversion-extraversion. *J. abnorm. soc. Psychol.*, **28**, 377–399, 1934.
13. —— & ——, Personality factors S, E and M and their measurement. *J. Psychol.*, **2**, 109–127, 1936.
14. —— & ——, Personality factors, D, R, T and A. *J. abnorm. soc. Psychol.*, **34**, 21–36, 1939.
15. —— & ——, Personality factors N and GD. *J. abnorm. soc. Psychol.*, **34**, 239–248, 1939.
16. HILDEBRAND, H. P., A factorial study of introversion-extraversion by means of objective tests. Ph.D. Thesis, University of London, 1953.
17. LOVELL, C. A study of the factor structure of thirteen personality variables. *Educ. and Psychol. Measmt.*, **5**, 335–350, 1945.
18. NICHOLS, E. G., The relation between certain personality variables and the figural after-effect. Ph.D. Thesis, University of London, 1956.
19. NORTH, R. D., An analysis of the personality dimensions of intro-version-extraversion. *J. Pers.*, **17**, 352–367, 1949.
20. VERNON, P. E., *The Assessment of Psychological Qualities by Verbal Methods*. London: H.M.S.O., 1938.

7

A Factorial Study of Introversion-Extraversion

H. P. HILDEBRAND

First published in *British Journal of Psychology*, **49**, 1–11, 1958

PREVIOUS research suggested that Jung's Theory of Psychological Types could best be examined by factorial methods. Two orthogonal factors of neuroticism and introversion-extraversion were hypothesized in order to explain Jung's theory. A varied neurotic population was examined on a large battery of tests and factors identified as 'neuroticism', 'g' and 'introversion-extraversion' extracted. Further evidence confirming Jung's theories was given by using regression equations and factor scores which enabled criterion groups not included in the original matrix to be correctly identified.

INTRODUCTION: DEFINITION

Jung is commonly acknowledged to have coined the terms 'introversion' and 'extraversion' (Ref. 19) to describe a typology which he traces back to its earliest beginnings—the well-known division into 'habitus phythisicus' and 'habitus apoplecticus' elaborated by Galen. Other modern authors before Jung, notably Jordan (Ref. 18) and Gross (Ref. 13), had put forward psychological theories based on a type division, but Jung was the first to gain widespread acceptance for the type theory. Since his descriptions of the introvert and the extravert have been the basis for much of the subsequent work in this field, it would seem advisable to quote them in some detail.

'Introversion: means a turning inward of the libido whereby a negative relation of subject to object is expressed. Interest does not move towards the object but recedes towards the subject. Everyone whose attitude is introverted thinks, feels and acts in a way that clearly demonstrates that the subject is the chief factor of motivation while the object at most receives only a secondary value. Introversion may possess either a more intellectual or a more emotional character just as it can be characterized by either intuition or sensation. Introversion is active when the subject wills a certain seclusion in the face of the object: it is passive when the subject is unable to restore again to the object the libido which is streaming back from it. When Introversion is habitual, one speaks of an introverted type (Ref. 19, p. 567).

'Extraversion: means an outward turning of the libido. With this concept I denote a manifest relatedness of subject to object in the sense of a positive movement of subjective interest towards the object. Everyone in a state of extraversion thinks, feels and acts in relation to the object and moreover in a direct and clearly observable fashion, so that no doubt can exist about his positive dependence upon the object. In a sense, therefore, extraversion is an outgoing transference of interest from the subject to the object. If it is an intellectual extraversion, the subject thinks himself into the object; if a feeling extraversion then the subject feels himself into the object. The state of extraversion means a strong, if not exclusive, determination by the object. One should speak of an active extraversion when deliberately willed and of a passive extraversion when the object compels it, i.e. attracts the interest of the subject of its own accord, even against the latter's intention. Should the state of extraversion become habitual the extraverted type appears' (Ref. 19, p. 543).

Three further points are of importance. First, Jung states that:

'although there are individuals in whom one can recognize the type at first glance, this is by no means always the case. As a rule only careful observation and weighing of the evidence permits a sure classification. However clear and simple the fundamental principle of the opposing attitudes may be, this concrete reality is none the less complicated and obscure, for every individual is an exception to the rule. Therefore, one can never give a description of a type, no matter how complete, which absolutely applies to one individual, despite the fact that thousands might, in a sense, be characterized by it.'

Secondly, following the implications that I-E is a continuum, Jung identifies the poles of the distribution of I-E with two of the main groups of neurotic disorders—the extravert with the conversion hysterias and the introvert with Janet's psychasthenias. He says: 'Hysteria is, in my view, by far the most frequent neurosis with the extraverted type' (Ref. 19, p. 421), while psychasthenia is identified as the typical neurotic disorder of the introvert. This neurosis is characterized on the one hand by marked sensitivity, and on the other by great exhaustion and constant tiredness. Eysenck has suggested the term 'dysthymic' to cover this syndrome of affective disorders. In modern psychiatric terminology dysthymic would cover such syndromes as anxiety states and reactive depressions.

Thirdly, Jung stresses the independence of introversion and neurosis: he says—'It is a mistake to believe that introversion is more or less the same as neurosis. As concepts the two have not the slightest connection with one another.'

Jung's formulation was widely accepted and a great number of studies carried out in an attempt to provide an experimental basis for the theory. But as Collier & Emch point out, there was considerable confusion as to the definition of the traits it was hoped to define (Ref. 4). The main lines of Jung's arguments were ignored, while the terms introversion and extraversion were retained and redefined according to the authors' theoretical preferences. Collier & Emch remark that there are three main varieties of redefinitions which still claim to have some connection with Jung's original dichotomy. First, there is the attempt at simplification; secondly, the identification of introversion with neurotic tendency— extraversion being given 'per contra' a connotation of normality; and thirdly, the relating of introversion to the schizophrenic and extraversion to the manic depressive psychoses.

Not surprisingly the experimental evidence is very inconclusive. Experiments based on the first variety of redefinitions are quite inadequate to explain the wide variety of phenomena cited by Jung. The second type of definition is based on Freud's adaptation of the term introversion. For Freud, introversion is 'one of the invariable and indispensable considerations in every case of psycho-neurosis—a substitution for actual objects of phantasies of these objects' (Ref. 10). It is Freud's belief that Jung's use of the term is 'indiscriminate'. As Collier & Emch point out 'Freud's definition of the term represents a rigid contraction both in meaning and in use'. They maintain that Freud's definition of introversion has been particularly pervasive in the work of writers interested in the subject, but paradoxically the writers concerned seem to regard it as a natural extension of Jung's concept rather than a contraction. It is beyond the scope of this paper to examine this aspect of the controversy, but it is apparent that any work based on Freud's use of the term introversion can have little relation to the original formulation. Similarly, of course, any attempt to identify introversion with psychotic manifestations goes far beyond Jung's formulations and can be disregarded in terms of validation of the hypothesis.

There seems no point in carrying the argument further, particularly as all early experimental work is summed in three excellent reviews of work carried out to establish the empirical basis of I-E. They are those of Guilford (Ref. 14), Collier & Emch (Ref. 4) and Eysenck (Ref. 5) and are devoted in the main to small-scale experiments. Two further causes of confusion presented by these authors are, first, the clinical identification of introversion with neurosis referred to above and, secondly, the identification of extraversion with sociability first put forward by Freyd (Ref. 11). This identification was disproved when put to an empirical test by Russell Frazer (Ref. 9). Lack of sociability must be regarded as an index of neuroticism, not as a sign of introversion (Ref. 5).

Eysenck has also presented a review of factorial studies (Ref. 6) with some bearing on Jung's hypothesis. In the main these studies agreed in finding 'a bi-polar factor variously called "surgency-desurgency" (Ref. 3), "c" (Ref. 12), "aggressive-inhibitive" (Ref. 21) or whatever terms seem appropriate . . . these factors closely agree with one another as well as our own hysteria-dysthymia factor'. All the studies named above are based upon rating scales and have their origin in the pioneer work of Heymans & Wiersma (Ref. 15) and of Webb (Ref. 27). The name given to a factor arising from the intercorrelation of a number of traits seemed mainly to depend on the theoretical bias of the author. The low reliability and validity of such studies make caution necessary when identifying such factors with Jung's introversion-extraversion hypothesis, but the similarity of the results is striking.

Further evidence is available from questionnaire studies. Of these the questionnaire constructed by Guilford is outstanding in terms of reliability and soundness of statistical construction. Guilford himself would explain I-E in terms of a number of oblique factors, but Lovell (Ref. 22) and North (Ref. 25) have shown that the questionnaire in fact gives rise to two second-order factors, the second of which shows a distinct resemblance to the factors found by the rating method (Ref. 17).

THE PRESENT STUDY

Rationale

In the brief summary of previous work reported above, it has been shown that while small-scale testing has generally been ineffective to test Jung's hypotheses, various factorial studies have reported factors which seemed to resemble I-E. The evidence in favour of such a factor is suggestive but not convincing. In the present study, however, it was decided to test Jung's hypothesis directly, using factorial methods and a battery of tests designed to describe introversion-extraversion as completely as possible. The following hypotheses were derived from Jung's original statement by the writer. Hypothesis 1: That I-E (introversion-extraversion) is an underlying dimension of personality, common in some degree to all men. Hypothesis 2: That I-E is distinct from a second underlying dimension, namely, neuroticism. Deduction 2.1: That if a factor analysis is carried out on a group of tests purporting to measure I-E and neuroticism two general factors should emerge, which can most meaningfully be explained as I-E and neuroticism. Deduction 2.2: That these two factors would be significant and orthogonal. Hypothesis 3: That extraverts would tend as a group to suffer from a hysterical type of neurosis; that introverts as a group would tend to suffer from an anxiety neurosis. Deduction 3.1: That hysterics as a group would tend to score high on the neuroticism factor and also tend to cluster at the E pole of the I-E factor; conversely although anxiety states as a group would also tend to score high on the neuroticism factor they would tend to cluster at the I pole of the I-E factor. Deduction 3.2: That mixed neurotic groups would score on the neuroticism factor, but would tend towards a central distribution on the I-E factor. Deduction 3.3: That normal subjects would have a central tendency on the I-E factor and low scores on the neuroticism factor. The deductions made from these hypotheses are available to proof or disproof by experimental investigation.

In view of the nature of the investigation it was decided to use so-called objective behaviour tests. ('Objective behaviour tests', as here used, implies only that the tests are scored objectively and not that the tests themselves are objective. Such tests are scored by a standard set of instructions which do not require subjective interpretation by the interpreter.) The reasons for this decision were that the use of such tests would enable the experiment to be repeated independently if required, that the reliability and validity of the tests were usually known and that no evidence was at that time available about the interaction of these tests with regard to the factors under investigation.

According to the criteria laid down above, two groups of tests were chosen, one of which had been shown by previous experiments to differentiate between groups of normals and neurotics and a second which had been shown to differentiate significantly between dysthymics and hysterics in previous investigations. It was, of course, necessary that such differentiation did not depend upon subjective judgments but was a function of the test scores themselves. A group of tests with high loadings on the third factor 'g' was also included as previous work had suggested that there was some relationship between I-E and intelligence (Ref. 5).

It was proposed to resolve the crucial point of the generality of the I-E factor in the following manner. If the writer's interpretation of Jung's hypothesis was correct, then the exclusion of the two groups, which he describes as being the most typical of the poles of the dimension, from a factorial experiment should not affect the extraction of a factor which would be most meaningful psychologically when described as I-E. The hysteric and anxiety groups would be treated as criterion groups and not included in the factor analysis. Similarly, the normal control group was regarded as a criterion group for the neuroticism factor.

After the analysis had been carried out it was further proposed to make estimations of the regression coefficients of each variable and to plot the groups in a two-factor space with regard to the two factors of neuroticism and I-E. If the anxiety states and hysterics were found to be significantly different on the I-E factor after their score had been estimated and not significantly different on the neuroticism factor then Deduction 3.1 would be proved. A plot of the mixed neurotic groups would afford proof or disproof of Deduction 3.2 and a plot of the normals would do the same for Deduction 3.3.

An additional strength of this method is that it would confirm or disprove differentiation between criterion groups by means of analysis of variance techniques and indicate where such differentiation was due to specific causes or the action of the I-E factor. It was also decided to include subjects suffering from all types of neurotic disorder, in order that the different syndromes could be related to the relevant personality dimensions of neuroticism and I-E. A normal control group was also tested. It should be noted that the results found are those from a neurotic population and cannot immediately be generalized to cover the behaviour of a normal population.

Subjects

All neurotic subjects were drawn from in-patients at Belmont Hospital, Sutton, Surrey. All subjects were male. Minski gives the following details: 'Approximately 1500 to 2000 patients are admitted to Belmont annually for an average length of stay of 2 to 3 months. By far the majority of admissions are neurotics and come from all over the country. All patients are voluntary (Ref. 24).'

All admissions over an 8-month period were screened. From these 145 patients were selected as falling within the following categories. (1) Over 18 and under 50 years of age. (2) Considered by psychiatrist to show no sign of organic lesion. (3) Considered by psychiatrist to show no sign of psychotic illness. (4) I.Q. above 90. (5) Not undergoing physical treatment (E.C.T. or Insulin Therapy). All patients were severe neurotics, having been given up by both G.P. and out-patient clinics and the amount of mixed symptomatology was great. Cases where the psychiatrist felt justified in making a clear-cut diagnosis were few and the groups into which the patients were sorted should be regarded as classifications in terms of outstanding syndromes.

Details of the breakdown of subjects into groups are given in Table 1. The total number of patients tested was 145. Overall analyses of variance between the groups showed no significant difference in age. As a group, however, the obsessionals and depressives tended to be somewhat older. The mean age was 33·9 years, with a standard deviation of ±8·1.

TABLE 1

Group	No.	Abbreviation
Conversion hysterics	25	Dys.
Psychopaths	20	P.P.
Reactive depression	10	Dep.
Obsessional neurosis	10	Obs.
Anxiety states	25	Anx.
Mixed symptomatology	55	Mx.

The normal control group consisted of 25 male soldiers taken at random from a reallocation centre in the neighbourhood. Eysenck states of a preceding and similar group to that tested by the writer: 'It is known that soldiers going through such a centre tend to have a higher degree of neurotic and psychotic abnormality than do soldiers not reallocated. In addition these soldiers tend to be slightly below average in intelligence and therefore constitute a distinctly poor sample of the normal population.' That it is possible, in spite of this difficulty, to obtain highly significant differentiation between such a group and abnormal groups has been shown already (Ref. 7). The mean age of the Normal group equals 24·5±6·6 years. The C.R. between the mean age of this group and the mean age of the neurotic group is significant (C.R. = 5·53). However, the difficulty of obtaining a homogeneous normal sample imposed the use of this group. The testing of the control group was carried out at the Maudsley Hospital and the same procedure was used as with the neurotic groups at Belmont.

Experimental variables

In order to test the hypotheses propounded above a review was made of the literature and three groups of tests selected. The first of these was a group of three intelligence tests. Eysenck had suggested that intelligence might have some bearing on I-E and this group of tests was selected as covering the cognitive field. The tests were the Progressive Matrices, the Mill Hill Vocabulary and the Nufferno Power Test. Detailed descriptions of all tests and the rationale for use may be found in the writer's Ph.D. thesis (Ref. 16).

The second group of tests consisted of those which, it was hoped, would define the Neuroticism factor. They were as follows. (4) The Maudsley Medical Questionnaire. (5) The Maudsley Medical Questionnaire—lie scale. (6) An Annoyances Questionnaire—a list of thirty possible annoyances adapted from Pressey's X-O test. Previous research suggested that neurotics would be more irritable than normal groups.

The third group of tests included those which previous workers had suggested might have some bearing on the I-E dimension. They were (7) A Humour Scale—subjects were presented with thirty cartoons and asked to classify them according to preference. There were ten cartoons each for Sex humour, Incongruous humour and Extra-punitive humour. (8) The Guilford Martin Inventory of Factors S, T, D, C and R. Factors S and R had been found by previous workers to have some bearing on I-E and factors T, D and C on neuroticism (Ref. 17). (9) Static ataxia and (10) Suggestibility: four scores each were taken for static ataxia and for suggestibility to autosuggestion—maximum forward sway, maximum backward sway; total sway in half-inch units; and number of reversals (oscillations) in quarter-inch units. (11) The Porteus Maze Test—adapted Q score. Scoring categories were Starting time, Tracing time, Weighted wrong directions, Lifted pencils, Crossed lines. (12) Ratio stature/Transverse chest diameter in inches. (13) Leg persistence—the time in which the subject holds his leg above a chair. Analyses of variance were calculated for all variables, in order to test hypotheses relating to the ability of the tests to differentiate between neurotic groups. Critical ratios between means of the neurotic groups and that of the normal control group were also calculated where this seemed advisable. Full details will be found in Hildebrand (Ref. 16).

RESULTS

(i) Statistical analysis. Selection of variables for the final factor analysis was based on the following criteria. (1) That all subjects should have completed the test; (2) That the score of the total population on the test should have a normal distribution or a close approximation to it. It will be recalled that it was proposed to exclude the criterion groups from the matrix in order to provide external criteria of I-E and Neuroticism and the population included in the final matrix was thereby reduced to 95 subjects and consisted of 55 mixed neurotics, 10 obsessionals, 10 reactive depressives and 20 psychopaths. There were in all 22 variables that satisfied the criteria. All scores of the population on the 22 selected variables were transformed into standard scores on a nine point scale. Product moment correlations were then calculated for all variables.

In view of the requirements of the hypotheses and the lack of satisfactory tests of significance which might be applied to the ordinary centroid method of factor analysis (Ref. 2), it was decided to use Lawley's Maximum Likelihood Method (Ref. 26). This technique has the great advantage of applying what Burt calls the best test of significance of extracted factors, namely, a derivation of Bartlett's method (Ref. 1). Lawley's method assumes specific factors; it aims at minimizing the residuals and so accounting for the intercorrelations to the greatest possible extent. 'The method has the property of using the largest amount of information available in the data and gives "efficient" estimates which roughly speaking, are on the average nearer the true values than those obtained by other "inefficient" methods of estimation' (Ref. 20). Lawley makes two initial assumptions before using this method. These are, first, that the test scores and the factors of which they are linear functions are approximately normally distributed; secondly, that a hypothesis must be set up as to the number of factors present. Both these assumptions have been met in the present study.

A full centroid analysis was performed on the data to give first estimates of factor loadings and three factors were extracted. The hypothesis was set up that these three factors, which were tentatively identified as 'Neuroticism', 'g' and 'I-E' were sufficient to account for the observed correlations. Two iterations by Lawley's method were carried out as recommended by Lawley and the adjusted factor loadings subtracted from the original matrix.

The resulting residual correlations were tested for significance by Bartlett's correction (Ref. 1) of Lawley's test of significance and it was found that there were still significant factors remaining in the matrix. A fourth factor was accordingly extracted. On the basis of this evidence it is suggested that all four extracted factors are significant. Two rotations were sufficient to adjust the factors to psychologically meaningful positions. Full statistical details of these operations will be found by the interested reader in Hildebrand (Ref. 16).

(ii) Interpretation of the factors. The four factors as finally stabilized accounted for 32 per cent of the total variance. Factor loadings are given in Table 2. The first factor accounted for 12 per cent of the total variance and was easily identified as a neuroticism factor. As will be seen from Table 2, the four variables with the highest loadings differentiated

TABLE 2

FINAL LOADINGS FOR THE FOUR FACTORS

Factors

Variable	No.	I	II	III	IV	h^2
Prog. Matr.	1	179	750	−014	153	618
M.H.V.	2	−036	508	110	119	285
M.M.Q.	3	739*	−006	−257	055	615
Lie-scale	4	−380	050	−371	−009	284
Annoyances	5	429	−273	−012	068	263
S	7	739*	047	−472†	−043	773
T	8	467*	018	099	−142	248
D C	9	831*	−136	057	−127	728
R	10	−246	−236	563‡	−114	446
Power	11	098	744	012	−111	575
Sex humour	12	301	005	222	−198	179
Leg persistence	13	113	−007	−066	167	045
T.D. } Static ataxia	15	086	−082	180	520	317
R.	16	−041	143	073	513	290
T.D. } Reversals	18	176	−006	052	292	118
R.	19	021	161	261†	364	227
Body index	20	015	025	−255	035	067
Starting time	21	−167	055	−195	197	107
Total time	22	−062	−307	−071	321	206
Weighted wrong direction	23	257	−423	360†	−114	387
Lifted pencils	24	070	−211	006	098	059
Crossed lines	25	067	−168	425‡	−155	237
Totals		1·220	0·877	0·613	0·502	3·215

* The variables marked thus showed a significant difference $p > 0.01$ between normals and neurotics.

† Discriminates between the 45 hysterics and 45 dysthymics $p > 0.05$.

‡ Discriminates between the 45 hysterics and 45 dysthymics $p > 0.01$.

significantly between normals and neurotics. Moreover, previous studies had shown these tests to be highly saturated in neuroticism, emotional instability or similar factors.

The second factor extracted was identified as 'g' or general intelligence. This factor accounted for 9 per cent of the total variance. The second factor was confidently identified as an intelligence factor. The first three variables were the three tests of intelligence included in the matrix, and a high negative correlation between intelligence and mistakes and length of time taken on the Porteus maze test seems appropriate.

The third factor extracted was identified as I-E. This factor accounted for 6 per cent of the variance. For the purposes of this table critical ratios were calculated for the scores of the most highly loaded variables between the 45 hysterics and the 45 dysthymics. It will be seen that the tests do in fact discriminate between the groups. For these reasons the factor was identified as an I-E factor.

The fourth factor extracted was identified as arising from the inter-correlations of static ataxia and suggestibility scores. It does not seem possible to identify it more meaningfully.

Regression coefficients and factor scores

The factors having been identified, three deductions remained to be tested. It will be recalled that the experimental design called for discrimination between the various clinical groups by means of measurements made on the basis of scores based on the two factors of Neuroticism and I-E. It was felt that even though the factors were both significant and general they would have no more than a theoretical value unless such a discrimination could be made.

Ledermann's modification of Aitken's Pivotal Condensation method (Ref. 26) was used to estimate each individual's score on a given factor. The regression estimates so obtained 'are the best in the sense that they give the highest correlation, taken over a large number of men, between the estimates and the true value of a criterion when the latter can be separately ascertained'. As these requirements had been met in the present experiment, the scores of all groups were converted to standard scores, the eight highest regression coefficients for the factors Neuroticism and I-E were selected and the inner products of the standard scores and the regression coefficients calculated to give estimated factor scores for each member of the population on these two factors.

An overall analysis of variance was then made of the estimated scores on the Neuroticism factor, the results of which may be found in Table 3.

As will be seen from Table 3, the analysis of variance showed no significant differences among the neurotic population, but a very significant difference when the normal group was included. A t-test was carried out between the neurotic population and the normal group and the C.R. equalled 3·74 which is highly significant. This is in correspondence with the experimental results and demonstrates that the battery does discriminate between normals and neurotics at a high degree of confidence.

TABLE 3

	Anx.	Obs.	Dep.	Hys.	P.P.	Mx.	Total	Normal
No.	25	10	10	25	20	55	145	25
Mean	5·949	5·424	4·647	4·866	5·916	5·364	5·409	3·402
S.D.	1·686	2·068	1·808	1·927	1·803	1·716	1·816	1·686

$F = 1·591$ with normals excluded. N.S.
$F = 5·858$ with normals included. Significant beyond the 1 per cent level.

TABLE 4

	Anx.	Obs.	Dep.	Hys.	P.P.	Mx.	Total	Norma
No.	25	10	10	25	20	55	170	25
Mean	1·407	1·082	1·295	2·241	2·637	1·593	1·925	2·875
S.D.	0·986	1·489	1·131	1·271	1·384	1·384	1·399	1·084

$F = 5·896$, which is significant beyond the 1 per cent level.

An analysis of variance was also carried out on the factor scores for the I-E factor. Results are found in Table 4. Inspection of the means demonstrates clearly that the distribution follows the prediction. The hysterics and psychopaths are clustered at the extravert end of the distribution and the dysthymics at the introvert end of the distribution, with the mixed neurotics occupying a central position. The position of the normal group at the extravert end of the I-E continuum does not support 3.3, but is consistent with the experimental results obtained from this, which suggested that as a whole they could be expected to be highly extraverted. t-tests run between the groups showed no significant differences within the introvert and extravert clusters, but anxiety states were differentiated from hysterics at the 5 per cent level and the other groups at higher levels of significance. Fig. 5 gives a graphic picture of the means of each group in relation to the two axes. The I-E axis has been drawn so as to cut off 10 per cent of the normals and include them in the neurotic group, according to Russell Frazer's hypothesis that 10 per cent of the normal population is in fact neurotic (Ref. 9).

DISCUSSION OF RESULTS

Jung's theory of introversion-extraversion is essentially descriptive in nature. The procedure used in the present study enabled the writer to support Jung's theoretical formulations on a more experimental basis than had hitherto been possible. It was found possible to divide the experimental population into three categories, which were in accordance with the original hypothesis. These were neurotic introverts, neurotic extraverts and the normal group.

(1) The introvert category is made up of anxiety states, reactive depressives and obsessionals. They score high on the Neuroticism factor and cluster at the I pole of the I-E factor. Descriptively, Eysenck's amalgamation of the three groups into a single category of dysthymics seems substantiated by the experiment. On the factor scores there are no significant differences between the means of the groups making up this category. The factor-score criterion is probably a better one than one made on the basis of one or two tests.

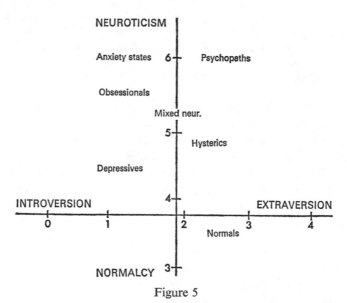

Figure 5

(2) The extravert category is made up of hysterics and psychopaths. There is no significant difference between the means of the factor scores of these two groups. The actual result of the experiment which finds psychopaths scoring higher on the I-E factor than do the hysterics

perhaps needs some discussion. It is inferred that the psychopaths were less inhibited in their test performance then were the hysterics and it is interesting to note that Mayer-Gross, Moore & Slater found that on their second canonical variate, which seems to be a measure of I-E, the psychopaths scored higher than did the hysterics (Ref. 23).

(3) The normal group did not in fact fulfil the prediction made for it originally. In terms of the other groups it was extremely extraverted although it differed significantly from the neurotic population on the Neuroticism factor. One possible explanation for this extreme degree of extraversion may perhaps be found in Eysenck's study of ratings (Ref. 5), where he found that such items as 'unskilled', 'narrow interests' and low I.Q. all had significant loadings on what he took to be an I-E factor. These three adjectives describe the control group well and this may well have contributed to their degree of extraversion. Although it was not possible to test another group on the complete battery, another group of normals was tested on the R scale, which is the highest ranking test on the E pole of the I-E continuum. The control group was found to be significantly more extraverted than this second normal group (Ref. 17). It is possible that if a less homogeneous and more representative civilian sample of the normal population had been tested on the battery the predictions concerning this group would have been fulfilled. However, there does seem some possibility that the battery may measure I-E within the normal population with perhaps the same efficiency as among the neurotic population.

It is interesting to note that using the rather sophisticated statistical procedures of the present experiment, it was possible to submit Jung's hypothesis to a much more searching test than had hitherto been possible. It is claimed that all the deductions derived from the original theory have been supported at a high degree of significance, with the exception of deduction 3.3 and reasons have been advanced why this deduction was not confirmed. It should, however, be noted that the entire experiment was purely on a descriptive basis. To quote yet again from Eysenck: 'Factor analysis is a mathematical procedure which resolves a set of descriptive variables into a small number of categories, components or factors. These factors, themselves, must in the first instance, be regarded as having a purely descriptive function. Under certain circumstances factors may be regarded as hypothetical causal instances underlying and determining the observed relationships between a set of variables. It is only when regarded in this light that they have interest and significance for psychology' (Ref. 6).

142   *Theoretical and Methodological Issues*

Whether or not the factors found in this experiment, particularly the I-E factor, may be considered to have hypothetical and causal instances underlying them is not, of course, a question that can be answered on the basis of the data here presented. Yet although the I-E factor as it is found in this experiment seems beyond dispute, it does seem worth while to point out that a certain amount of caution must be used before the factor can be used as a basic postulate in personality research. First, although the experiment was designed to amplify the factor as much as possible, yet the total variance accounted for by the factor amounted to only 6 per cent, only 1 per cent more than that of a factor that it was found impossible to identify satisfactorily. Secondly, of the tests which were suggested as possible measures of I-E, only two differentiated between introverts and extraverts at the 1 per cent level of significance. That, in spite of these results, the battery was as successful as it was is very satisfactory but the next step in any further investigation of this area of personality would seem to be further descriptive studies rather than a search for the hypothetical causative instance.

This article is based on the writer's unpublished Ph.D. thesis for London University (Ref. 16). The writer wishes to thank Dr L. Minski, Physician Superintendent of Belmont Hospital, for kind permission to test patients within the hospital and Dr M. M. Desai and Mr R. Secker of the Psychology Department, Belmont Hospital, for their many kindnesses. He also wishes to thank his supervising teacher, Dr H. J. Eysenck, for his advice and assistance.

REFERENCES

1. BARTLETT, M. S., Tests of significance in factor analysis. *Brit. J. Psychol. Statist. Sect.*, **3**, 77–85, 1950.
2. BURT, C., Tests of significance in factor analysis. *Brit. J. Psychol. Statist. Sect.*, **5**, 109–133, 1952.
3. CATTELL, R. B., *The Description and Measurement of Personality*. New York: World Book Co., 1966.
4. COLLIER, R. & EMCH, M., Introversion-extraversion—the concepts and their clinical use. *Amer. J. Psychiat.*, **94**, 1045–1075, 1938.
5. EYSENCK, H. J., *Dimensions of Personality*. London: Routledge & Kegan Paul, 1947.
6. ——, *The Structure of Human Personality*. London: Methuen, 1953.

7. ——, Research report under contract no. 62558s–56 with the Bureau of Medicine, U.S. Navy. (Unpublished), 1953.
8. ——, The logical basis of factor analysis. *Amer. Psychologist*, **8**, 105–114, 1953.
9. FRAZER, R., *The Incidence of Neurosis among Factory Workers*. London: H.M.S.O., 1947.
10. FREUD, S., *A General Introduction to Psycho-Analysis*. New York: Liverwright, 1920.
11. FREYD, M., Introverts and extraverts. *Psychol. Rev.*, **5**, 74–87, 1925.
12. GARRETT, J. C. M., General ability, cleverness and purpose. *Brit. J. Psychol.*, **9**, 345–366, 1918.
13. GROSS, O., *Die Cerebrale Sekundarfunktion*. Leipzig, 1902.
14. GUILFORD, J. P., Introversion-extraversion. *Psychol. Bull.*, **31**, 331–354, 1934.
15. HEYMANS, G. & WIERSMA, E., Beitrage zur speziellen Psychologie auf grund einer Massenufersuchung. *Z. Psychol.*, **42**, 81–127 et seq., 1906.
16. HILDEBRAND, H. P., A factorial study of introversion-extraversion by means of objective tests. Unpublished Ph.D. thesis, University of London Library, 1953.
17. ——, On the use of Guilford's introversion-extraversion questionnaire with a neurotic population. *Rev. Psychol. App.*, **6**, 179–185, 1956.
18. JORDAN, W. F., *Character as seen in Body and Parentage*. London: Macmillan, 1890.
19. JUNG, C. J., *Psychological Types*. London: Routledge & Kegan Paul, 1924.
20. LAWLEY, D. N., The maximum likelihood method of estimation of factor loadings. In Thomson, G.: *The Factorial Analysis of Human Ability*. London: London University Press (5th ed.), 1950.
21. LINE, W. & GRIFFIN, J. D. M., The objective determination of factors underlying mental health. *Amer. J. Psychiat.*, **91**, 833–842, 1935.
22. LOVELL, C., A study of the factor structure of 13 personality variables. *Educ. Psychol. Measmt.*, **5**, 335–50, 1945.
23. MAYER-GROSS, W., MOORE, J. T. N. & SLATER, P., Forecasting the incidence of neurosis in officers in the army and navy. *J. ment. Sci.*, **95**, 80–100, 1949.
24. MINSKI, L., *Belmont Hospital Annual Report*. (Privately printed), 1950.

25. NORTH, R. D., An analysis of personality dimensions of introversion-extraversion. *J. Pers.*, **17**, 552–567, 1948.
26. THOMSON, G., *The Factorial Analysis of Human Ability*. London: London University Press (5th ed.), 1950.
27. WEBB, E., Character and intelligence. *Brit. J. Psychol. Monogr. Suppl.*, **1**, No. 3, 1915.

8

The Dual Nature of Extraversion: A Replication

N. H. SPARROW & JOHN ROSS

First published in *Australian Journal of Psychology*, **16,** 214–218, 1964

A REPLICATION of a study by Eysenck & Eysenck confirms their finding that extraversion items from the M.P.I. and elsewhere produce two clusters when factor analysed. The common characteristics of the clusters are sociability and impulsiveness respectively. A method of testing Eysenck & Eysenck's factor interpretation of their results is suggested.

INTRODUCTION

In a recent study (Ref. 1) Eysenck & Eysenck have reported results on the 'dual' nature of extraversion which they interpret to imply that extraversion, though unitary, is a factor which is made up of two main traits, sociability and impulsiveness. While Eysenck & Eysenck's interpretation may be questioned, depending as it does on an unusual meaning of the term unitary (which usually means unifactorial) and on unusual tactics of factor interpretation, their results are interesting and straightforward. Briefly, a factor analysis of 66 extraversion-introversion (E) and neuroticism (N) items (plus the score from a Lie Scale) produced four factors. One factor was N and the space of the next two supported four item clusters, sociability and non-sociability and impulsiveness and non-impulsiveness. The factors which support this space are identified as extraversion (E) and a bipolar sociability-impulsiveness (S-Imp.).If the introversion items are reflected in the two-space, the finding is that the items, now all extraversion keyed, split into sociability and impulsiveness clusters. The aim of the present study was to try to replicate the Eysenck & Eysenck finding with respect to the split of E items.

METHOD

An experimental questionnaire was constructed which contained (1) Eysenck's original Maudsley Personality Inventory (M.P.I.), which

F

contains 24 E and 24 N items and, (2) an additional 12 items selected from Eysenck & Eysenck's questionnaire (Ref. 1), 8 from their impulsiveness cluster and 4 from their sociability cluster. Since some of the M.P.I. items were included in Eysenck & Eysenck's factor analysis, there were 27 items common to both studies, 16 from the impulsiveness cluster and 11 from the sociability. As an adjunct to the main experiment a 40 item scale was made from two sets of 20 items selected at random from the California Psychological Inventory's (C.P.I.) sociability and self-control scales. Two scores, each based on 10 items, were obtained from each set of items.

SUBJECTS

The Ss were male junior naval recruits (N = 170) with a common age of 16 and with I.Q.s of mean 104·8 and standard deviation 7·7. The Otis Higher C intelligence test was used. The homogeneity of the group should be noted.

PROCEDURE

Testing was carried out in groups of 25 to 30 in normal class periods. The E was introduced as a research worker. Names were not entered on the answer sheets.

RESULTS AND DISCUSSION

The product moment correlation matrix was computed for all 64 vaiables (the 60 items, scored 0, 1 or 2 and the 2 sociability and the 2 self-control scales). The matrix was factor analysed by the principal components method and an inspection of the latent roots showed three large factors. The three factors were rotated analytically by the varimax method.

Factor I was a clean neuroticism factor. Of the 24 N items from the M.P.I., 23 had loadings above 0·30. Of the remaining 36 items only 2 had loadings as high as 0·30. It may be remarked in passing that the two C.P.I. derived self-control scales had (negative) loadings of magnitude above 0·60 on the N factor. One sociability scale had a negative loading of −0·35, the other −0·15.

Factors II and III together produced a subspace very similar to that supported by Eysenck & Eysenck's E and S-Imp factors. If all items keyed towards introversion are reflected, there are two clusters. One cluster contains 12 of the 16 S items and the C.P.I. Sociability scales and the other 7 of the 11 Imp items and the C.P.I. self-control scales (reflected). A rotation was carried out to find factors corresponding as closely as possible to the E and S-Imp factors of Eysenck & Eysenck. The factor loadings are given in Table 1. When this was done the factor loadings from the present study were plotted against those from the Eysenck & Eysenck study for E and S-Imp factors separately. There was a linear relationship in each case; the product moment correlation between the loadings on the E factors from the two studies was 0·92 and on the S-Imp factors 0·80.

TABLE 1

ROTATED FACTOR LOADINGS

	N	E	S-Imp
1. Are you happiest when you get involved in some project that calls for rapid action?	−0·10	0·11	0·16
2. Do you sometimes feel happy, sometimes depressed, without any apparent reason?	0·53	0·06	−0·03
3. Does your mind often wander while you are trying to concentrate?	0·51	0·15	−0·30
4. Do you usually take the initiative in making new friends?	0·01	0·26	0·12
5. Would you rate yourself as an impulsive individual?	0·01	0·35	0·00
6. Are you inclined to be quick and sure in your actions?	−0·41	0·10	0·21
7. Are you frequently 'lost in thought' even when supposed to be taking part in a conversation?	0·56	−0·02	−0·11
8. Are you sometimes bubbling over with energy and sometimes very sluggish?	0·31	0·07	0·00
9. If you want to learn about something, would you rather do it by reading a book on the subject than by discussion?	−0·06	−0·36	−0·06
10. Would you rate yourself as a lively individual?	−0·12	0·24	0·28
11. Would you be very unhappy if you were prevented from making numerous social contacts?	0·23	0·22	0·27
12. Are you inclined to be moody?	0·55	0·08	−0·02
13. Would you describe yourself as an easy-going person not concerned to be precise?	0·26	0·31	−0·30

TABLE 1 *continued*

ROTATED FACTOR LOADINGS

	N	E	S-Imp
14. Do you have frequent ups and downs in mood, either with or without apparent cause?	0·51	−0·05	−0·02
15. Do you prefer action to planning for action?	−0·02	0·20	−0·20
16. Does your natural reserve generally stand in your way when you want to start a conversation with an attractive stranger of the opposite sex?	−0.13	−0.55	0·04
17. Are your daydreams frequently about things that can never come true?	0·29	−0·12	−0·05
18. Are you inclined to keep in the background on social occasions?	−0·15	−0·47	0·48
19. Are you inclined to ponder over your past?	0·36	−0·04	0·04
20. Do you often act on the spur of the moment without stopping to think?	0·27	0·21	−0·22
21. Is it difficult to 'lose yourself' even at a lively party?	−0·08	0·00	0·00
22. Do you ever feel 'just miserable' for no good reason at all?	0·62	0·02	0·09
23. Are you inclined to be overconscientious?	−0·21	−0·08	0·05
24. When people shout at you, do you shout back?	0·20	0·20	−0·22
25. Do you often find that you have made up your mind too late?	0·34	−0·13	−0·21
26. Do you like to mix socially with people?	0·05	0·26	0·47
27. Have you often lost sleep over your worries?	0·48	0·08	−0·07
28. Are you inclined to limit your acquaintances to a select few?	−0·21	−0·26	0·32
29. Are you often troubled about feelings of guilt?	0·41	−0·01	−0·21
30. Do you ever take your work as if it were a matter of life or death?	−0·09	−0·03	−0·40
31. Are your feelings rather easily hurt?	0·38	−0·24	−0·13
32. Do you like to have many social engagements?	0·20	0·44	0·31
33. Would you rate yourself as a tense or 'highly-strung' individual?	0·34	0·02	0·05
34. Do you generally prefer to take the lead in group activities?	0·12	0·26	0·34
35. Is your motto to take matters of everyday life with proper seriousness rather than to 'laugh and be merry'?	−0·03	−0·34	−0·34

TABLE 1 *continued*

ROTATED FACTOR LOADINGS

	N	E	S-Imp
36. Do you often experience periods of loneliness?	0·51	−0·26	−0·04
37. Are you inclined to be shy in the presence of the opposite sex?	−0·18	−0·65	0·19
38. Do you like to indulge in a reverie (daydreaming)?	0·39	0·29	−0·03
39. Do you nearly always have a 'ready answer' for remarks directed at you?	−0·04	0·19	0·29
40. Do you tend towards an over-cautious pessimism?	−0·21	−0·17	0·15
41. Do you spend much time in thinking over good times you have had in the past?	0·45	0·03	−0·06
42. Would you rate yourself as a happy-go-lucky individual?	0·08	0·39	−0·01
43. Have you often felt listless and tired for no good reason?	0·54	0·02	−0·01
44. Are you inclined to keep quiet when out in a social group?	−0·11	−0·56	0·40
45. After a critical moment is over, do you usually think of something you should have done but failed to do?	0·38	−0·11	0·04
46. Can you usually let yourself go and have a hilariously good time at a gay party?	0·05	0·50	0·29
47. Do ideas run through your head so that you cannot sleep?	0·46	0·02	−0·10
48. Do you like work that requires considerable attention?	0·15	−0·17	−0·50
49. Would you do almost anything for a dare?	0·07	0·34	−0·37
50. Have you ever been bothered by having a useless thought come into your mind repeatedly?	0·47	0·01	−0·10
51. Are you inclined to take your work casually, that is, as a matter of course?	0·06	0·32	−0·44
52. Are you touchy on various subjects?	0·36	0·07	0·04
53. Do other people regard you as a lively individual?	0·01	0·34	0·19
54. Do you often feel disgruntled?	0·50	−0·24	−0·08
55. Would you rate yourself as a talkative individual?	0·32	0·34	0·26
56. Do you have periods of such great restlessness that you cannot sit long in a chair?	0·59	0·08	−0·07
57. Do you like to play pranks upon others?	0·05	0·48	−0·34

TABLE 1 *continued*

ROTATED FACTOR LOADINGS

	N	E	S-Imp
58. Do you enjoy opportunities for conversation so that you rarely miss a chance of talking to a stranger?	0·21	0·39	0·21
59. Do you tend towards a rather reckless optimism?	0·13	0·37	−0·16
60. Would you rather spend an evening by yourself than go to a rather dull party?	−0·15	−0·36	−0·03
SC₁ } Self control	−0·63	−0·25	−0·17
SC₂	−0·63	−0·24	−0·12
CPI			
SO₁ } Sociability	−0·15	0·47	0·45
SO₂	−0·35	0·45	0·22

The finding of this study is that the results of Eysenck & Eysenck are clearly replicated under Australian conditions and with a homogeneous group of younger subjects. A small preliminary study with University students obtained substantially the same result. The interpretation of the two clusters as sociability and impulsiveness is confirmed by the behaviour of the C.P.I. Sociability and Self-Control Scales. A word of caution about interpretation may be sounded about the Impulsiveness since the C.P.I. Scales of Self-Control both loaded more strongly on the Neuroticism factor than on any dimension within the E, S-Imp subspace. Whether Eysenck & Eysenck's rotation and interpretation can be confirmed remains an open question. If the E factor does correspond with a more fundamental, constitutional C.N.S. property as they say, then performance derived measures of E should load along the E factor in the subspace in question. This would seem to provide a method for testing Eysenck & Eysenck's interpretation.

REFERENCES

1. EYSENCK, S. B. G. & EYSENCK, H. J. On the dual nature of extraversion. *Brit. J. soc. clin. Psychol.*, **2,** 46–55, 1963.

9

A Short Questionnaire for the Measurement of Two Dimensions of Personality

H. J. EYSENCK

First published in *Journal of Applied Psychology*, **42**, 14–17, 1958

IN a previous paper, the writer has described the construction of two 24-item questionnaires for the measurement of neuroticism and extraversion (Ref. 2). The studies described in this paper were based on item analyses of some 250 questions appearing in well-known inventories, as well as a factor analysis of the finally chosen 48 questions, carried out separately for 200 men and 200 women. The reliabilities of the new questionnaires were reasonably high, in spite of their relative shortness, being 0·88 for neuroticism and 0·83 for extraversion. The independence of the two scales was demonstrated by the low correlation of −0·09 for the original sample of 400 men and women and the even lower correlation of −0·07 for a further male group of 200. Factorially, too, the items chosen for the two scales fell into two clearly separated groups making rotation to simple structure easy. A limited number of validation studies have been carried out and are quoted in *The Dynamics of Anxiety and Hysteria* (Ref. 3).

For many practical purposes, such as work in market research, for instance, even a relatively short questionnaire containing 48 questions may be too long, and the present study was designed to investigate the possibility of using an even shorter version containing only 6 questions for each of the two scales.

SUBJECTS AND METHOD

The subjects of the investigation were approached on a quota sample basis by the interviewers of one of the largest and most experienced British Market Research Organizations; these interviews are carried out all over England, correct proportions of urban and rural dwellers and of the different regions of the country being ensured. In addition to sex, the sample was divided according to age, 35 being the dividing line. Social

151

class was assessed in the usual manner, the dividing line being taken between classes A, B and C on the one side and D and E on the other.

The total sample consisted of 1,600 subjects, divided into 8 groups of 200 each on the basis of the three selection criteria taken in all possible combinations. The reliability of sex and age classifications is known to be reasonably high; that for class is rather low (Ref. 1). We may expect these unreliabilities to lead to a varying degree of attenuation in our results.

In the interview, a number of questions were first asked relating to a variety of commercial products; these constituted the ostensible purpose of the interview. A few personal questions about age and occupation followed and finally the interview was terminated with the 12-item personality questionnaire given below. The questions were asked by the interviewer and the answers written down by him. The proportion of subjects approached who refused outright was 7 per cent; the proportion of subjects who consented to answer the questions in the first part of the interview and refused to answer the questions in the personality inventory was only 2 per cent.

The questions used in the study are given in Table 1. Each question answered 'Yes' was scored plus one point for neuroticism (marked 'N' in the key) or extraversion (marked 'E' in the key); each question answered 'No' was scored minus one point for neuroticism or extraversion, respectively, as shown in the key. No points were given for answers which could not be clearly classified as either 'Yes' or 'No' by the interviewer. The possible range of scores on either factor is therefore from plus six points to minus six points, a total of twelve points.

RESULTS

Tetrachoric correlations were run between the twelve questions and the resulting table of correlations factor analysed. Thurstone's procedure was followed and the two highly significant factors emerging were rotated in accordance with the principle of simple structure (Ref. 4). Table 2 gives the factor loadings of the rotated factors. Also given in Table 3 are the loadings of the 12 items which they had originally had in the analyses carried out on the whole population of 200 men and 200 women for all 48 items (Ref. 2). The comparison shows that the figures are remarkably similar from one occasion to the other, although methods of selection have changed considerably and although in the original analyses the 12 items were only a small part of the total number of items factor analysed. In some ways the new set of factor loadings is even more clear-cut than the original one. None of the E items has loadings on N as large as 0·10 and none of the N items has loadings on E as large as 0·10; in the original study several loadings exceeded this figure. We may conclude, then, that the factor structure has stood up well to repetition.

The correlation between extraversion and neuroticism is $-0·05$; this is very similar to the correlations reported previously for our samples of men and women. Again, therefore, the figures from the present study bear out in an important direction the conclusions from the original work. The split-half reliabilities (corrected) are 0·79 for N and 0·71 for E; these values are acceptable for group comparisons. (Test-retest reliabilities on small groups have been found to be slightly, but not significantly, in excess of these figures.)

Results of an analysis of variance for neuroticism and extraversion scores respectively are reported in Tables 3 and 4. Significant differences due to some of the main effects appear in the scores for both factors, but they are more conspicuous on the N scores, where they account for 7·41 per cent of the total variance, than on the E scores, where they only

TABLE 1

Questions	+1 Key Yes	−1 No
A. Do you sometimes feel happy, sometimes depressed, without any apparent reason?	N	
B. Do you prefer action to planning for action?	E	
C. Do you have frequent ups and downs in mood, either with or without apparent cause?	N	
D. Are you happiest when you get involved in some project that calls for rapid action?	E	
E. Are you inclined to be moody?	N	
F. Does your mind often wander while you are trying to concentrate?	N	
G. Do you usually take the initiative in making new friends?	E	
H. Are you inclined to be quick and sure in your actions?	E	
I. Are you frequently 'lost in thought' even when supposed to be taking part in a conversation?	N	
J. Would you rate yourself as a lively individual?	E	
K. Are you sometimes bubbling over with energy and sometimes very sluggish?	N	
L. Would you be very unhappy if you were prevented from making numerous social contacts?	E	

F*

TABLE 2

| | Present Sample | | Original Sample | | | |
Item	E	N	E_m	N_m	E_f	N_f
A	0·01	0·75	−0·10	0·79	−0·05	0·72
B	0·48	0·01	0·70	−0·09	0·73	0·03
C	−0·06	0·74	0·03	0·82	0·08	0·58
D	0·59	0·04	0·59	0·12	0·66	0·10
E	−0·09	0·71	−0·04	0·75	0·04	0·69
F	0·02	0·58	−0·13	0·57	0·00	0·50
G	0·59	−0·06	0·72	−0·15	0·66	0·14
H	0·49	−0·04	0·58	−0·09	0·51	−0·04
I	−0·06	0·58	−0·06	0·67	−0·03	0·59
J	0·68	−0·02	0·87	−0·05	0·65	−0·16
K	0·09	0·63	0·23	0·55	0·17	0·43
L	0·64	0·09	0·67	0·03	0·58	−0·08

TABLE 3

ANALYSIS OF VARIANCE OF THE NEUROTICISM SCORES

Source of Variance	Sum of Squares	df	m.s.v.
Total	20269·7775	1599	
Main effects			
Sex	995·4025	1	995·4025*
Class	311·5225	1	311·5225*
Age	142·8025	1	142·8028*
First order interactions			
Sex: Class	36·6025	1	
Sex: Age	0·0225	1	
Class: Age	1·3225	1	
Second order interactions	14·8225	1	
Totals			
All interactions	52·7700	4	13·1925
All differences between groups	1502·4975	7	214·6425
Residual variance within groups	18767·2800	1592	11·7885

* Signifies statistical significance at 5 per cent level.

TABLE 4

ANALYSIS OF VARIANCE OF THE EXTRAVERSION SCORES

Source of Variance	Sum of Squares	df	m.s.v.
Total	14263·8975	1599	
Main effects			
Sex	79·2100	1	79·2100*
Class	16·8100	1	16·8100
Age	28·6225	1	28·6225
First order interactions			
Sex: Class	3·4225	1	
Sex: Age	4·0000	1	
Class: Age	1·2100	1	
Second order interaction	0·9025	1	
Totals			
All interactions	9·5350	4	2·3838
All differences between groups	134·1775	7	19·1682
Residual variance within groups	14129·7200	1592	8·8755

* Signifies statistical significance at 5 per cent level.

account for 0·94 per cent. The sex difference is the greatest in relation to N and the only significant one in relation to E. On N, the women have a score roughly ½ SD higher than the men (i.e., women are less stable); on E, the men have a score roughly ⅙ SD higher than the women (i.e., men are more extraverted). Class and age differences are also significant for N, the lower class and younger age groups being slightly more unstable emotionally by ⅓ SD and ¼ SD, respectively. None of the interactions give rise to mean square variances significantly greater than the residual error; on the whole they tend to be small. In fact, most of the observed differences are slight and only significant because of the large number of cases; little psychological importance would appear to attach to any of them except the sex difference on N, which is large and in line with previous work (Ref. 2).

The mean scores for N and E, respectively, are 0·15 and 1·96 for our sample; corrections for different proportions in the total populations would not give appreciably different estimates of population parameters and would appear to be a task of supererogation. Distributions of scores are sufficiently normal to permit the use of correlational statistics,[1] and the variances of the different groups are sufficiently

[1] The distribution of the E scores has a noticeable negative skew, but it is doubtful if this is sufficient to make desirable the use of logarithmic or other types of transformation.

homogeneous to permit analysis of variance to be carried out without transformation. The variances for N are slightly higher than those for E, being 11·73 as compared with 8·83.

A question regarding drinking habits was included in the questionnaire. A division was made between 'drinkers', i.e., those who drank frequently or sometimes and 'non-drinkers', i.e., those who drank very rarely or never. The N scores of these two groups were very similar, being −0·37 as compared with 0·04; if anything, it appears that 'non-drinkers' as here defined are very slightly more unstable than drinkers. The small size of the difference does not warrant our taking this conclusion too seriously. The E scores of the two groups are very significantly different, the scores being 2·48 and 1·55. Thus drinkers are about ⅓ SD more extraverted than non-drinkers.

SUMMARY

An investigation has been carried out to demonstrate the possibility of constructing short reliable personality questionnaires which might be of use in industrial and applied work and which could be administered in the usual interview situation.

An analytic sample of 1,600 adult subjects, equally divided as to age, sex and social class, was selected on a quota-sampling basis and administered a 12-item questionnaire. Six questions bearing on neuroticism and 6 questions bearing on extraversion had been selected from a previous item-analytic and factor-analytic study in order to cross-validate certain conclusions. Correlations were calculated between the 12 items and a factor analysis performed; this disclosed two orthogonal factors clearly identical with those of the previous analysis. Analysis of variance gave evidence of certain score differences due to sex, age and social class, although with the exception of the sex differences these were of minor importance. The 12-item questionnaire was found to have reasonable reliability and the two personality variables measured by it were found to be uncorrelated. The practical usefulness of instruments of this kind was discussed.

REFERENCES

1. EYSENCK, H. J., *The Psychology of Politics*. London: Routledge & Kegan Paul, 1954.
2. ——, The questionnaire measurement of neuroticism and extra-version. *Riv. Psicol.*, **50,** 113–140, 1956.
3. ——, *The Dynamics of Anxiety and Hysteria*. London: Routledge & Kegan Paul, 1957.
4. THURSTONE, L. L., *Multiple Factor Analysis*. Chicago: Univ. of Chicago Press, 1947.

10

Perception of Children's Personalities by Experienced Teachers

H. J. HALLWORTH

First published in *Educational Review*, **19**, 3–12, 1966

TEACHERS' DESCRIPTION OF PUPILS

THE very fact of living in a society involves all of us in a continued classification and description of other people. Teachers inevitably and necessarily make judgments about the personalities of their pupils. Such judgments commonly issue in the form of words and involve the use of a large vocabulary of personality trait names.

A visitor to a school staff room does not have long to wait before hearing conversation concerning pupils who are persistent, lazy, solitary, confident, aggressive, popular, withdrawn, cheerful, co-operative, etc. The words are entered on report forms; they are used as headings on record cards. They are the coin for exhanges of information among staff; they are the heads under which a welfare state requires information concerning its future citizens for purposes of educational and vocational guidance.

The assumption appears to be that a teacher has a vast store of information about the personalities of his pupils, which may be simply tapped by using appropriate words such as those which form much of the currency of staff room conversation. Obviously this assumption has a firm basis in fact. But the question we wish to ask is, in what sense is it justified? When personality trait names are used to describe children, either in conversation or on report and record cards, to what extent are they used independently and to what extent are they organized into one or several groups of traits?

RESEARCH ON TEACHERS' PERSONALITY RATINGS

A series of researches carried out from the Education Department in the University of Birmingham has attempted to answer this question. Teachers were asked to rate their pupils on 14 personality traits which are in common use. The ratings were made in a controlled situation devised to avoid any spurious relationship between them. The procedure has already been described in this journal (Ref. 4). Each teacher considered a class of boys or girls well known to him and with an age range of not more than one year. Ratings were made on a linear scale, one trait at a time for the whole group, with the average for the group being the centre of the scale, and with the distribution following the percentages of the normal curve.

In each of these studies it was found that the teachers used the personality trait names as if they were organized into two main groups. The first group, which has been labelled 'emotional stability' or 'reliability and conscientiousness', consists of four traits: emotional stability, trustworthiness, persistence and co-operation with teachers. In most cases, the trait of maturity also falls into this group, as does ability in school work. The second group, labelled 'social extraversion', consists of five traits: cheerfulness, sense of humour, sociability, self-assertion and spontaneity. Ability in games is sometimes included in this group. Two other traits, popularity and confidence, frequently fall between the two main groups of traits.

When these fourteen traits are used, it is usual for some three-fifths of all the variance to be accounted for by these two groups of traits. In other words, the teachers judge on fourteen traits, but three-fifths of their judgments may be said to be made in terms of these two 'factors' or 'dimensions'. It is easily seen that the two factors are similar to the two factors of neuroticism-emotional stability and introversion-extraversion described by Eysenck (Ref. 3). They are also similar to the two second-order factors of anxiety-adjustment and introversion-extraversion described by Cattell (Ref. 1). The similarity between his factors and those obtained by Eysenck has been discussed recently by Cattell (Ref. 2).

DIMENSIONS OF MEANING

The dimensions obtained from teachers' ratings appear to be comparable to the main dimensions of personality. They are also comparable, however, to Osgood's dimensions of 'meaning'.

Osgood (Ref. 8) obtained a large number of opposing pairs of adjectives from *Roget's Thesaurus*. Each pair was used to define two ends of a seven-point scale, such as:

good :　:　:　:　:　:　:　: bad

100 subjects each used 76 such scales to make assessments of 20 concepts. A concept might be CHURCH or MYSELF. Each subject used every scale to rate every concept. The ratings were then correlated over all subjects and all concepts and the technique of factor analysis was employed to determine whether scales were used independently or in groups.

In a large number of such researches with varied subjects and concepts, it has been found that the scales fall into three main groups or factors named 'evaluation', 'activity' and 'potency' (Refs. 9 and 10). These are interpreted by Osgood as factors of 'connotative meaning': they indicate that subjects do not use each scale independently; rather, they use the scales as if they are associated in these three main groups. The subject does not ask himself a different question for every scale. He asks himself three main questions: first, 'How much do I approve or disapprove of the concept?'; second, 'How active or passive is it?'; and third, 'How strong or weak is it?'

It has already been suggested that the first of these factors is similar to the factor of 'emotional stability' or 'reliability and conscientiousness' obtained from teachers' ratings (Ref. 8). The use of two names for this group of traits is unsatisfactory and a more general description may be obtained on the supposition that the teacher asks himself the question: 'How much do I approve or disapprove of this child as a pupil?' This is the dimension of evaluation or general attitude used within the setting of school life. The second factor of 'social extraversion' may be similarly explained by the assumption that the teacher asks himself the question: 'How active is this child in the social life of the school?'

In order to determine whether the two sets of factors are identical, a preliminary investigation was made and has already been reported (Ref. 6). The results indicated the need for the larger research which became practicable with the development of a new system of computer programmes, and which is reported in the present article (Refs. 7 and 10).

THE INVESTIGATION

Ratings and Scales

It was necessary to have teachers rate their pupils on the fourteen personality traits which were used in the earlier researches and which are listed in Table 1, variables 1–14 inclusive. These ratings were made in the manner described above, taking all the usual precautions to avoid spurious correlations between the traits.

TABLE 1

LOADINGS ON FIVE VARIMAX FACTORS

Variable	I	II	III	IV	V
1. Emotional stability	64	18	00	06	47
2. Trustworthiness	83	08	00	04	10
3. Persistence	75	17	31	09	06
4. Co-operation with teachers	78	22	−11	06	−03
5. Cheerfulness	30	76	−18	07	09
6. Sense of humour	17	79	−10	02	00
7. Sociability	15	83	−11	08	12
8. Self-assertion	−06	71	40	−01	06
9. Maturity	44	29	42	06	41
10. Popularity	22	74	−01	15	32
11. Anxiety-confidence	07	70	24	−03	32
12. Spontaneity	03	80	−06	−03	−13
13. School work	64	24	39	19	02
14. Games	15	58	26	−02	07
15. Lenient-severe	−12	−06	74	−12	−08
16. Successful-unsuccessful	−68	−35	−39	−16	−03
17. Still-moving	00	77	21	04	−35
18. Slow-fast	21	69	36	15	−22
19. Beautiful-ugly	−24	−27	00	−76	−19
20. Cruel-kind	67	09	−49	06	01
21. Difficult-easy	71	03	−36	07	12
22. Clean-dirty	−43	−04	−07	−62	−10
23. Masculine-feminine	09	−13	−34	69	−09
24. Wise-foolish	−77	−05	−32	−12	−19
25. Dishonest-honest	81	01	−16	08	−01
26. Hard-soft	20	−18	−63	29	−13
27. Light-heavy	−04	−07	32	−42	23
28. Good-bad	−85	−01	11	−12	−04
29. Worthless-valuable	75	23	14	19	−04
30. Strong-weak	−37	−45	−51	15	−21
31. Excitable-calm	42	−43	03	−03	60
32. Active-passive	12	−77	−31	−02	28
33. Cautious-rash	−53	58	01	−02	−24
34. Yielding-tenacious	23	29	67	−02	01
Percentage of Total Variance	23·65	21·89	10·62	5·79	4·57

Decimal points are omitted before figures for all loadings.

The description of each variable shows the direction of scoring in the research and the sign of the loading remains as on the computer print-out (except where all signs were reflected for Factor I). Within the text, the description of certain variables has been reversed to make easier reading and signs of loadings have been reversed accordingly.

It was also necessary to have the same teachers rate the same pupils on a number of seven-point scales chosen from each of the three 'semantic' dimensions. In Osgood's terms, a teacher regarded each of his pupils in turn as a concept to be judged. The twenty selected scales are variables 15–34, inclusive, in Table 1. The dimensions from which they were taken are indicated below, where 'E' means 'evaluation', 'A' means 'activity' and 'P' means 'potency', the letters in each case being placed at the high end of the scale:

15.	Lenient-severe	P	25.	Dishonest-honest	E
16.	Successful-unsuccessful	E	26.	Hard-soft	P
17.	Still-moving	A	27.	Light-heavy	P
18.	Slow-fast	A	28.	Good-bad	E
19.	Beautiful-ugly	E	29.	Worthless-valuable	E
20.	Cruel-kind	E	30.	Strong-weak	P
21.	Difficult-easy	A	31.	Excitable-calm	A
22.	Clean-dirty	E	32.	Active-passive	A
23.	Masculine-feminine	P	33.	Cautious-rash	A
24.	Wise-foolish	E	34.	Yielding-tenacious	P

Eight scales were from the evaluative dimension, six from the activity dimension and six from the potency dimension.

It was predicted that the teachers would use personality traits from the emotional stability or reliability and conscientiousness dimension and semantic scales from the evaluation dimension, in the same manner; in other words, that these two sets of measures would be associated in a single factor. It was also predicted that the teachers would use personality traits from the social extraversion dimension and semantic scales from the activity dimension, in the same manner; in other words, that these two sets of measures also would be associated on a second factor. Two factors were therefore predicted with high loadings in the following measures respectively:

Factor I: Emotional Stability, Reliability and Evaluation:
  Traits: (1) emotional stability, (2) trustworthiness, (3) persistence, (4) co-operation with teachers, (5) attainment in school work.
  Scales: (16) successful, (19) beautiful, (20) kind, (22) clean, (24) wise, (25) honest, (28) good, (29) valuable.

Factor II: Social Extraversion:
  Traits: (5) cheerfulness, (6) humour, (7) sociability, (8) self-assertion, (12) spontaneity, (14) ability in games.
  Scales: (17) moving, (18) fast, (31) excitable, (32) active, (33) rash.

It was considered that if two clearly defined clusters of traits and scales were obtained such as the above, this would be sufficient to establish that the two sets of dimensions are identical. After a consideration of results from preliminary work, it was considered that another factor of 'masculinity-femininity' could be predicted; and a factor of 'potency' produced by a clustering of Osgood's potency scales.

SUBJECTS

The teachers who made these ratings were 42 advanced students in the Education Department at the University of Birmingham. All were qualified teachers with considerable experience and outstanding in their own part of the profession. Some were class teachers, some were heads, some were lecturers. Each rated a group of pupils or students well known to him and ranging from juniors aged 10+ to men and women aged 19+ years. The total number rated was 834.

Each group was homogeneous in age and sex, but the variety of groups was such that, unless all teachers and lecturers tend to rate along the same dimensions, it was unlikely that the hypothesis would be substantiated. Since the teachers and lecturers who made the ratings formed a highly selected group from the teaching profession and as such would be more likely to use traits and scales independently, this aspect of the sampling also tended to make the substantiation of the hypothesis less probable.

STATISTICAL ANALYSIS

Each teacher (or lecturer) rated every member of his class (or group of students) on each of the 34 traits and scales listed in Table 1. Using an electronic computer, a correlation matrix was obtained for each of the 42 such sets of ratings, and the matrices were combined, using z-scores. The combined correlation matrix was analysed by the method of principal components, five components being extracted; and the axes were rotated in accordance with the Varimax criterion. Together, the five Varimax factors accounted for 66·52 per cent of the total variance.

RESULTS

Against each of the 34 variables in Table 1 is shown its loading on each of the five Varimax factors. Within the column for each of these factors, high loadings show the clusters of ratings and scales which are sought. The percentage of variance at the foot of each column indicates the relative importance of the factor.

Factor I: The Good Pupil: Evaluation

Factor I accounts for 23·65 per cent of the total variance and has high loadings as follows (Table 2):

'Good Pupil' Ratings		Evaluation Scales	
1 emotional stability	0·64	16 successful	0·68
2 trustworthiness	0·83	20 kind	0·67
3 persistence	0·75	24 wise	0·77
4 co-operation	0·78	25 honest	0·81
13 school work	0·63	28 good	0·85
		29 valuable	0·75

These loadings substantiate the first part of the hypothesis and are comparable to those obtained in the earlier research. With two exceptions, all traits from the dimension of reliability and conscientiousness and all scales from the evaluative dimension are represented. Further, with one exception, no other traits and scales have high loadings.

The two missing evaluative scales are 19 beautiful and 22 clean. However, it has previously been found that teachers do not use the former scale when they are evaluating a pupil; and the latter has, in fact, a moderate loading of 0·43. The scale which is not classed by Osgood as part of the evaluative dimension but which has a high loading on this factor is 21 easy. This scale generally appears on the evaluative dimension when teachers are rating pupils, apparently owing to their concern with discipline (Ref. 6).

Other variables with moderate loadings are the rating 9 maturity and the activity scales 31 calm and 33 cautious. Again, these have previously been found in association with this factor.

The general picture is of a stable, trustworthy, persistent and co-operative child who is good at school work and of whom teachers approve. He is considered mature, generally well balanced and reliable, successful and good at his school work. When a teacher makes an assessment of the personality of his pupil, it would appear that an important question he always asks himself is: 'How much do I approve of him?' or 'Do I consider him a good pupil?'

Factor II: Activity: Social Extraversion

Another question the teachers asks himself, of equal importance, appears to be: 'How active is he socially?' This question is represented by Factor II, which accounts for 21·89 per cent of the total variance. The Factor has high loadings on the traits from the social extraversion dimension and scales from the activity dimension as shown in Table 1.

All traits and scales from these two dimensions are present, with the exception of 21 difficult-easy, which was found on Factor I. The factor

Extraversion Traits		Activity Scales	
5 cheerfulness	0·76	17 moving	0·77
6 humour	0·79	18 fast	0·69
7 sociability	0·83	31 excitable	0·43
8 self-assertion	0·71	32 active	0·77
12 spontaneity	0·80	33 rash	0·58
14 games	0·58		

lends support to the second part of our hypothesis that dimensions from ratings and semantic scales are part of the same universe. However, one other semantic scale also has a considerable loading, namely 30 strong, which lies on Osgood's dimension of potency. Also the two traits of 10 popularity and 11 confidence have high loadings. Instead of lying between Factors I and II as anticipated, they lie on Factor II.

Factor III: Potency

The third Varimax factor is of considerably less importance and extracts 10·62 per cent of the variance only. Its highest loadings are as follows:

Potency Scales		Other Variables	
15 severe	0·74	8 self assertion	0·40
26 hard	0·63	9 maturity	0·42
30 strong	0·51	13 school work	0·39
34 tenacious	0·67	16 successful	0·39
		20 cruel	0·49

Four potency scales have high loadings and the remaining two, 23 masculine and 27 heavy, have moderate loadings. This is hardly the factor of masculinity which has sometimes been obtained, however. The remaining variables with moderate loadings suggest a picture of potency, ruthlessness and success.

Factor IV: Femininity

The fourth factor is smaller again, accounting for only 5·79 per cent of the variance and is a factor of femininity. High loadings are on 19 beautiful, 23 feminine, 22 clean and 27 light. As often found, good looks and cleanliness go together.

Factor V

Factor V accounts for 4·57 per cent of the variance only and has its highest loadings on 31 calm, 1 emotional stability, 9 maturity, 17 still and 11 confidence. A suggested name is 'emotional stability'.

CONCLUSION

Factors III, IV and V

In so far as they contribute relatively little to the general hypothesis, the last three factors should perhaps be disposed of first. The fifth factor, not obtained previously, suggests that if appropriate variables were included it would be possible to show that when classifying their pupils, teachers make some distinction between those who are good pupils and those who are emotionally stable.

Similarly, by including other variables and by forming separate combined matrices for ratings of the two sexes, it may be possible to show that teachers differentiate between feminine and less feminine girls and between masculine and less masculine boys. This is to imply that the scale 'masculine-feminine' is associated with different classes of variables accordingly as it is applied to boys or to girls. Unpublished evidence suggests that this is so and the paucity of high loadings on the present Factor IV, as compared with the factor of masculinity obtained in the earlier study of boys, lends support to this hypothesis.

The present factors are independent one of the other. It is, of course, possible to define factors which are 'oblique', or correlated with each other. The advantage is that they will define the clusters of traits and scales with less ambiguity. Such factors have been obtained from the Varimax factors described above. They are not dealt with in the present article both because they differ relatively little from the Varimax factors, and because the latter afford a direct comparison with the other researches to which reference is made and which have used an analysis comparable to that described here. However, it should be mentioned that the oblique transformation gives a factor of potency more nearly comparable to the factor of like name obtained in the first research of this kind (Ref. 6).

Factors I and II

The main clusters of traits and ratings are plainly seen, however, whether the factors are independent or correlated. It is clear that the factors obtained from teachers' ratings and the factors obtained from Osgood's semantic differential are part of the same universe. What is the implication?

The common assumption is that, when a teacher refers to a pupil and uses a personality trait name such as 'perseverance', he is describing some quality of the pupil. Recent work on teachers' personality ratings, however, has emphasized that they provide evidence not of the pupils' personalities, but of the teachers' perceptions of such personalities and of the meanings which teachers attach to words. Osgood's work has been directed to the analysis of 'meaning'. It demonstrates that there are three major clusters into which words used to connotate meaning are placed. The present research shows that certain important traits used for teachers' ratings fall into two of these same clusters. It suggests that, when teachers rate the personalities of their pupils, they do so in terms of a system of meaning which has been shown to characterize much human thinking, and which in this case is adapted to a school context.

In effect, ratings may or may not be an adequate representation of a child's personality; they certainly are indicative of the system of meaning through which a teacher observes and classifies his pupils. This does not imply that ratings may not be useful; it does, however, suggest that more attention should be given to the systems of meaning which teachers use.

REFERENCES

1. CATTELL, R. B., *Personality and Motivation Structure and Measurement*. London: Harrap, 1957.
2. ——, Objective personality tests: a reply to Dr Eysenck. *Occup. Psychol.*, **38**, 69–86, 1964.
3. EYSENCK, H. J., *The Structure of Human Personality*. London: Methuen, 2nd edit., 1957.

4. HALLWORTH, H. J., A teacher's perception of his pupils. *Educ. Rev.*, **14,** 124–133, 1962.
5. ———, Personality ratings of adolescents: a study in a comprehensive school. *Brit. J. educ. Psychol.*, **34,** 171–177, 1964.
6. ———, Dimensions of personality and meaning. *Brit. J. soc. clin. Psychol.*, **4,** 161–168, 1965.
7. ——— & BREBNER, ANN, A System of Computer Programmes for Use in Education and Psychology. London: Brit. Psychol. Soc.
8. OSGOOD, C. E., SUCI, G. J. & TANNENBAUM, P. H., *The Measurement of Meaning*. Urbana: Univ. of Illinois Press, 1957.
9. OSGOOD, C. E., Studies on the generality of affective meaning systems. *Amer. Psychol.*, **17,** 10–28, 1962.
10. WAITE, G., A study of attitudes using the Semantic Differential. M.A. Thesis, Univ. of Birmingham Library, 1961.

11

A Scale Analysis of Introversion-Extraversion[1]

ERICH MITTENECKER [2]

First published in

Zeitschrift für Philosophie, Psychologie und Pädagogik, **4,** 183–193, 1954

THE PROBLEM of measurement in psychology is closely connected with the question of isolating individual variables. There is no sense in quoting data for a concept A, if it turns out that A represents a complex of factors which are independent of each other (i.e. are orthogonal factors). Each statement about A will simply consist of putting together the data for the individual factor and nothing else. However, if the factors are dependent on each other in the sense that they share a characteristic of A (i.e. a general factor) then the datum A will be a reasonably good evaluation of the general factor. The evaluation will of course be improved by the inclusion of more items which measure the general factor represented by A, especially if the items are independent of any specific factor.

In psychological testing the correlations between tests are used as the basis for factor analysis. The factor analytical procedures developed by Spearman, Thurstone, Burt and others have, as is well known, led to contradictory results in the study of such psychological processes as perception, intelligence, thinking and memory. With regard to intelligence, for example, some workers find a number of independent factors such as spatial ability, numeracy, immediate memory, etc. and no general property of intelligence which can be meaningfully measured. Other investigators, however, find a general factor of intelligence and a number of specific factors.

In personality studies many tests are not amenable to quantitative analysis and therefore it is not possible to apply factor analysis to them.

[1] Translated by W. H. Fox.

[2] A grant in aid made by the Rockefeller Foundation to the Psychological Institute, University of Vienna, facilitated this work and made it possible to employ Mr R. Neumann as assistant in the carrying out of several of the experiments. I would like to acknowledge his efforts.

With attitude scales and personality inventories the individual items are either questions of the kind: *Would you like to be a great politician?* (*Yes/No*) or statements like: *I am very sad* (*often/rarely/never*). In social psychology there are two important theoretical approaches to the problems of isolating independent concepts from a pool of qualitative data. One approach, Lazarsfield's (Ref. 5) Latent Structure Analysis, is really a non-metrical formulation of the factor-analytic model and is simply based on the response alternatives (e.g. Yes/No; Correct/Incorrect) found in questionnaires. Like factor analysis, Latent Structure Analysis enables one to develop individual tests for each latent variable found. Both methods therefore result in the development of truly one-dimensional tests.

The second approach is that of Guttman (Ref. 3). Guttman's technique is not suitable for analysing data into independent factors but it does provide the means for refining a test which on the basis of factor analysis or intuitive knowledge is considered to be largely unidimensional. The technique, which Guttman calls Scale Analysis, was developed during World War II for the study of soldiers' attitudes to various aspects of army life. The underlying idea of the technique can be illustrated as follows. Let a series of people's weights represent the test items: 50 kg, 55 kg, 60 kg, 70 kg; the responses to these items being 'heavier than' and 'lighter than'. This series forms a true scale as persons who are heavier than a given individual weight always have a higher score (i.e., a higher rank order) than persons who are lighter than the given weight. If one uses five weights, everybody must be arranged according to the following 6 rank-order positions:

Rank Order	Heavier than					Lighter than				
	70	65	60	55	50	70	65	60	55	50
1.	/	/	/	/	/					
2.		/	/	/	/	/				
3.			/	/	/	/	/			
4.				/	/	/	/	/		
5.					/	/	/	/	/	
6.						/	/	/	/	/

The heaviest people are in rank-order 1, the next heaviest people in rank-order 2 and so on. The resulting diagram is called a scalogram. Since the five weights form a true scale any other distribution of responses (heavier-lighter) is impossible. For example, if a subject yielded the following results:

Heavier than					Lighter than				
70	65	60	55	50	70	65	60	55	50
/	/	/		/				/	

one would attribute the anomaly to an error in measurement or to the influence of an extraneous distorting variable. A subject who is heavier than 70 kg must also be heavier than 65, 60, 55 and 50; one who is heavier than 65 and lighter than 70 must be heavier than 60, 55 and 50, etc. The particular feature of test items which make up a scale is that they are cumulative. In a series of test items whose unidimensionality is not known (in our example of people's weights the unidimensional nature of the scale was quite obvious from the start) any departure from the cumulative requirement also represents a departure from unidimensionality.

There are many examples of test items in psychology which possess cumulative characteristics; they take the form of a series of questions which, when answered affirmatively, express different degrees of a variable. If the answers to the questions depend on one individual variable, the scalograms will be continuous. For example, the answers to the following three questions depend only on the attitude to science:

1. Science is of advantage to human progress
2. Science is a blessing to Man
3. Without science, mankind has no meaning

These three items are cumulative. If one affirms the third item, one will in any case also affirm the first and second; if one affirms the second and denies the third, one will also affirm the first.

In practice one rarely finds scalograms without some degree of error. Guttman himself accepts scales with up to 10 per cent of the responses as errors, i.e. outside the expected parallelogram structure. It is not necessary here to go into the methodological details of Guttman's technique as these have already been published (Ref. 3).

Certain areas of personality which have long been subjected to measurement on a unidimensional basis are obviously scalable in the Guttman manner. One such personality dimension is that of introversion-extraversion. It is also one of the categories of the PI test which includes 15 of the most reliable introversion-extraversion items (e.g. *I have many acquaintances whom I often meet—Correct/Incorrect*).

The present paper describes the development of a Guttman-type scale using the 15 introversion-extraversion items from the PI test together with a few additional items from Laird's extraversion-introversion test (Ref. 4). Three response categories were evolved for each question, these being reduced to two categories at a later stage of the analysis.

A sample of 100 subjects (including 70 students) of both sexes were read the following statements and each subject had to select one of three possible answers, a, b or c.

1. If I have an argument I keep control over myself
   - a   very well
   - b   well
   - c   moderately or not at all
2. Before I do something I
   - a   always
   - b   sometimes
   - c   never
       think it over
3. A lonely life in a hut in the forest or in the mountains could
   - a   always
   - b   sometimes
   - c   never
       make me happy
4. I
   - a   like
   - b   dislike
   - c   intensely dislike
       doing several things at the same time
5. If I fail to achieve something it annoys me
   - a   a lot
   - b   a little
   - c   not at all
6. I
   - a   never
   - b   rarely
   - c   usually
       have a ready quip to answer jokes made against me
7. I find it
   - a   very difficult
   - b   difficult
   - c   easy
       to get some life into a boring party

8. It is
   a always
   b sometimes
   c never
      a good idea not to trust people
9. I have
   a often
   b sometimes
   c only rarely
      experienced disappointment in my life
10. I succeed
    a only very rarely
    b sometimes
    c always
       in consoling someone who is unhappy
11. I have
    a very few
    b some
    c many
       acquaintances whom I often meet
12. I spend my leisure time alone
    a preferably
    b willingly
    c unwillingly
13. I find it
    a usually
    b sometimes
    c never
       difficult to suppress a feeling of inferiority to other people
14. I am
    a usually
    b sometimes
    c never
       cautious in choosing friends
15. I go to noisy, jolly parties
    a with great pleasure
    b with pleasure
    c unwillingly
16. Before I ask others for help I struggle with a problem
    a a very long time

    b   a long time

    c   only a short time

17. I am

    a   usually

    b   sometimes

    c   rarely

       confused when I find myself in front of a large number of people

18. I treat my belongings with particular care

    a   always

    b   sometimes

    c   very rarely

19. I

    a   usually

    b   sometimes

    c   very rarely

       worry about anything in the world

20. I

    a   always

    b   sometimes

    c   very rarely

       prefer to work alone in a room rather than with others

21. I prefer reading books and quality journals to playing games

    a   agree

    b   both equally

    c   disagree

The responses of each subject were recorded on graph paper.

    Using a procedure similar to Guttman's scalogram board technique, involving on one side the rank order of the subjects and on the other side the rank order of the response categories, the data was adjusted until a structure resembling a scalogram resulted. This, however, contained a large number of errors and formed what Guttman calls a 'quasi-scale'. The errors were rather irregularly distributed over the scale indicating the presence of a 'general dimension' and of a considerable number of distorting variables. By omitting those items which were particularly associated with errors and by collapsing response categories (e.g. 7b and c becoming 7bc) a scalogram was eventually produced which satisfied the scale criteria. Thus the seven items used can be placed in a rank order to show their cumulative relationships. It is worth mentioning that all seven items are to be found in the PI test while the seven additional items from Laird's test had to be dispensed with. The order, beginning with the most introverted response, runs as follows: 12a, 10a, 11a, 7a, 14a, 9ab, 16ab, 12bc, 10bc, 11bc, 7bc, 14bc, 9c, 16c.

Guttman quotes several criteria for a true scale. The first concerns the relative frequency of errors; in our study it amounted to 10·01 per cent being more or less equal to the standard (about 10 per cent) proposed by Guttman. The experiment with the seven refined items was repeated on a group of 129 subjects in order to ascertain the presence of possible chance factors. Once again there was a very similar frequency of errors—11·3 per cent. Guttman records variations in error frequency of up to 4 per cent on the repetition of experiments with new samples of subjects. As a further criterion he requires that errors be equally distributed over the scale. The pronounced accumulation of errors in certain regions of the diagram indicates the presence of one or more distorting variables. There is, however, no evidence of this in our scalogram—the errors are distributed over all variables and categories.

Guttman further maintains that as many items as possible should lead to 50 per cent of subjects responding in the opposite sense. Questions answered in a very one-sided fashion would lead only to an artificial attenuation of the possibility of error. In our series of statements the answers were distributed as follows:

12a	10 per cent	12bc	90 per cent
10a	19 per cent	10bc	81 per cent
11a	30 per cent	11bc	70 per cent
7a	27 per cent	7bc	73 per cent
14a	59 per cent	14bc	41 per cent
9ab	77 per cent	9c	23 per cent
16ab	88 per cent	16c	12 per cent

But this does not satisfy the requirements proposed by Guttman. It can, however, be shown quite easily with the help of the weights experiment that the criterion of as many 50–50 items as possible leads precisely to the effect which it is supposed to circumvent, as well as having another serious advantage. In our weights example one would have to use a series like 56, 58, 59, 60, 62, 64 and this implies that the middle weight of the whole group studied is about 60 kg. This would comply with Guttman's demand for items which were responded to 50 per cent in one sense and 50 per cent in the opposite sense; but what would be the result of such a selection? A group with normally distributed weights would then necessarily contain a very large number of extreme variables (all the people weighing more than 64 kg would be ranked as 1 and all those weighing less than 56 kg would be ranked as 7). In a non-ideal scale this extraordinary accretion of extreme cases (i.e. extreme in respect of the selected items) would lead necessarily to a pronounced diminution in the possibility of error. In addition to this, some distortion in the distribution in individual ranks would appear, which in the case of personality traits would lead to a frequency distribution of a highly improbable form. The frequencies in individual ranks would become almost equal and under certain circumstances may even lead to a U-shaped distribution. In fact, among the scalograms published by Guttman there actually are cases in which extreme values of the variables being measured are more numerous than middle values. This is of course very important in attitude scales where it is desirable to reflect extremes in attitude expression but the individual items must constitute a good sample of all the possible items which test this attitude in the normal (non-extreme) population. However, this conclusion cannot be drawn if at the outset 50/50 items are given preference in the construction of the scalogram. With a personality variable like introversion-extraversion one expects a bell-shaped rather than a U-shaped distribution curve in any heterogeneous group. If our series of seven selected items is a good sample it will produce a distribution of response percentages which extends over a large area (from 10 to 90 per cent) in one direction; and the frequencies of the individual ranks will be distributed more or less as one expects with personality traits, that is, they will be normally distributed. Both of these latter requirements are met in our seven items. The foregoing frequency distribution of responses clearly indicates that the response tendencies to the individual items range over the whole scale from extreme introversion to extreme extraversion. The frequency distribution of individual ranks is shown in the scalogram below where the ranks are indicated in Roman numerals in the left-hand margin, first column. For example, in rank order I (with all 7 questions answered in the direction of introversion) there are only 4 cases; there are 7 cases in rank II; 12 in rank III; etc. This distribution corresponds almost exactly to the distribution of degrees of introversion yielded by all 21 items originally used and of course it approaches a normal distribution. It is thus much more likely that the criterion of item distribution over the whole range is the more important one if one is concerned with producing a unidimensional scale. This problem also relates to two further methodological questions of current interest: Brunswick's question of sampling the situations in which behaviour occurs (Ref. 1) and the questions of selecting test items for intelligence tests (Ref. 6).

Finally, what about the general significance of the foregoing analysis? Apart from the statistical advantages to be obtained from a scale as opposed to a non-scale (Guttman could, for example, demonstrate that the multiple correlation of a series of scalable items with an external criterion is the same as the simple correlation of the scale ranks with the latter), I believe it is possible to throw a little more light on the essential nature of introversion-extraversion. This can be done by looking more closely at the actual content of the seven selected items. Of course

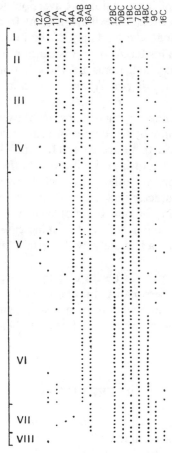

Figure 6

G

we should bear in mind that it was not the content of the items that was scaled but the subjects' reactions to the items. However, there is obviously a connection between content and response in our seven statements, since the distribution of the response-categories for each question on both the introversion and extraversion side of the scalogram agrees with what one would expect for content as well. For example, item 10 (I succeed (a) only very rarely, (b) sometimes, (c) always in consoling someone who is unhappy) is found on the introversion side with category (a only very rarely) and on the extraversion side with categories (b sometimes and (c always).

If we analyse the individual items in the scalogram what emerges is the well-known picture of introversion-extraversion developed by research in recent years—a picture somewhat different from early work on the concept of C. G. Jung—the tendency of the introvert to be alone, his tenuous contact with his fellow men, his caution in dealing with others, etc. However, the unscalable items, i.e. those left out of the analysis, are probably worth commenting on. Apart from items 3, 6 and 8, which were omitted because they evoke responses mainly in one direction (96–99 per cent), the remaining unscaled items are those which the responses are determined not only by the degree of introversion but also by other factors. Of these items there are some (1, 5 and 15) which apparently depend on the general control or inhibition of affect as well as on introversion; and there are yet other items which would appear to be influenced by work characteristics and general interests (2, 4, 18, 20, 21). From the content point of view it is not clear why items 13 and 17 had to be omitted but these items may at least indicate that many introverts have learned to deal adequately with certain aspects of the social environment.

The aim of this paper has been not only to present a detailed scale analysis of a specific personality dimension with the associated benefits of greater accuracy and economy of measurement but also to present scale analysis as a method which could be usefully applied in a variety of research settings.

REFERENCES

1. BRUNSWICK, E., *Systematic and Representative Design of Psychology Experiments*, California: Univ. of California, 1949.
2. CATTELL, R. B., *Factor Analysis.* New York: Harper & Brothers, 1952.

3. GUTTMAN, L., Chapters 3–9 in *Measurement and Prediction: Studies in Social Psychology in World War II*, by S. A. Stouffer *et al.*, Princeton: Princeton Univ. Press, 1950.

4. LAIRD, D. A., Inventory of extraversion-introversion. *J. abnorm. soc. Psychol.*, **20**, 128 et seq., 1925.

5. LAZARSFIELD, P. F., Chapters 10 and 11 in *Measurement and Prediction: Studies in Social Psychology in World War II*, by S. A. Stouffer *et al.*, Princeton: Princeton Univ. Press, 1950.

6. MITTENECKER, E., Über Elementanalyse psychologischer Tests. *Statist. Viertelj.-Schr.*, **IV**, 125 et seq., 1951.

12

Second Stratum Personality Factors Defined in the Questionnaire Realm by the 16 P.F.[1]

R. L. GORSUCH & R. B. CATTELL

First published in *Multivariate Behavioral Research*, **2**, 211–214, 1967

Abstract

To determine the factors in the correlations between the 16 P.F. scales on the basis of a heterogeneous sample, a correlation matrix (N = 1, 652) was determined by combining data from several samples. Eight factors were extracted on the basis of mathematical and statistical considerations and rotated to simple structure.

INTRODUCTION

The major factors were Anxiety, Exvia-Invia (extraversion vs. introversion but with limited social orientation), Cool Rationality-Pathemia (affectivity) and Independence-Subduedness. Smaller factors included Cultured Tact-Spontaneity and Untamedness-Sensitive Practicality. The present study suggests that several stable second order factors may possibly be established in addition to the usual ones of Anxiety and Exvia-Invia.

The determination of the structure of human personality has been moving distinctly forward in the past fifteen years. Through factor analytic procedures based on measurement of individual differences (e.g., Refs. 7 and 25), many relatively independent dimensions of personality have been established. In the questionnaire realm, as distinct from that of life data and objective tests (Ref. 7), the Sixteen Personality Factor Questionnaire (16 P.F.) was designed as a comprehensive instrument for measuring the factors uncovered from research based on ratings as well as questionnaire studies (Ref. 13). However, since the primary factors (and therefore the 16 P.F. scales) are correlated, one can factor

[1] This investigation was supported, in part, by a grant (MN 01733–17) to the second author from the National Institute of Mental Health, Public Health Service. The authors are indebted to Dr Charles Spielberger for his comments on this paper.

these correlations between the primary factors and eventually arrive at second stratum factors within the domain.

The question of the second stratum structure of the 16 P.F. is of theoretical and applied interest because it may lead to better description of the individual and prediction of his behaviour. In particular, the following three problems necessitate knowledge of second stratum factors such as those found in the 16 P.F.: (1) studies to explore hypotheses concerning personality structure and behaviour in specific populations and across cultures are incomplete without reference to the higher stratum factors in the general U.S. population as well as to the primary factors; (2) a current debate between Cattell (Ref. 9) and Eysenck (Ref. 22) (in which the former argues for measurement predominantly in primary factor terms and the latter in terms of the second level of factors) cannot be adequately researched until the second stratum structure is known for even small factors, without possibly prejudicing the research in Cattell's favour; and (3) the relationship between second stratum factors in the questionnaire medium and first stratum objective test factors has been hypothesized as one in which each second stratum questionnaire factor has a parallel objective test factor (Refs. 5, 6 and 17), providing one knows the second stratum questionnaire factors.

Several studies have reported the second order factor structure of the 16 P.F. in limited populations—such as students (Refs. 2, 33 and 39) and mental patients (Refs. 23, 30 and 31), as well as specialized populations or combinations of populations (Refs. 6, 10, 16, 28, 35 & 40). Although the studies on limited and specialized populations are valuable in their own right, the generalization of their factor structure is limited as compared to studies based on sampling from a more heterogeneous universe. This limited generalization may be restrictive in developing general hypotheses concerning the nature of the second stratum factors and in developing combinations of the subscales to measure them for the purpose of research and the development of norms for applied use.

An early attempt to give the second stratum structure applicable to a wide range of populations was implied in the 16 P.F. Handbook (Ref. 18, p. 17) which gives weights to estimate two higher order factors. In a more comprehensive attempt, Cattell & Scheier (Ref. 17, pp. 45–48) examined several studies and suggested generalized factor patterns for four second stratum factors: Anxiety, Exvia-Invia (extraversion-introversion), Pathemia (affectivity) and Promethian Will vs. Resignation. Unfortunately, the numerous published studies have used such varying procedures in the factoring and rotating of the data that such comparisons across studies are more suggestive than conclusive. There-fore, the present study regards the Cattell & Scheier factors primarily as hypotheses for investigation.

The purpose of the present study was to determine the exact second order factor structure of a more heterogeneous population than has yet been examined. The authors expect that the factor structure itself will prove to have more general applicability than the results of previous research.

METHOD

Subjects

To obtain as diversified a total sample as possible, the data were gathered from many divergent sources. The use of several testing situations and different administrators for each subsample also helped to provide a guarantee against spurious results due to a unique situation or particular administrator. The composition of each subsample, with its number of subjects, is shown in Table 1. The 1957 version of the 16 P.F. (Form A) was used in all cases except for the sample gained from Cattell (Ref. 6) and the high school seniors. From Cattell (Ref. 6), it was possible to obtain correlations between the actual factors them-selves. The high school senior subsample used Form B as well.

TABLE 1

SUBJECTS

No.	Description
320	High school seniors (176 females).
96	Randomly drawn sample from several thousand basic airmen, Karson (Ref. 30).
408	181 undergraduates of both sexes; 227 Air Force men in training, Cattell (Ref. 6).[2]
172	33 college undergraduates, 65 Air Force, and 74 convicts, all males, Horn (Ref. 28).[2]
142	Harvard students (males) studying in the humanities and sciences.[1]
214	Illinois adults (149 male farmers; 65 female secretarial applicants).[1]
300	Parents (150 females) of children referred to a clinic for treatment.[1]
1652	Total

[1] The authors are indebted to Drs S. Karson, Ann Roe and Arthur Sweney for their co-operation in providing data.

[2] Did not include B intelligence. Therefore the correlations of scale B are based on an N of 1072.

Procedure

The elements of the correlation matrix from each subsample were transformed to Fisher's Z coefficients, weighed according to the subsample's size and added to the same elements of the other matrices. The resulting values were then divided by the total number of subjects (1652 for all scales except B, which was 1072) and converted back into correlation coefficients. This procedure eliminates the influence on the correlations from mean differences between the groups and reduces the effects from differences in range. Therefore, the resulting matrix gives the personality structural relationships from within the subsamples, rather than being a combination of individual differences and subsample differences.

Factor Analysis

Four criteria for the number of factors to extract were examined: (1) Guttman's criterion for the fewest number of factors to extract based on mathematical considerations (Ref. 26); (2) Sokal's statistical criterion which treats the residuals as partial correlation coefficients (Ref. 37); (3) Bartlett's statistical test of the latent roots of the matrix (Ref. 1); and (4) the 'point of inflection' method (Refs. 8 and 11) based on the change in the slope of the plotted latent roots. Both significance tests were applied with a significance level of 0·05. Based on the estimate of the proper number of factors to extract, an iterative centroid factor analysis was repeated to estimate communalities until the greatest change in a variable's communality from one iteration to the next was less than 0·005. The matrix was then factored by the principal axis method.

To obtain the most psychologically meaningful position for the factors, the criterion of maximizing simple structure as seen in the hyperplane count (i.e., finding that position where the largest number of variables have negligible loadings on the factors) was reached by the Cattell & Foster Rotoplot programme (Ref. 14). The rationale and evidence for the psychological meaningfulness of this simple structure criterion are given by Cattell & Dickman (Ref. 12), Cattell & Gorsuch (Ref. 15), Cattell & Sullivan (Ref. 19) and Thurstone (Ref. 38).

RESULTS

The four criteria for the number of factors to extract gave the following results: (1) Guttman's criterion indicated at least five factors; (2) Sokal's significance test indicated nine factors; (3) Bartlett's significance test indicated twelve factors; and (4) the point of inflection method suggested ten factors. The divergence in results is partially explained by the fact that Guttman's procedure gives the lower mathematical bound while Sokal's and Bartlett's procedures are attempts to determine the upper statistical bound. Since unique convergence of communalities is, with 16 variables, difficult to obtain for more than eight factors and the variance of individual factors would be minute beyond this, eight factors were extracted. Eighteen iterations were necessary to determine appropriate communalities for the principal axis factor analysis.

In the 26 overall Rotoplot rotations (728 single plane comparisons), two factors had only one major loading each and were slightly loaded by other primaries in only a few of the plots. Therefore, they were rotated as specifics (i.e., set orthogonal to the other factors). The rotational exploration suggested that this is an example of the discrepancy between the meaning of factor orders and factor strata discussed theoretically by Cattell (Ref. 10). This is to say, Factor VII: B (intelligence) and Factor VII: G (superego strength) are from the beginning actually at the second stratum level but appear as similar to specifics in these data due to the lack of other similar variables and were therefore rotated accordingly.[1] Table 2 gives a summary of the factor loadings greater than an absolute value of 0·20 as defined by the primary factor pattern.

The correlations among the factors are given in Table 3. The factors are arranged in decreasing order of total variance directly accounted for by each factor. All calculations were to at least four decimal places to avoid accumulating rounding error and results were rounded to two places only on preparing the tables.

FACTOR INTERPRETATION AND DISCUSSION

Table 2 shows the factor of greatest magnitude in the present study to be Anxiety. It appears to be the result of high tension level ($+Q_4$) and a high guilt level ($+O$) along with suspiciousness of others ($+L$). The combination of these particular variables could be the result of external circumstances alone, but it seems reasonable, in view of the lack of self-sentiment control and low integration ($-Q_3$) and low ego strength

---

[1] Varimax orthogonal (Ref. 29), Kaiser-Dickman oblique (Ref. 27) and Maxplane oblique (Ref. 21) analytical rotation procedures were also used. The Rotoplot solution was selected for presentation since only it had a high hyperplane count while rotating two factors out as specifics.

TABLE 2

PRIMARY FACTOR PATTERN

	Factors[1]							
	I	II	III	IV	V	VI	VII	VIII
A: Sociable (vs. cool, aloof)	—	46	-54	-23	—	—	—	—
B: Intelligence	—	—	—	—	—	—	87	—
C: Ego Strength	-52	—	—	—	—	—	—	—
E: Dominance	—	44	—	36	—	—	—	—
F: Surgency	—	59	—	—	—	—	—	—
G: Superego Strength	—	—	—	—	—	—	—	85
H: Adventurousness (vs. timidity)	-42	62	—	—	—	—	—	—
I: Sensitive (vs. tough, realistic)	—	—	-66	—	—	-31	—	—
L: Paranoid suspiciousness	54	—	—	—	—	—	—	—
M: Unconcerned (vs. practical, conventional)	—	—	—	38	—	44	—	—
N: Shrewdness (vs. naivete)	—	—	27	—	49	—	—	—
O: Guilt proneness	70	—	—	46	—	—	—	—
Q₁: Radical (vs. conservative)	—	—	—	—	22	—	—	—
Q₂: Self-sufficiency (vs. group dependency)	—	-34	—	41	—	—	—	—
Q₃: Self-sentiment control (vs. lack of integration)	-54	—	—	—	25	—	—	—
Q₄: Ergic tension	76	—	—	—	—	—	—	—

[1] Only loadings above 0·20 are included. Decimal place omitted.

TABLE 3

CORRELATIONS BETWEEN FACTORS

	I	II	III	IV	V	VI	VII	VIII
I. Anxiety (vs. Integration)	100[1]							
II. Exvia (vs. Invia)	−06	100						
III. Cool Rationality (vs. Pathemia or Affectivity)	−15	32	100					
IV. Independence (vs. Subduedness)	26	06	03	100				
V. Cultured Tact (vs. Spontaneity)	−16	14	10	−06	100			
VI. Untamedness (vs. Sensitive Practicality)	−01	−16	−23	−17	06	100		
VII. B. Intelligence	00	00	00	00	06	01	100	
VIII. G. Superego Strength	00	01	00	00	08	08	08	100

[1] Decimal points omitted

(—C), to suggest that the internal personality balances play an important role. The influence of temperamental predisposition (—H) to anxiety is important in that the person who reacts more to threatening circumstances of any kind is somewhat more likely to be anxious. The factor interpretation is relatively unchanged from that presented by Cattell & Scheier (Ref. 17) and Scheier & Cattell (Ref. 36).

The second factor in terms of magnitude in the present research is Exvia-Invia, a name given to this factor to differentiate it from popular connotations of extraversion-introversion which overstress the role of sociability (however, the classical psychological definition of extraversion as being externally oriented is fitting). The continuum represented by this factor is characterized by a more adventurous disposition (+H), which, since it is predominantly an inherited characteristic from the evidence so far gathered (Ref. 7), may be a major causative component of it. Whereas +H thus probably represents a component from constitutional insusceptibility to threat, the primary rivalling it for highest loading, namely surgency (+F), represents an actual low experience of threat, punishment and inhibition in early and present life (Ref. 7).

An interpretation which holds that the positive pole of this factor is the person who is less susceptible to the intimidations presented by his environment is supported by the other variables loading the factor. They show a person more inclined to be aggressive and less inclined towards a submissive response (+E), less aware of general ergic frustration in social relations (+A) and less inclined towards that group conformity which would reduce occasions of frustration (—Q_2). Supplementary evidence for this interpretation is found in the greater conditionability of introverts through punishment in Komazakis' study of high school children (Ref. 32).

Although the correlational agreement of Eysenck's extraversion scale with the present factor probably indicates an excellent match,[1] the theory presented here of Exvia-Invia differs. The present theory suggests that it results from an interaction of H, the degree of constitutional insusceptibility to threat connected with autonomic reactivity (as seen by the pulse rate and EKG associations with H [Ref. 7]) and of F, the actual degree of life experience of inhibiting influences. The other loading

---

[1] Eysenck's main marker is Guilford's R which loaded this factor when it was included in Becker's study (Ref. 2). Gorsuch & Adcock (unpublished) found a 26 item extraversion scale, selected from the 16 P.F. on the basis of their correlations with the components of Exvia, to correlate 0·78 with Eysenck's scale (N = 41 randomly selected introductory psychology students).

variables are probably responses, broadly speaking, to the same influence.

The third factor has been named Cool Rationality at the positive pole and Pathemia (or affectivity) at the negative to indicate the common core running through the primaries. This interpretative title defines the high person as cortically alert (accompanied by the handling of problems at the rational level), whereas a low score represents more action at the hypothalamic level and infusing all reactions with feelings, hence 'Pathemia' from the Greek root for feeling. It appears to be a good match for Burt's sthenic vs. asthenic emotionality factor (Ref. 3). The questionnaire primaries agree with and further hint that this Pathemia is an overprotected and unrealistic emotionality. Since men and women differ significantly in the appropriate directions on each of the three primaries brought together in this factor (Ref. 18), women are expected to be lower than men on Factor III. However, it does not seem to be a masculinity-femininity factor *per se*, since other scales not related to this factor also have sex differences (e.g., Scale E). Family background and training could play an important part developmentally in this factor since 1 is largely environmentally determined; the sex differences indicate that the role of the female child probably contributes to it.

The fourth factor is almost as large in terms of variance as the third and is titled Independence-Subduedness. The basic characteristic for which it is named, independence, would be necessary to reject the *status quo* in favour of change $(+Q_1)$ and would provide for leading a person away from a group orientation and towards a greater self-sufficiency $(+Q_2)$, especially when the person's original membership group is on the more conservative side. It is possible that persons scoring high on this factor will be rated by others as hostile in many situations because of the high scoring individual's lack of concern over being accepted by the group. Similarly, in his leadership efforts, he is more likely to be oriented towards task competition rather than maintaining the level of group cohesiveness.

But to develop an approach to life producing a high score on this factor, dominance $(+E)$ would appear to be a necessary prerequisite; the unconcernedness and tendency to be absorbed in one's own concerns $(+M)$ may likewise be interpreted as contributing to the factor's development whereas the more aloof and cool lack of sociability $(-A)$ would be the result of negative reinforcement for such activities from interpersonal conflict over some of his more radical positions. Presumably, a long series of defeats in life in general would tend to lower one's score on this factor.

In factors V and VI appear two patterns of a relatively new nature.

In this study they were somewhat difficult, initially, to settle in a simple structure position and a large fraction of the rotation time was in fact devoted to them; they need further confirmation to warrant much theorizing concerning them.

The fifth factor, Cultured Tact-Spontaneity, exemplifies the polished, sophisticated person ($+$N) who has a fair degree of integrated self-control ($+Q_a$), with perhaps some departure from group norm ($+Q_1$). At the negative pole appears a person of more spontaneous, conservative and possibly undiplomatic social integration.

The sixth factor, Untamedness vs. Sensitive Practicality, is a somewhat unexpected combination of high autia ($+$M) with toughness ($-$I). It suggests at the positive pole a combination which might be found in delinquency (or at least in Samuel Boswell's 'yaho-manity'), but at present it is tentatively called Untamedness.

Finally, factors VII and VIII remain the primaries that they were in the original 16 P.F. No further interpretation of intelligence (B) and superego strength (G) is therefore necessary, except to note that they may belong as peers with the second stratum anxiety, exvia, etc.

While the factors found in this study generally confirm the pattern set forth by Cattell & Scheier (Ref. 17, p. 45ff), several discrepancies have occurred. In particular, Anxiety accounts for more variance in the present study than Exvia-Invia which was previously listed first to indicate it accounted for more variance. The difference here is quite high with Anxiety accounting directly for 60 per cent more variance than Exvia-Invia. Otherwise, as noted above, the Anxiety factor has exactly the same variables in the same rank order (except that $+$L and $-$C are here tied for fourth place whereas Cattell & Scheier had $-$C loading slightly higher) as given in Cattell & Scheier's Table 4–3 (Ref. 17, p. 46) and is therefore an excellent match. Nothing in the present factor suggests any revision of the interpretations of this second stratum factor given elsewhere (Refs. 17 and 36).

Past the first factor, the match becomes less than perfect. Exvia-Invia, while undoubtedly the same factor, has two major changes: (1) $+$A has decreased its loading while $+$H and $+$F have both made definite increases and (2) M has dropped out while $+$E has entered as a strong component. Since $+$E has appeared in this factor in rating data (Ref. 7) and has often occurred in other 16 P.F. studies (Refs. 2, 20, 28, 31, 33 and 35), it may now rate a place in the concept of the second stratum factor represented. The disappearance of $+$M may possibly be accounted for by changes in the scale after the first revision or it may be specific to a particular subpopulation; more research needs to be done to determine exactly when it does load the factor.

Since the Exvia-Invia factor, or a slightly similar one, has not only appeared in many 16 P.F. studies but also in Eysenck's work (Ref. 22) and in analysis of the higher order factors in the Guilford questionnaires (e.g., Ref. 34), the solidarity of this factor in the present study of the 16 P.F. in a heterogeneous population provides confirmatory evidence of the importance of such a factor and limits Carrigan's conclusion in her review,of extraversion-introversion (Ref. 4).

Although $+A$ and $+N$ have changed places in the rank ordering of loadings, Cool Rationality vs. Pathemia (affectivity) has appeared as similar to Cattell and Scheier's Pathemia factor. In factor IV, Independence vs. Subduedness, however, a considerable difference was found between the result hypothesized on the basis of previous research and that obtained in the present study. In this study $+N$, which has been one of the highest loaders in the adult trait, does not occur, whereas $+M$, $+Q_2$ and $-A$ have joined the factor. Therefore, the factor name previously used—Promethian Will vs. Resignation—was not deemed appropriate, although the two factors still have considerable conceptual variance in common as shown through the loadings of $+E$ and $+Q_1$.

REFERENCES

1. BARTLETT, M. S., Tests of significance in factor analysis. *Brit. J. Psychol., Stat. Sect.*, **3**, 77–85, 1950.
2. BECKER, W. C., A comparison of the factor structure and other properties of the 16 P.F. and the Guilford-Martin personality inventories. *Educ. and Psychol. Measmt.*, **21**, 393–404, 1961.
3. BURT, C. L., *The Factors of the Mind.* New York: Macmillan, 1941.
4. CARRIGAN, P. M., Extraversion-introversion as a dimension of personality: a reappraisal. *Psychol. Bull.*, **57**, 329–360, 1960.
5. CATTELL, R. B., Psychiatric Screening of Flying Personnel. Personality Structure in Objective Tests—a Study of 1,000 Air Force Students in Basic Pilot Training. USAF School of Aviation Medicine (Project No. 21.0202–0007), Report No. 9, 1–50, 1955.
6. ——, Second-order personality factors in the questionnaire realm. *J. consult. Psychol.*, **20**, 411–418, 1956.
7. ——, *Personality and Motivation Structure and Measurement.* New York: World Book, 1957.

8. ——, Extracting the correct number of factors in factor analysis. *Educ. and Psychol. Measmt.*, **18**, 791–838, 1958.

9. ——, Objective personality tests: The distinction of anxiety, neuroticism and motivation: a reply to Dr Eysenck, *Occup. Psychol.*, **38**, 69–86, 1964.

10. ——, Higher order factor structures. In C. Banks (ed.), *Contributions in Honour of Sir Cyril Burt.* (Chap. 10). London: Univ. of London Press, 1965.

11. ——, The scree test: a brief first test for the number of factors. *Multivariate Behav. Res.*, **1**, 245–276, 1966.

12. —— & DICKMAN, K., A dynamic model of physical influences demonstrating the necessity of oblique simple structure. *Psychol. Bull.*, **59**, 389–400, 1962.

13. —— & EBER, H., *The 16 Personality Factor Questionnaire* (3rd edit.). Champaign, Ill.: Institute of Personality and Ability Testing, 1961.

14. —— & FOSTER, M. J., The Rotoplot programme for multiple single plane, visually-guided rotation. *Behav. Sci.*, **8**, 156–165, 1963.

15. —— & GORSUCH, R. L., The uniqueness and significance of simple structure demonstrated by contrasting organic 'natural structure' and 'random structure' data. *Psychometrika*, **28**, 55–67, 1963.

16. —— & NESSELROADE, J., Untersuchung der interkulturellen konstanz der persoenlichenkeitfactorem in 16 P.F.-text. *Psychol. Beitraege*, **8**, 502–515, 1965.

17. —— & SCHEIER, I. H., *The Meaning and Measurement of Neuroticism and Anxiety.* New York: Ronald Press, 1961.

18. —— & STICE, G., *Handbook for the Sixteen Personality Factor Questionnaire.* Champaign, Ill.: Institute for Ability and Personality Testing, 1957.

19. —— & SULLIVAN, W., The scientific nature of factors: A demonstration by cups of coffee. *Behav. Sci.*, **7**, 184–193, 1962.

20. —— & WARBURTON, F. W., A cross-cultural comparison of patterns of extraversion and anxiety. *Brit. J. Psychol.*, **52**, 3–15, 1961.

21. EBER, H. W., Toward oblique simple structure: Maxplane. *Multivariate Behav. Res.*, **1**, 112–125, 1966.

22. EYSENCK, H. J., *The Structure of Human Personality* (2nd ed.). New York: John Wiley & Sons, 1960.

23. GORDA, E. F. & MARKS, J. B., Second-order factors and the 16 P.F. test and MMPI inventory. *J. clin. Psychol.*, **17**, 82–85, 1961.

24. GUILFORD, J. P., *Fundamental Statistics in Psychology and Education.* New York: McGraw-Hill, 1956.

25. —— & ZIMMERMAN, W. S., Fourteen dimensions of temperament. *Psychological Monographs*, **70,** 1–26, 1956.
26. GUTTMAN, L., Some necessary conditions for common factor analysis. *Psychometrika*, **19,** 149–161, 1954.
27. HARMAN, H. H., *Modern Factor Analysis*. Chicago, Ill.: Univ. of Chicago Press, 1960.
28. HORN, J., Second order factors in questionnaire data. *Educ. and Psychol. Measmt.*, **23,** 117–134, 1963.
29. KAISER, H., The varimax criterion for analytic rotation in factor analysis. *Psychometrika*, **23,** 187–200, 1958.
30. KARSON, S., Second-order personality factors in positive mental health. *J. clin. Psychol.*, **17,** 14–19, 1961.
31. KARSON, S. & POOL, K. B., Second-order factors in personality measurement. *J. consult. Psychol.*, **22,** 299–303, 1958.
32. KOMAZAKIS, T., Sho-batou to gakushu: Toluni shindan-sei koes-betan shudan ni orte (Relations between reward-punishment and learning. Especially in groups diagnosed for introversion and extraversion). *Japanese Journal of Educational Psychology*, **4,** 41–45, 1956.
33. LAFORGE, R., A correlational study of two personality tests: the MMPI and Cattell 16 P.F. *J. consult. Psychol.*, **26,** 402–411, 1962.
34. LOVELL, CONSTANCE, A study of the factor structure of thirteen personality variables. *Educ. and Psychol. Measmt.*, **5,** 335–350, 1945.
35. MICHAEL, W. D., BARTH, C. & KAISER, H. F., Dimensions of temperament in three groups of music teachers. *Psychol. Rep.*, **9,** 701–704, 1961.
36. SCHEIER, I. H. & CATTELL, R. B., *The IPAT Anxiety Scale Handbook*. Champaign, Ill.: Institute for Personality and Ability Testing, 1963.
37. SOKAL, R. R., A comparison of five tests for completeness of factor extraction. *Trans. Kansas Academy of Science*, **62,** 141–152, 1959.
38. THURSTONE, L. L., *Multiple-factor Analysis*. Chicago, Ill.: The Univ. of Chicago Press, 1947.
39. TOLLEFSON, D., Differential Responses to Humor and Their Relation to Personality and Motivation Measures. Unpublished doctoral dissertation, Univ. of Illinois Library, 1961.
40. TSUJIOKA, BIEN & CATTELL, R. B., A cross cultural comparison of second-stratum questionnaire personality factor structure—anxiety and extraversion—in America and Japan. *J. soc. Psychol.*, **65,** 205–219, 1965.

13

The Age Generality of Personality Factors Derived from Ratings[1]

DONALD R. PETERSON

First published in
Educational and Psychological Measurement, **20,** 461–474, 1960

RECENTLY Cattell and various colleagues (Refs. 7, 8 and 12) have reported a series of factor analytic investigations of personality in children. Subjects in early, middle and late childhood have been examined through use of ratings, questionnaires and objective tests, factor analyses have been conducted and the results compared with those previously obtained from study of adults. Although some age-related changes have been reported, the major conclusion of these studies has been that personality structure does not change radically from early childhood to maturity, that the factors previously isolated in adults are found in similar number and with similar meaning in children. This is an important proposition. If the age generality of certain fundamental personality dimensions can indeed be demonstrated, a firm rational and empirical basis will have been formed for longitudinal study of developmental change in personality expression, for long-term prediction of adult personality tendencies from knowledge of trends appearing in early childhood and for various other kinds of investigation whose pursuit may require a systematically-defined conception of stable personality structure.

In the studies cited above, such terms as 'clear' and 'unmistakable' are frequently used in asserting identity between certain aspects of adult and child personality and the general conclusion has typically been stated 'with considerable confidence'. Part of this report is concerned with a statistical evaluation of those claims. The degree of similarity between the various sets of factors will be quantitatively assessed. From that evaluation, it will become obvious that the similarity between allegedly invariant early and late factor patterns is not impressively

[1] This analysis was done while the writer was on a summer fellowship supported by the University Research Board, University of Illinois.

close. The descriptive efficiency of the factors isolated by Cattell and his colleagues will then be examined and criteria for factor inclusion different from the ones employed in the original articles will be developed. Finally, alternative factor solutions, based on those criteria, will be proposed and compared with the original ones in terms of factor reliability and reproducibility.

PROCEDURE

If a personality factor is to offer maximal promise of predictive utility, it must display at least two properties. First, it must be statistically invariant. Second, it must be descriptively efficient. In an unsuitably narrow but properly operational way, let us define one important aspect of statistical invariance as the degree of correspondence between loadings on common variables for any pair of factors for which identity is claimed. More precisely, if two studies possess a high proportion of variables in common and if a given factor in one study is identified with a factor in the other study, the invariance of the single influence which both factor patterns are alleged to represent can be partially defined as the magnitude of the correlation between paired loadings of the common variables on the two factors.

This analysis deals with the results of four studies. The first, by Cattell (Ref. 2), is based on peer ratings of young college men. The second, by Cattell & Gruen (Ref. 8), is based on peer ratings of children between the ages of 10 and 14 years. The third, by Cattell & Coan (Ref. 7), is an analysis of ratings by teachers of children from six to eight years of age. The last, by Peterson & Cattell (Ref. 12), is based on teacher ratings of four- and five-year-old children. With the exception of the last study, identification of factors has been founded on two criteria—namely, the apparent meaning of highly loaded variables and the co-occurrence of common markers in each group of salient variables. The purely judgmental quality of the first criterion and the quasi-judgmental nature of the second render them considerably less rigorous than the techniques described below. In the present analysis, the following operations have been performed: (a) common elemental variables have been identified for each pair of studies; (b) loadings on common variables have been tabulated for all factors in each pair of studies; (c) intercorrelations between the loadings have been computed.[1]

[1] The merits and faults of this matching technique have been discussed elsewhere (Ref. 6). Its faults are many, but the present article rests only on the contention that

TABLE 1

CORRELATIONS BETWEEN FACTOR LOADINGS FOR ADULTS
AND FOR CHILDREN AT VARIOUS AGE LEVELS
(DECIMALS OMITTED)

Factor	Age 11	Age 7	Age 4
A		08	57
E	09	32	44
F	49	49	38
G	33	61	60
H	12	70	31
I		41	73
J		37	33
K			55
L	33	40	67
M		14	31

RESULTS

Table 1 presents correlations between factor loadings for adults and those for allegedly similar factors among children. A casual glance at the correlations creates the general impression that they are not very high and more careful scrutiny precludes any other evaluation.[1] Consider the column of intercorrelations between adult factors and those for 11-year-olds. Loadings on E (Dominance) for children correlate 0·09 with those for the 'same' factor in adults. According to the present findings, identification of the child factor as anything other than E would have been preferable to the interpretation Cattell & Gruen actually chose. Correlation with the adult version of G, for example, is 0·47 and with I it is 0·56. The correlation of 0·09 is the lowest one in the entire pertinent row of correlations. Approximation for F is better, but the correlation for G, 'very clearly' identified as the modification it would be likely to take in children, is only 0·33. Identification of H and L was regarded as 'tentative' and correlations of 0·12 and 0·33 with loadings for the adult analogues attest to the appropriateness of that term.

The study of seven-year-old children (Ref. 7) was generally more

---

these correlations are more objective, precise indices of factor similarity than the original criteria.

[1] Complete tables of intercorrelation have been deposited with the ADI Auxiliary Publications Project, Photoduplication Service, Library of Congress, Washington 25, D.C. Order Document number 6283, remitting $1.25 for photoprints, or $1.25 for 35 mm microfilm.

adequate than the one with 11-year-olds, especially in respect to data-gathering procedure (adults performed the ratings, rather than children) and quality of factor resolution (the criteria of simple structure were far more closely met). These improvements are reflected in generally better matches and the results of comparison for G and H are fairly encouraging. Factors F, I and L also show acceptable similarity with the adult forms, but some of the others do not. Cattell & Coan comment on some 'minor anomalies' in identifying their sixth factor as A. Loading correlation between it and the analogous adult factor is 0·08. The authors state that their second factor is '. . . clearly the typical dominance-submission source trait', but the correlation with loadings on E in adults is only 0·32.

The third column of Table 1, obtained by comparing loadings on adult factors (Ref. 2) with those found in the study of four-year-olds (Ref. 12), must be interpreted in a different way from the other figures in Table 1. In the studies of seven- and 11-year-olds, factor identification was based on criteria other than magnitude of loading correlation and indices of such correspondence provide a measure of the extent to which independently-reached conclusions confirm hypotheses of factor similarity. The authors of the study of four-year-olds, however, obtained the loading correlations before identifying the factors and identification was based in part on the information which those correlations provided. The more strongly positive results are therefore understandable.

All in all, results are rather unconvincing. Inferential evaluation of correlations of the kind reported here is difficult, but can be approached through empirical examination of the actual distribution of all correlations obtained. This is a positively skewed distribution, with a mean of 0·19 and median of 0·16. Five per cent of the correlations exceed 0·48 and while that figure can hardly be regarded as a limit of statistical significance, it does permit an empirical comparison between the magnitude of correlations drawn from allegedly 'matching' factors and those where no assertions of identity have been made. Over all three comparisons, 24 such 'matches' are claimed. Only nine of the related correlations fall in the upper five per cent of the actual distribution of correlations. If figures for the Cattell-Peterson study (Ref. 12) are excluded because they involve capitalization on chance effects, the mean loading correlation for all factor pairs for which identity is claimed is 0·36; inclusion of results from the study of four-year-olds elevates the figure to 0·42. Previously noted deficiencies in the study of 11-year-olds might justify omitting it from consideration. When this is done, the mean correlation for putatively matching factors is still only 0·46. The mean correlation for all other (nonmatching) factor pairs is 0·17. The difference between this and the previously stated correlations may be statistically reliable, but it is not particularly striking.

AN ALTERNATIVE SOLUTION

Descriptive Efficiency

The primary goal of factor analysis is to achieve scientific parsimony. Methodologically related to this goal is the problem of completeness of factor extraction. If the purpose of most factor analytic research is to educe a limited set of dimensional concepts which can be employed in designating a far greater number of diverse phenomena, then it is necessary to establish criteria for determination of the number of dimensions needed to accomplish the descriptive task.

Current methodological focus is clearly on the elaboration of procedures for determining whether or not a given factor is statistically significant. Burt's well-known review (Ref. 1) deals with no other issue, though Burt concedes that for certain problems other concerns than statistical significance may be paramount. To the writer, this emphasis seems entirely misplaced. It has apparently arisen from a misunderstanding of the meaning of parsimony and from historically accidental covariation between competence to deal with issues such as these and inability to think in any terms other than those of statistical significance. 'Parsimony' can have many meanings, but its primary meaning in the factor analytic context is not at all relevant to the achievement of a differentiation between true and accidental, real and error, significant and nonsignificant factors. Instead, parsimony implies the achievement of descriptive efficiency, the attainment of the greatest possible designative power from the smallest possible number of dimensional concepts.

Cattell has recently discussed the extraction of the 'correct' number of factors in factor analysis (Ref. 5) and his major concern, like that of most others who have dealt with this issue, has been with the differentiation of true from error factors. Cattell's solution is based, in part, on the extraction of enough factors to account for a conventionally established, very high proportion of variance. Now the amount of variance for which a given factor accounts is a thoroughly sound basis from which to evaluate the factor and Cattell presents an excellent defence of his choice, but the way in which he applies such criterion information seems unwisely directed. The descriptive efficiency of a factor can be sensibly and precisely defined in terms of the amount of variance which it comprehends, but neither for practical nor theoretical purposes is it necessary to isolate all the influences operating in a correlation matrix, or in a set of them. Literally, it is impossible to attain such completeness. For most practical and theoretical purposes it is enough to isolate the most important, powerful, useful and economical ones. This, unlike the aim of sufficiency, is defensible because it can be attained. One of Cattell's proposals is unassailably sound, i.e., '. . . any decision as to the number of factors to be extracted from a naturally occurring correlation matrix is bound to be arbitrary' (Ref. 5, p. 18). But if the goal of factor analysis is efficiency rather than sufficiency in the specification of dimensions, the criteria for deciding when to stop extracting factors reduce to those operations which lead to a maximization of designative power and a minimization of the number of dimensions in terms of which such designation is performed.

Let us turn now to an examination of the descriptive efficiency of the factors isolated in the studies with which this paper is concerned. The proportion of total variance comprehended by each of the unrotated centroid factors in each of the four studies is given in Figure 7. The average of these functions resembles a hyperbola of the general form $xy = k \, (x > 0)$ and its most striking characteristic is the extreme negative slope of y for small values of x. The first factor accounts for 31·4 per cent of the total variance on the average and the second for 14·5 per cent. No other factor accounts for more than six per cent of total variance and all the factors beyond the first two account for approximately equal amounts of variance. For any function of this kind, an objectively specifiable point of diminishing return in efficiency could be established by defining and minimizing a radius of curvature, but such elegant procedures would be pretentious alongside the quality of the data which rating studies typically offer and the analysis to follow deals rather arbitrarily with only the first two obviously very efficient factors in each of the studies. Together, they account for an average of 46 per cent of total variance. This, clearly, is not all the true common variance. Some of the smaller factors may be perfectly real. But from the viewpoint of descriptive efficiency they are trivial.

The Alternative Solution

The first two centroid factors in each of the four studies were plotted and blind orthogonal rotations performed. Results are presented in

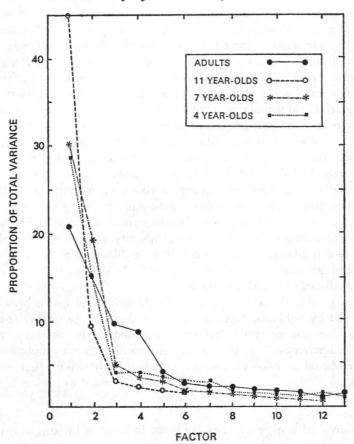

Figure 7. Proportion of total variance accommodated by centroid factors.

Table 2. Each of the four solutions was reached independently. They are presented together because of the statistical similarity which obtains between them and because of the evident resemblance in meaning to be discussed below.[1]

The same correlational test of invariance applied earlier to the original factors was employed with these newly-derived dimensions. Over all comparisons, the average loading correlation for Factor I is 0·90, for Factor II 0·66 and for all claimed matches 0·81. Average loading

[1] A rating schedule derived from this analysis can be obtained by writing to the author.

correlation for all factor comparisons with respect to which identity is denied is 0·33 and an inordinate share of the variance in the distribution on which that average is based is contributed by the study in which child-defined variables were employed and the children themselves did the ratings. From results of the present comparison and from the fact that the first factor accounted for 45 per cent of total variance in the study of 11-year-olds, it would appear that children can successfully differentiate their peers in respect to general adjustment, but not much else. In the analysis of similarity correlation was 0·42. An average of 0·81 for the present factors bespeaks their more substantial resemblance.

Factor I, defined by the first 24 variables in Table 2, is primarily marked by obedience (in children), stability of interests and attitudes, responsibility, conscientiousness, good-natured, easygoing tendencies, patience, trust, good manners, freedom from jealousy, determination and perseverance, co-operativeness, modesty and emotional stability. Let us call it General Adjustment. Its resemblance to a reflection of the general neuroticism factor which Eysenck (Refs. 9 and 10) has so extensively discussed is rather striking.

Factor II is defined by variables 25–35 in Table 2 and is principally marked by boldness, outgoing social tendencies, open expressiveness, gregariousness, energetic alertness, cheerfulness, attentiveness to others and assertiveness. The resemblance to another factor emphasized by Eysenck, introversion-extraversion, is again fairly striking. Let us call it that.

Reliability

Individual item reliabilities are given in three of the original studies on which the present analysis is based, but not one report contains information on reliability of factor scores. Since application of results would generally involve use of the latter and not individual item scores, information on factor reliability is more clearly pertinent to proper evaluation of the findings. Factor scores[1] were therefore calculated from data available from the study of four-year-old children (Ref. 12) and inter-judge correlations computed. Results (uncorrected correlations) are presented in Table 3. In only one case (Factor D, r = 0·73)

[1] To assure the greatest possible precision in computing factor scores based on the original solution (Ref. 12), exact factor loadings rather than reference vector loadings were employed in weighting variables. Factor scores for General Adjustment and introversion-extraversion were derived by unweighted summation of scores on the 10 most highly loaded variables for each factor, as these are presented in Table 2.

TABLE 2

LOADINGS ON FACTORS I AND II
(DECIMALS OMITTED)

Variable	Adult I	II	Age 11 I	II	Age 7 I	II	Age 4 I	II	Means X_i	X_{ii}
(Factor I)										
Obedient			82	20			88	−19	85	01
Stable interests	74	18			82	10			78	14
Responsible	65	−31	76	28	85	06	69	25	74	07
Conscientious	53	−32	79	21	79	−01	80	−26	73	−10
Good-natured	56	06	69	17			75	38	67	20
Patient	69	34	76	22	45	−48	73	12	66	−12
Trusting	62	−06	67	−53	59	−01	77	24	66	18
Mannerly	42	14	77	20	69	29	74	16	66	20
Free of jealousy	69	07	61	10	64	29	59	28	63	05
Persevering	57	−18	70	39	70	20	52	22	62	15
Co-operative	58	24	81	31	85	08	20	20	61	21
Self-effacing	60	−40	61	12	54	−55	54	−55	57	−35
Calm	45	−49	30	−18	70	−15	68	−27	53	−35
Adaptable	38	27			48	56	74	38	53	40
Self-sufficient	49	74	72	27			32	04	51	17
Quiet	12	−81	75	19	50	−67	64	−38	50	−42
Socially mature	59	10	46	43			45	18	50	24
Orderly	40	−22	19	−03	72	−08	66	−20	49	−13
Tender	13	−02					64	04	39	01
Not hypochondriacal	40	−08	38	55					39	24
Learns fast	21	04			55	49			38	26
Tolerant of stress	35		11	64			66	12	37	25
Conventional	12	−52	46	17			36	10	31	−08
Practical	03	−31	47	52	34	−34			28	04
(Factor II)										
Bold	−03	72	24	76	−40	77	−41	70	−15	74
Outgoing	15	76			19	71			17	74
Expressive	−01	64			−04	73			−02	69
Gregarious	−13	77	42	59		61	12	67	10	66
Energetic	41	64	34	69	41	66	−11	58	26	64
Cheerful	16	59	50	63	31	65	38	64	34	63
Attentive to others	38	55	33	61			11	51	27	56
Assertive	−08	59	−58	22	−12	76	−26	62	−26	55
Prefers playmates of opposite sex	−07	48			−12	38			−10	43
Self-reliant	54	10	52	54	32	53	30	53	42	43
Happy-go-lucky	33	−06	36	61	21	53	06	61	24	42
(Residual)										
Aesthetically sensitive	23	35			−14	−39			04	02

does the reliability for an originally reported factor reach the level attained for Factors I and II and the average reliability of 0·49 over all factors derived in the earlier solution is not outstandingly high. The figures of 0·73 and 0·70 for Factors I and II represent an obvious improvement and the reliabilities which could probably be obtained through use of pooled judgments are not markedly inferior to those for some of the objective measures of intelligence in current use.

TABLE 3

FACTOR RELIABILITIES

Factor	r	Factor	r	Factor	r	Factor	r
A	0·41	F	0·41	J	0·60	O	0·33
C	0·52	G	0·44	K	0·57		
D	0·73	H	0·63	L	0·57	I	0·73
E	0·40	I	0·60	M	0·10	II	0·70

DISCUSSION

In terms of the usual criteria of simple structure, the factor solutions just offered leave much to be desired, but simple structure is only a means to an end, not an end in itself. If one factor solution nicely approaches simple structure, but produces factors which do not match closely on replication and if another solution leads to factors which are reproducible but fail to meet simple structure criteria, choice must be determined by a decision as to which set of standards is more fundamental. This decision in turn can only rest on still more basic considerations and those which are most clearly pertinent are issues attendant on predictive power. If one set of factors permits relatively accurate prediction of developed personality tendencies from knowledge of early manifestations and another offers less precision, the superiority of the former set will be established. From this broader perspective, invariance itself is less an end than a means. The importance of this analysis and the earlier research on which it is based will be sharply limited unless careful studies of predictive power are made and these, perhaps the ultimate tests of factor quality, have not yet been done. A critical group of such studies should be longitudinal in design. One empirical basis for such investigation has been presented in the reports of Cattell and his collaborators. An alternative basis is presented here.

The degree of resemblance between the factors described above and those which constitute the framework for most of Eysenck's work offers further possibilities for productive research. It seems likely that a major basis for the difference between Cattell's and Eysenck's formulations is purely statistical, and in a sense artifactual. More careful control over sampling, both of individuals and of variables, would be required to confirm the hypothesis that theoretical disparity is a simple function of discrepancy in the number of factors the two investigators characteristically extract, but if such a proposition can be demonstrated as fact a major empirical and theoretical integration will have been achieved.

Until further evidence is accumulated as to meaning, it seems unwise to regard the factors derived herein as personality 'influences' in the usual sense of that term. The basic data are not direct products of the behaviour of subjects. They constitute products of the behaviour of raters in reference to perceived characteristics of subjects in certain more or less narrowly restricted settings. It is quite as plausible to assume that covariation among such indicants occurs as a function of perceptual factors in the raters, or constant influences in the situations, as to assume that they are direct reflections of the characteristics of the subjects themselves.

Indeed we may be dealing with nothing more than an instance of the very general tendency among mankind to construe conceptual referents of all kinds in terms of a very limited number of major dimensions. Osgood and his collaborators have repeatedly demonstrated a tendency for human beings to structure tremendously varied kinds of meanings in terms of (a) goodness-badness, (b) strength-weakness and (c) activity-passivity (Ref. 11). The first dimension isolated in this analysis may be only an expression of the general tendency to perceive objects in an evaluative way. Introversion-extraversion, as considered above, may represent a combination of the second two conceptual dimensions isolated by Osgood. This consideration should lead to some modification in currently popular views of the meaning of factors derived from ratings, but it need not eventuate in a total rejection of such factors as are demonstrated here. This is a social world and man's destiny is probably determined as much by what others think of him, regardless of the origin of those beliefs, as by the characteristics he 'truly' possesses as an individual.

The relatively high reliabilities for Factors I and II are encouraging. Personality research has long been enfeebled by the paucity of adequate measuring instruments and the development of the latter has in turn been impeded by the absence of reliable criteria. The dimensions defined above offer a reasonably solid basis for the development of more objective, more economical measures of two evidently important personality traits. Though factorial composition of the dimensions may be 'in the heads' of raters, the ratings themselves must have something to do with the behaviour of the subjects, or reliabilities could not be as high as they are. Whatever the dimensions mean, they are consistently judged, they appear in recognizable and statistically reproducible form regardless of subject age and they probably constitute as firm a basis for objective measurement, long-term prediction and theory construction as any dimensions isolated to date.

SUMMARY

This analysis was conducted in an effort to locate personality dimensions which appear as factors regardless of the age at which subjects are examined. Definition of such dimensions is an important step in the investigation of personality development and the construction of adequate personality theory. Cattell and his colleagues have recently presented a series of factor analytic studies of ratings on children at three different age levels. In comparing results with those previously obtained for adults, they claim that most of the factors found in children from four years of age and upward are essentially the same as those which appear in mature subjects. In the present analysis, a correlation test of factor similarity was applied to the results of the studies by Cattell *et al.* and while the authors' conclusions were sometimes supported, the degree of resemblance between child and adult factor patterns was generally unimpressive.

Alternative factor solutions were then presented. Only two factors of high relative variance were retained for rotation in each study. On interpretation these were found to resemble Eysenck's general neuroticism and introversion-extraversion factors and support was offered for the contention that disparity between Eysenck's and Cattell's factor theories lies chiefly in a difference in the number of factors with which the two investigators characteristically deal. The degree of resemblance between representations of these two factors at the various age levels was then assessed, and correlations between loadings on common marker variables were found to be in the neighbourhood of 0·80.

Two sets of factor scores, one based on the original solution and one on the present alternative, were computed from teacher ratings of four-year-old children and estimates of factor reliability were obtained. Uncorrected interjudge correlations of approximately 0·70 were found for the two factors isolated herein and both displayed reliability superior to that of all but one of the factors isolated in the original analysis. The use of factor scores as criteria for the development of more economical and objective measures of adjustment and introversion-extraversion seems justified.

If the immediate goal of factor analysis is to achieve simple structure, the factor solutions offered in this analysis are inferior to those presented in the original studies. If the immediate goals of factor analysis are to attain efficient description with dimensions of acceptable factor reliability and statistically demonstrable reproducibility, the factors derived in this analysis offer appreciable advantages. But the ultimate goal of factor analysis is beyond all these. The final aim and the final test of factor quality is predictive power and that test remains to be performed.

REFERENCES

1. BURT, C. L., Tests of significance in factor analysis. *Brit. J. Psychol. Stat. Sect.*, **V**, 109–133, 1953.
2. CATTELL, R. B., Confirmation and clarification of primary personality traits. *Psychometrika*, **XLII**, 402–421, 1947.
3. ——, *Factor Analysis*. New York: Harper & Brothers, 1952.
4. ——, *Personality and Motivation Structure and Measurement*. Yonkers, N.Y.: World Book Company, 1957.
5. ——, *Extracting the Correct Number of Factors in Factor Analysis*. Adv. Publ. No. 8, Urbana, Ill.: Laboratory of Personality Assessment, University of Illinois, 1957.
6. —— & BAGGALEY, A. R., *The Salient Variable Similarity Index—S —For Factor Matching*. Adv. Publ. No. 4, Urbana: Laboratory of Personality Assessment, University of Illinois, 1954.
7. —— & COAN, R. W., Child personality structure as revealed by teachers' behaviour ratings. *J. clin. Psychol.*, **XIII**, 315–327, 1957.
8. —— & GRUEN, W., The personality factor structure of 11-year-old children in terms of behavior rating data. *J. clin. Psychol.*, **IX**, 256–266, 1953.
9. EYSENCK, H. J., *Dimensions of Personality*. London: Routledge & Kegan Paul, 1947.

10. ——, *The Structure of Human Personality*. London: Methuen, 1953.
11. OSGOOD, C. E., SUCI, G. J. & TANNENBAUM, P., *The Measurement of Meaning*. Urbana, Ill.: University of Illinois Press, 1957.
12. PETERSON, D. R. & CATTELL, R. B., Personality factors in nursery school children as derived from teacher ratings. *J. consult. Psychol.*, **XXIII,** 562, 1959.

SECTION THREE

Response Sets

Editor's Introduction

THE NOTION of response set is a crucial one for the questionnaire measurement of personality; if our subjects do not answer in response to the meaning of the questions which we pose to them and their habitual behaviour patterns are not in fact revealed in their answers because these are determined by extraneous factors, then the validity of questionnaires will be dramatically lowered and may in fact disappear altogether. Subjects may show an acquiescence response set and answer most questions, irrespective of content, with 'Yes', or they may show negative response set and answer most questions with 'No' or subjects may be determined in their answers by some form of desirability response set and give those answers which they think will put them in the best light. Possibilities like these have given rise to a large body of research, much of which is concerned with social attitudes and hence irrelevant to personality inventories. However, a number of studies have been done specifically in relation to response sets as they affect extraversion-introversion and the outcome of this work seems to be that such response sets undoubtedly exist but that fortunately their distorting influence is relatively slight. Desirability response set appears to affect the measurement of neuroticism more than that of extraversion; fortunately scales are available which measure to some extent the strength of this response set, thus making it possible to correct results up to a point.

One difficulty which has not often been discussed, but which finds some support in Lemaine's imaginative study, lies in the fact that extraverts and introverts find different traits desirable. It has been taken for granted that 'desirability' of traits was a constant, but this notion is almost certainly wrong; Lemaine has shown it to be wrong for extraverts and introverts, but it may be surmised that similar differences exist between people high and low on neuroticism, for instance. Much fruitful work could be done on this problem, which has so far only been attacked in a very limited way.

Another problem on which Farley's excellent study throws some light is the vexed one of contamination of desirability response set and content response in instruments supposed to measure the former, such as the Edwards Social Desirability Scale. His pioneering effort deserves to be followed up, at least to the point where instruments are available which measure social desirability without content contamination; to produce a scale which achieves this and which is not prone to the other difficulty pointed out, i.e. differential desirability response, will certainly tax the ingenuity of psychologists to the limit. Until such scales are available, however, we shall not know for sure to what extent our measuring scales for extraversion are in fact in error because of response sets.

H.J.E.

14

Effects of 'Salesman Candidate' Sets
on the Eysenck Personality Inventory

BARBARA J. GOMEZ & JOHN R. BRAUN

First published in *Psychological Reports*, **20**, 192, 1967

BRAUN AND GOMEZ studied effects of two faking sets on Eysenck Personality Inventory (EPI) scores (Ref. 1). Scores were significantly decreased on Neuroticism (N) and significantly increased on Lie (L) under both sets. 'Attempt-to-conceal-faking' set produced significantly smaller increase in L at the cost of significantly smaller decreases in N. Extraversion (E) scores were not significantly changed by either set. Star found that an 'ideal-self' set significantly increased E scores on the Maudsley Personality Inventory from which the EPI was derived (Ref. 2). The present study employed 'salesman candidate' faking sets which might have a similar effect on EPI E scores.

Introductory psychology students took the EPI anonymously under regular instructions and immediately thereafter under faking instructions. Group I's (N = 56) instructions were to answer '... so as to appear an ideal candidate for a position as a salesman'. Group II's (N = 50) instructions were similar but also stated that the EPI contained provisions for detecting faking and that Ss should fake so as not to be detected. Regular administration means for Group I (Group II) were 9·48 (9·72), 12·88 (13·08) and 2·23 (2·08) on N, E and L, respectively, with SDs of 4·83 (4·30), 3·93 (3·54) and 1·63 (1·43). Faked administration means were 2·93 (3·28), 14·84 (15·02) and 6·89 (4·30), with SDs of 3·17 (2·28), 2·47 (2·56) and 1·89 (2·30). For both groups t tests for correlated means showed significant differences (p < 0·01) between regular and faked administration for N, E and L. N decreased under faking while E and L increased. Separate analyses of covariance revealed F to be significant (p < 0·01) for L but not for N or E. Thus, the 'attempt-to-conceal-faking' set produced a significantly smaller increase in L, but, contrary to the findings of Braun & Gomez (Ref. 1), it did not come at the cost of a smaller decrease in N. Using an L score of 4 as cut-off point, under regular administration there were 20 per cent false positives in Group I

211

and 18 per cent in Group II. Under faking sets, 95 per cent of Group I and 56 per cent of Group II had L of 4 or above; this difference was significant ($p < 0.001$). Thus, the 'salesman' faking set produced significant changes in EPI N, E and L scores. L scores were again shown to be of value in detecting faking but not to so great an extent as in the original study.

REFERENCES

1. BRAUN, J. R. & GOMEZ, B. J., Effects of faking instructions on the Eysenck Personality Inventory. *Psychol. Rep.*, **19**, 388–390, 1966.
2. STAR, K. H., Ideal-self response set and Maudsley Personality Inventory scores. *Psychol. Rep.*, **11**, 708, 1962.

15

Acquiescence Response Set in Personality Questionnaires

S. B. G. EYSENCK & H. J. EYSENCK[1]

First published in *Life Sciences*, **2**, 144–147, 1963

KEEHN (Ref. 3) has suggested the possibility that response set might play a part in the results obtained by means of the Maudsley Personality Inventory (Ref. 1) and this possibility has been investigated in part (Ref. 2) by the present writer who found that the tendency of subjects to show an acquiescence response set is uncorrelated with scores on the two M.P.I. scales, i.e., extraversion and neuroticism. In this investigation, however, response set was measured by reference to the F scale, which is made up of social attitude items and as was pointed out in that paper, 'it is, of course, possible that many different "acquiescence" response sets exist, each confined to one type of material; if this were so questionnaires relating to personality items might form a class independent of the response set generated by social attitude items'. The present investigation was carried out in an attempt to provide evidence on this point.

Two scales were constructed for the measurement of neuroticism, each containing 24 items similar to those used in the M.P.I. but worded in a slightly simplified fashion so as to make them suitable for subjects with below average intelligence and education. These two scales, designated 'N_A' and 'N_B', are all scored in such a way that a 'Yes' answer is indicative of neuroticism and a 'No' answer indicative of stability. In addition, four eight-item scales of extraversion were constructed in a similar manner; these will be referred to as A, B, C and D. In scales A and C a 'Yes' answer was indicative of extraversion, while in scales B and D a 'No' answer was indicative of extraversion. The correctness of the system of scoring was checked by means of a factor analysis of all the items concerned in this study.

Two sets of predictions were made on the hypothesis that response set might play a part in answers to questions of this type. If there was

[1] We are indebted to the Maudsley and Bethlem Royal Hospital Research Fund for the support of this investigation, and to Mr Alan Hendrickson for programming the computer and supervising the processing of the data.

indeed a tendency for people to answer 'Yes' regardless of the actual content of each question, then extraversion scales A and C should correlate positively with N_A and N_B, as on all these scales the 'Yes' answer would be indicative of extraversion in the one case, neuroticism in the other, thus producing a positive correlation between extraversion and neuroticism. On the other hand extraversion scales B and D should correlate negatively with N_A and N_B, because on these scales a 'No' answer measures extraversion while the 'Yes' answer measures neuroticism. The size of the differences found would then be an index of the extent of the influence exerted by response sets on these questionnaires.

The other hypothesis relates to the intercorrelations between the four sets of extraversion items. If response set plays a part in the answering of the questions then the correlations between congruent sets (AC and BD, i.e. sets where 'Yes' or 'No' answers respectively contribute towards a high score on extraversion) should be larger than the correlations between incongruent sets (AB, AD, BC, CD, i.e., sets where in the one case 'Yes', in the other case 'No', is the answer contributing to a high score on extraversion).

The questionnaire was applied to a sample of 500 subjects, roughly equally divided as to sex and containing a great variety of subjects from both working and middle class occupations. While the sample could on no account be considered representative, it would be much more similar to a proper representative sample than is usual in inquiries of this kind.

The results of the study as they relate to hypotheses 1 and 2 are given in Tables 1 and 2; it will be seen that they bear out the hypothesis of the existence of a small but definite response set in these data. Scales A and C correlate approximately $+0\cdot12$ with N_A and N_B while scales B and D correlate approximately $-0\cdot14$ with N_A and N_B. These results, when viewed against the fact that a correlation of $0\cdot085$ would be significant at the 5 per cent level and one of $0\cdot115$ at the 1 per cent level, significantly support the hypothesis. It will, of course, be noted that the results, although statistically significant, are so only because of the very large number of subjects involved; in absolute terms the correlations are, of course, very low and indicate that for most practical purposes response set can be disregarded in inquiries of this kind and is of academic rather than practical interest. The figures from Table 2 suggest a similar conclusion; here also there is little doubt about the significance of the differences between the congruent and incongruent group correlations, but these differences are not large and it will be seen that two of the four incongruent group correlations are actually larger than one of the two congruent group correlations.

TABLE 1

	N_A	N_B
A	0·16	0·16
B	−0·13	−0·16
C	0·08	0·06
D	−0·15	−0·15

TABLE 2

Congruent Groups:	Incongruent Groups:
AC = 0·60	AB = 0·48
BD = 0·45	AD = 0·35
	BC = 0·46
	CD = 0·34

The results reported here link up quite well with those achieved by using another approach, namely that of studying directly the validity of the extraversion and neuroticism questionnaires (Ref. 3). It has been demonstrated there that persons nominated as high or low, respectively, on extraversion or neuroticism by outside judges do, in fact, achieve appropriate scores on the Maudsley Personality Inventory; this would have been unlikely, or indeed impossible, had response set played as large a part in personality questionnaires as it has been shown to do in social attitude questionnaires.

SUMMARY

Five hundred subjects filled in two neuroticism questionnaires and four extraversion questionnaires; the former were all keyed for 'Yes' responses, whereas two of the latter were keyed for 'Yes' and two for 'No' responses. An analysis of the relationships between these different questionnaires substantiate the hypothesis of the existence of response set in questionnaires, but also demonstrate that these response sets, while statistically significant, are practically of little importance.

REFERENCES

1. EYSENCK, H. J., Response set, authoritarianism and personality questionnaires. *Brit. J. soc. clin. Psychol.*, **1,** 20–24, 1962.
2. EYSENCK, S. B. G. The Validity of a personality questionnaire as determined by the method of nominated groups. *Life Sciences*, **1,** 13–18, 1962.
3. KEEHN, J. P., Response sets and the Maudsley Personality Inventory. *J. Soc. Psychol.*, **54,** 141–146, 1961.

16

Social Desirability, Extraversion and Neuroticism:
A Learning Analysis

FRANK H. FARLEY

First published in *Journal of Psychology*, **64**, 113–118, 1966

INTRODUCTION

In an analysis of social desirability (SD) in the Maudsley Personality Inventory (MPI), Martin & Stanley found that the Neuroticism (N) Scale had a significant negative correlation of -0.61 with their own SD Scale, but that the Extraversion (E) Scale did not contain SD variance (Ref. 14). The Lie (L) Scale had a significant positive correlation of 0.39 with their SD Scale.

The MPI has since been thoroughly restandardized and refactored with alterations in item content (Ref. 7) and has been named the Eysenck Personality Inventory (EPI). The present paper reports an analysis of SD responding in Extraversion and Neuroticism as measured by the EPI.

In the Martin & Stanley study, SD was assessed by an SD Scale constructed by the authors. However, the most widely used scale, that of Edwards (Ref. 4), was not employed. In light of the large body of literature on the Edwards Scale (ESD), it would seem worth while employing this instrument when investigating relationships between SD and personality inventories.

The ESD is based on the conceptualization that a socially desirable response is a true response to any item with a high social desirability scale value (as assigned by judges) and a false response to any item with a low social desirability scale value. The ESD has been constructed in terms of this definition of SD responding. It consists of 39 items drawn from the MMPI with nine true-keyed items of high social desirability scale value, and 30 false-keyed items of low social desirability scale value. Edwards' approach to SD research is essentially an item-bound one; it concerns itself with the scale-value of items along a judged Social Desirability dimension.

Another approach to SD research is represented by Crowne &

Marlowe (Ref. 3), who have contrasted the purely psychometric analysis of SD with the investigation of a subject's motivation to respond in the socially desirable direction, and the extent to which this behaviour generalizes to nontest situations. They have interpreted SD responding as a reflection of a subject's need for social approval. In an extensive series of studies, they have demonstrated that SD responding in testing situations can be predictive of a subject's conforming, approval-seeking behaviour in a wide range of nontest situations. They have criticized the ESD as a measure of social desirability on the grounds that it is contaminated by psychopathological item content. That Edwards has demonstrated consistently high correlations between the ESD and MMPI Scales may be due to the effects of SD upon endorsement of items in the latter, or simply be due to the psychopathology in both scales. It is not possible to sort out SD response bias from genuine endorsement of symptomatology. Crowne & Marlowe have developed an SD scale (MC-SD) that is supposedly free of pathological item content and is based on a generalized motivational interpretation of SD responding (Ref. 2). They consider that the MC-SC reflects more than SD response bias; it is a measure of the personality trait need-for-approval. Martin & Stanley have emphasized that SD seems to be a common factor in effective pathological scales and that it may be requisite of such scales (Ref. 14).

Heilbrun has reviewed the whole issue of SD and psychopathology and has proposed that psychological health and social desirability are 'in large measure' one and the same thing (Ref. 12). '... it becomes important to distinguish between the tendency to behave in socially desirable ways, which must be mirrored in test performance to the extent veridical self-appraisal is achieved and the tendency to respond to test items without regard to fact but only with regard to the social appearance which the person wishes to create by his test performance' (Ref. 12, p. 385). Block distinguished between a facade or superficial brand of socially desirable behaviour and socially desirable behaviour that is a correlate of adjustment (Ref. 1). Heilbrun identified Block's first type as a 'fake good' set and the second as a basic product of social learning.

In an early study (Ref. 11), Heilbrun demonstrated that the more socially undesirable were the keyed responses on any MMPI scale, the better that scale was at differentiating psychologically disturbed Ss from normal ones. 'Since the pathological groups invariably received the higher scale scores, it follows that they were endorsing the keyed, socially undesirable and psychopathological behaviour more frequently. There-fore, the more socially undesirable the behaviour endorsed by an individual, the more likely he will evidence a manifest psychological disturbance' (Ref. 12, p. 384).

On the basis of the above discussion, one might consider SD respond-ing and the Extraversion and Neuroticism Scales as follows. Any correlations between SD Scales and N Scales could be due to shared psychopathological item content, or essential SD variance reflecting the respondent's adjustment to social and cultural norms and, therefore, his learning history. From Crowne & Marlowes' analysis (Ref. 12), it would be expected that ESD and N correlations would largely be a product of similarity of pathological-type content. But correlations between their scale (MC-SD) and the N Scale would be interpreted as reflecting the presence or absence of socially conditioned, approval-motivated traits (indicative of positive adjustment) along the neuroticism dimension. The latter relationship would seem to represent Heilbrun's equation of psychological health and Social Desirability. To the extent that an ESD and N correlation might reflect the operation of at least both reasons outlined above, the ESD would be expected to have a higher negative correlation with the N Scale than would the MC-SD. The MC-SD would, in effect, be controlling for that confounding due to similarity of pathological item content.

As there is no psychopathological item content in the EPI-E Scale and Martin & Stanley found no relationship between their SD Scale and the MPI-E, it was expected that no significant correlation would be found between the EPI-E and ESD. Where the MC-SD is concerned, as it seems to refer less to the SD characteristics of questionnaire items and more to a socialized, conforming, approval-motivated characteristic of personality, it is conceivable on the basis of the personality-behaviour theory of Eysenck (Ref. 5) that, to the extent that the extravert is less socially conditioned than the introvert, he will respond less in the approval-motivated direction. That is, the EPI-E would correlate negatively with the MC-SD. The stronger social conditioning of the introvert would be reflected in his endorsement of socially desirable items as contained in the MC-SD. Using the same learning-conditioning analysis, a negative correlation would be expected between the N Scale and MC-SD. This would represent the neurotic's endorsement of socially undesirable items as simply one part of his maladaptive (asocial) behaviour pattern; he is reflecting a history of maladjustive learning.

METHOD

One hundred male subjects were used. Sixty-eight of these were apprentices at a large motor works near London and the remaining 32 were paid volunteers taking part in a number of experiments at the Institute of Psychiatry, University of London. These latter subjects were largely drawn from Civil Service occupations in the greater London area. In conjunction with other studies, the subjects were administered Form A of the EPI, the Edwards' 39-item SD Scale and the Marlowe-Crowne 33-item SD Scale. The EPI was scored for E, N and L.

RESULTS AND DISCUSSION

Product-moment correlations were computed between the SD Scales and the EPI Scales. These correlations were as follows: ESD-Extraversion, $r = 0 \cdot 133$; ESD-Neuroticism, $r = -0 \cdot 603$ ($p < 0 \cdot 01$); ESD-Lie, $r = 0 \cdot 069$; MC-SD-Extraversion, $r = -0 \cdot 218$ ($p < 0 \cdot 05$); MC-SD-Neuroticism, $r = -0 \cdot 299$ ($p < 0 \cdot 01$); and MC-SD-Lie, $r = 0 \cdot 554$ ($p < 0 \cdot 01$).

It can be seen that, with 98 df, the ESD correlates significantly only with the N Scale, but the MC-SD correlates significantly with all EPI Scales.

It should be noted here that of the 33 items comprising the MC-SD, 18 are keyed true and 15 false, so that an interpretation of MC-SD correlations in terms of an acquiescence response set is highly improbable. This may not be asserted with confidence where the ESD is concerned, as this scale contains nine items keyed true and 30 items keyed false. Hand & Brazzell (Ref. 10) have reported data suggesting that the ESD does, and the MC-SD does not, harbour acquiescence variance.

Where the correlations between extraversion and the SD Scales are concerned, the lack of a significant correlation between the E Scale and the ESD clearly suggests that the E Scale is free of SD variance in the symptomological sense. This suggestion is reinforced by the high negative correlation between the N Scale and the ESD. The very considerable drop in the magnitude of correlation between the N Scale and the MC-SD, coupled with the lack of correlation between E and ESD, strongly suggests that the ESD is contaminated to a considerable extent with psychopathological item content and that correlations between the ESD and pathological scales cannot be interpreted as necessarily reflecting SD variance in the latter.

The negative correlation of the E Scale with the MC-SD is in accord with a social conditioning analysis of extraversion and suggests that points of contact may be made between Eysenck's personality theory and recent work on approval motivation (Ref. 3). As the correlation of E and MC-SD is low but of particular interest where the theoretical analysis of SD responding is concerned, replication of this relationship seemed desirable. Accordingly a further 58 male apprentices were administered the E Scale and MC-SD. In this replication the correlation was -0.38 ($p<0.01$). It is apparent that the correlation has held up, and indeed is much higher.

The correlations between the N Scale and the ESD and MC-SD are in line with the considerations advanced earlier; the correlation of -0.603 between N and ESD most likely reflects similarity of pathological item content; the correlation of -0.299 between N and MC-SD most likely mirrors essential 'adjustive' SD variance (the learning analysis) and may possibly also reflect a slight degree of pathological content in the MC-SD (Ref. 13).

The 0.069 correlation between the EPI-L and ESD is somewhat lower than the usual insignificant, positive correlations between the ESD and Lic Scales as reported in the literature (Ref. 3) and strongly suggests that the ESD is not unambiguously measuring an individual's tendency to describe himself in a socially desirable light. That the EPI-L is largely an SD measure has been demonstrated by Eysenck & Eysenck (Ref. 8) employing a preliminary form of that scale. The correlation of 0.554 between the EPI-L and MC-SD is virtually identical with the correlation between the MMPI-L Scale and MC-SD of 0.54 reported by Crowne & Marlowe (Ref. 3) for a sample of 37 male and female American college students and with the 0.57 correlation between the MC-SD and the Lie Scale of the Maudsley Personality Inventory found by Farley (Ref. 9) for a sample of 70 male Canadian university students and the unpublished correlation of 0.49 between the MC-SD and the MPI-L Scale found by the writer for 30 male and female Canadian introductory psychology students.

SUMMARY

On the hypotheses that introverts socially condition more strongly than extraverts and should therefore emit more socially desirable (SD) responses than extraverts, and that Ss high in neuroticism (N) should endorse fewer SD responses than low N Ss as a reflection of the neurotic's maladaptive learning history, measures of extraversion (E) and N (Eysenck Personality Inventory) were correlated on 100 male English Ss with two measures of SD responding (Edwards SD Scale and Marlow-Crowne SD Scale). In line with expectation, both E and N were significantly negatively associated with SD responding. There was, however, no significant relationship between E and the Edwards Scale. The magnitude of the relationships between SD and each of the personality dimensions was highly dependent on the SD measures employed and was consistent with theoretical analyses of these measures.

REFERENCES

1. BLOCK, J., Some differences between the concepts of social desirability and adjustment. *J. consult. Psychol.*, **26**, 527–530, 1962.
2. CROWNE, D. P. & MARLOWE, D., A new scale of social desirability independent of psychopathology. *J. consult. Psychol.*, **24**, 349–354, 1960.
3. ——, *The Approval Motive: Studies in Evaluative Dependence.* New York: Wiley & Sons, 1964.
4. EDWARDS, A. L., *The Social Desirability Variable in Personality Assessment and Research.* New York: Dryden, 1957.
5. EYSENCK, H. J., *The Dynamics of Anxiety and Hysteria.* London: Routledge & Kegan Paul, 1957.
6. ——, *Manual of the Maudsley Personality Inventory.* London: Univ. of London Press, 1959.
7. —— & EYSENCK, S. B. G., *Manual of the Eysenck Personality Inventory.* London: Univ. of London Press, 1964.
8. EYSENCK, S. B. G. & EYSENCK, H. J. An experimental investigation of desirability response set in a personality questionnaire. *Life Sci.*, **5**, 343–355, 1963.
9. FARLEY, F. H., Global Self-ratings, the Independence of Questionnaire Drive and Anxiety and Social Desirability Variance. Unpublished manuscript, Institute of Psychiatry Library, University of London, 1965.
10. HAND, J. & BRAZZELL, C. O., Contamination in measures of acquiescence and social desirability. *Psychol. Rep.*, **16**, 759–760, 1965.
11. HEILBRUN, A. B., Revision of the MMPI K correction procedure for improved detection of maladjustment in a normal population. *J. consult. Psychol.*, **27**, 161–165, 1963.

12. ——, Social-learning theory, social desirability and the MMPI. *Psychol. Bull.*, **61**, 377–387, 1964.
13. KATKIN, E. S., The Marlowe-Crowne social desirability scale: independent of psychopathology? *Psychol. Rep.*, **15**, 703–706, 1964.
14. MARTIN, J. & STANLEY, G., Social desirability and the Maudsley Personality Inventory. *Acta Psychol.*, **21**, 260–264, 1963.

17

Extraversion and Judgments of Social Desirability[1]

JEAN-MARIE LEMAINE

First published in *Bulletin de Psychologie*, **19**, 419–426, 1965

INTRODUCTION

SOCIAL desirability, both as a term and as an area of psychological research, originated with the Minnesota Multiphasic Personality Inventory (MMPI). A. L. Edwards has hypothesized that the responses of normal subjects to the MMPI are more likely to reflect what is socially acceptable or desirable than true judgments (Ref. 2). I shall not develop this point here as I have described the statistical evidence underlying this hypothesis elsewhere (Ref. 4). In an attempt to circumvent the methodological problems raised by the social desirability tendency, Edwards has developed a special measuring instrument. This instrument, which is itself open to methodological criticism, comprises 30 statements taken from the MMPI and which are unambiguous with regard to the social desirability of the traits or behaviours they describe—the ambiguity of a statement being operationally defined in terms of the dispersion of the desirability judgments given by the respondents. The tendency of a person to reply in a socially desirable manner is measured by the number of statements on the scale which he selects as describing himself.

However, the work on social desirability cannot be restricted to the social desirability measure. There are other fundamental aspects of the problem as the work of E. L. Cowen and his colleagues at the University of Rochester suggests. The special interest of the Rochester research lies in the fact that it is not limited to measuring the social desirability tendency *per se* but is concerned with the actual nature and content of what is regarded as socially desirable. While the Rochester research emphasizes the similarities of social desirability values among different groups of judges, it is also concerned with intergroup differences with regard to these values. The mean levels of the values attributed to different characteristics on a scale of estimation are, for the most part, a function of the *dispersion* of judgments which of course is the same as the lack of agreement between judges in a given group.

[1] Translated by A. and J. Basilevitch & R. Cooper.

PROBLEMS AND HYPOTHESES

The foregoing historical account has highlighted the problem of differences in judgments as a result of the desirability of personal characteristics. The differences are indicated principally by the dispersion of judgments which form two quite different series originating from two different groups of judges. The present paper offers some hypotheses to explain such data.

As the proposed personal characteristics (see Table 1) referred to social behaviour, it seemed that a socially-oriented personality variable such as extraversion would influence social desirability judgments. In particular this influence would affect (1) the estimation means and (2) the dispersion estimations. In other words, if we were dealing with two groups, one introverted and one extraverted, we could hypothesize as follows:

1. the estimation means of the desirability of the proposed characteristics will not necessarily be the same in the group of extraverts as in the group of introverts;
2. the indices of agreement between the judges will not necessarily be the same in the group of introverts and in the group of extraverts.

The first hypothesis will not be examined in detail. It would be wrong to expect that the simple difference in social behaviour of extraverts and introverts would be reflected in their estimates of characteristics presented to them in a testing situation (see Table 5). However, it seemed to me that the second hypothesis could be more precisely framed inasmuch as one could postulate (1) the existence of a social norm and (2) the existence of a predisposition to perceive this norm, which would depend upon the personality.

As described by Eysenck, extraverts are characterized by a strong desire for contact with other people. (According to Eysenck, the concept of extraversion is conceptually bound up with the general idea of 'sociability'.) In respect of the present study, it is felt that extraverts, because of their marked sociability, are likely to have acquired a conceptual and practical knowledge of the social norm whereas this knowledge would be lacking in introverts. In particular, perception of the norm by introverts would be more uncertain and would be more open to different interpretations which would be reflected in greater variability of judgments.

In order to study this problem we need to define: (1) the measure of extraversion, (2) the conditions in which the social norm operates and (3) the experimental material and measure of the dependent variable.

THE EXPERIMENT

(1) *The Measure of Extraversion*

Hans J. Eysenck has developed a questionnaire to measure extraversion and neuroticism. I have extracted 40 questions from the most recent version of the test (Ref. 3)—20 of these questions relate to extraversion, according to criteria I have discussed elsewhere (Ref. 5). A factor analysis of the replies to these questions produced four factors, two of which could be identified with Eysenck's extraversion factor. Of the two factors, one consisted of 11 questions (an 'expansiveness' or 'sociability' scale) and the other of 6 questions (with loadings of at least 0·40) representing an 'optimism' scale.

The questionnaire was administered to 180 subjects of both sexes (students of the Sorbonne and the School of Applied Psychology) at the same time as a list of characteristics on which they had to make desirability preferences. From the distribution of scores on the 'sociability' and 'optimism' scales, subjects were classified as 'most sociable' and 'least sociable', 'most optimistic' and 'least optimistic'. Those subjects who fell in the 'most sociable' *and* 'most optimistic' categories were defined as extraverts, while the 'least sociable' *and* the 'least optimistic' subjects were defined as introverts (the 'sociability' and 'optimism' scales correlated at approximately 0·40). This process left 82 subjects (all females) for the experiment, of whom 46 were introverts and 36 were extraverts.

(2) *The Conditions*

Subjects were allocated on a random basis to the following three conditions:

Condition No. 1. Please indicate how far each characteristic is considered socially desirable by people of your age and sex. (This instruction was intended to bring a social norm into operation.)

Condition No. 2. Please indicate how far each characteristic is desirable from your personal point of view,

whether, having this characteristic, you would be satisfied with it; whether, not having the characteristic, you feel you would be better off with it.

Condition No. 3. Please indicate the extent to which you personally would like to see each characteristic in people of your age and sex whom you meet every day.

On completion of the questionnaire booklets, it was found that there were unequal numbers of subjects in the two personality categories, i.e., introversion, extraversion. In Condition 1 there were 10 introverts and 11 extraverts; in Condition 2, 18 introverts and 14 extraverts; and in Condition 3, 18 introverts and 11 extraverts. However, these unequal numbers are unlikely to affect the hypothesis which is concerned largely with within-group dispersions and not, for example, with mean levels of judgment.

(3) *The Experimental Material and Measure of the Dependent Variable*

The purpose of the study was to analyse the dispersion of 'social desirability' judgments as a function both of personality and the ability of situations (conditions) to activate a social norm in the individual. The list of 56 characteristics evaluated by the subjects is shown at Table 1. A rating scale consisting of 5 points (1, most desirable; 5, most undesirable) was used by the subjects in making their judgments.

TABLE 1

LIST OF CHARACTERISTICS PRESENTED TO SUBJECTS

To have varied interests
To respect normal conventions

To be easily dominated
To be kind to others
To control one's impulses and to be able to refuse personal pleasures
To be capable of friendship
To be relaxed

To have an expressive face and/or hands
To give priority to intellectual values and knowledge
Not to be self-satisfied
To set high standards for oneself
To be conciliatory
To converse easily with strangers
To be readily accepted as a confidant
To please people of the opposite sex
To know how to speak well on many subjects
To be someone who gives his time etc. to other people

To like experiences which bring the senses and feelings into play (e.g., to touch, to taste, to be in physical contact with others etc.)

To have a clear mind
To agree with other people's ideas and expectations
To take pleasure in exercising power
To be amusing in company
To be on familiar terms with people

To like gambling
To be natural and unaffected in one's speech
To be very intelligent
To make others want to protect you

To feel guilty easily
To be a non-conformer
To be very interested in the opposite sex
To like giving advice
To express moral rights and wrongs

TABLE 1 *continued*

To be protective towards relatives and close friends	To avoid limited social relationships
	To be charming
To have a sense of humour	To prefer a small number of friends
To act quickly	rather than many acquaintances
	To like to associate with other people
To let yourself daydream	without necessarily having a specific
To prefer not putting off the satisfaction	purpose
of your desires and wishes	To seek the opinions of others
To like to argue with others	To be interested in other people's
	reasons for behaving
To believe in declarations of friendship	To be advised
To prefer solitude	To stick to your own opinions
To appreciate what gives pleasure to	
others	To say things without regard to other
To be objective about oneself	people's feelings
To seek reassurance from others	To make your own way in life
To be able to accept other people's	To have no routine
criticisms of you	To take things as they come in life

We have therefore 6 groups of judges (2 types of judges, 3 conditions). Each of the characteristics shown to the subjects will be assigned an index of disagreement among the judges in each of the 6 groups; this disagreement index will represent the dispersion of the individual estimations in each group. In all, we will have to deal with 336 indices of disagreement (6 groups, 56 characteristics).

According to our hypothesis, the disagreement will be stronger for the introverts, particularly so in Condition 1; in other words, while we may not necessarily expect a major effect of personality or of condition on the disagreements among the desirability judgments, we would certainly expect an interaction between the condition *and* the personality—the variability attributable to the characteristics themselves being held constant.

RESULTS

The data of Table 2 show that the hypothesis is not verified. There is no interaction between personality and condition; only a major effect of personality ($p < 0.01$)—the dispersion of introverts' judgments (independently of the characteristics themselves and of conditions) being greater than that of the extraverts' judgments.

TABLE 2

INDICES OF DISAGREEMENT FOR THE DESIRABILITY OF PERSONAL CHARACTERISTICS
AS A FUNCTION OF THE CHARACTERISTICS THEMSELVES, SITUATIONAL CONDITIONS
AND SUBJECT'S PERSONALITY TYPE (INTROVERSION-EXTRAVERSION)

Source of variation	df	Sum of squares	Means of squares	F	P
Total	335	11463·00			
I. Between characteristics (Ch)	55	5249·17	95·44	4·30	<0·01
II. Within characteristics	280	6213·83			
A. Between groups (G)	5	473·77			
(a) Conditions (C)	2	100·76	50·38	2·41	
(b) Personality (P)	1	354·24	354·24	16·97	<0·01
(c) C×P	2	18·77	9·38	0·45	
B. Error (Ch×G)	275	5740·06	20·89		
(a) Ch×C	110	2006·57	18·24	0·97	
(b) Ch×P	55	1665·59	30·28	1·61	<0·05
(c) Ch×C×P	110	2067·90	18·80		

Means of disagreement in the different groups

	Condition 1	Condition 2	Condition 3
Introverts	0·99	1·01	0·94
Extraverts	0·91	0·88	0·84

TABLE 3

INDICES OF DISAGREEMENT FOR THE DESIRABILITY OF PERSONAL CHARACTERISTICS
AS A FUNCTION OF THE CHARACTERISTICS THEMSELVES, SITUATIONAL CONDITIONS
AND SUBJECT'S PERSONALITY TYPE (STABILITY-INSTABILITY)

Source of variation	df	Sum of squares	Means of squares	F	P
Total	335	9081·81			
I. Between characteristics (Ch)	55	5278·14	95·97	7·97	<0·01
II. Within characteristics	280	3803·67	13·58		
A. Between groups (G)	5	112·38			
(a) Conditions (C)	2	54·86	27·43	2·04	
(b) Personality (P)	1	50·30	50·30	3·75	
(c) C×P	2	7·22	3·61	0·27	
B. Error (Ch×G)	275	3691·29	13·42		

Table 5 shows a number of characteristics which produced differences in mean desirability estimations between introverts and extraverts. I have only retained those results for which the mean estimations were of the same side (whether desirable or undesirable) of the neutral point of the scale, i.e., a scale value of 3. We can assume that if a mean is nearer 3, then its dispersion will be greater. From this assumption we can make ten specific predictions in relation to the data of Table 5: that in 6 cases the introverts' estimations must have the larger dispersions and that in the other 4 cases the extraverts' estimations will have the larger dispersions. If we calculate the differences of dispersion in the predicted direction for all ten cases (I-E if predicted I E and E-I if we predicted E I), we find that the mean of these differences is not significantly greater than zero (t's of $1 \cdot 58$, $1 \cdot 01$ and $1 \cdot 49$ for Conditions 1, 2 and 3 respectively). But if we consider only the predictions I E, the same operation, in spite of the reduced degrees of freedom, gives us t values which enable us to reject the hypothesis of no difference ($4 \cdot 07$ for Condition 1, $p < 0 \cdot 01$; for Condition 2, $p < 0 \cdot 02$; $2 \cdot 34$ for Condition 3, $p < 0 \cdot 10$).

Disagreement and Emotional Instability

Representative items, with their factor loadings, of the Stability-Instability scale are:

—Do you often have the feeling that you are missing something in life? ($0 \cdot 45$)
—Do you sometimes feel happy, sometimes depressed for no apparent reason? ($0 \cdot 75$)
—Do you sometimes feel full of energy, sometimes lifeless? ($0 \cdot 44$)
—Are you moody? ($0 \cdot 66$)
—Do you sometimes feel very unhappy for no reason? ($0 \cdot 75$)
—Do you frequently have highs and lows in mood without any apparent cause? ($0 \cdot 89$)
—Do you sometimes feel apathetic and tired for no apparent reason? ($0 \cdot 72$)

Table 3 shows that the only significant variation in desirability disagreements concerns the characteristics to be judged. The Stability-Instability of the judges produces no significant effect. However, the data of Table 3 do at least suggest a greater (though not significant) variability in each of the experimental conditions for the unstable subjects.

Disagreement and Extraversion

We should also note that the *differences* in judgment variability as a function of extraversion-introversion are quite independent of the methods that subjects use to anchor their judgments on the scale of desirability. Subjects normally respond to the scale in two ways:

1. they tend to choose a mean which is either more socially desirable or more socially undesirable, and
2. they tend to use the extremes of the scale (values 1 and 5) irrespective of the desirability or undesirability of the actual items.

TABLE 4

MEAN EXTREMISM LEVELS OF (A) FAVOURABLE AND (B) UNFAVOURABLE ESTIMATES AS A FUNCTION OF THE EXPERIMENTAL CONDITION AND SUBJECTS' INTROVERSION-EXTRAVERSION, TOGETHER WITH EXTREMISM DIFFERENCES AS A FUNCTION OF PERSONALITY

| | Extremes in favour | | Extremes in disfavour | |
	Introversion	Extraversion	Introversion	Extraversion
Condition 1	0·459	0·412	0·394	0·395
Condition 2	0·435	0·534*	0·245	0·385†
Condition 3	0·434	0·384	0·355	0·284

* $p < 0.08$
† $p < 0.04$

The first tendency produces inter-individual differences which are not necessarily related to the personality characteristics being investigated here. While the second tendency is not usually as strongly expressed as the first, it is still sufficiently marked to be taken into consideration.

Before discussing the independence between the disagreement in a group and the extremism of its member's estimations, it is necessary to describe how the indices of extreme responses have been calculated. For every subject there were two indices of extreme response: one for extreme responses in favour and the other for extreme responses not favoured. It was hypothesized that a general factor of extreme response did not exist. (In fact, it was eventually found that the Bravais-Pearson coefficient, expressing the correlation between the two indices of extreme response, rose to $0·58$ for the introverts and to $0·46$ for the extraverts). The neutral value of 3 being excluded, there were for each subject two groups of figures: the favourables (1 and 2) and the unfavourables (4 and 5). The ratio of the number of scale values, 1, to the number of scale

TABLE 5

DIFFERENCES IN 'DESIRABILITY' MEANS AS A FUNCTION OF SUBJECTS' PERSONALITIES (INTROVERSION-EXTRAVERSION) (N.B. A HIGHER MEAN INDICATES THAT THE CHARACTERISTIC IS LESS DESIRED)

Characteristics	Extraverts	Introverts	χ^2	Degrees of freedom
To be amusing in company	1·67	2·52	17·21*	2
Interest in the opposite sex	2·33	3·00	12·70*	ditto
To be admired	1·89	2·59	11·93*	ditto
To be charming	1·25	1·80	10·68*	ditto
To like sensual experiences	2·56	3·30	10·02*	ditto
To have a clear mind	2·14	1·63	8·98†	ditto
To be objective about oneself	3·75	3·35	7·14†	ditto
To take pleasure in power	2·81	3·37	6·84†	ditto
To make your own way in life	1·33	1·80	6·47†	1
To take things as they come	3·39	4·02	6·41†	2
To like solitude	2·97	2·39	5·10‡	ditto
To stick to own opinions	2·25	1·96	4·69‡	ditto

Differences obtained for the Stability-Instability factor

	Stable	Unstable		
To prefer a small number of friends	1·77	1·67	6·67†	2
To have no routine	3·46	2·93	5·25†	

* p<0·01   † p<0·05   ‡ p<0·10

TABLE 6

DIFFERENCES IN 'DESIRABILITY' MEANS AS A FUNCTION OF CONDITIONS SUBJECTS BEING INTROVERTED OR EXTRAVERTED

Characteristics	Conditions 1	2	3	χ^2
To be admired	2·24	2·13	3·32	(2 df)
To like giving advice	3·76	3·25	4·04	15·98*
To give priority to intellectual values	2·38	2·56	3·25	11·84*
To like to exercise power	3·09	3·13	3·64	9·67*
To make others want to protect you	3·62	3·09	4·07	8·32†
To be protective to others	2·48	1·70	2·50	8·15†
To avoid limited social relationships	2·67	3·34	3·64	7·30†
To be capable of friendship	1·05	1·28	1·38	5·46‡

* p<0·01   † p<0·05   ‡ p<0·10

values 1 and 2 and the ratio of the number of scale values 5 to the number of scale values 4 and 5 were the indices of extreme response.

From Table 4 we can see that, compared to the extraverts, the introverts' extreme responses are more marked in Conditions 1 and 3 and less marked in Condition 2, while the introverts' estimations variability is always greater than that of the extraverts.

DISCUSSION

Conditions and Systems of Reference

That the original hypothesis has not been verified does not appear to be the fault of the experimental conditions. In fact, looking at Table 6 we can see that the extent of the differences reflected in the indices of desirability of the different conditions are quite considerable and are not due to chance.

How did we obtain the results given in Table 6? For each characteristic evaluated by the judges there is a mean index in each group, defined by the condition and the personality. For each type of judge, these mean indices allow us to arrange the conditions according to the mean index of desirability which characterizes them. When this order is exactly the same for the introverts and the extraverts, it is assumed that a systematic difference of degree exists. The estimations of introverts and extraverts are then combined and, because the distributions of these estimations take different forms and are often non-parametric, we apply a median test with two degrees of freedom.

The only significant differences concern the following items:

I like to be admired (Condition 2) and do not like to see admiration expressed for someone else (Condition 3).

I personally do not care to give advice (Condition 2); I don't at all like those who give advice (Condition 3).

Both introvert and extravert groups value intelligence and knowledge (Condition 1); I do not care for people who value intelligence very highly (Condition 3).

I dislike the idea of personally exercising power (Conditions 1 and 2) and I dislike even more those people who enjoy exercising it (Condition 3).

I personally do not care for making other people act towards me in a protective way (Condition 2) and dislike people who wish to be protected in this way (Condition 3).

I want to act in a protective way towards others (Condition 2); I am not unduly influenced by those who display a protective attitude (Condition 3).

People say that it is nice to possess the ability to create friendship (Condition 1) but it is not so nice to be with people who have this ability (Condition 3).

As children, it was impressed on us that superficial social relationships were to be avoided (Condition 1) but I personally dislike people who avoid superficial relations with me (Condition 3).

The conditions have therefore been successful in creating reference systems. However, 'reference system' suggests that differences in norms operate in a special way. Obviously there can be 'more of a norm' with one system of reference than another. More likely we shall find that different reference systems are subject to different constraints. Do we possess the date which will permit us to study the distribution of constraints associated with relatively different characteristics, as a function of the conditions used in the experiment?

Personality, Conditions and Distributions of the Indices of Constraint

The indices used for the verification of the hypotheses are, in Thurstonian terms, indices of ambiguity. A characteristic for which the desirability or undesirability is ambiguous is apparently a characteristic for which no norm of desirability exists. However, the desirability of a characteristic is probably better described as having relative ambiguity. Let us assume for practical purposes that the ambiguity of a characteristic can vary with the reference system and therefore with the condition that activates the desirability reference system. In the situation represented by the condition there exists for *one characteristic* (trait or particular behaviour) a particular norm which serves to constrain behaviour in one way or another. Consequently, in respect of a group of characteristics, there will be a structure of ambiguities which applies to a particular situation or even to all situations. What can we say about the way in which the constraints vary as a function of the present experimental situations which were created by combining condition and personality?

From the results already described we can see that in general terms the characteristics do form a hierarchy as a function of their ambiguity: the reliability of the disagreement indices, independently of the experimental situations, can be considered as having highly significant F values (see Tables 2 and 3). These highly significant indices, however, only correspond to reliability coefficients of 0·35 and 0·50 (values which are statistically equivalent). In other words, it is highly likely that one factor alone cannot produce the intercorrelations observable between the series of disagreement indices reflecting the ambiguity characteristic to the six groups in the experiment.

TABLE 7

STRUCTURE OF AGREEMENT ACCORDING TO PERSONALITY TYPES AND EXPERIMENTAL
CONDITIONS (EXTRAVERTED SUBJECTS = E; INTROVERTED SUBJECTS = I; E–1 FOR
EXAMPLE, REFERS TO EXTRAVERTED SUBJECTS IN CONDITION 1, ETC.); CORRELATIONS
ARE BETWEEN THE DISAGREEMENT ENCOUNTERED IN THE DIFFERENT GROUPS

| | INTERCORRELATIONS | | | | | LOADINGS | |
	E–2	E–3	1–1	1–2	1–3	General factor	Bipolar factor
E–1	0·46	0·52	0·25	0·24	0·34	0·58	0·24
E–2		0·38	0·50	0·35	0·46	0·78	0·06
E–3			0·38	0·19	0·40	0·73	0·40
1–1				0·24	0·34	0·58	−0·13
1–2					0·34	0·40	−0·07
1–3						0·74	−0·50

I have therefore calculated the correlations between the indices of ambiguity of the characteristics presented to each group, the group being defined by combining condition and personality. The results of these calculations, together with the results of a factor analysis, can be seen at Table 7. Factor rotation produces two oblique factors of extraversion and introversion but since their correlation is greater than 0·70 I preferred to work with the two gross factors which showed up more clearly. The first factor expresses the generality in the system of constraints, the norm being more potent for certain characteristics than for others, irrespective of the subject's personality and the condition to which he may have been exposed. The unequal values of the loadings follow no systematic pattern and can be easily explained by the relatively small number of characteristics taken into consideration ($N = 56$). This first factor accounts for 42 per cent of the variance. The second bipolar factor is far less important than the first (8·2 per cent of the variance); in fact the disposition of the signs and the numerical values of the loadings produces a factor which overall is of minimal significance. Firstly, the loadings of the introvert groups and those of the extravert groups have opposite signs (from Table 2 we can see that the interaction between items and personality is appreciably more marked than the second-order interaction). Secondly, the highest loading of either sign belongs to the series of Condition 3 (that which is desirable to find in others) and the lowest loading in the series of Condition 2 (that which is desirable to have oneself) and the intermediate position being occupied by the series of Condition 1 (that which the group of pairs is supposed to think about what is desirable or undesirable). The conditions, therefore, appear to combine with differential *norm structures* rather than simple scalar differences in norms (i.e., the existence of more or less of a norm).

The two principal results of this study can be stated as follows:

1. introverts, when compared with extraverts, experience more ambiguity and less cognitive constraint when they have to judge the desirability of certain behavioural characteristics, irrespective of experimental conditions;

2. there is an interaction between the experimental condition and the personality, unrelated to the level of ambiguity but related to the order of the ambiguities.

Conclusions and Future Implications

The initial hypothesis of this study has of course not been supported—probably because of the problems introduced with the concepts of norm and reference system. Although the overall results are somewhat complex and are not amenable to a simple, straightforward interpretation, they do nevertheless provide a number of points worthy of further discussion.

We have at least established that introverts agree with each other less often than do extraverts. With respect to the estimation operations required of them, this indicates that the extraverts are more likely than the introverts. In other words, if we factor analyse the correlations between subjects, the group of extraverts, when compared to the introverts, will have substantially higher loadings on the first factor (which is undoubtedly the most important). As a general finding this probably does not really extend our knowledge—to do this it is necessary to examine in detail the most utilized items relating to the initial hypothesis.

In the initial hypothesis we introduced the idea of social contact as in intervening variable accounting for an additional, unobserved variable— accuracy in perceiving the norm. It was then argued, in probability as distinct from causal terms, that extraverts should have a more regular and more active participation in social life than introverts. However, it is also worth pointing out that the exigencies of everyday life and other environmental demands can on occasion force an introvert into regular social intercourse and into a knowledge of the accepted norms and customs.

Since we have seen that the reference system is quite unrelated to the differences between introverts and extraverts, any future work must look at the relationship between introversion-extraversion and social parti- cipation (depending of course on the availability of a measuring instrument for the latter). In order to check that an individual's percep- tion does differ from the norm, the factor loadings of introverts with little social experience must be smaller than those of introverts with a great deal of social experience and, in turn, extraverts must have still higher loadings.

REFERENCES

1. COWEN, E. L., La variable désirabilité sociale dans l'étude de la personnalité, *Psychol. franc*, **8,** 1–15, 1963.
2. EDWARDS, A. L., *The Social Desirability Variable in Personality Assessment and Research*, New York: Dryden, 1957.
3. EYSENCK, S. B. G. & EYSENCK, H. J., The validity of questionnaire and rating assessments of extraversion and neuroticism and their factorial stability. *Brit. J. Psychol.*, **54,** 51–62, 1966.
4. LEMAINE, J. M., Dix ans de recherche sur la désirabilité sociale. *Ann. Psychol.*, **65,** 117–130, 1965.
5. ——, Extraversion et nevrosisme. *Bull. Psychol.*, **19,** 13–15, 1966.

18

Desirability Response Set in Children

SYBIL B. G. EYSENCK, I. A. SYED & H. J. EYSENCK

First published in
British Journal of Educational Psychology, **36**, 87–90, 1966

THE JUNIOR form of the Eysenck Personality Inventory, measuring extraversion, neuroticism and tendency to lie, was administered to two groups of children totalling 575, both boys and girls, ranging in age from 11–15. Children in the control group were tested and retested under identical instructions; children in the experimental group were tested under standard instructions but retested under instructions to 'fake good'. As predicted there were highly significant changes in the experimental group towards greater lying and less neuroticism; there were no changes in extraversion as compared to the control group. Test/retest reliability in the experimental, as compared with the control group, was slightly lower for extraversion, considerably lower for neuroticism and very much lower for the lie scale. The results were interpreted as giving evidence that social desirability response set was unlikely to have accounted for more than a small portion of the variance in the original test scores.

INTRODUCTION

There has been much argument in recent years about the possibility of response sets or response styles affecting results obtained by use of questionnaires. Rorer has discussed this evidence at great length (Ref. 6) and has come to the conclusion that 'the data accumulated to date must be interpreted as indicating that response styles are of no more than trivial importance in determining responses to personality, interest and attitude inventories'. This conclusion is very similar to that arrived at independently with respect to the M.P.I. and E.P.I. by Eysenck & Eysenck (Refs. 3, 4 and 5) and by Eysenck (Ref. 1). The recent publication of a junior form of the E.P.I. (Ref. 2) suggested the desirability of investigating the possibility that response sets might be more powerful in the case of children whose responses do not seem to have been studied in detail in this connection. The present study is, therefore, concerned with a test of the hypothesis that the so-called 'desirability' response set is of little importance in connection with the answers given by children on the Junior E.P.I.

This questionnaire contains 24 questions relating to extraversion, 24 questions relating to neuroticism and 12 questions which form a lie scale, the purpose of which is to detect faking on the part of the subjects. The scales are reliable and norms are available for quite large age and sex groups. Full information on the test is given in the manual (Ref. 2).

For the purpose of this test ten groups of children altogether were tested, divided into age groups (11–15 years, inclusive), as well as into sex groups. 289 children were given the test and were then retested within one month, instructions on both occasions being identical and as suggested by the manual. 286 children were given the first test in the same way but were then retested after one month with instructions to 'fake good'; the specific words used were that they 'should try to put themselves in the best light'. In essence, therefore, this experiment was a repetition of the one carried out by Eysenck & Eysenck on adults (Ref. 3) and the underlying idea was that if the original test data had been strongly influenced by social desirability response set, then the deliberate adoption of such a response set should not lead to any great change in scores. If, on the other hand, the original responses had been made without much regard to social desirability, then we would expect considerable changes in the scores of the experimental group, as compared with the control group, particularly in relation to the neuroticism and lie scales. It was not expected that the extraversion scale would be much affected as neither extraversion nor introversion is as obviously more socially desirable as is a low score on neuroticism or a high score on the lie scale.

The detailed results of the experiment are given in Tables 1 and 2. Table 1 shows the actual scores and the changes of the various groups on the three scales, as well as the test/retest correlations under straightforward test/retest conditions. Table 2 gives the same information under experimental conditions. Some of the groups are too small to make their results very convincing but the overall results are quite clear cut. With respect to extraversion, the changes in the experimental group are almost exactly as large as those in the control group, demonstrating that, as in the case of the adult sample, extraversion is not to any reasonable degree subject to conscious faking. When we turn to neuroticism the position is quite different. Changes in the control group average around 0·5,

Table 1

Control Group

	Age	n	M			M			M			Test-Retest Correlations		
			E_1	E_2	E_2-E_1	N_1	N_2	N_1-N_2	L_1	L_2	L_2-L_1	E	N	L
Girls	11	38	17·474	17·789	0·315	12·658	11·974	0·684	3·921	3·921	0	0·690	0·628	0·575
	12	32	18·656	18·906	0·250	10·500	9·281	1·219	3·312	3·000	−0·312	0·786	0·804	0·636
	13	36	17·389	18·028	0·639	11·778	10·889	0·889	3·778	3·444	−0·334	0·715	0·748	0·780
	14	27	17·296	17·926	0·630	12·148	11·926	0·222	3·444	3·444	0	0·828	0·827	0·827
	15	7	16·143	17·143	1·000	13·000	12·143	0·857	3·571	3·000	−0·571	0·902	0·891	0·811
Boys	11	42	17·643	17·429	−0·214	12·286	10·952	1·334	4·357	4·238	−0·119	0·694	0·670	0·654
	12	34	17·824	18·176	0·352	11·500	10·559	0·941	3·529	3·176	−0·353	0·603	0·755	0·782
	13	30	18·100	17·933	−0·167	11·100	10·667	0·433	3·067	3·467	0·400	0·502	0·740	0·810
	14	25	17·760	18·840	1·080	9·560	10·760	−1·200	2·120	1·440	−0·680	0·617	0·727	0·613
	15	18	18·111	18·556	0·445	8·500	7·444	1·056	2·444	2·000	−0·444	0·821	0·861	0·786
Boys and Girls	11	80	17·563	17·600	0·037	12·463	11·437	1·026	4·150	4·087	−0·063	0·688	0·655	0·627
	12	66	18·227	18·530	0·303	11·015	9·939	1·076	3·424	3·091	−0·333	0·680	0·774	0·711
	13	66	17·712	17·985	0·273	11·470	10·788	0·682	3·455	3·454	−0·001	0·595	0·743	0·781
	14	52	17·519	18·365	0·846	10·904	11·365	−0·461	2·433	2·481	0·048	0·737	0·787	0·797
	15	25	17·560	18·160	0·600	9·760	8·760	1·000	2·760	2·280	−0·480	0·841	0·872	0·799

TABLE 2

EXPERIMENTAL GROUP

	Age	n	M			M			M			Test Retest Correlations		
			E_1	E_2	E_2-E_1	N_1	N_2	N_1-N_2	L_1	L_2	L_2-L_1	E	N	L
Girls	11	18	17·111	18·111	1·000	11·500	8·278	3·222	5·222	6·944	1·722	0·742	0·529	0·681
	12	44	18·727	18·864	0·137	12·364	9·955	2·409	2·818	5·318	2·500	0·573	0·692	0·210
	13	43	18·070	19·023	0·953	12·349	7·047	5·302	2·837	7·372	4·535	0·875	0·562	0·049
	14	54	17·630	19·037	1·407	14·278	8·926	5·352	2·407	7·241	4·834	0·415	0·597	—0·093
	15	30	17·167	17·600	0·433	14·733	10·200	4·533	2·200	5·767	3·567	0·751	0·524	—0·008
Boys	11	17	18·176	18·765	0·589	10·000	10·000	0	3·471	3·647	0·176	0·362	0·804	0·552
	12	28	18·893	18·893	0	11·250	8·071	3·179	3·071	6·536	3·465	0·598	0·486	—0·332
	13	34	18·235	19·529	1·294	10·647	6·324	4·323	2·618	6·941	4·323	0·698	0·675	0·282
	14	9	17·556	18·556	1·000	9·667	5·000	4·667	2·111	8·444	6·333	—0·560	0·829	0·010
	15	9	18·889	17·889	—1·000	11·333	6·444	4·889	1·111	7·667	6·556	0·225	0·690	0·134
Boys and Girls	11	35	17·628	18·429	0·801	10·771	9·114	1·657	4·372	5·343	0·971	0·559	0·644	0·691
	12	72	18·792	18·875	0·083	11·931	9·222	2·709	2·916	5·792	2·876	0·563	0·621	—0·020
	13	77	18·143	19·246	1·103	11·597	6·728	4·869	2·740	7·182	4·442	0·782	0·604	0·150
	14	63	17·619	18·968	1·349	13·619	8·365	5·254	2·365	7·413	5·048	0·348	0·643	0·075
	15	39	17·564	17·667	0·103	13·948	9·333	4·615	1·949	6·205	4·256	0·697	0·596	—0·037

I

TABLE 3

| | Control Group | | | | Experimental Group | | |
	E	N	L	n	E	N	L	n
Boys (11–15) years	0·640	0·726	0·743	149	0·509	0·632	−0·021	97
Girls (11–15) years	0·754	0·759	0·709	140	0·635	0·516	0·151	189
Total Age and Sex	0·691	0·741	0·728	289	0·596	0·608	0·093	286

whereas in the experimental group they are some six or eight times as high. This difference is very highly significant statistically. It is interesting to note that the changes in the experimental group increase with age from 11 through 12 to 13; there is no further increase after 13. This is not an unexpected result, of course, as one might expect increasing age to bring greater sophistication with respect to knowledge of what is and is not socially desirable.

Results on the lie scale are even more impressive than those on the neuroticism scale. For the control group there is a slight tendency for the children to lie less on repetition, but for the experimental group there is a tremendous increase in lying, which again is very highly significant statistically. This increase is almost identical with that shown on the neuroticism scale but is, of course, achieved with a scale having only half as many items and must thus be regarded as being something like twice as large. Again, there is an increase in degree of change from 11 through 12 to 13 and a failure for this increase to continue beyond the age of 13.

The test/retest reliability for both conditions are given in Tables 1 and 2; they have also been calculated for the total group, boys and girls separately and also boys and girls together; these figures are given in Table 3. It will be seen that reliabilities for the extraversion scale are somewhat lower under experimental as compared to control conditions; those for neuroticism show a further lowering, while those for the lie scale become completely insignificant under experimental conditions. These results are in good accord with the changes in means reported above; although it is, of course, possible for a considerable shift in mean to occur without any change in test/retest correlation, this is unlikely to happen in practice because the added factor of 'faking good' instructions is likely to affect different children differently and, therefore, to lower test/retest correlations.

Our results will be seen to be very similar to those of the adults reported by Eysenck & Eysenck (Ref. 3) in that much greater changes were found for the neuroticism and lie scales than for the extraversion scale. These changes were in the predicted direction, i.e., towards greater lying and less neuroticism and their size indicates that desirability response set is unlikely to have played a large part in the causation of the original scores.

ACKNOWLEDGEMENTS

We wish to acknowledge the support of the Bethlem Royal and Maudsley Hospital Research Fund. We are also indebted to Mr K. A. Hooton, Headmaster of South Hackney School, whose co-operation made this study possible and to Mr. A. Hendrickson, who programmed the data for computer analysis.

REFERENCES

1. EYSENCK, H. J., Response set, authoritarianism and personality questionnaires. *Brit. J. soc. clin. Psychol.*, **1**, 20–24, 1962.
2. EYSENCK, S. B. G., *Manual of the Junior Eysenck Personality Inventory*. London: Univ. of London Press, 1965.
3. —— & EYSENCK, H. J., An experimental investigation of 'desirability' response set in a personality questionnaire. *Life Sci.*, **2**, 343–355, 1963.
4. —— & EYSENCK, H. J., Acquiescence response set in personality questionnaires. *Life Sci.*, **2**, 144–147, 1963.
5. —— & ——, 'Acquiescence' response set in personality inventory items. *Psychol. Rep.*, **14**, 513–514, 1964.
6. RORER, L. A., The great response-style myth. *Psychol. Bull.*, **63**, 129–156, 1965.

Correlational Studies

Editor's Introduction

CORRELATIONAL studies, i.e. studies in which a measure of extraversion is correlated with other measures of trait or type concepts, are legion; they are comparatively easy to run, can be analysed routinely and written up without difficulty—they are also unfortunately quite uninformative in the majority of cases. Middling high correlations have been found in hundreds of investigations, usually in an expected direction, but the relevance of such results to the building up of a scientific account of personality structure is not high. Such correlations are so much subject to changes in the composition of the sample that great differences from one sample to another are the rule rather than the exception; little faith can usually be put in single correlations, even when the sample used was reasonably large.

This is not to say that such studies should never be undertaken; under certain circumstances results can be of considerable value. There is a long-continued controversy, for instance, relating to the independence of extraversion and neuroticism; it is clearly of considerable importance to know whether any particular measuring instruments for E and N do in fact give results which show these scores to be independent or not. Again, it is of interest to know whether certain hypotheses regarding, say, the relationship between extraversion and repression can be verified with a given set of questionnaires. Such studies widen our knowledge and understanding of the dynamics involved in these various behaviour patterns and are worthwhile to the extent that they have a sound theoretical basis.

A rather different type of correlational study is also included in this section, i.e. one in which questionnaire measures are correlated with ratings. The value of this type of study lies in the demonstration of validity which emerges from a positive outcome of the investigation. Correlating one inventory with another can never give acceptable evidence of validity; at best such procedures demonstrate the reliability of the questionnaires used. Of course there is no absolutely clear distinction between reliability and validity; scientific arguments are in the long run circular and the difference between validity and reliability lies mainly in the larger size of the circle when we speak of validity. Nevertheless the distinction is worth retaining.

H.J.E.

19

On the Independence of Extraversion and Neuroticism

FRANK H. FARLEY[1]

First published in *Journal of Clinical Psychology*, **23,** 154–6, 1967

PROBLEM

EYSENCK has developed a personality-behaviour theory in which the structural framework has been defined by the four higher-order factors of extraversion-introversion (E), neuroticism (N), psychoticism and intelligence (Ref. 3). These factors are asserted as representing the major sources of variance in the description of personality and as being mutually uncorrelated. It is with the latter aspect that this note is concerned.

Interest in the present context is centred specifically on the extraversion-introversion and neuroticism dimensions as measured by the Eysenck Personality Inventory (EPI) (Ref. 5). The EPI was developed as an improvement on the Maudsley Personality Inventory (MPI) (Ref. 4), which had previously been Eysenck's principal measure of the E and N dimensions. Some writers have reported significant correlations between the E and N scales of the MPI (Refs. 1, 8, 9 and 11), results clearly not in accord with the supposed independence of these dimensions. One of the major questions in Carrigan's extensive evaluation of extraversion-introversion as a dimension of personality (Ref. 2) was the extent to which it could be considered as independent of a neuroticism or more generally defined adjustment dimension. As early as 1934 Guilford noted that, 'There is the very troublesome situation found by those who construct tests of I-E and of "neurotic tendency", a difficulty in keeping the two types of tests from correlating significantly with one another'. (Ref. 7, p. 343).

The findings to date with the EPI have usually indicated a small but quite non-significant negative correlation between E and N, with introversion being positively associated with neuroticism. Eysenck & Eysenck (Ref. 5) have reported no significant correlations between E and N in both the EPI and the Junior Eysenck Personality Inventory (JEPI)

---

[1] These data were gathered while the author was at the Institute of Psychiatry, University of London.

(Ref. 6), employing a number of different standardization samples. Savage recently confirmed the latter findings using the JEPI on 93 junior school children of both sexes, for which the correlation between E and N was 0·068 (Ref. 10). The present note reports further data on this issue, employing the EPI.

METHODS AND RESULTS

Two equivalent forms (A and B) of the EPI are available; form A was used in the samples reported below. A high score on either the E or N scale represents extravertedness or high degree of neuroticism respectively. Data on a number of samples was available (Table 1).

TABLE 1

MEANS, STANDARD DEVIATIONS AND CORRELATIONS BETWEEN
EPI EXTRAVERSION AND NEUROTICISM SCORES

Sample	N	Sex	EPI–E Mean	SD	EPI–N Mean	SD	r	P
1. Technical College Students	623	M	11·6	4·0	9·3	4·4	−0·03	NS
2. Civil Servants[1]	148	M	11·8	4·5	10·5	5·0	0·12	NS
3. Civil Servants[1]	91	M	11·1	5·1	9·8	5·5	0·05	NS
4. Trades Apprentices	223	M	12·9	3·1	7·3	3·8	−0·06	NS
5. Trades Apprentices	58	M	13·4	3·0	8·3	3·3	0·00	NS
6. Trades Apprentices	309	M	13·8	3·9	10·0	4·1	−0·16	NS
7. College Students[2]	26	F	13·1	3·8	14·2	5·2	0·00	NS

[1] Mainly Civil Servants, but with other white collar and clerical workers, as well as a few firemen, soldiers, etc.
[2] Includes a very few clerks, secretaries and housewives.

Employing a probability level of 5 per cent, it can be seen from Table 1 that none of the correlations is significant. Of the seven correlations, three are positive and four negative. The median correlation is zero.

Earlier work with the MPI suggested that E and N might be slightly correlated in extreme samples, e.g., certain psychiatric patients (Ref. 4). None of the present samples allowed a test of this possibility, that is, where psychiatric patients were concerned. However, to check that extremes of age or response distortion were not affecting the E and N

I*

relationship, a further analysis was undertaken. As sample 2 had the greatest age variability of the different samples, it was used in comparing Ss of 45 years of age or more (N = 28) with a similar-sized group of the youngest Ss in the sample (N = 25) on the E and N relationship. These results are found in Table 2. As response distortion might possibly be expected to influence the E and N relationship, extreme groups on the 9 item EPI Lie Scale (L) were compared. The largest sample (1) was used for this purpose. All Ss with L scores of 0 (N = 67) were compared with all Ss who obtained L scores of 6 or greater (N = 68). From Table 2 it may be concluded that the present extremes of age and response distortion in normal Ss did not significantly affect the E and N relationship. No significant correlation was found in any of the 4 groups.

TABLE 2

CORRELATIONS OF EPI EXTRAVERSION AND NEUROTICISM
SCORE FOR AGE AND LIE SCORE GROUPS

	Mean age	Range	r	P		r	P
Oldest Ss	48·8	45–55	0·13	NS	High Lie Ss	−0·08	NS
Youngest Ss	19·1	18–21	−0·10	NS	Low Lie Ss	0·03	NS

Altogether, the analyses reported above, based on 1478 Ss, may be interpreted as strong support for the independence of extraversion and neuroticism as measured by the EPI.

SUMMARY

To verify the theoretically important independence of the personality dimensions of extraversion (E) and neuroticism (N) as measured by the Eysenck Personality Inventory (EPI), correlations between the E and N scales were computed for 7 separate samples with a total of 1478 Ss. No significant correlations were obtained; values of the coefficients ranged from 0·122 to −0·158, with a median r of −0·004. E and N correlations computed on extreme groups constituted on the basis of age and response distortion (lie scale scores) yielded similarly small and quite non-significant values.

REFERENCES

1. BRONZAFT, A., HAYES, R., WELCH, L. & KOLTUV, M., Relationships between extraversion, neuroticism and ascendence. *J. Psychol.*, **50,** 279–285, 1960.
2. CARRIGAN, PATRICIA M., Extraversion-introversion as a dimension of personality; a reappraisal. *Psychol. Bull.*, **57,** 329–360, 1960.
3. EYSENCK, H. J., *The Dynamics of Anxiety and Hysteria.* London: Routledge & Kegan Paul, 1957.
4. ——, *Manual of the Maudsley Personality Inventory.* London: Univ. of London Press, 1959.
5. —— & EYSENCK, SYBIL B. G., *The Eysenck Personality Inventory.* San Diego, Calif.: Educational and Industrial Testing Service, 1963.
6. EYSENCK, SYBIL G., *Manual of the Junior Eysenck Personality Inventory.* London: Univ. of London Press, 1965.
7. GUILFORD, J. P., Introversion-extraversion. *Psychol. Bull.*, **31,** 331–354, 1934.
8. JENSEN, A. R., The Maudsley Personality Inventory. *Acta Psychol.*, **14,** 314–325, 1958.
9. LYNN, R. & GORDON, I. E., The relation of neuroticism and extraversion to intelligence and educational attainment. *Brit. J. educ. Psychol.*, **31,** 194–203, 1961.
10. SAVAGE, R. D., Personality factors and academic attainment in junior school children. *Brit. J. educ. Psychol.*, **36,** 91–92, 1966.
11. SPENCE, K. W. & SPENCE, JANET T., Relation of eyelid conditioning to manifest anxiety, extraversion and rigidity. *J. abnorm. soc. Psychol.*, **68,** 144–149, 1964.

20

Ego-Defence Patterns in Extraverts and Introverts[1]

GILBERT BECKER

First published in *Psychological Reports*, **20**, 387–392, 1967

PRESENT findings among normal Ss extend previous findings among psychiatric Ss. Male and female undergraduates were administered the Byrne Repression-Sensitization (R-S) Scale and the scales in Guilford's GZTS representing factors R, S and T, three varieties of extraversion-introversion (E-I). Results indicate that (a) relationships between R-S and E-I in normals are similar to but smaller than those in psychiatric patients; (b) S (sociability) is the best general predictor of R-S scores; (c) R-S depends on the presence or absence of an extraversive tendency of any of the 3 varieties; (d) females tend to be more repressive than males; and (e) sex differences in R-S are more pronounced in extraverts.

In 1963 Weinberg obtained data from a psychiatric population which suggested that extraverts tend to use ego-defence mechanisms such as repression, denial and reaction-formation (Ref. 8); these permit minimal awareness or sensitization to threatening stimuli. Introverts, on the other hand, tend to use ego-defence mechanisms such as isolation, intellectualization and rumination, which permit maximal awareness to those same stimuli. In addition, females tend to use repression (and related mechanisms) in greater degree than do males. This tendency is especially pertinent because no sex differences have been found in studies of normal populations (Refs. 2 and 4). In view of the discrepancy in sex differences found in normal and psychiatric populations, we must be cautious in extending Weinberg's unpublished findings to normal populations.

The main purpose of the present study was to test whether or not Weinberg's findings can be extended to normal populations. A second purpose was to test whether or not (and if so, how) various forms of extraversion-introversion (E-I) interact among themselves and with sex, in the determination of ego-defence pattern.

[1] This investigation was supported in part by a grant (08.195.64) from the Graduate Studies Expansion Fund of the University of Manitoba.

METHOD

Subjects

Eighty-four male and 72 female students enrolled in various introductory psychology sections at Louisiana State University in New Orleans served as Ss. The course is open to freshmen and predominantly first-year students were enrolled.

Measuring Instruments

The testing material was administered during a regular class period in the form of two booklets. The first booklet consisted of items taken from the revised repression-sensitization (R-S) Scale (Ref. 4). A high score indicates a tendency to use isolation (and related mechanisms) and a low score indicates a tendency to use repression and related mechanisms).

For a review of the development and construct validity of the R-S scale see Byrne (Ref. 3, pp. 169–220).]

The second booklet contained the 90 items used to measure Factors R, S and T as taken from the Guilford-Zimmerman Temperament Survey (GZTS) (Ref. 7). Factor R is identified as restraint vs. rhathymia. Factor S is called sociability and was previously referred to by its polar opposite, social introversion. Factor T is named thoughtfulness (or reflectiveness) and was previously called thinking introversion. [For a review on the measurement and meaning of the three E-I traits see Guilford (Ref. 6, pp. 183–187, 413, 444–445, 454).] Three changes were introduced in the administration and scoring of the E-I scales. First, all items were changed from a second-person format to a first-person format. Second, S was asked to respond to the items by answering True or False rather than by checking Yes, ? or No (cf. Ref. 1). These two changes are in line with response indicators used in the R-S scale and simplify test administration and scoring. Third, scoring procedures were changed, where necessary, to effect uniform polarities among the three scales. A high score on all three scales indicated extraversion and a low score, introversion. If Weinberg's findings were to be replicated, negative correlations would be expected between R-S scores and each of the R, S and T scores.

Statistical Treatment

Data were summarized by means of a product-moment correlational analysis and by a factorial variance analysis. rs were calculated between scores on the R-S scale and scores on the E-I scales for each sex separately and combined. For the second analysis, the distributions of the three E-I scores were dichotomized at the mean for males and females separately. On the basis of these dichotomies, each S was categorized as high or low on each E-I trait. Since a $2 \times 2 \times 2 \times 2$ ($R \times S \times T \times Sex$) factorial design would have reduced the number of observations in some cells too drastically for reliable analysis, it was decided that R-S scores would be analysed as a function of the number of E-I factors scored high on, or simply the number of highs (NH). NH scores ranged from zero to 3. The factorial design used, then, was based on a 4×2 (NH $\times$ Sex) arrangement.

Correlational Findings

Correlation coefficients are reported in Table 1 together with those derived from Weinberg's data for ready comparison.[1] With respect to the sample and disregarding sex differences for the moment, the relative positions of the coefficients are the same as in the psychiatric sample (i.e., starting from negative unity, S, T and R). However, the area covered has shifted somewhat away from the negative pole. This can mean either that psychiatric populations reflect relationships found in normal groups, but in greater extreme, or that the two groups differ with regard to test-taking attitude in terms of response set or interpretation of the items.

Normal male and female social extraverts indicated a tendency toward use of repressive mechanisms (in line with the general tendency in the psychiatric group). Normal male thinking extraverts showed neither a tendency toward repression nor isolation, whereas their female counterparts indicated a preference for repressive mechanisms (in line with the general tendency in the psychiatric group). Normal female rhathymics also showed neither tendency, whereas their male counterparts showed a tendency toward isolation (contrary to the general tendency found in the psychiatric group and the only statistically reliable positive correlation in either sample). The direction of sex differences in R is opposite in the

---

[1] Weinberg used Factors R, S and T as taken from Guilford's Inventory of Factors STDCR (Ref. 5) from which GZTS items are derived. One purpose of creating the GZTS was to avoid some of the higher intercorrelations among some of the scales. Also used was the original R-S scale (Ref. 2) on which an item analysis produced the revised scale used in the present study. Coefficient signs have been changed, where necessary, to correspond with the data of the present study. These data are based on scoring procedures designed to effect uniform polarities among the E-I scales. High scores on all E-I scales indicate Extraversion; high R-S scores indicate sensitization.

TABLE 1

PRODUCT-MOMENT COEFFICIENTS OF CORRELATION
WITH REPRESSION-SENSITIZATION SCORES

Sex	N	R	S	T
	Extraversion-Introversion Factors in the GZTS			
Male	84	0·238*	−0·376†	0·056
Female	72	−0·081	−0·362†	−0·304†
Total	156	0·126	0·377†	−0·101
	Coefficients Derived from Weinberg's Unpublished Data[1]			
Male	17	−0·643†	−0·577†	−0·440
Female	45	−0·116	−0·601†	−0·425†
Total	62	−0·278*	−0·579†	−0·439†

* $0 < 0·05$.
† $p < 0·01$.

two samples. Why male repressors tend to be rhathymic in psychiatric populations but tend to show restraint in normal populations is not clear. That female repressors showed neither tendency in both populations is consistent but also not clear.

In summary, (a) coefficients obtained in the present population were smaller than those found in a psychiatric population (especially among the males) and (b) similarities in the two populations between the sexes were found only with respect to S, making that dimension the best general predictor of R-S scores across both the normal-abnormal and the male-female dichotomies.[2]

Factorial Findings

Table 2 reports the means and standard deviations for all rows, columns and cells of the factorial arrangement. Fig. 8 depicts R-S and sex differences in R-S, as functions of NH. F tests indicated reliable main effects for both NH ($F = 4·41$, df = 3/148, $p < 0·01$) and Sex ($F = 4·60$, df = 1/148, $p < 0·05$).

R-S seems to be a function not of the NH variable as such (quantitative) but rather of the absence or presence of highs in any number

[1] This comparison is made possible by Dr Norris H. Weinberg's kindly providing a copy of his raw data.
[2] A transcript of raw data has been filed with the American Documentation Institute, Auxiliary Publications Project, Photoduplication Service, Library of Congress, Washington, D.C. 20540. Remit $1.25 for photocopies or 35 mm microfilm of Document No. 9291.

TABLE 2

MEAN REPRESSION-SENSITIZATION SCORES FOR MALES AND FEMALES IN SUBGROUPS FOR VARIOUS NUMBER-OF-E-I-FACTORS-SCORED-HIGH-ON

Sex	Number of E-I Factors Scored High									
	0		1		2		3		Total	
	N	M±SD	N	M±SD	N	M±SD	N	M±SD	N	M±SD
Male	13	58·38±16·70	34	42·97±19·72	25	50·04±19·75	12	50·83±15·75	84	48·42±18·89
Female	14	57·57±20·35	17	39·76±18·79	26	41·46±19·21	15	35·93±19·24	72	43·30±21·17
Total	27	57·96±18·68	51	41·90±19·47	51	45·67±19·92	27	42·56±19·24	156	46·03±20·25
Difference		00·81		03·21		08·58		14·90		05·12

(qualitative). This notion is supported by the results of an additional, one-way analysis of variance of R-S scores for all Ss in the 1-, 2- and 3-NH subgroups (omitting the O-NH subgroup) which produced an F ratio of less than unity. Differently put, R-S depends on whether or not an individual scores low on all three E-I dimensions; scoring low on two of them has the same effect as scoring low on none of them. It seems that, while a 'restricted' or nonpervasive extraversion indicates a tendency toward repression, only an 'unrestricted' or pervasive introversion indicates a tendency toward isolation.

As reported above, sex differences in R-S scores were non-existent in two studies of normal populations (Refs. 2 and 4). Ss in both studies were drawn from first- and second-year students enrolled in introductory psychology sections at the University of Texas. The data of the more recent study, in which the revised R-S scale was used, permit a direct comparison with the present data. In that study 1304 students (733 males, 571 females) were tested over a 2-year period. The means obtained for males and females were 42·25 and 42·68, respectively. Comparison of these data with the data of the present study shows that the difference lies almost solely in the male scores (42·25 as compared to 48·42; the

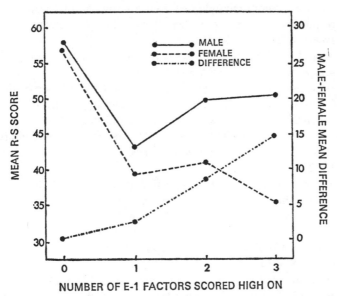

Figure 8. Repression-Sensitization (R-S), and sex differences in R-S, as functions of the number of Extraversion-Introversion (E-I) factors scored high on.

female scores are very similar (42·68 as compared to 43·30). Why male students attending LSUNO tend to be more sensitizing than male students attending the University of Texas is an interesting question not readily answerable.

Fig. 8 indicates that sex differences in R-S increase as NH increases (and do so steadily in contrast to the qualitative function obtaining between R-S as such and NH). Although a t test between male and female R-S scores in the combined 2-NH and 3-NH subgroups yielded a ratio of 2·50 (df = 76, p<0·02), the F ratio indicating the reliability of the overall interaction variance was less than unity. This lack of overall reliability suggests caution in interpretation.

In summary, (a) R-S depended on the presence or absence of an extraversive tendency of any of the three varieties; (b) females tended to be more repressive than males; and (c) sex differences in R-S were a positive monotonic function of NH.

REFERENCES

1. BENDIG, A., Score reliability of dichotomous and trichotomous item responses on the Maudsley Personality Inventory. *J. consult. Psychol.*, **23,** 181–184, 1959.

2. BYRNE, D., The repression-sensitization scale: rationale, reliability and validity. *J. Pers.*, **29,** 334–349, 1961.

3. ——, Repression-sensitization as a dimension of personality. Pp. 169–220 in B. A. Maher (ed.), *Progress in Experimental Personality Research.* Vol. 1. New York: Academic press, 1964.

4. ——, BARRY, J. & NELSON, D. Relation of the revised repression-sensitization scale to measures of self-description. *Psychol. Rep.*, **13,** 323–334, 1963.

5. GUILFORD, J. P., *An Inventory of Factors STDCR.* Beverly Hills, Calif.: Sheridan Supply Co., 1940.

6. ——, *Personality.* New York: McGraw-Hill, 1959.

7. —— & ZIMMERMAN, W. S. *The Guilford-Zimmerman Temperament Survey: Manual of Instructions and Interpretations.* Beverly Hills, Calif.: Sheridan Supply Co., 1949.

8. WEINBERG, N. H., Word Association Style, Field Dependence and Related Personality Variables. Unpublished manuscript. Los Angeles, Calif.: Neuropsychiatric Institute, UCLA Centre for the Health Sciences, 1963.

21

Extraversion and Stimulus-Seeking Motivation

FRANK FARLEY & SONJA V. FARLEY

First published in
Journal of Consulting Psychology, **31**, 215–216, 1967

FROM EYSENCK'S personality theory and recent notions of stimulus-seeking behaviour, it was predicted that extraversion would correlate with stimulus seeking as measured by the Sensation Seeking Scale (SSS) of Zuckerman, Kolin, Price & Zoob (Ref. 10). The correlation found was 0·47, p<0·01. It was concluded that this result was consistent with previous findings and that it aids in establishing the construct validity of the SSS.

In a recent paper Zuckerman, Kolin, Price & Zoob (Ref. 10) reported the development of an objective questionnaire measure of sensation seeking—Sensation Seeking Scale (SSS)—in an attempt to quantify psychometrically the construct of optimal stimulation. This was a forced-choice factored scale of 34 items, with 4 items scored for males, 8 for females and 22 for both sexes. They reported preliminary validation for the scale in terms of a positive correlation with field independence as measured by the Embedded Figures Test—field independent subjects (Ss) being more responsive to internal sensations than field dependent ones—and a negative correlation with anxiety, as sensation seeking involves an enjoyment of tension-raising situations.

Eysenck (Ref. 3) has summarized the evidence supporting the view that because of the hypothesized greater inhibitory potential of the extravert as compared to that of the introvert (Ref. 2), the extravert will seek arousal-producing stimuli so as to maintain some optimum level of 'arousal potential' (Ref. 1), whereas introverts, with a hypothesized high excitatory potential, will attempt to avoid arousal-producing stimuli. This conception has received some experimental confirmation (Ref. 3), though the amount of relevant research is not extensive.

The present paper reports on the relationship between extraversion and stimulus seeking as purportedly measured by the SSS.

One hundred male Ss were administered the SSS and the Eysenck Personality Inventory (EPI, Ref. 4). Sixty-eight of the Ss were apprentices at a motor works near London and the remaining 32 were paid volunteers for a series of experiments at the Institute of Psychiatry. These latter Ss were largely civil service employees. Only the 26 items on the SSS which loaded 0·30 or higher for males on the major sensation-seeking factor established in the scale construction (Ref. 10) were used. Extraversion was measured by the extraversion (E) scale of the EPI.

RESULTS

The mean SSS score was 14·57, SD = 3·93. The mean E score was 15·14, SD = 4·36. The product-moment correlation between the SSS and the E scale was 0·47, p<0·01. An item analysis was done between the 26 SSS items and the E scores. Of the 26 items, 10 had correlations with E significant at or beyond the 0·05 level. The alternatives chosen by extraverts on each of these 10 forced-choice items are presented below, using the original item numbering of Zuckerman *et al.* (Ref. 10).

7. I like to explore a strange city or section of town by myself, even if it means getting lost.
9. I would like to try some of the new drugs that produce hallucinations.
11. I sometimes like to do things that are a little frightening.
17. I would like to take off on a trip with no preplanned or definite routes, or timetables.
21. I would like to have the experience of being hypnotized.
22. The important goal of life is to live it to the fullest and experience as much of it as you can.
23. I would like to try parachute jumping.
26. I prefer friends who are excitingly unpredictable.
28. I often find beauty in the 'clashing' colours and irregular forms of modern paintings.
33. When I feel discouraged I recover by going out and doing something new and exciting.

DISCUSSION

Certainly each of the 10 items listed above reflects stimulus-seeking motivation and preference for sensory variability. This fits with the high risk-taking of the extravert (Ref. 6), his more frequent alternation behaviour (Ref. 5), his greater alcohol and cigarette consumption (Ref. 3), his greater extent of physical movement (Ref. 8), his less stimulus-deprivation tolerance (Ref. 9) and his greater pain tolerance as compared with introverts (Ref. 7).

The present results aid in establishing the construct validity of the SSS as a measure of stimulus seeking, in that the correlation with extraversion could be deduced from a theoretical framework of stimulus-seeking behaviour from which other related predictions had been confirmed.

REFERENCES

1. BERLYNE, D. E., *Conflict, Arousal and Curiosity*. New York: McGraw-Hill, 1960.
2. EYSENCK, H. J. (ed.), *Experiments in Personality*, 2 vols. London: Routledge & Kegan Paul, 1960.
3. —— (ed.), *Experiments with Drugs*. Oxford: Pergamon Press, 1963.
4. —— & EYSENCK, S. B. G. *Manual of the Eysenck Personality Inventory*. San Diego: Educational and Industrial Testing Service, 1964.
5. —— & LEVEY, A. Alternation in choice behaviour and extraversion. *Life Sci.*, **4**, 115–119, 1965.
6. LYNN, R. & BUTLER, J. Introversion and the arousal jag. *Brit. J. soc. clin. Psychol.*, **1**, 150–151, 1962.
7. —— & EYSENCK, H. J. Tolerance for pain, extraversion and neuroticism. *Percept. mot. Skills*, **12**, 161–162, 1961.
8. Rachman, S., Psychomotor Behaviour and Personality with Particular Reference to Conflict. Unpublished doctoral dissertation. Univ. of London, 1961.
9. PETRIE, A., COLLINS, W. & SOLOMON, P., The tolerance for pain and for sensory deprivation. *Amer. J. Psychol.*, **73**, 80–90, 1960.
10. ZUCKERMAN, M., KOLIN, E. A., PRICE, L. & ZOOB, I., Development of a sensation-seeking scale. *J. consult. Psychol.*, **28**, 447–482, 1964.

22

Validity of the Eysenck Extraversion
Scales as Determined by Self-Ratings in Normals[1]

F. T. VINGOE

First published in
British Journal of Social and Clinical Psychology, **5**, 89–91, 1966

THE E.P.I. was administered to 58 normal Ss who were students in three adult psychology classes. Immediately after responding to the E.P.I., Ss were asked to rate themselves on a seven-point Introversion-Extraversion Scale. The Ss were divided into introverts and extraverts on the basis of their self-ratings. The Ss were also dichotomized into introverts and extraverts on the basis of E scores. Introvert and extravert criterion groups were found to be significantly different from each other and from the total group. The results indicate that introverts as defined by self-ratings are somewhat more aware of their position on the introversion-extraversion continuum than are extraverts. Results support the validity of the E scale of the E.P.I. when using introvert and extravert criterion groups as defined above.

INTRODUCTION

The Eysenck Personality Inventory (E.P.I.) measures '... two major dimensions of personality, extraversion-introversion (E) and neuroticism-stability (N)' (Ref. 1). It is very similar to the Maudsley Personality Inventory (M.P.I.), incorporating, however, many improvements over this earlier instrument (Ref. 1).

Eysenck & Eysenck (Ref. 1) note that the E.P.I. will require validation studies from many independent sources. S. B. G. Eysenck has used the method of nominated groups in order to assess the validity of the E.P.I. Independent judges were asked to nominate extraverted and introverted Ss, after which the nominees were asked to complete the E.P.I. The results indicated that '... individuals who impress others as showing

[1] This investigation was supported in part by the research grant No. 63–10–17 from the California State Department of Mental Hygiene.

262

introverted or extraverted behaviour patterns ... answer the E.P.I. in a corresponding manner' (Ref. 1). This study attempts to assess validity of the E scale by self-ratings of American Ss. The major assumption of this study is that on such a personality variable as extraversion, normal Ss can rate their relative position.

PROCEDURE

Fifty-eight Ss from adult psychology classes were asked to complete the E.P.I. according to the regular instructions. After completing the inventory, they were asked to rate themselves on a seven-point Intro-version-Extraversion Scale. Data for nine Ss were eliminated on the following bases: (a) those with a lie score greater than four, (b) inventories completed by foreign students. The number of Ss was thus reduced to 49, 24 males (mean age 33·1, range 18–52) and 25 females (mean age 32·4, range 18–55). The total mean age was 32·7. The Ss were divided into introverts (those whose self-ratings were 3 and below) and extraverts (those whose self-ratings were 3 and above). This procedure classified 24 Ss as introverts and 25 Ss as extraverts. In order to determine if these groups could be differentiated on the basis of their obtained E scores, t-tests were calculated.

There was also a comparison made of introverts as defined by the E.P.I. (those who obtained an E score below the median) and extraverts (those who obtained an E score at and above the median). Dichotomized on this basis there were 31 and 18 Ss respectively in the two groups.

RESULTS

Although the E.P.I. has been standardized and used mainly with British Ss, Eysenck & Eysenck (Ref. 1) indicate that the 'Results with the M.P.I. (upon which the E.P.I. is based) suggests that comparable American groups do not differ appreciably from English groups'. Based on a sample of normal British Ss (n = 1931), the mean extraversion score and standard deviation are 12·08 and 4·37 respectively, while the mean neuroticism score and standard deviation are 9·04 and 4·80 respectively. The obtained mean extraversion score and standard deviation are 12·73 and 3·74; the obtained mean neuroticism score and standard deviation are 8·45 and 5·31. These results then lend support to Eysenck & Eysenck's statement above.

The means and standard deviations of the introvert and extravert criterion groups may be found in Table 1.

TABLE 1

DATA FOR INTROVERT AND EXTRAVERT CRITERION GROUPS

Group	n	M	SD	t	
Introvert	24	10·33	2·78	1·718*	(Intro-extra)
Extravert	25	15·04	3·16	1·974*	(Extra-total)
Total	49	12·73	3·74	2·051†	(Intro-total)

* p<0·05
† p<0·025

The significance of the difference between the means is also indicated in this table. The introvert and extravert group means were significantly different from each other and from the total means. While the t-value between the extravert and total group was significant beyond the 5 per cent point, the analogous t-value between the introvert and total group was significant beyond the 2·5 per cent point. Table 2 presents data on the Introvert and Extravert groups as defined by the E.P.I. While the introvert and extravert group means were significantly different from each other, they were not significantly different from the total mean. In general, the results support the validity of the E.P.I. scale.

TABLE 2

DATA FROM INTROVERT AND EXTRAVERT EPI GROUPS

Group	n	M	SD	t	
Introvert	31	3·45	0·88	4·469*	(Intro-extra)
Extravert	18	4·61	0·83	1·035	(Extra-total)
Total	49	3·88	2·91	0·791	(Intro-total)

* p<0·0005

DISCUSSION

One major difference between this study and the study using nominated groups referred to in Eysenck & Eysenck (Ref. 1) is that in Eysenck's study the judges were provided with a descriptive statement of the typical extravert and introvert. No definition or descriptive statement was given to the Ss in the present study. It would be interesting to replicate this study, using a larger n and including a group of Ss who were given the description of the typical introvert and extravert as used by Eysenck. The use of a nine- rather than a seven-point scale might also improve the design. The data from Table 2 indicate that introvert and extravert groups as defined by E scores could be differentiated from each other but not from the total group. One factor which seemed to contribute to this was the apparent reluctance of many Ss to select extreme self-ratings such as 1 or 7.

The results indicate that introverts are more aware of their position on the introversion-extraversion continuum than are extraverts.

A question that may be raised is: are introverts more successful than extraverts in assessing other aspects of their personality makeup? Some research on neurotic groups carried out by Eysenck (Ref. 2) gives support to the hypothesis that introverts have more insight about themselves in general than extraverts. He characterizes hysterics and psychopaths as extraverted neurotics; and the dysthymic group, such as depressives and those with anxiety states, as introverted neurotics. It is a common clinical observation that the dysthymic group are more insightful about themselves than hysterics and psychopaths.

The data on neuroticism from the present study was surveyed for trends: examining those Ss with high neuroticism scores, there was no apparent relation between these high scores and the efficacy of self-rating. This suggests that neurotics are as aware of their position on the introversion-extraversion continuum as are normals. This concurs with the general observation that many neurotics have good insight.

REFERENCES

1. EYSENCK, H. J. & EYSENCK, S. B. G., *Manual for the Eysenck Personality Inventory*. San Diego, California: Educational and Industrial Testing Service, 1963.
2. EYSENCK, H. J., Classification and the Problems of Diagnosis. In H. J. Eysenck (ed.), *Handbook of Abnormal Psychology*. New York: Basic Books, 1961.

23

The Personality of Judges as a Factor in the Validity of Their Judgment of Extraversion-Introversion

SYBIL B. G. EYSENCK & HANS J. EYSENCK[1]

First published in
British Journal of Social and Clinical Psychology, **3**, 141–144, 1964

THE QUESTIONNAIRE responses of nominated extraverts and introverts on the Extraversion and Neuroticism Scales of the Eysenck Personality Inventory were studied, in conjunction with the E and N scores of the judges and their intelligence test scores. High validity of choice was observed, but no relationship found between personality or intelligence of the judges and the excellence of their judgments.

Personality is most frequently described in terms of behaviour patterns and these in turn are most frequently indexed in terms of (a) self ratings, as on questionnaires, or (b) ratings by others. Both methods are open to criticism, but these criticisms are different in character; accordingly agreement between the two methods would argue in favour of the validity of both (Ref. 3). Two recent studies have used the method of nominated groups (Ref. 1) to test the validity of ratings of extraversion and neuroticism, by having judges nominate persons supposedly extremely high or low on either of these dimensions of personality; personality inventories were then administered to these nominees and their scores on relevant scales compared. S. B. G. Eysenck and Eysenck & Eysenck both found evidence of considerable validity in studies using relatively small numbers of judges (Refs. 4 and 9); they also found some presumptive evidence that some judges were better able than others to nominate persons correctly for the categories in question. The present study presents a repetition of the former experiments, with a much larger sample of judges and extends the argument by attempting to relate the intelligence and personality of the judges to their success in judging the

[1] We are indebted to the Royal Bethlem and Maudsley Hospital Research Fund for financial support, to 'Mensa' for co-operation in securing subjects, and to Mr A. Hendrickson for preparing the computer programmes.

extraversion or introversion of their nominees. The influence of 'desirability' and 'acquiescence' response sets having been shown in earlier researches to be of relatively little import in relation to the questions used in the EPI (Refs. 4, 10 and 11) no special measurement was undertaken to assess their influence on our results.

The test of personality used was the Eysenck Personality Inventory (Ref. 6), an improved version of the Maudsley Personality Inventory (Ref. 2). This test has two parallel forms, but we shall here be concerned only with the combined scores from both forms. The measure of intelligence used was a well-standardized British test; this was administered in person to candidates who applied to become members of an organization (Mensa) which made the possession of a high I.Q. the prime requisite of membership. Candidates were first required to complete Form A of the test under unsupervised conditions; only those who succeeded were then admitted to the supervised test (Form B). Testing was carried out by the organization, not by the present writers, but appears to have been done conscientiously and well. From the results, two groups were formed which differed in intelligence, as defined by the test chosen. The intelligent group, with I.Q.'s above 148 on this test, will be donated M in this study and was made up of individuals who passed the test; the less intelligent group, with I.Q.'s below 148 on this test, will be denoted P in this study and was made up of individuals who failed the test. (The S.D. of this test being unusually high, the tested I.Q. of 148 corresponds roughly to one of 130 on the Binet or the Wechsler scale.) Names of members of both groups were kindly furnished us by the secretary of 'Mensa'. These two groups constitute the judges; they were circulated with the EPI and invited to take part in the general scheme of research (which was not at this stage specified). Out of about 1500 M-group members, 751 filled in the original questionnaire; out of 317 P-group members, 229 did. Details regarding the E and N scores of these subjects are given in Table 1, together with the scores for the EPI standardization group of 1931 (which, of course, did not contain either M or P members).

It will be seen that apart from being more intelligent than the general population, the M group and to a lesser extent the P group, is slightly less neurotic and much less extraverted. The former may be a reflection of the preponderance of middle-class members in both M and P (Refs. 5 and 7); the latter is possibly a function of the rather cognitively-oriented type of society to which subjects belonged, or aspired to belong. Ninety-two M and 27 P members were retested about one year later in

TABLE 1

E AND N SCORES OF M AND P GROUPS, AS COMPARED
WITH NORMAL STANDARDIZATION SAMPLE

	E		N		
	M	σ	M	σ	n
M	20·213	7·541	17·177	8·985	751
P	22·699	7·709	18·432	8·840	229
Control group	26·264	7·742	19·557	9·038	1931

person when they came to the Institute of Psychiatry in order to carry out some personality tests; the retest reliability for E and N was found to be 0·88 and 0·84 for M members and 0·94 and 0·92 for P members. The correlation between E and N for the standardization group was −0·04; for the M and P groups it was −0·24 and −0·15.

M and P members were asked to act as 'judges' or selectors, and to choose one extreme extravert and one extreme introvert each from among their acquaintances. They were furnished with descriptions of 'typical' extraverts and introverts, as follows:

'The typical extravert is sociable, likes parties, has many friends, needs to have people to talk to and does not like reading or studying by himself. He craves excitement, takes chances, often sticks his neck out, acts on the spur of the moment and is generally an impulsive individual. He is fond of practical jokes, always has a ready answer and generally likes change; he is carefree, easygoing, optimistic and likes to "laugh and be merry". He prefers to keep moving and doing things, tends to be aggressive and lose his temper quickly; altogether his feelings are not kept under tight control and he is not always a reliable person.

'The typical introvert is a quiet, retiring sort of person, introspective, fond of books rather than people; he is reserved and distant except to intimate friends. He tends to plan ahead, "looks before he leaps" and distrusts the impulse of the moment. He does not like excitement, takes matters of everyday life with proper seriousness and likes a well-ordered mode of life. He keeps his feelings under close control, seldom behaves in an aggressive manner and does not lose his temper easily. He is reliable, somewhat pessimistic and places great value on ethical standards.'

From nominations made by M and P members, 302 and 92 replies respectively were received from nominated extraverts and 335 and 88 replies respectively from nominated introverts. The mean E and N scores of these groups are shown in Table 2. It will be seen that the nominated extraverts have E scores of 31, while the nominated introverts have E scores of 16, i.e., almost exactly one-half as large. Both differ significantly from the population mean of 26, the introverts more so than the extraverts. On N the nominated extraverts have lower scores than the nominated introverts, but the difference is slight (18 as against 20). This may be compared with the population mean of 20. It is apparent that, as in the previous studies, judges have no difficulty in identifying individuals who are extreme in extraversion or introversion and it is also apparent that in doing so they do not fall into the error of confounding introversion and neuroticism to any considerable degree. The more intelligent M-group members do not judge extraversion better than the less intelligent P-group members. This argues against I.Q. as an important element in judging personality, although at lower levels it may of course exert a stronger influence.

TABLE 2

MEAN E AND N SCORES OF NOMINATED EXTRAVERTS AND INTROVERTS

	M	σ	M	σ		n
M	31·106	6·702	17·215	9·129	Extraverts	302
P	31·773	6·758	18·761	9·054		92
M	16·030	6·968	19·812	9·333	Introverts	335
P	15·924	6·064	19·739	10·284		88

Among the nominees discussed above, many had no partners; i.e., some judges nominated an extravert who forwarded his questionnaire to us, but either failed to nominate an introvert, or nominated one who failed to forward his questionnaire. Similarly, some introverts had no matching extraverts. In all, there were 225 matched pairs nominated by M members and 75 matched pairs nominated by P members. Table 3 gives the correlations between the E and N scores of judges and the E and N scores of nominees, separated into extraverted and introverted nominees. The argument underlying this calculation was as follows. In the group of extraverted nominees, a high E score constitutes a 'good' choice, while in the group of introverted nominees, a high E score constitutes a 'poor' choice. If extraverted judges are better (or worse) than introverted judges in making good choices, then their E scores should correlate positively (or negatively) with the E scores of their choices. A similar argument applies to the N scores of the nominees, although there of course both a positive or a negative correlation would indicate that judges of the particular type of personality being correlated with N were erroneously choosing too many (or too few) extraverts or introverts because in their minds this dimension was adulterated with N. The figures in Table 3 do not suggest any relationship between judges' personality and accuracy of judgment, being uniformly low. (Levels of significance required for the 5 per cent and 1 per cent level of significance for the M and P groups respectively are 0·13 and 0·18 for M and 0·22 and 0·29 for P.)

TABLE 3

CORRELATIONS BETWEEN E AND N SCORES OF NOMINATED GROUPS ($E_{nom.}$ AND $N_{nom.}$) AND E AND N SCORES OF JUDGES (E_x AND N_x)

	$E_{nom}.E_x$	$E_{nom}.N_x$	$N_{nom}.E_x$	$N_{nom}.N_x$		n
E group	0·104	−0·069	0·028	−0·023	Mensa	225
	−0·039	−0·128	−0·048	−0·006	P	75
I group	0·139	0·056	−0·094	0·044	Mensa	225
	0·105	0·090	−0·146	0·221	P	75

It will have been noticed that in the M and P groups, both of which were more introverted than the standardization group, N and E correlated negatively, while in the standardization group the correlation was quite negligible. These figures suggest the possibility that introverted groups in general may be characterized by a negative relationship between E and N, while the opposite may be true of extraverted groups. This hypothesis can, of course, be tested on our nominated E and I groups. The actual correlations for M-nominated introverts and P-nominated introverts were −0·19 and −0·10; those for the nominated extravert groups were −0·06 and +0·01. The evidence is slight but significantly in favour of the existence of a negative relationship between E and N among introverts; this is in good agreement with the finding of a curvilinear regression line reported in connection with the MPI (Ref. 2).

REFERENCES

1. EYSENCK, H. J., *The Psychology of Politics.* New York: Harper, 1954.

2. ——, *The Maudsley Personality Inventory*. London: Univ. of London Press, 1959. San Diego: Educ. and Indust. Test. Serv., 1962.

3. ——, *The Structure of Human Personality*. New York: Macmillan, 1960.

4. ——, Response set, authoritarianism and personality questionnaires. *Brit. J. soc. clin. Psychol.*, **1,** 20–24, 1962.

5. ——, Smoking, personality and psychosomatic disorders. *J. psychosom. Res.*, **7,** 107–130, 1963.

6. —— & Eysenck, S. B. G., *The Eysenck Personality Inventory*. San Diego: Educ. and Indust. Test. Serv. Also: London, Univ. of London Press, 1963.

7. Eysenck, S. B. G., Social class, sex and response to a five part personality inventory. *Educ. psychol. Measmt.*, **20,** 47–54, 1960.

8. ——, The validity of a personality questionnaire as determined by the method of nominated groups. *Life Sci.*, **1,** 13–18, 1962.

9. —— & Eysenck, H. J., The validity of questionnaire and rating assessments of extraversion and neuroticism and their factorial stability. *Brit. J. Psychol.*, **54,** 51–62, 1963.

10. —— & ——, Acquiescence response set in personality questionnaires. *Life Sci.*, **2,** 144–147, 1963.

11. —— & ——, An experimental investigation of 'desirability' response set in a personality questionnaire. *Life Sci.*, **2,** 343–355, 1963.

24

An Assessment of Some Structural Properties of the Jungian Personality Typology[1]

LAWRENCE J. STRICKER & JOHN ROSS

First published in
Journal of Abnormal and Social Psychology, **68**, 62–71, 1964

SOME structural properties of Jung's typology were investigated, using a self-report inventory, the Myers-Briggs Type Indicator. The findings were that: (a) the type classifications had moderate stability; (b) Indicator score distributions were not bimodal; (c) with one exception, the regressions of other variables on Indicator scales did not change at the zero point of the Indicator scales; (d) the Indicator scales did not interact; (e) the Indicator scales did not moderate the regressions of other variables on one another; and (f) type indeterminacy was unrelated to ineffective behaviour and maladjustment. It was concluded that these results offer little support for any of the structural properties attributed to the typology.

The merits of the typological approach to personality measurement have long been a source of controversy. It is undeniable, however, that personality typologies (Refs. 17, 28 and 29) have had and continue to have important influences on psychological theorizing and research. Jung's typology (Refs. 16, 17, 18 and 19) is one of the most influential.

[1] The following people graciously furnished data for the studies reported in this article: William C. Craig of Stanford University; James W. Dean of Westinghouse Electric Corporation; D. J. Gibson of Westinghouse Electric Corporation; Robert F. Grose of Amherst College; C. Hess Haagen of Wesleyan University; Thomas L. Hilton of Carnegie Institute of Technology; Clark W. Horton of Dartmouth College; David Keirsey of the Covina, California School District; Harold A. Korn of Stanford University; Joseph Marron and John F. Morse of Rensselaer Polytechnic Institute; Donald H. Moyer of Cornell University; John O. Nelson of Yale University; Douglas O. Pederson of Rensselaer Polytechnic Institute; Kathryn Pruden of Long Island University; John T. Rule of Massachusetts Institute of Technology; Rixford K. Snyder of Stanford University; John C. South of Westinghouse Electric Corporation; Ernest C. Tupes and John R. Weir of California Institute of Technology.

Like the other typologies, it has stimulated a considerable amount of research, but very little of this research has been primarily concerned with verifying the typology *per se*. Such direct research is needed for a proper assessment of Jung's typology. The studies, using a self-report inventory, the Myers-Briggs Type Indicator, which are described here, were undertaken to contribute to such an assessment of Jung's typology, as well as to the construct validation of the Indicator.

SOME PROPERTIES OF JUNG'S TYPOLOGY

Jung postulates two attitudes—extraversion and introversion—and four functions—sensation, intuition, thinking and feeling—which interlock in the sense that extraversion and introversion indicate the focus of cognitive activity and the four functions describe its specific varieties.

Extraversion and introversion describe the direction of a person's interest. Extraversion involves an interest in the external world and introversion involves an interest in the interior world. Sensation and intuition are two distinct ways of perceiving. Sensation is a direct form of perception; intuition is indirect, holistic and typically enriched by information which the perceiver adds to what is given by the stimulus. Thinking and feeling are two distinct and contrasting means of evaluating phenomena. Thinking is a logical process, capable of being formalized, that results in impersonal judgments of right or wrong; feeling is a more subjective process which results in the acceptance or rejection of phenomena and judgments of like or dislike.

Jung attributes several structural properties to the elements of his typology. The attitudes and functions are viewed as:

Stable

There is a predisposition to develop certain attitudes and functions. Consequently, even though the extent of their actual development depends upon the environment, changes in type are not apt to occur in the normal course of events.

Categorical or Qualitative Dichotomous

The extent to which a person's type is actually developed may be a continuous variable, but type *per se*—the direction of the development— is conceived as being categorical. Hence, a person is an extravert or an introvert; sensing or intuitive; thinking or feeling.

K

Interacting

The various attitudes and functions, when taken in combination, tend to modify each other and produce unique effects, e.g., extraverted thinking is qualitatively different from introverted thinking and an extravert with intuition and thinking is considerably different from an introvert with intuition and thinking.

Giving Rise to Different Compounds of Surface Traits

The predisposition towards the development of certain attitudes and functions results in more reliance on and increased effectiveness with them. This reliance on particular attitudes and functions determines the pattern of personality characteristics, values, interests and other surface traits which develop.

In addition, type indeterminacy is viewed as producing ineffective and maladjusted behaviour. Type indeterminacy arises when the members of a pair of attitudes or functions are at the same level, instead of one member of the pair being stronger. This situation is believed to occur because both members of the pair are undeveloped, rather than being equally developed. The outcome is conflicting, vacillating and, consequently, ineffective behaviour.

MYERS-BRIGGS TYPE INDICATOR

In order to investigate these structural issues, the Myers-Briggs Type Indicator (Ref. 22) was employed.[1] The Indicator is particularly suited for use in such investigations because it was explicitly developed to make the measurements and assessments called for by the Jungian typology, or at least a typology which follows the broad outlines of Jung's, although it may differ in some details (Ref. 32). Since the Indicator was designed to classify people into type categories which have real meaning, the type theory guided all phases of its construction, including the writing of items, their selection and weighting, and the derivation of a scoring system.

The Indicator consists of four scales: Extraversion-introversion (E-I), sensation-intuition (S-N), thinking-feeling (T-F), and judging-perceiving (J-P).[2] Items on the scales consist of behaviour reports, value judgments

---

[1] Unless otherwise indicated, the research described in this article involved the current version—Form F—of the Indicator.

[2] No separate and explicit variable of this kind is found in Jung's typology, but Jung does classify each of the four functions as either rational (or judging) or irrational (or perceiving).

and word pairs. All items have at least two alternatives; one alternative reflects a particular attitude or function and the other alternative reflects the opposite attitude or function. Each alternative is weighted separately to reflect the extent of the alternative's relationship to the scale classification and to set the scale's zero point. The zero point of each scale (i.e., where the scores for the two opposing attitudes or functions are equal) was so chosen that those who are on one side of it and, hence, in one type category, are presumed to be qualitatively different from those who are on the other side of it and, hence, in the opposite type category.

The score on a scale is the difference between the sums of the weights (or scores) for the two kinds of alternatives which were chosen. A person's E score, for example, is the sum of the weights for the extravert alternatives he chose, and similarly, his I score is the sum of the weights for the introvert alternatives he chose. His E-I score is the difference between the E and I scores. The direction of this difference indicates which of the two categories is dominant. For example, if the E score is 4 and the I score is 16, the E-I difference score is I 12 and the person is classified as an introvert. If the E score is 16 and the I score is 4, the person's difference score is E 12 and the person is classified as an extravert. If the two scores are equal, the person's difference score is zero and the type is considered indeterminate and denoted 'X'.[1]

TABLE 1

AGREEMENT IN ORIGINAL AND RETEST TYPE CATEGORY
OF AMHERST COLLEGE STUDENTS

| Scale | Proportion of agreement | | Kappa |
	Chance	Actual	
E–I	0·47	0·68	0·40†
S–N	0·58	0·85	0·65†
T–F	0·50	0·73	0·46†
J–P	0·48	0·63	0·30*

Note $-N = 41$
* $p < 0.05$ † $p < 0.01$

[1] After the studies reported in this article were completed, the Indicator's scoring was changed so as to eliminate indeterminate type categories. This goal was accomplished by linearly transforming the original continuous scores and combining a scale's indeterminate type category with one of the two other type categories on that scale. The use of the new scoring would not alter these studies' continuous score results and, in view of the small number of subjects in the indeterminate type categories, would have no appreciable effect on these studies' type category results.

STUDY I: STABILITY OF TYPE CLASSIFICATIONS

The stability that is attributed to the types implies that they should not, in general, change over time.

METHOD

42 members of an elementary psychology class at Amherst College were retested with the Indicator 14 months after they had taken it with their entire freshman class shortly after entering college.[1]

RESULTS

The original-retest agreement in the three type categories on each scale (e.g., classification as E, X or I originally and on retest) was measured by kappa coefficients (Ref. 4)—kappa is the proportion of agreement after correction for agreement expected by chance. These coefficients, which appear in Table 1, ranged from 0·30 to 0·65. All were significant ($\leqslant 0·05$).

The original-retest agreement of the four-variable type combinations (e.g., extraversion, sensation, thinking, judging) was also computed. The proportion of agreement expected by chance was 0·07, the actual proportion of agreement was 0·20 and the kappa coefficient was 0·13; it was significant ($p < 0·01$).

The product-moment correlations between the original and retest continuous scores were 0·73 for the E-I scale, 0·69 for the S-N scale, 0·48 for the T-F scale and 0·69 for the J-P scale; all were significant ($p \leqslant 0·01$).

STUDY II: BIMODALITY IN SCORE DISTRIBUTIONS

If there are qualitatively different kinds of people, as the typology suggests, and if individual items each fit alternatives designed to attract one type or the other against one another, as each scale of the Indicator does, the true score distributions of each scale should be bimodal and, hence in so far as the obtained scores reflect the true scores, the obtained score distributions should also be bimodal.

[1] Neither chi square analyses of type distributions on each of the four scales, t tests of differences in mean scores, nor F tests of differences in variances on each of the four scales yielded any differences between the 41 students and the 217 other members of their entering class which were significant ($p < ·05$).

METHOD

The Indicator was administered to 21 samples, each of which consisted of virtually every member of some clearly defined group. In order to increase sample size, homogeneous groups (e.g., male freshman classes at highly selective liberal arts colleges) were combined, resulting in 14 composite samples. These samples included groups of high school, college and graduate school students, recently employed college graduates and public school teachers.[1]

Samples varied in size from 60 to 2,389. The frequency distributions of scores on each of the four Indicator scales in the 14 samples were obtained and inspected for bimodality.

RESULTS

None of the distributions, which appear in Tables A to D,[2] seemed to exhibit any marked evidence of bimodality, although there was considerable skewness. As an illustration of the nature of the obtained distributions, Figure 9 shows the distributions of E-I scores for the two

[1] The 14 composite samples are: 146 twelfth-grade boys in the college preparatory programme in eight Massachusetts high schools; 230 twelfth-grade boys in the general-vocational programme in eight Massachusetts high schools; 148 girls in the college preparatory programme in eight Massachusetts high schools; 433 girls in the general-vocational programme in eight Massachusetts high schools; 2,177 male liberal arts college students—258 Amherst, 821 Dartmouth, 844 Stanford, and 254 Wesleyan freshmen of the Class of 1963; 2,389 male engineering students—201 California Institute of Technology, 515 Cornell College of Engineering, 792 Massachusetts Institute of Technology, and 881 Rensselaer Polytechnic Institute freshmen. The California Institute of Technology and RPI students were in the Class of 1962, the other two groups were from the Class of 1963; 1,000 service academy students—freshmen of the Class of 1962 at two of the armed services academies; 300 male freshmen in the Class of 1963 at Long Island University; 184 female freshmen in the Class of 1963 at Long Island University; 99 Yale Divinity School students who entered in September 1958; 60 students in the Graduate School of Industrial Administration at Carnegie Institute of Technology who entered in September 1958; 350 recent male college graduates hired by Westinghouse between June and August 1959; 86 men teaching in the Covina, California, elementary schools; 248 women teaching in the Covina, California, elementary schools.

[2] Tables A to H and Figures A to E have been deposited with the American Documentation Institute. Order Document No. 7600 from ADI Auxiliary Publications Project, Photoduplication Service, Library of Congress, Washington 25, D.C. Remit in advance $1.75 for microfilm or $2.50 for photocopies and make cheques payable to: Chief, Photoduplication Service, Library of Congress.

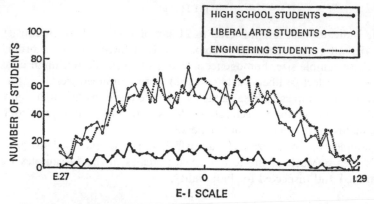

Figure 9. Distribution of E-I scores for three student groups.

largest samples—2,389 male engineering students and 2,177 male liberal arts college students—and, for comparison, a sample of 397 male high school students.

STUDY III: NONLINEAR REGRESSIONS

If there are distinct types and if score distributions within type categories are less important than differences of any magnitude between type categories, the regression of type relevant variables on type scores should change in slope or level at the boundary between types—the zero point of the Indicator scale.[1]

STUDY IIIA: REGRESSIONS OF APTITUDE TESTS FOR HIGH SCHOOL STUDENTS

METHOD

Experimental forms of vocabulary and arithmetic reasoning tests were administered to the tenth-grade students in certain academic and vocational high schools in Massachusetts (Ref. 9). Two years later, the Indicator (Forms E and F) was administered to the same samples. The regression of each of the two aptitude tests on each Indicator scale was

[1] This sign of the existence of underlying types was suggested by Isabel Briggs Myers.

determined separately for 722 male and 718 female students who were present in both test administrations.[1]

RESULTS

F tests of the difference between the corresponding correlation coefficients and correlation ratios, which appear in Table 2, indicated that 6 of the 16 regressions departed significantly ($p < 0.05$) from linearity. Five of these 6 regressions involved the vocabulary test. The U shaped regression of the vocabulary test on the T-F scale for the boys, which appears in Figure 10, seemed to change in slope in the area of the T-F scale's zero point. None of the other significantly nonlinear regressions, which appear in Figures A to C (see p. 277, footnote[2]) seemed to change markedly or to be discontinuous in the region of the zero point.

TABLE 2

SIGNIFICANCE OF NONLINEAR REGRESSIONS OF VOCABULARY AND ARITHMETIC
REASONING TESTS ON INDICATOR SCALES FOR MALE AND FEMALE HIGH SCHOOL
STUDENTS

Scale	k	Males[a] r	η	F	k	Females[b] r	η	F
			Vocabulary test regressions					
E–I	18	0·03	0·19	1·67*	18	−0·02	0·17	1·30
S–N	17	−0·30	0·36	2·08†	17	−0·38	0·42	1·88*
T–F	13	0·12	0·24	3·09†	14	−0·02	0·14	1·22
J–P	19	−0·17	0·26	1·66*	19	−0·15	0·24	1·54
			Arithmetic reasoning test regressions					
E–I	18	0·03	0·10	0·43	18	0·02	0·16	1·10
S–N	17	−0·17	0·20	0·67	17	−0·22	0·27	1·34
T–F	13	−0·02	0·16	1·75	14	0·01	0·15	1·35
J–P	19	−0·13	0·21	1·23	19	−0·10	0·23	1·73*

[a] N = 722
[b] N = 718
* $p < 0.05$
† $p < 0.01$

[1] In Study IIIa and Study IIIb Indicator scores were grouped in intervals of three units each and extreme intervals were combined so that each interval contained at least six students. Scores for the other intervals, which were all two digits, were grouped into intervals of two units each, except for the arithmetic reasoning test scores in Study IIIa, which were left ungrouped.

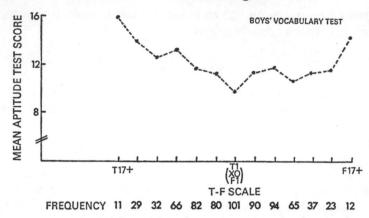

Figure 10. Nonlinear regression on the T-F scale for high school students.

STUDY IIIB: REGRESSIONS OF APTITUDE TESTS AND GPA FOR COLLEGE STUDENTS

METHOD

The Indicator was administered to the entering male freshmen class at Stanford University. Scores on the Scholastic Aptitude Test's (Refs. 5 and 7) Verbal (SAT-V) and Mathematical (SAT-M) sub-tests and freshman-year grade point average (GPA) were later obtained for 828 of these students. The regression of each of these variables on each Indicator scale was determined for this sample.

RESULTS

F tests of the difference between the corresponding correlation coefficients and correlation ratios, which appear in Table 3, indicated that the regression of SAT-V on the S-N scale and the regression of GPA on the T-F scale both departed significantly ($p < 0.05$) from linearity. Neither of these regressions, which appear in Figures D and E (see p. 277, footnote[2]), seemed to change markedly or to be discontinuous in the region of the zero point.

TABLE 3

SIGNIFICANCE OF NONLINEAR REGRESSIONS OF SAT–V, SAT–M, AND
GPA ON INDICATOR SCALES FOR MALE STANFORD UNIVERSITY FRESHMEN

		Regressions							
		SAT–V			SAT–M			GPA	
Scale	k	r	η	F	r	η	F	r	η	F
E–I	18	−0·13	0·17	0·65	−0·14	0·21	1·17	−0·04	0·11	0·58
S–N	18	−0·40	0·44	2·16	−0·19	0·24	1·07	−0·13	0·18	0·76
T–F	17	−0·02	0·17	1·55	0·08	0·17	1·30	−0·03	0·22	2·69*
J–P	19	−0·21	0·25	0·98	−0·07	0·17	1·14	0·07	0·13	0·66

Note N = 828
  * $p < 0.01$

STUDY IV: INTERACTIONS AMONG TYPE DIMENSIONS

The notion of interaction among the Indicator scales which is explicit in the typological theory implies that the scales should interact in relation to other variables affected by typological differences; statistically, the values obtained for the other variables should not be reducible to sums of main effects for each separate type category.

METHOD

The subjects were drawn from the sample of male Stanford University freshmen used in Study IIIb. At least 10 students were in each of the 16 type classifications (indeterminate type classifications were ignored), so 10 were randomly selected from each of the type classifications and classified by their type classification in a $2 \times 2 \times 2 \times 2$ factorial design. Separate analyses of variance were made for four variables: SAT–V, SAT–M, freshman-year GPA and freshman-year over-under achievement (actual GPA less GPA predicted from SAT–V and SAT–M, as computed for the same group of 160 students).

RESULTS

The mean squares and F ratios for these analyses of variance appear in Table E (see p. 277, footnote[2]). The main effects of two Indicator scales
K*

(S-N and J-P) were significant ($p<0.05$), each for two dependent variables (SAT-V and SAT-M), but no first-, second-, third-, or fourth-order interactions among the Indicator scales were significant ($p<0.05$) for any dependent variable.

STUDY V: MODERATOR VARIABLE PROPERTIES

The typological theory makes an implicit distinction between phenotypical and genotypical behaviour. People of different types may behave similarly, but their behaviour is thought to result from different combinations and patterns of surface traits which are peculiar to their type. One implication of this notion is that the regression equations for predicting a given behaviour from other variables would depend upon the subjects' type classification; different weights for the predictors or entirely different predictors would be required for subjects in the various type classifications. In short, the Indicator should moderate the regressions of other variables upon one another (Ref. 26).

METHOD

The Indicator was administered to the entering freshman class at Wesleyan University and California Institute of Technology. These students' SAT-V and SAT-M scores and freshman GPA, freshman over-under achievement (actual GPA less GPA predicted from SAT-V and SAT-M, as computed from the same sample) and freshman dropout (available for the California Institute of Technology only) were obtained later. The results for 225 Wesleyan men and 201 California Institute of Technology men were analysed separately. Standard partial regression coefficients for predicting each of the academic criteria from the SAT scales were computed for students within the two major type categories on each scale (e.g., the SAT scales' regression coefficients for students classified as extraverts and the students classified as introverts). Indeterminate categories were not analysed because few students were in them.

RESULTS

The standard partial regression coefficients appear in Table F (see p. 277, footnote[2]). There were no significant ($p<0.05$) differences in regression coefficients between the two type categories on any Indicator scale.

STUDY VI: EFFECTS OF TYPE INDETERMINING

According to the Jungian typology, failure to develop one member of each pair of attitudes or functions results in fluctuating and ineffective behaviour. Consequently, type indeterminacy on the Indicator should be related to variables which reflect such behaviour.

METHOD

The subjects were the Wesleyan University and California Institute of Technology students used in Study V. The two samples were analysed separately. Two measures of type indeterminacy were derived for each Indicator scale: a dichotomous measure—indeterminate or not indeterminate—based on the conventional criterion of a zero difference in scores for the two categories on each scale; and a continuous score based on the actual difference in scores for the two categories on each scale. Correlations were computed between these indeterminacy measures and four kinds of variables presumed to reflect ineffective or maladjusted behaviour which were available for either of the two samples: freshman GPA, freshman over-under achievement, freshman dropout—available for California Institute of Technology only—and Minnesota Multiphasic Personality Inventory (Ref. 14) scores—available for Wesleyan University only.

RESULTS

None of the correlations between the indeterminacy measures and GPA, over-under achievement, or dropout, which appear in Table G (see p. 277, footnote[2]), was significant ($p < 0.05$).

Correlations between the indeterminacy measures and the MMPI scales (corrected for K where appropriate) appear in Table H (see p. 277, footnote[2]). There were only four significant ($p < 0.05$) correlations with the clinical scales, which might be expected by chance because of the large number (80) of significance tests applied to the correlations between the Indicator scales and the clinical scales. However, J-P indeterminacy, in terms of both dichotomous and continuous measures, had a consistent pattern of low but significant ($p < 0.05$) correlations with the validity scales. The continuous indeterminacy measure correlated -0.16 with ?, -0.15 with L and 0.13 with F; the dichotomous measure correlated -0.24 with ? and 0.14 with K.

DISCUSSION

These studies, with one or two exceptions, offer little support for the structural properties attributed to the typology.

The moderate stability of the type classifications which was found, whether the type classifications were considered separately or in combination, is contrary to the notion that the Indicator type classifications reflect underlying categories which are relatively unchangeable, but it is understandable in view of the moderate internal consistency reliability of the type classifications and continuous scores (Ref. 32); the subjects (college freshmen), who were at an age when changes might well be comparatively large; and the fact that a change in score of one point can shift a person from one type classification to another. This study should be repeated with a larger sample.

Neither the shape of the Indicator score distributions nor the regressions of other variables on Indicator scales—with the exception of one regression on the T-F scale—support the existence of dichotomous types.

The failure of the Indicator score distributions to exhibit any marked evidence of bimodality is consistent with the results of investigations of the score distributions of an earlier version of the Indicator (Ref. 20) and the current one (Ref. 22). However, these findings conflict with several studies of other inventories which measure one or more of the Jungian personality type variables. Gray (Ref. 11) found bimodality in the distributions of the E-I, S-N and T-F scales of an inventory that is very similar to the Indicator, the Gray-Wheelwright Psychological Type Questionnaire (Refs. 10, 11, 12 and 13) and some indications of bimodality were found in the distributions of other extraversion-introversion scales by Ball (Ref. 1), Heidbreder (Ref. 15), Neymann (Ref. 23), Neymann & Kohlstedt (Ref. 24) and Schwegler (Ref. 27), but not by Campbell (Ref. 3), Conklin (Ref. 6), nor Root & Root (Ref. 25). In addition, Bash (Ref. 2) found marked bimodality in the distributions of a Rorschach extraversion index—arc tan (M/C).

No ready explanation can be offered for the apparent contradiction between the results of this study and those earlier studies which typically found quite marked bimodality. These contradictory findings are worth pursuing. Perhaps the first steps in such an enterprise should be attempts at replicating the earlier studies and a careful examination of the psychometric properties of the scales that they used.

Attempts to identify underlying types from bimodalities in distributions have serious limitations which cast doubt on the usefulness of this approach: regardless of the underlying variable's distribution, a scale's score distribution depends upon its items, e.g., high item intercorrelations can produce bimodality and item heterogeneity can suppress it (Ref. 8); scale scores may be confounded with extraneous variables (Ref. 8), such as social desirability response style; and no entirely satisfactory statistical test for bimodality exists, although an existing test (Ref. 20) does have interesting properties.

Although some nonlinear regressions of other variables on Indicator scales were found, only the regression of a vocabulary test on the T-F scale for high school boys seemed to change noticeably in the region of the zero point of the Indicator scale. This one regression would seem to have limited meaning since corresponding regressions of the vocabulary test on the T-F scale for the high school girls and of SAT-V on the T-F scale for the male Stanford University students were not significantly nonlinear. These studies have been limited to academic variables; other kinds of variables should also be investigated.

These generally negative findings about the nature of the regressions of other variables on Indicator scales conflict with other reported results (Refs. 21 and 22) which have been interpreted as demonstrating that regressions change sharply or even discontinuously in the region of each Indicator scale's zero point and, hence, support the existence of underlying types. Although the absence of information about the significance of the nonlinearity in these other regressions precludes a satisfactory assessment of their meaning, these other results do underline the desirability of more investigations in this area.

In any event, attempts to verify the existence of underlying types from sharp changes in regressions of other variables at the zero point on Indicator scales have two limitations: the variables which should display such a regression are difficult to identify on *a priori* grounds, unless the type theory is much more explicit than in the present case; and no statistical test exists for determining the point at which a change in the level or slope of the regression occurs, although a statistical test for discontinuity has been developed (Ref. 33). However, nonlinear regressions can be identified by the standard statistical test and then inspected for shifts at the zero point.

The interaction among the four dimensions, which has such a central place in the typology and largely distinguishes it from the usual trait approach, was not evident in the analyses of variance of academic aptitude and performance measures. But, again, the choice of appropriate dependent variables is crucial and other kinds of variables, particularly those from the personality sphere, should be investigated.

The finding that the Indicator scales did not moderate the regressions of the variables which were investigated implies that different patterns of surface traits are not associated with each type classification. The Indicator's moderator variable properties should be investigated further, using other variables and, perhaps, continuous Indicator scores instead of dichotomous type classifications.

Contrary to theoretical expectations, indeterminacy measures were unrelated to academic performance variables and personality measures, possibly because of ambiguities in the Indicator's measurement of type indeterminacy. Type indeterminacy, as it is measured by the Indicator, can be due to lack of development of the two polarities, which corresponds to Jung's conception and should have adverse consequences; or equal development of both polarities, which is unrelated to Jung's conception of type indeterminacy and, rather than being undesirable, is the goal of individuation.

To turn to the larger implications of these studies, a finding that the Indicator reflected the features of its underlying typological framework would have lent support to Jung's typology and partially validated the Indicator. The negative findings which, in fact, were obtained cannot be interpreted as clearly. They seem to mean either that Jung's typology is not consistent with the real world, or the Indicator does not correspond to the theoretical formulation of the typology, i.e., the Indicator does not operationally define the typology.

The available data do not allow a choice between these two interpretations. A comprehensive assessment of Jung's typology would seem to require studies employing a variety of techniques and measuring instruments. Obverse factor analysis is particularly suited to such investigations (Ref. 31). In a model study of this kind, Stephenson identified eight clusters of people corresponding to the eight Jungian types (Ref. 30). The extent to which the Indicator faithfully reflects the typology can only be gauged by an examination of the procedures used in constructing the Indicator, the content of the scales, their reliability and the network of the scales' relationships with other variables.

It should be noted that the findings about the typological framework reported in this article, even though they are, in the main, negative, have no necessary implications for the validity of the Jungian attitudes and functions, either as formulated by Jung or measured by the Indicator, which are integrated by this framework. Even if the typological framework has no reality—and the present results point in that direction—the attitudes and functions still may exist as continuous traits and have considerable meaning, while lacking the structural properties attributed to them. It would be wise to bear this possibility in mind in studies of the attitudes and functions, and their utility as measures in the personality domain.

REFERENCES

1. BALL, R. J., Introversion-extraversion in a group of convicts. *J. abnorm. soc. Psychol.*, **26**, 422–428, 1932.
2. BASH, K. W., Einstellungstypus and Erlebnistypus: C. G. Jung and Hermann Rorschach. *J. proj. Tech.*, **19**, 236–242, 1955.
3. CAMPBELL, KATHERINE J., The application of extraversion-introversion tests to the insane. *J. abnorm. soc. Psychol.*, **23**, 479–481, 1929.
4. COHEN, J., A coefficient of agreement for nominal scores. *Educ. and Psychol.*, *Measmt.*, **20**, 37–46, 1960.
5. COLLEGE ENTRANCE EXAMINATION BOARD, *A Description of the College Board Scholastic Aptitude Test*. Princeton, N.J.: College Entrance Examination Board, 1962.
6. CONKLIN, E. S., The determination of normal extravert-introvert interest differences. *J. genet. Psychol.*, **34**, 28–37, 1927.
7. DYER, H. S. & KING, R. G., *College Board Scores No. 2: Their Use and Interpretation*. Princeton, N.J.: College Entrance Examination Board, 1955.
8. EYSENCK, H. J., *Dimensions of Personality*. London: Routledge & Kegan Paul, 1947.
9. FRENCH, J. W., *Comparative Prediction of Success and Satisfaction in High School Curricula*. (Res. Bull. No. 62–4) Princeton, N.J.: Educational Testing Service, 1962.
10. GRAY, H., Jung's psychological types: meaning and consistency of the questionnaire. *J. gen. Psychol.*, **37**, 177–186, 1947.
11. ——, Jung's psychological types in men and women. *Stanford med. Bull.*, **6**, 29–36, 1948.
12. ——, Jung's psychological types: ambiguous scores and their interpretation. *J. gen. Psychol.*, **40**, 63–88, 1949.
13. —— & WHEELWRIGHT, J. B., Jung's psychological types: their frequency of occurrence. *J. gen. Psychol.*, **34**, 3–17, 1946.

14. HATHAWAY, S. R. & MCKINLEY, J. C., *Minnesota Multiphasic Personality Inventory: Manual.* (Rev. ed.) New York: Psychological Corporation, 1951.

15. HEIDBREDER, EDNA, Measuring introversion and extraversion. *J. abnorm. soc. Psychol.*, **21**, 120–134, 1926.

16. JACOBI, J., *The Psychology of C.G. Jung.* (Rev. ed.) New Haven: Yale Univ. Press, 1951.

17. JUNG, C. G., *Psychological Types.* London: Routledge & Kegan Paul, 1923.

18. ——, *Modern Man in Search of a Soul.* New York: Harcourt, Brace, 1933.

19. ——, *Collected Works.* Vol. 7. Two essays on analytical psychology. New York: Pantheon, 1953.

20. LORD, F. M., *Multimodal Score Distributions on the Myers-Briggs Type Indicator.* (Res. Memo. No. 58–8). Princeton, N.J.: Educational Testing Service, 1958.

21. MYERS, ISABEL B., Inferences as to the dichotomous nature of Jung's types, from the shape of regressions of dependent variables upon Myers-Briggs type indicator scores. *Amer. Psychologist*, **17,** 364, 1962.

22. ——, *The Myers-Briggs Type Indicator: Manual.* Princeton, N.J.: Educational Testing Service, 1962.

23. NEYMANN, C. A., The relation of extraversion-introversion to intelligence and tuberculosis. *Amer. J. Psychiat.*, **9,** 687–696, 1930.

24. —— & KOHLSTEDT, K. D., A new diagnostic test for introversion-extraversion. *J. abnorm. soc. Psychol.*, **23,** 482–487, 1929.

25. ROOT, A. R. & ROOT, ELIZABETH B., A study of the Neymann-Kohlstedt diagnostic test for introversion-extraversion. *J. abnorm. soc. Psychol.*, **26,** 415–421, 1932.

26. SAUNDERS, D. R., Moderator variables in prediction. *Educ. and Psychol. Measmt.*, **16,** 209–222, 1965.

27. SCHWEGLER, R. A., *A Study of Introvert-extravert Responses to Certain Test Situations.* New York: Teachers College, Columbia University, Bureau of Publications, 1929.

28. SHELDON, W. H., *The Varieties of Temperament.* New York: Harper, 1942.

29. SPRANGER, E., *Types of Men.* New York: Hafner, 1928.

30. STEPHENSON, W., Methodological consideration of Jung's typology. *J. ment. Sci.*, **85,** 185–205, 1939.

31. ——, *The Study of Behavior.* Chicago: Univ. Chicago Press, 1953.

32. STRICKER, L. J. & ROSS, J., *A Description and Evaluation of the Myers-Briggs Type Indicator*. (Res. Bull. No. 62–6) Princeton, N.J.: Educational Testing Service, 1962.

33. THISTLETHWAITE, D. L. & CAMPBELL, D. T., Regression-discontinuity analysis: an alternative to the ex post facto experiment. *J. educ. Psychol.*, **51**, 309–317, 1960.

25

Effects of Impulsivity, Introversion and Individual Values upon Association under Free Conditions[1]

SANDRA DUNN, JOAN BLISS & ELSA SIIPOLA

First published in *Journal of Personality*, **26**, 61–76, 1958

THE STANDARD word-association test has, in general, been disappointing as a diagnostic tool. Despite its sensitivity to symptoms of emotional maladjustment, it has failed to provide measures of other important aspects of the personality. Since modern clinical and experimental evidence indicates that temperament, attitudes and values do influence associative processes, it seems plausible to suspect that the special conditions imposed in the standard test are responsible for its failure to reflect these basic aspects of the personality.

Recently Siipola, Walker & Kolb (Ref. 7) described a modified technique of word association which approximates the degree of freedom provided in other projective tests. Through the device of relaxing time pressure and giving S freedom to choose any type of associate, this new technique produced a fundamental change in the character of the whole associative process. Instead of mechanically giving prompt, impersonal associations related to his immediate impression of the stimulus, the S usually delayed, experienced rich imagery and actively searched for the associate which seemed most satisfying to him personally. The authors labelled the unique character of the associative process under free conditions as 'subject-bound' and contrasted it with the 'stimulus-bound' type of process characteristic of association under time pressure.

The present study is based upon the assumption that such aspects of the personality as temperament, attitudes and values are more likely to show a strong influence on associative processes under conditions sufficiently free from external restraints to allow the S to choose freely among widely varying interpretations of the task and of the speed of operation. That the modified technique described in the earlier study provides such freedom is supported by the results obtained. The tempo

---

[1] This study is based upon Honours theses submitted by Joan Bliss (Part 1) and Sandra Dunn (Part II).

290

spontaneously set by individuals under these free conditions varied from a rapid pace of 2 sec. to a leisurely pace of 26 sec. and the content of the associations varied from objective, common associates for some Ss to subjective, personal associates for others. Under free conditions, then, some Ss impose upon themselves a task attitude of extreme time pressure which induces a relatively stimulus-bound associative process, whereas others, taking full advantage of the freedom to delay, experience a subject-bound associative process.

This study concerns the relation of these wide individual differences in self-imposed task attitudes to certain specific temperamental and attitudinal variables: impulsivity-inhibition, extraversion-introversion and individual values. One would expect that, given the freedom to choose, impulsive, extraverted, or practical individuals will prefer a stimulus-bound manner of associating, while inhibited, introverted, or aesthetically inclined individuals will prefer a subject-bound approach. Thus, these contrasting personality characteristics should be related in a predictable manner to contrasting patterns of associative reaction. The objective criteria utilized to distinguish the two types of associative patterns are as follows: a stimulus-bound pattern is indicated by shorter reaction time, more contrast, associates, and less awareness of associative processes intervening between stimulus and response, as compared to a subject-bound pattern indicated by longer reaction time, more adjective-noun associates and more frequent awareness of complex intervening associative processes.

A theory describing the significance and interrelations of these criteria is fully presented in the previous study (Ref. 7). In brief, a stimulus-bound associative pattern is, by definition, tied to a set for speed, which automatically induces a limitation of the associations to the type that come most quickly, namely, contrast associates. Since this type of associative process stops quickly at the early stage of mere identification of the stimulus, the S has no complex intervening processes to report. A subject-bound pattern is tied to a set to find a personally meaningful association, which involves a time-consuming intervening process, typified by concrete visual images of objects or events. Since this type of intervening process features concrete objects, the final word selected by S to express the personal meaning of the process is likely to be the name of a concrete object, a noun. Thus a noun response to an adjective stimulus provides a convenient index of the subject-bound type of pattern.

PART I: IMPULSIVITY-INHIBITION AND EXTRAVERSION-INTROVERSION

In terms of specific hypotheses, the problem here can be stated as follows. (a) Ss who are typically impulsive are more likely to select a relatively stimulus-bound manner of associating under free conditions, as evidenced by faster reaction time, more contrast associates and less frequent awareness of intervening processes; whereas typically inhibited Ss are more likely to select a relatively subject-bound approach, as evidenced by slower reaction time, more adjective-noun associates and more frequent awareness of intervening processes. (b) Ss who are thinking-extraverts are more likely to select the relatively stimulus-bound pattern under free conditions; whereas Ss who are thinking-introverts are more likely to select the relatively subject-bound pattern.

The temperamental variable of impulsivity-inhibition was selected to feature the difference in tempo of reaction in the two associative patterns. It is assumed that under conditions which offer S free choice of associative tempo, the temperamentally impulsive person, quick to react under most conditions, will spontaneously prefer to associate also at a fast tempo; the temperamentally inhibited person will prefer to delay and control his impulsivity even in an association test. The variable of extraversion-introversion of the thinking type was selected to focus upon the difference in the objective-subjective aspect of the two patterns of association. It is assumed that the typical thinking-extravert will be readily satisfied with giving objective, impersonal associates related to his immediate impression of the stimulus; whereas the thinking-introvert will prefer the introspective search for a subjectively oriented, personally meaningful associate.

PROCEDURE

The Guilford Inventory of Factors STDCR (Ref. 4) was used as a measure of impulsivity-inhibition (scale R) and of extraversion-introversion (scales T and S). It was administered to all 222 female students in an elementary course. Extreme high and low groups (with cutting points at the 15th and 85th percentiles) were then selected on scales R, T and S. Several weeks later the Ss in these selected groups were individually given Tendler's list of 25 neutral stimulus words (Ref. 8) under exactly the same free conditions as used by Siipola, Walker &

Kolb (Ref. 7). The atmosphere was relaxed and S, unaware of being timed, was free to select any single associate which she wished to report.

Scale R (rhathymia) provides a direct measure of impulsivity-inhibition, while scale T provides a direct measure of extraversion-introversion of the thinking type (defined as absence or presence of an inclination towards meditative or introspective thinking). It was predicted that Ss in the Low R impulsive group (N = 28) and in the Low T extraverted group (N = 22) would show the stimulus-bound pattern, whereas Ss in the High R inhibited group (N = 28) and in the High T introverted group (N = 24) would show the subject-bound syndrome. Scale S, which provides a measure of another dimension of extraversion-introversion (shyness and seclusiveness in contrast to sociability), was excluded from our specific predictions above. While, on theoretical grounds, one would not expect social extraversion-introversion to be directly related to our two associative patterns, the high correlation of scale S with Scale T would suggest an indirect relation (Ref. 5). Thus Ss in the Low S extraverted group (N = 29) might show a pattern similar to that of the Low T group, while Ss in the High S introverted group (N = 26) might show a pattern similar to that of the High T group. Scale S was included to clarify the importance of differentiating the two types of extraversion-introversion.

RESULTS

The results were analysed in terms of the reaction time and content of the associative responses. The statistical treatment is restricted to an analysis of the results for the 15 adjective stimulus words, since adjective stimuli have been found to be well suited to yield differentiation between stimulus-bound and subject-bound associates (Ref. 7).

Table 1 presents a comparison of the spontaneous tempo of associative reaction (based upon individual medians) adopted by Ss low or high on scales R, T and S. Ss with low scores on any of the three scales were relatively prompt in their reactions, whereas Ss high on these scales delayed their reactions. However, only in the case of scale R is there a statistically reliable difference (p = 0·025) between the low and high groups. Thus the results clearly confirm our prediction that individuals who are typically impulsive choose to react more promptly than do inhibited individuals on an association test administered under free conditions. The results for scale T fail to confirm our prediction.

TABLE 1

MEAN REACTION TIMES (SEC.) OF HIGH AND LOW GROUPS

Guilford Scale	Low Group	High Group	Diff.	t	p
R	3·4	5·1	1·7	2·05	<0·025[1]
T	3·4	4·0	0·6	0·78	>0·10
S	3·8	4·9	1·1	1·09	>0·10

[1] One-tailed test

The content of the associations was analysed according to the method of scoring adopted in the previous study. It consists of classifying the responses according to a system based on purely formal grammatical categories. In this study we are concerned with only two categories: adjective-adjective responses of the contrast type (e.g., quiet-loud) and adjective-noun responses (e.g., quiet-peace). For the present list of stimulus words, it has been established that the frequency of contrast responses is negatively correlated with reaction time and the frequency of adjective-noun responses is positively correlated with reaction time (Ref. 7). Hence, a fast tempo of reaction and contrast responses are related criteria of a stimulus-bound pattern, whereas a slow tempo and adjective-noun responses are related criteria of a subject-bound pattern.

Table 2 presents the frequencies with which responses in the two significant categories of content occurred. As would be expected, the groups low on scales R, T and S gave a higher frequency of contrast responses and a lower frequency of adjective-noun responses than did the groups high on these scales. Again, only in the case of scale R is there a statistically reliable difference between the low and the high groups in support of our prediction that impulsive individuals will give more contrast associates while inhibited individuals will give more adjective-noun associates. The results for scale T, although yielding differences in the correct direction, again fail to confirm our prediction.

Immediately after giving her associations to the Tendler list, S was questioned in detail as to the nature of the associative process intervening between the stimulus words and the responses given. The critical question concerned the issue of whether or not S was aware of any intervening process. No process was recorded if S reported that her responses were direct or automatic ('they just popped into my head') and if, upon direct inquiry, S denied awareness of specific intervening processes. Some process was recorded if S reported specific mediating

TABLE 2

MEAN FREQUENCIES OF CONTRAST AND ADJECTIVE-NOUN RESPONSES

| | Contrast Responses | | | | |
Guilford Scale	Low Group	High Group	Diff.	t	p
R	2·6	0·8	1·8	2·82	<0·01[1]
T	2·6	1·5	1·1	1·19	>0·10
S	2·4	2·0	0·4	0·56	>0·10
	Adjective-Noun Responses				
R	9·2	11·2	2·0	2·17	0·02[1]
T	10·3	11·0	0·7	0·58	>0·10
S	9·0	10·5	1·5	1·46	>0·10

[1] One-tailed test

processes aroused by the stimulus word (concrete visual images, moods or feelings, words other than the response word, or other processes). If several types of processes were reported, S was asked to select the dominant one, that which applied to the largest number of items.

Table 3 presents the evidence on the nature of the intervening processes drawn from the Ss' introspections. As would be expected, the majority of the Ss high on scale R, T and S reported some process intervening between stimulus and response, whereas only a minority of Ss low on these scales so reported. Chi^2 tests based upon the frequencies for the final summary values in Table 3 reveal statistically significant

TABLE 3

PERCENTAGES OF SS REPORTING INTERVENING PROCESSES

| | Scale R | | Scale T | | Scale S | |
Dominant Process	Low	High	Low	High	Low	High
Images	21	39	18	38	17	31
Moods	4	4	5	13	14	8
Words	4	14	0	8	0	8
Others	4	7	9	0	7	12
Some Process (Total)	32	64	32	58	38	58
No Process	68	36	68	42	62	42
	$\chi^2 = 5·79$		$\chi^2 = 3·25$		$\chi^2 = 2·15$	
	p = <0·10[1]		p = <0·05[1]		p = <0·10[1]	

[1] One-tailed test

differences in the cases of scales R and T. These findings support our prediction that while impulsive and non-introspective individuals will be generally unaware of meditating processes, inhibited and meditative individuals will usually report complex intervening processes. These data also establish more firmly the fact that concrete visual imagery is the dominant intervening process most frequently reported under free conditions.

DISCUSSION

The results for Part I support our first hypothesis to the effect that opposite temperamental qualities of impulsivity and inhibition are related respectively to the stimulus-bound and subject-bound patterns of association under free conditions. It is not surprising that the personality dimension of impulsivity-inhibition identifies a pertinent variable which controls the self-selected rate of associative reaction. But exactly how shall we interpret the effects of impulsivity-inhibition upon the nature of the intervening associative process and the final associative product? A parsimonious explanation would hold that the variable of impulsivity-inhibition has a direct influence on response latency but only an indirect influence (through latency) on the quality of the intervening process and the associative content. Thus, as an expression of his temperament, the impulsive person prefers to associate at a fast tempo, and hence responds directly, without reflection, and automatically gives more contrast associates. The person of inhibited temperament prefers to associate at a leisurely pace, and hence experiences complex intervening processes of a type most readily expressed as adjective-noun associates.

The fact that the results generally fail to support our prediction of a relation between extraversion-introversion of the thinking type and the two patterns of association may be an artifact produced by the close relation of Guilford's scale T to maladjustment. Since it has already been shown that maladjustment scores are reliably related to the two associative patterns (Ref. 7), it seems plausible to assume that the maladjustment variable worked in opposition to the extraversion-introversion variable in the present study. According to Guilford, both our Low T and High T groups were maladjusted, so that their associative patterns would tend to be similar because of this factor in common.

PART II: INDIVIDUAL VALUES

The broad question investigated in this part is whether different individual values, as measured by the Allport-Vernon-Lindzey Study of Values (Ref. 1), are related to the stimulus-bound and subject-bound patterns of association under free conditions. This measure of six value systems was introduced here to include another aspect of the objective-subjective dimension of personality which might be more closely related to our two patterns of association (and less directly related to maladjustment) than Guilford's measures of extraversion-introversion. Knowledge of an individual's dominant value system should provide very definite information about the specific standard of evaluation that he will apply, in situations providing freedom of choice. One should be able to predict from his values the general manner in which a person will interpret the task of word association, the kind of evaluative choices he will make between alternative responses and the kind of responses that he will find personally most meaningful. Moreover, on the basis of a theoretical analysis of the relation of the six value systems to our problem, we came to the conclusion that these values could be classified under the following two relevant categories:

1. Extraceptive values: economic (E), theoretical (T), political (P).

2. Intraceptive values: aesthetic (A), religious (R), social (So).

These two categories are based directly upon Murray's concepts of extraception and intraception, which he carefully distinguishes from Jung's broader categories of extraversion and introversion (Ref. 6, pp. 210 ff.). They seem to catch a special quality of the objective-subjective dimension of personality directly related to our problem. To characterize the extraceptive individual Murray uses the following relevant terms: objective, tough-minded, impersonal, practical, utilitarian, scientific, materialistic, psychologically superficial, denotative in speech. In contrast, he characterizes the intraceptive individual as: subjective, tenderminded, personal, egocentric, impractical, imaginative, intuitive, idealistic, artistic or religious, psychologically penetrating, connotative in speech.

The classification of the six values under these two contrasting categories is obviously more appropriate in some cases than in others. The extraceptive category is most clearly represented by the economic value, with the theoretical and political values less clearly related. The intraceptive category is clearly represented by both the religious and aesthetic values, with the social value of somewhat doubtful relevance. Following this line of thinking, it seems quite safe to predict that Ss with a dominant economic value will show measurable associative differences from Ss with either a dominant religious or aesthetic value. Certainly the practical efficiency of a stimulus-bound approach which provides very quick denotative responses should appeal to the tough-minded 'economic man'. And the opportunity to exploit subjective imagery, feelings and penetrating connotations should appeal to the 'aesthete' or the 'religious man'. It seems plausible also, though much less certain, to predict that Ss with a dominant social value will associate similarly to those with aesthetic and religious values, and that Ss with theoretical and political values will associate similarly to those with economic values.

PROCEDURE

The present experiment was designed with a twofold purpose. The first was to determine whether six groups of Ss, each with a different dominant value, fall into a predicted order as to the speed of associative reaction which they adopt, and whether their reaction-time results justify empirically the separation of the six value groups into the two categories, extraceptive and intraceptive. If this should prove true, the second purpose was to determine whether groups with extraceptive values show the total stimulus-bound associative pattern while groups with intraceptive values show the total subject-bound syndrome.

Six groups representing the six value systems were obtained from a class of 246 female students in introductory psychology. The 15 Ss representing the most extreme 'pure type' with a single dominant value were chosen for each of the six groups: groups A, R, So, E, T, P. These 90 Ss were given individually the Tendler word association list under exactly the same free conditions described in Part I.

The problem can be stated, then, in terms of the following three hypotheses. (a) In speed of associative reaction the order of groups from fastest to slowest will be as follows: group E, groups T and P, group So, groups R and A. (b) There will be significant differences between the reaction times of groups E, T and P, on the one hand and groups A, R and So on the other hand. (c) As a group, Ss with extraceptive values (group ETP) will show the total stimulus-bound pattern of association under freedom as evidenced by faster reaction time, more contrast associates and less frequent awareness of intervening processes. As a group, Ss with intraceptive values (group ARSo) will show the total subject-bound pattern as evidenced by slower reaction time, more adjective-noun responses, and more frequent awareness of intervening processes.

RESULTS

The associative responses were first analysed in terms of reaction time. The spontaneous tempo of reaction (based upon each S's median reaction time) is revealed by the following group means in seconds: group E, 3·4; group P, 4·1; group T, 4·3; group So, 6·5; group R, 7·1; group A, 8·7. By using the reciprocals of these mean reaction times, the scores were converted into speed scores.

Table 4 gives the summary of an analysis of variance of the six groups based on the measure of speed of reaction. The significant F ratio for 'between' values indicates only that one or more of the possible differences among the six group means is significant, but it does not specify which differences are significant. Therefore, two further tests were carried out.

TABLE 4

SUMMARY OF ANALYSIS OF VARIANCE OF REACTION TIMES

Source	df	MS	F	p
Between Values	5	0·0784	5·41	<0·01
Trend	1	0·3694	25·48	<0·01
Residual	4	0·0056	<1·00	ns
Within Groups	84	0·0145		
Total	89			

In order to test the specific first prediction of the trend or order of group means, orthogonal polynomials were applied according to a method suggested by Abelson.[1] The predicted regressions weights for groups A, R, So, T, P, E were, in that order, −4, −4, −1, +2, +2, +5. When applied to the data, this set of weights yields an F for the predicted trend which is significant considerably beyond the 0·01 level, as is shown in Table 4. The residual is not significant, indicating that no other trend orthogonal to the predicted one is necessary to explain the results obtained. These results, then, confirm our first prediction. In so

[1] The authors are indebted to Robert P. Abelson of Yale University for his adaptation of the method published by Grant (Ref. 3).

far as speed of reaction is concerned, group E was the most stimulus-bound and groups A and R were the most subject-bound, with the other three groups falling in between in the order predicted.

In order to test the second prediction that there would be significant differences between the reaction times of groups E, T, P on the one hand and groups A, R, So on the other hand, Duncan's Range Test (Ref. 2) was applied. The results, presented in Table 5, show that the six value groups separated into two subsets as predicted.

TABLE 5

SUMMARY OF APPLICATION OF DUNCAN'S TEST TO REACTION TIMES

	Groups					
	A	R	So	T	P	E
[1]Results: Means (reciprocals)	0·1488	0·1584	0·1778	0·2740	0·2846	0·3128
Shortest Significant Ranges						
p	2	3	4	5	6	
Rp (0·05)	0·0880	0·0927	0·0958	0·0977	0·0995	

[1] Any two means not underscored by the same line are significantly different; any two means underscored by the same line are not significantly different.

There was a statistically significant difference between each extraceptive value and each intraceptive value, while at the same time there were no significant differences between the values falling within each of these two major categories. This finding fully justifies the separation of the six value groups into two main groups: the extraceptive (group ARSo) and the intraceptive (group ETP). In addition, we have automatically confirmed our third prediction in so far as it concerns reaction time.

Our next task is to determine whether, in addition to the differences in reaction time, the extraceptive group showed the stimulus-bound pattern in content as indicated by a higher frequency of contrast associates and whether the intraceptive group showed the subject-bound pattern with a higher frequency of adjective-noun responses.

Table 6 presents the frequencies with which responses in the two significant categories of content occurred. These results fully support our prediction. Group ETP, in comparison to group ARSo, gave a higher frequency of contrast responses and a lower frequency of adjective-noun responses; both of these differences between the groups are significant at the 0·001 level. The results demonstrate, then, that the two groups do not merely associate at different rates; they produce different types of associates as well. The group with extraceptive values produces relatively more associations which merely define or denote the stimulus; a contrast response is an effective device for quick identification (long is not short). The group with intraceptive values produces more associations which express or connote the concrete imagery of processes intervening between stimulus and response, that is, noun responses to adjective stimuli.

TABLE 6

MEAN FREQUENCIES OF CONTRAST AND ADJECTIVE-NOUN RESPONSES

	Contrast Responses				Adjective-Noun Responses			
Group	Mean	Group	Mean		Group	Mean	Group	Mean
A	0·5	E	3·5		A	11·1	E	8·3
R	0·9	T	3·3		R	11·1	T	7·9
So	1·6	P	2·5		So	10·1	P	9·2
ARSo	1·0	ETP	3·1		ARSo	10·8	ETP	8·5

$$\text{Diff.} = 2·1 \qquad\qquad \text{Diff.} = 2·3$$
$$t = 3·66 \qquad\qquad\qquad t = 3·01$$
$$p = 0·001^1 \qquad\qquad\quad p = 0·001^1$$

[1] One-tailed test

There is finally the question of whether group ARSo, in comparison to group ETP, shows more frequent awareness of processes intervening between stimulus and response. Table 7 presents the evidence from the introspections.

In order to obtain a more detailed record, the method of collecting and analysing the introspective data was changed from that described for Part I. In addition to the general inquiry following the Tendler list of items, a special extended inquiry was included. It was based upon five additional stimulus words, with the questioning following immediately after the response to each item. This special inquiry was designed to avoid the possible errors of memory in the method utilized for Part 1. Since many Ss now reported their intervening processes in great detail and often reported several processes as equally prominent (e.g., a visual image and alternative words to express this image), all processes reported during the special inquiry were recorded for each S instead of merely

TABLE 7

PERCENTAGES OF Ss REPORTING INTERVENING PROCESSES IN SPECIAL INQUIRY

Type of Process	Groups							
	A	R	So	P	T	E	ARSo	ETP
Images	100	80	70	50	43	43	82	45
Moods	25	30	20	17	0	0	25	6
Words	63	90	40	50	29	29	64	36
Some Process (Total)	100	90	70	83	57	43	87	61
No Process	0	10	30	17	43	57	13	39

$$\chi^2 = 4\cdot10$$
$$p = <0\cdot025^1$$

¹ One-tailed test

the dominant process as in Part I. The data in Table 7 are based upon 54 Ss, divided equally between the two groups, who were given the complete inquiry.

The results presented in Table 7 confirm our prediction concerning intervening processes. Group ARSo, in comparison to group ETP, showed a significantly higher frequency of cases reporting some process; a Chi² test based on the final summary values indicates that the difference is significant at the 0·025 level. In comparing the general magnitude of these figures with those of Table 3 one realizes that the special type of inquiry used here probably encouraged the Ss not merely to report, but actually to experience, more intervening processes.

DISCUSSION

The results for Part II, in confirming all three of our predictions, prove that the broad extraceptive-intraceptive dimension of values is related to the two distinguishable patterns of association which we have designated by the terms stimulus-bound and subject-bound. In so far as the specific value systems are concerned, Ss with economic values are consistently most stimulus-bound and Ss with aesthetic or religious values are consistently most subject-bound, while Ss with the other values fall in between. The fact that the same list of common, neutral stimulus words given to individuals with different values yields associative reactions so decisively different in content and latency adds firm support to the contention that, under certain conditions, individual values can constitute a critical determinant of simple cognitive processes.

In Part II, as in Part I, we have found three closely related dependent variables (latency, kind of associates and type of mediating processes) to be significantly tied to a personality variable. The critical question raised now is whether the same explanation should be applied here as in Part I where, for the dimension of impulsivity-inhibition, latency was considered the primary dependent variable with the others representing secondary effects. Our tentative answer must be negative. In the case of values, we hold that the primary dependent variable is the kind of associative process and product preferred by the S and that response latency varies as a related consequence of such preferences. Ss with extraceptive values prefer an objectively orientated associative process closely tied to the stimulus and often culminating in a contrast response; hence their response latency tends to be short. Ss with intraceptive values prefer a subjectively orientated, personally meaningful, type of associative process tied to concrete imagery and often culminating in an adjective-noun response, hence their response latency tends to be long.

Thus we maintain that different hypotheses are required to account for the relation of our two associative patterns to values and to impulsivity-inhibition. Conclusive evidence to support this position could be supplied only by extensive further experimentation. The main argument that we can offer to support the need for the different hypotheses presented is that the present research, which successfully confirmed several specific predictions, would have been impossible to design without these particular hypotheses. The personality variable of impulsivity-inhibition was selected for investigation only because of its obvious relation to speed of reaction, while the variable of individual values was selected wholly on the basis of its promise of relating to differences in evaluative preferences among various kinds of associations. In Part II we proceeded by first making an analysis of the kind of associative processes and products which would appeal to individuals with each of the six different values, and in the course of this analysis, we found that the value systems could be grouped or arranged along an intraceptive-extraceptive dimension likely to relate to specific qualitative differences in association. Only on the basis of this complex reasoning could we arrive by inference at the specific predictions made concerning the relation of value systems to response latency. The grouping (group ARSo, group ETP) and arrangement in order of the value systems, essential to predicting the patterns and latency of association, could not have been achieved had we proceeded from the bare assumption that latency was the primary dependent variable in associative reaction as related to personality variables. Although such an assumption would have the virtue of parsimony, it lacks predictive value since it does not suggest what particular relations might be expected between specific values and speed of associative reaction to common, neutral words.

A final question is whether the high degree of relatedness and the particular kinds of relations to temperament and values found under the free conditions of this study would hold under the standard test conditions of time pressure. The degree to which individual temperament and values can influence associative responses seems clearly dependent on the extent to which the conditions allow the individual to take the initiative and to choose freely between various possible interpretations of his task. It seems likely that it is dependent also on whether the general pace of reacting expected of S is slow enough to allow full engagement of such ego-involving factors as personal values. Pressure conditions practically prohibit personal involvement by forcing S to perform a rigidly defined task at the fastest tempo possible. As to the particular kind of relations found, previous evidence indicates that a given behavioural index will have a different kind of relation to personality factors under pressure from that which holds under free conditions (Ref. 7). Thus, fast reaction time and many contrast associates obtained under time pressure may not indicate impulsivity and extraceptive values but may have a completely different meaning there for personality dynamics.

SUMMARY

The problem investigated concerned the issue of whether the temperamental variable of impulsivity-inhibition and two attitudinal variables, extraversion-introversion and individual values, are related in a predictable manner to patterns of associative reaction when an association test is administered under free conditions without time pressure. The Guilford STDCR Inventory was used to select extreme groups in impulsivity-inhibition and in extraversion-introversion; the Allport-Vernon-Lindzey Study of Values was used to select extreme groups in the six value systems. Tendler's list of neutral stimulus words was administered under free conditions to these groups composed of women undergraduates.

In general, the results supported our prediction that under free conditions impulsivity-inhibition and individual values would be consistently related to certain patterns of associative reaction. The prediction related to the variable of extraversion-introversion was not confirmed.

Individual Values under Free Conditions 305

Specifically, the results showed that the typically impulsive S and the S with extraceptive values (economic, theoretical, political) both select a relatively stimulus-bound pattern of association; both have shorter reaction times, give more contrast associates and report that responses tend to come directly without mediating processes. In contrast, the typically inhibited S and the S with intraceptive values (aesthetic, religious, social) select a relatively subject-bound pattern; both have longer reaction times, give more adjective-noun associates and generally report complex processes, especially visual imagery, intervening between stimulus and response.

REFERENCES

1. ALLPORT, G. W., VERNON, P. E. & LINDZEY, G., *Study of Values: Manual of Directions.* New York: Houghton Mifflin, 1951.
2. DUNCAN, D. B., Multiple range and multiple F tests. *Biometrics,* **11,** 1–42, 1955.
3. GRANT, D. A., Analysis-of-variance tests in the analysis and comparison of curves. *Psychol. Bull.,* **53,** 141–154, 1956.
4. GUILFORD, J. P., *An Inventory of Factors STDCR: Manual of Directions.* Beverley Hills: Sheridan Supply Co., 1940.
5. —— & GUILFORD, R. B., Personality factors D, R, T and A. *J. abnorm. soc. Psychol.,* **34,** 21–36, 1939.
6. MURRAY, H. A., *Explorations in Personality.* New York: Oxford Univ. Press, 1938.
7. SIIPOLA, E., WALKER, W. N. & KOLB, D., Task attitudes in word association, projective and nonprojective. *J. Pers.,* **23,** 441–459, 1955.
8. TENDLER, A. D., Significant features of disturbance in free association. *J. Psychol.,* **20,** 65–89, 1945.

L

Genetic Studies

Editor's Introduction

THE TERM 'genetic' in the title of this section has two meanings in psychology, both of which are represented in the contents of the section. In the older sense of the term, preserved for instance in the title of the *Journal of Genetic Psychology*, it refers to the developmental aspects of behaviour. In the more recent sense it refers to hereditary mechanisms in the causation of behaviour. Behavioural genetics is a field of study which is receiving more and more attention, but unfortunately good, brief and not-too-technical papers relating to extraversion were hard to find, so that this aspect of the genetic field is underrepresented. A detailed survey of the main findings, criticisms and controversies concerning the genetic causation of personality differences is given in *The Biological Basis of Personality* (Ref. 2); the main upshot of this survey is a stress on the importance of genetic causes in our type of society, as well as on the need to think of psychological measurements in phenotypic terms. Roughly two-thirds to three-quarters of individual differences in extraversion-introversion are linked with genetic causes; this still leaves much room for environmental modification, but it also sets limits to these modifications which we disregard at our peril.

Developmental studies are much more numerous, and concern themselves with a variety of matters ranging from the season of the year in which the infant is born, through his position in the family (only child, first-born, last-born, etc.) to the congruity of his behaviour from birth to maturity. Can we foretell with any degree of accuracy how a child with a given personality will grow up? Sir Cyril Burt has shown, in a 35-year follow-up study of 763 children who at school had been rated by their teachers on extraversion and emotionality, that 15 per cent and 18 per cent respectively later became habitual offenders or neurotics. Of the former, 63 per cent had been rated as high on emotionality; 54 per cent had been rated high on extraversion, but only 3 per cent on introversion. Of the latter, 59 per cent had been rated as high on emotionality; 44 per cent had been rated as high on introversion, but only 1 per cent on extraversion. Thus emotional introverts tend to become neurotics, emotional extraverts criminals, very much as predicted in the writer's *Crime and Personality* (Ref. 3); considering the known lack of reliability of teachers' ratings the true relationships are almost certainly even more marked than would appear from these figures (Ref. 1). Apparently as the twig is bent . . .

Theories regarding the relation between childhood and adult personality require proper testing, however; it cannot be assumed that hypothesized relations will always eventuate. It has been a veritable psychiatric shibboleth that schizophrenics are introverted as children; the facts, as we shall see, do not bear this out. There is a dearth of good, thorough follow-up studies of large groups of children (the groups have to be large in order to contain any appreciable number of criminals, neurotics, schizophrenics, etc.); it is to be hoped that with our better and more reliable methods for measuring personality in young children more follow-up studies will be undertaken to verify or reject theories widely held at the moment.

H.J.E.

REFERENCES

1. Burt, C., Factoral studies of personality and their bearing on the life of a teacher, *Brit. J. educ. Psychol.*, **35,** 368–378, 1965.
2. Eysenck, H. J., *The Biological Basis of Personality*. Springfield, Ill.: Charles C. Thomas, 1967.
3. ——, *Crime and Personality*. London: Routledge & Kegan Paul, 1964.

26

Month and Season of Birth in Relation to Intelligence, Introversion-Extraversion and Inferiority Feelings

GEORGE FORLANO & VIRGINIA ZERILLI EHRLICH

First published in *Journal of Educational Psychology*, **32,** 1–12, 1941

THE PROBLEM of the relationship between the month of birth and physiological and psychological development of the human organism has been a fascinating and important one to many investigators. Sanders (Ref. 7) has reviewed studies concerning the relationship between birth month and physiological condition of the child. The major part of the evidence that he reviewed indicates that children born in Summer or in Autumn are heavier than those born in the other seasons.

A review of the studies on the psychological factors in relation to birth month reveals a unanimity in the general conclusion drawn; namely, that children born in the Winter months (December–March) are, as a group, duller than those born in the other seasons. Blonsky (Ref. 1) found the lowest mean IQ for children born in Winter. Pintner (Ref. 3) in 1931 studied 4925 cases and found the lowest IQ among those born in Winter. Pintner & Forlano (Ref. 4) in 1933 grouped 17,502 cases according to socio-economic status and found the lowest mean IQ to occur in the Winter months (January–March) regardless of whether the children came from low, average, or high socioeconomic status. Their findings definitely showed that month of birth is a factor in the intelligence test scores of children. Later, in 1937, Pintner & Maller (Ref. 6) studied the possible variations that might be caused by combining different ethnic groups. Their sample of cases consisted of school children belonging to three ethnic groups; namely, Italian, Jewish and Negro. The results of the Pintner-Maller study indicated that those born in the warm months (June–November) are on the average brighter than those born in the cold months (December–May). This general difference prevailed in each of the three ethnic groups. More recently, Fialkin & Beckman (Ref. 2) studied the test scores of 3189 adults. The test scores were obtained from the records of clients of the Adjustment Service of New York City. The results obtained from this study of the scores of adults, in general, agree with those obtained with children.

In 1939 Pintner & Forlano (Ref. 5) raised the question as to whether the same tendency found in the Northern Hemisphere, namely, the slightly lower average IQ of children born in Winter, would be found also in the Winter months on the Southern Hemisphere where the seasons are reversed. Their data from the Southern Hemisphere tend slightly to confirm previous findings in the Northern Hemisphere.

The study to be reported here seeks: first, the relation between month of birth and intelligence scores of adolescent males and, second, the relation between month of birth and certain aspects of personality; namely, introversion-extraversion and inferiority feeling.

DESCRIPTION OF THE POPULATION

The total number of cases employed in this report was 7897.[1] All cases were male students of a large public college in New York City. The test records were selected at random from the college files for entering students for the years from 1929 through 1936 inclusive.

THE TESTS

All matriculated students at entrance to college are given the Thurstone Psychological Examination, an intelligence test, the I-X test and Feradcom test. The latter two were devised or adapted by Payne.[2]

The one referred to as the I-X test affords presumably a measure of introversion-extraversion. The greater the score the more extraverted the person is supposed to be. Simple statements from this test are as follows:

(a) I indulge in daydreams and reveries, thinking of what I would like to do   True   False
(b) I seldom like to argue and force people to accept my ideas   True   False

[1] Some students missed taking one or both of the personality tests so that for the I-X test the cases numbered 7827, whereas the number for the Feradcom test was 7837.

[2] We wish to thank Professor Arthur F. Payne, formerly Director of the Student Personnel Bureau of the College of the City of New York, for his permission to make use of the files. The I-X test is an adaptation of L. R. Marston's Personality Rating Scale.

(c) I never break in on the conversation of
people sitting near me   True   False

The reliability of the I-X test by the split-half technique was found to be 0·78 by the Spearman-Brown prophecy formula. It must be remembered that the terms introversion-extraversion are used in many different meanings. Various tests so named may show low or even negative correlations among themselves. In this study the terms will always be used in quotation marks to indicate only the kind of introversion-extraversion measured by the I-X test.

The Payne Feradcom test affords a measure of feeling of inadequacy. The greater the score on this scale and greater the tendency toward inferiority feeling. The name Feradcom is an abbreviation for the Adlerian inferiority complex. The split-half reliability for this test is about 0·76. Some items from this test are as follows:

(a) I am much troubled by doubts about God
and immortality   True   False
(b) I often feel that I am set apart and different
from other people   True   False
(c) I welcome responsibilities of all sorts   True   False

TABULATION OF DATA

A distribution of test scores for each test and for each month was made. In addition, the months of March, June, September and December were subdivided into two groups, one for the first twenty days and the other for the rest of the month. This made a total of sixteen distributions for each test. The division in the case of the four months just mentioned made it possible later to combine the months into seasonal groups of either trimonthly units or according to astronomical delimitations. According to the grouping by trimonthly units, the Winter season would either tri-monthly units or according to astronomical delimitations. it possible to present our data in a form comparable with those of previous investigators. The grouping by astronomical seasons, e.g. Winter, December 21st through March 20th, seemed a more accurate procedure to follow.

L*

DISTRIBUTION OF INTELLIGENCE SCORES
BY MONTH OF BIRTH

Table 1 shows a summary of the means and standard deviations of the intelligence scores by month of birth. In agreement with the findings of other investigators, the means for the Winter months tend to be lower than those for Summer months. The means for the months of November, December, January and February range from 209·17 to 211·64. The means for the other months excluding September range from 212·06 to 215·47. September is an exception, but its mean is approximately the same as that of February, which has the highest mean of the Winter months.

How statistically significant are these monthly differences? The standard ratios, that is, the ratio of the mean difference to the standard error of the difference, are presented in Table 3. The month with the highest intelligence score is April with a mean of 215·47. January has the lowest mean score of 209·17. The standard error of the difference between these two monthly means is 2·71. The standard ratio for this mean difference is 2·32. In other words, the chances are 989·9 in 1000 that a similar mean difference would be found if this investigation were to be repeated under similar conditions. The differences among the other months would probably be less than the one between January and April. The results are in line with those of previous investigators who found that the lowest mean IQ occurred in the Winter months.

When we group by tri-monthly units, for example, the Winter season consisting of the months of January, February and March, we find that Autumn and Winter have lower mean intelligence scores than either Spring or Summer. The results are presented in Table 2. The greatest mean difference is between Spring and Autumn or Winter. The ratio of the mean difference between Spring and Winter to the sigma difference is 1·63, which is not a statistically significant ratio. The results are presented in Table 3. A similar result can be expected for a comparison between Spring and Autumn.

Since there was a possibility that the method of grouping the months by seasons in tri-monthly units might affect the trend of results, a second analysis was made according to astronomical limits. The seasons were taken as beginning and ending with the dates of the vernal and autumnal equinoxes and the Summer and Winter solstices. This regrouping caused interesting changes in the mean intelligence scores. These are given in Table 2. By defining Autumn as beginning on September 21st and ending

Table 1

MEAN AND STANDARD DEVIATION OF INTELLIGENCE, I-X AND FERADCOM SCORES BY MONTH OF BIRTH

Month	Intelligence scores			I-X scores			Feradcom scores		
	No. of students	Mean	Standard deviation	No. of students	Mean	Standard deviation	No. of students	Mean	Standard deviation
January	689	209·17	47·99	656	63·22	11·60	658	40·85	12·45
February	619	211·64	50·88	602	63·16	10·80	595	39·82	11·85
March	668	213·29	49·50	657	62·58	11·25	660	40·60	12·05
April	630	215·47	50·37	631	63·45	11·25	633	40·25	12·40
May	692	213·21	46·46	689	60·75	11·75	694	40·85	11·95
June	721	214·30	48·40	717	62·77	11·10	719	40·28	12·90
July	627	212·06	48·40	623	62·87	11·40	626	41·14	12·85
August	641	213·50	50·28	640	61·89	11·15	641	41·04	12·45
September	725	211·50	49·40	734	63·08	11·35	727	41·20	12·40
October	651	214·33	48·90	648	63·57	11·35	650	40·63	12·40
November	594	210·40	47·75	592	63·12	11·40	595	40·86	12·60
December	640	210·50	49·60	638	63·50	10·85	639	39·76	13·00
Total	7897			7827			7837		

TABLE 2

MEAN AND STANDARD DEVIATION OF INTELLIGENCE, I-X AND FERADCOM SCORES BY SEASON OF BIRTH

Season[1]	Intelligence scores			I-X scores			Feradcom scores		
	No. of students	Mean	Standard deviation	No. of students	Mean	Standard deviation	No. of students	Mean	Standard deviation
Autumn: October 1–December 31	1885	211·80	48·80	1878	63·40	11·20	1884	40·36	12·60
Winter: January 1–March 31	1976	211·80	48·84	1915	62·98	11·25	1913	40·45	12·15
Cold: October 1–March 31	3861	211·80	48·80	3793	63·20	11·25	3797	40·40	12·40
Spring: April 1–June 30	2043	214·30	48·40	2037	62·86	11·25	2046	40·46	12·40
Summer: July 1–September 30	1993	212·30	49·40	1997	62·36	11·30	1994	41·14	12·55
Warm: April 1–September 30	4036	213·30	48·90	4034	62·75	11·25	4040	40·80	12·50
Autumn: September 21–December 20	1881	213·00	48·80	1884	63·40	11·30	1882	40·46	12·47
Winter: December 21–March 20	1973	209·90	49·50	1913	63·00	11·15	1910	40·45	12·48
Cold: September 21–March 20	3854	211·40	49·20	3797	63·20	11·25	3792	40·45	12·45
Spring: March 21–June 20	2045	214·40	48·50	2040	62·95	11·30	2048	40·38	12·29
Summer: June 21–September 20	1998	212·50	49·20	1990	62·47	11·25	1997	41·15	12·64
Warm: March 21–September 20	4043	213·50	48·80	4030	62·75	11·25	4045	40·75	12·45

[1] We have grouped the seasons in two ways. The grouping in the lower part of the table is according to astronomical delimitations; whereas, the grouping in the upper half of the table is not, but follows the grouping used in previous studies.

on December 20th, the warmer days of September were included and the colder days of December excluded, the mean scores rose 1·20 points. By defining Winter as beginning on December 21st and ending on March 20th, the warmer part of March was eliminated and the colder days of December included. The mean for Winter then fell by 1·90 points. The standard ratio for the mean difference between Spring and Winter is 2·90, which is practically statistically significant. The results are given in Table 3.

By grouping the colder seasons and the two warmer seasons by either method, we find that the mean intelligence score is greater for the warmer seasons in both cases (Table 2); but neither mean difference yields a statistically significant ratio. The standard ratios are given in Table 4. Pintner & Forlano (Ref. 4) using more than twice the number of cases employed here found a similar tendency which yielded a ratio of 3·57, which is considered statistically significant.

At this point it is worth while to note that the regrouping of seasons according to vernal and autumnal equinoxes and Summer and Winter solstices tended to increase the standard ratios in the comparisons involving Winter and Spring and the cold and warm months. These results were presented in Tables 3 and 4.

In what season can we expect the highest mean intelligence score and in what season can we expect the lowest? Table 5 summarizes all the results on this point to date. A perusal of Table 5 shows that there is no agreement as to which season gives the highest intelligence rating. However, five of the six studies reviewed here show the mean for Spring equalling or surpassing the means for the other seasons. Every study shows the lowest mean intelligence score occurring in the Winter months.

The means for Summer and Autumn are very much alike and in some cases practically identical. The seasonal tri-monthly groupings of the Forlano & Ehrlich study give identical means for Autumn and Winter. However, using a more accurate and standard grouping; namely, that according to astronomical delimitations, the mean for Winter is noticeably decreased while that for Autumn is substantially increased. Using the astronomical grouping for seasons, we may conclude that the highest mean intelligence score will most probably occur in Spring while the lowest mean IQ will most probably occur in Winter.

TABLE 3

COMPARISON BETWEEN HIGHEST AND LOWEST MEAN INTELLIGENCE SCORES

Month or season	Number	Mean	Standard deviation	Mean difference	σ difference	Difference[1] / σ difference
Month:						
April	630	215·47	50·37	6·30	2·71	2·32
January	689	209·17	47·99			
Season:						
April 1–June 30 (Spring)	2043	214·30	48·40	2·50	1·53	1·63
January 1–March 31 (Winter)	1976	211·80	48·84			
Season:						
March–June 20 (Spring)	2045	214·40	48·50	4·50	1·55	2·90
December 21–March 20 (Winter)	1973	209·00	49·50			

[1] In the text this ratio is referred to as the standard ratio in order to differentiate it from the critical ratio of McGaughy and the experimental coefficient of McCall.

TABLE 4

COMPARISON BETWEEN MEANS OF WARM AND COLD MONTHS ON INTELLIGENCE SCORES

Season	Number	Mean	Standard deviation	Mean difference	σ difference	$\dfrac{\text{Difference}}{\sigma \text{ difference}}$
Cold: October 1–March 31	3861	211·80	48·80	1·50	1·10	1·36
Warm: April 1–September 30	4036	213·30	48·90			
Cold: September 21–March 20	3854	211·40	49·20	2·10	1·10	1·91
Warm: March 21–September 20	4043	213·50	48·80			

TABLE 5

SEASONAL MEAN IQs OR INTELLIGENCE SCORES

Subjects	Blonsky, backward children	Pintner, school children	Pintner, Forlano, school children	Pintner-Maller, coloured and white children	Fialkin-Beckman, male adults	Forlano[1] Ehrlich, male college students	Forlano[2] Ehrlich, male college students
Number	453	4,925	17·502	6,353	3,189	7,897	7,897
Spring	84·3	97·20	102·35	94·9	6·69	214·30	214·40
Summer	81·5	97·20	102·06	96·4	6·66	212·30	212·50
Autumn	81·3	97·10	101·83	96·5	6·58	211·80	213·00
Winter	80·1	95·95	100·65	94·5	6·53	211·80	209·90

[1] According to trimonthly groupings
[2] According to astronomical groupings

MONTH OF BIRTH AND PERSONALITY

Investigation of this phase of the problem is exploratory and the conclusions that may be drawn are provisional until reports of other investigators are received and examined as to consistency of findings.

The greater the score on the I-X test indicates a greater tendency toward extraversion. The analysis of the data on the I-X test is given in Table 1. The results show slight variations among the mean scores from month to month. There seems to be a general tendency for the warm months from May through August to have lower mean scores than the other months. In other words, persons born during these warm months tend to be slightly more introverted than those born during other months. The greatest mean difference is between May with a mean of 60·75 and October with a mean of 63·57. The standard ratio for this difference is 4·48 which is statistically significant. This is given in Table 6.

Grouping the months by seasons either in astronomical or trimonthly units, we find that the tendency remains the same. The higher mean I-X scores, presented in Table 2, occur in the cold seasons of Autumn and Winter. The lower mean I-X scores occur during the warmer seasons of Spring and Summer. The greatest differences occur between Summer and Autumn; the standard ratios, given in Table 2, being 2·88 for the trimonthly grouping and 2·58 for the astronomical grouping.

We do not obtain as marked trends when the seasons are combined into the larger units of cold and warm months, but the general tendency is the same. The standard ratios are given in Table 7.

Turning now to an analysis of the results on the Feradcom test we find that the mean differences from month to month are very small. It will be remembered that the greater the score on the Feradcom test the greater the tendency toward feelings of inferiority. Table 1 shows the mean Feradcom score by months. The range of means is from 39·76 for December to 41·20 for September, a difference of 1·44 points. The standard error of this difference is 0·69 and the standard ratio 2·09. The latter ratio is given in Table 8.

Table 2 presents the Feradcom results according to seasonal groupings. When analysed according to trimonthly units, the greatest difference is that between Summer and Autumn. The mean difference is 0·78 and the standard ratio given in Table 8 is 1·95. When analysed according to astronomical seasonal groupings the highest mean Feradcom score given in Table 2 occurs again in Summer with a mean of 41·15.

Table 6

Comparison Between Highest and Lowest Mean on the I–X Scale

Month or season	No. of students	Mean	Standard deviation	Mean difference	σ difference	Difference / σ difference
Month:						
October	648	63·57	11·35	2·82	0·63	4·48
May	689	60·75	11·75			
Season:						
October 1–December 31 (Autumn)	1878	63·40	11·20	1·04	0·36	2·88
July 1–September 30 (Summer)	1997	62·36	11·30			
September 21–December 20 (Autumn)	1884	63·40	11·30	0·93	0·36	2·58
June 21–September 20 (Summer)	1990	62·47	11·25			

TABLE 7

COMPARISON BETWEEN MEANS OF WARM AND COLD MONTHS ON THE I-X SCALE

Season	No. of students	Mean	Standard deviation	Mean difference	σ difference	$\dfrac{\text{Difference}}{\sigma \text{ difference}}$
Cold: October 1–March 31	3793	63·20	11·25	0·45	0·25	1·80
Warm: April 1–September 30	4034	62·75	11·25			
Cold: September 21–March 20	3797	63·20	11·25	0·45	0·25	1·80
Warm: March 21–September 20	4030	62·75	11·25			

TABLE 8

COMPARISON BETWEEN HIGHEST AND LOWEST MEAN ON THE FERADCOM SCALE

Month or season	Number	Mean	Standard deviation	Mean difference	σ difference	$\dfrac{\text{Difference}}{\sigma \text{ difference}}$
Month:						
September	727	41·20	12·40	1·44	0·69	2·09
December	639	39·76	13·00			
Season:						
July 1–September 30 (Summer)	1994	41·14	12·55	0·78	0·40	1·95
October 1–December 31 (Autumn)	1884	40·36	12·60			
June 21–September 20 (Summer)	1997	41·15	12·64	0·77	0·39	1·97
March 21–June 20 (Spring)	2048	40·38	12·29			

The lowest mean Feradcom score occurs in Spring with a mean of 40·38. The standard ratio of this mean difference is 1·97.

Table 9 shows a comparison between the half-year groupings of cold and warm months. The comparison shows small mean differences of 0·40 and 0·30 with standard ratios of 1·43 and 1·07, respectively.

None of the standard ratios reported for the Feradcom test are large enough to be considered statistically significant. The significance of any of the results lies only in their consistency. There seems to be a trend for persons born during the Summer months to have feelings of inferiority.

We have seen that students who were born in warm months tend on the average to have scores indicating introversion and average scores indicating inferiority feelings. Moreover, persons born during the warm months were found to have a higher mean intelligence score than those born during the cold months. It will be noted that introversion, higher mean intelligence score and greater inferiority feelings appear during the warmer months. Perhaps at this point it might be well to ask: are the more intelligent more introverted and have they more inferiority feelings? In other words, is intelligence correlated with introversion and inferiority feelings?

To answer the question regarding the correlation between intelligence and our two personality traits, we employed four sets of data. We selected at random 280 cases from each of the following freshman years: September, 1930; September, 1931; September, 1933; and February, 1937. For each year three coefficients of correlation were computed; namely, that between Thurstone Psychological and I-X, Thurstone Psychological and Feradcom, and I-X and Feradcom. The correlations are presented in Table 10.

The correlations indicate that there is practically no relation between intelligence and each of our two personality traits. Persons with high intelligence scores may make high or low scores on the personality tests. We can confidently say, for example, that the warm months gave a lower introversion average score than the colder months not because introversion goes with higher average intelligence score. The correlations between I-X and Feradcom are greater than zero; they range from −0·27 to −0·39. The more introverted a person is the more likely it is that he has a greater feeling of inferiority. However, the correlations between I-X and Feradcom are comparatively low and indicate that whatever the tests are measuring, they are not measuring the same thing. Yet, we find that both introversion and inferiority feeling tend to go with persons born in the warmer months of the year.

TABLE 9

COMPARISON BETWEEN MEANS OF WARM AND COLD MONTHS ON THE FERADCOM SCALE

Season	Number	Mean	Standard deviation	Mean difference	σ difference	$\dfrac{\text{Difference}}{\sigma \text{ difference}}$
Cold: October 1–March 31	3797	40·40	12·40	0·40	0·28	1·43
Warm: April 1–September 30	4040	40·80	12·50			
Cold: September 21–March 20	3792	40·45	12·45	0·30	0·28	1·07
Warm: March 21–September 20	4045	40·75	12·45			

TABLE 10

COEFFICIENTS OF CORRELATION BETWEEN THE VARIABLES, THURSTONE
PSYCHOLOGICAL, INTROVERSION-EXTROVERSION AND FERADCOM

Number	Thurstone Psychological and I–X	Thurstone Psychological and Feradcom	Feradcom and I–X
288	$-0·07\pm0·04$	$0·11\pm0·04$	$-0·39\pm0·03$
288	$·00\pm0·04$	$·00\pm0·04$	$-0·27\pm0·04$
288	$-0·02\pm0·04$	$0·04\pm0·04$	$-0·33\pm0·03$
288	$0·10\pm0·04$	$-0·12\pm0·04$	$-0·38\pm0·03$

SUMMARY

The present study based on the scores of 7897 adolescents makes possible a comparison of the results with those based on children and adults. The results of the present study on the relation of intelligence and month or season of birth in general conform with those obtained with children and adults. Adolescents born in the Spring months (March 21–June 20) were on the average brighter than those born in Winter (December 21–March 20). The difference, 4·50, is statistically significant—2·90 times its standard error. However, the comparison of warm months (March 21–September 20) and cold months (September 21–March 20) gave a mean difference of 2·10, which is not statistically significant—1·91 times its standard error. Considered individually the differences observed are not entirely conclusive, but the differences are never in favour of a cold group whether compared against a corresponding warm month, season or half-year.

The results of the present study on the relation between month of birth and introversion-extraversion or inferiority feeling show that persons born in the cold seasons of Autumn and Winter seem to be more extraverted. The greater difference occurred between Summer and Autumn, the standard ratios being 2·88 and 2·58, respectively, according to the method of grouping months that was used. We do not obtain as marked trends when the seasons are combined into cold and warm months. The results for the test of inferiority are similar to those for the test of introversion-extraversion except that those for the former are less conclusive than the results for the latter. Yet, the tendency is always in the same direction; namely, that persons born in the Summer or warm months tend as a group to be introverted and exhibit feelings of inferiority.

When we review the results for all three measures; namely, intelligence, introversion-extraversion and inferiority feeling, we discern a consistent trend. We note that persons born during the warm months tend to have higher intelligence scores and that as a group they seem to be introverted and to exhibit feelings of inferiority. The conclusion in so far as the intelligence factor is concerned is clearer since it rests on a broader investigational and factual basis. The major value of our results on the intelligence factor lies in their consistency with each other and with the findings of other investigators. On the other hand, the results for the personality factor must not be emphasized too much. Needless to point out, the inconclusive standard ratios, the complexity and number of aspects of personality, the intricate connections between personality and intelligence, the comparative fallibility of personality tests, make it imperative to mark time until other investigators report before drawing any conclusion on the relation between month of birth and personality.

REFERENCES

1. BLONSKY, P. P., Früh- und Spätjahrkinder. *Jahrb. j. Kinderheilkunde,* **CXXIV,** 115–120, 1929.
2. FIALKIN, H. N. & BECKMAN, R. O., The influence of month of birth on the intelligence test scores of adults. *J. genet. Psychol.,* **LII,** 203–209, 1938.
3. PINTNER, R., Intelligence and month of birth. *J. appl. Psychol.,* **XV,** 149–154, 1931.
4. —— & FORLANO, G., The influence of month of birth on intelligence quotients. *J. educ. Psychol.,* **XXIV,** 561–584, 1933.
5. —— & ——, Season of birth and intelligence. *J. genet. Psychol.,* **LIV,** 353–358, 1939.
6. —— & MALLER, J. B., Month of birth and average intelligence among different ethnic groups. *J. genet. Psychol.,* **L,** 91–107, 1937.
7. SANDERS, B. S., *Environment and Growth,* p. 375. Baltimore, Md.: Warwick & York, 1934.

27

Introversion and Birth Order[1,2]

FRANZ HILLINGER

INTRODUCTION

THIS paper describes an investigation into the problem of whether first-born children tend to be more introverted[3] than later-born children. Conversations with parents invariably suggest that there is a difference between eldest children and their younger brothers and sisters, particularly in the way that first-born children display an inward-directed mode of experience. The present writer has also observed this phenomenon in schools where generally speaking first-born children with brothers and sisters appeared to be quieter, more withdrawn and less lively.

In particular, the study described here dealt with possible connections between a child's mode of experience and its attendance at a kindergarten, its pattern of leisure time activity and the mother's age at the time of the child's birth; the study also investigated whether differences exist between children who have only brothers and those who have only sisters.

The writer is not aware of any published work on the tendency of first-born children to be introverted. There are, however, papers on gifted children and birth-order by Hegnauer (Ref. 1), Juda (Ref. 3) and Rudin (Ref. 6); their results all agree that significantly more highly gifted children are to be found among first-born than among later-born children. Navratil (Ref. 5) has studied the physical constitution of the youngest child and the incidence of alcoholism and stomach ulcers among youngest children in large families, while Vogel (Ref. 7) reports on oligophrenia in later-born children.

---

[1] This is a summary of a dissertation bearing this title submitted to the Faculty of Philosophy of the University of Vienna.
[2] Translated by W. H. Fox.
[3] Introversion is used here in the sense used by Mitteneker & Toman (Ref. 4).

329

METHOD

A total of 587 children, 294 boys and 293 girls, acted as subjects in this study; all of the children were in the junior classes of grammar schools in Wiener Neustadt (Lower Austria). They were distributed in the following categories:

	Boys	Girls
Group I: First-born children with siblings	85	81
Group II: Only children	74	89
Group III: Later-born children	135	123

The children came from all social backgrounds but by occupation more than half of their fathers were middle class (civil servants and other professional men).

There are special difficulties in attempting to observe the behaviour of children in school groups. Particularly, it is only the extreme, more unusual children who attract attention. The children's progress records could not be used in this study because the judgments recorded were not based on standardized and precise concepts.

As far as the present writer is aware there exists no truly comprehensive test of extraversion-introversion for children. There is, however, such a test for adults (i.e., over 18 years of age)—Mitteneker & Toman's (Ref. 4) P-I test which includes 15 items relating to extraversion-introversion (score C of the P-I test).

Because of the close contacts afforded by family life parents can quite easily describe how their children would behave in actual real-life situations such as those referred to in the 15 items of the C score of the P-I test. Practically all these items involve a situation which demands a decision to be made on a real-life basis. The present study used parents' observations of children—the C score of the P-I being selected to assess introversion. The individual items had to be slightly modified for use with parents and also to correspond to the attitude situations of the children. Each of the 15 items were split into two alternatives, one indicating a tendency to introversion, the other indicating extraversion. For each item the parents selected one of the two alternatives.

Item 2 will serve as an example of the way in which the items were modified (for the other items see Refs. 2 and 4):

(a) If my child wants to do something, he/she thinks it all over for a long time.

(b) If my child wants to do something, he/she can make up his/her own mind quickly.

All the parents gave their comments on all the items of the test and it was therefore assumed that the test was actually assessing attitudes which they had been able to observe in their children.

The reliability of the parents' attitudes was checked by questions on the social behaviour of their children. The answers to these questions were referred to the class teachers, who of course knew their pupils well, so that they in turn could make their comments. If the teacher's view differed from a parent's answer, even if only on one point, then this assessment was not used. It thus may be assumed that questionnaires which were answered untruthfully for any reason at all were for the most part eliminated.

VALIDITY TEST OF THE MODIFIED C-SCALE

In order to check the applicability of the C-score modification, 30 introverted and 30 extraverted children attending a boys' grammar school in Wiener Neustadt were selected as a control group. These sixty children were given the test questionnaire to be completed by their parents.

RESULTS OF THE CONTROL STUDY:

Parents decided as follows:
Introverted Group

Attitude adopted for	I	II	III
Introversion	157 (69·8%)	70 (66·6%)	80 (66·6%)
Extraversion	68 (30·2%)	35 (33·3%)	40 (33·3%)

Decisions of the whole group
For introversion: 307 (68·2%), for extraversion: 143 (31·7%)

Extraverted Group

Attitude adopted for	I	II	III
Introversion	7 (15·6%)	29 (16·1%)	32 (14·3%)
Extraversion	38 (84·4%)	151 (83·9%)	193 (85·7%)

Decisions of whole group
For introversion: 68 (15·1%), for extraversion: 382 (84·8%)

If the number of decisions for introversion per subject are expressed

as a score, we have the following means and variances for the introvert
and extravert groups:

	Introvert Group	Extravert Group
M	10·233	2·267
σ^2	2·875	0·961

The difference between the means of the two groups is very significant
—t = 22·31 (df = 58). We may therefore assume that the test does
distinguish efficiently between the extremes of the personality dimension
being studied.

The positive results of the control study can be further illustrated with
an analysis of the individual items of the test. Table 1 gives the Chi²
value for the difference in frequency of each of the 15 statements of the
test as they were answered in the introverted direction by subjects in the
introvert and extravert groups.

TABLE 1

Item No.	Content of Item	Chi-squared (df = 1)
11	small circle of acquaintances	35·424
14	no noisy, jolly parties	33·200
12	feeling of inferiority	26·936
13	caution in choice of friends	26·696
1	self-control in argument	25·909
8	caution in dealing with others	21·818
15	spend leisure preferably alone	21·012
3	preference for lonely life	19·717
6	inability to spread joy	16·320
7	inability to reply to jokes	16·087
5	annoyance felt for long time	11·091
4	inability to deal with more than one thing at once	7·325
2	slowness in coming to decision	5·688
9	strong feeling of missing others	4·929
10	inability to console others	1·736 ns.

On average in the introvert group 69·08 per cent of the decisions on
each item were for introversion while only 15·08 per cent were so in the
extravert group.

On the basis of the results of the control study, it can be assumed that
the modified test is capable of discriminating sharply along the dimension of introversion-extraversion.

RESULTS OF THE MAIN INVESTIGATION

The number of items per subject answered by the pupils' parents in the introverted direction (I-score) was assessed.

A. Degree of introversion of first-born as compared with later-born children

1. *Boys:*
   Table 2 shows the I-scores for the boys.

TABLE 2

	I (First-born)	II (Only children)	III (Later-born)
N	85	74	135
M	6·706	5·527	5·207
σ^2	7·59	7·705	7·57

Tests of differences:
I–III: t = 3·93 (df = 218) significant
I–II: t = 2·68 (df = 157) significant
II–III: t = 0·80 (df = 207) not significant

The t-values indicate that first-born boys are significantly more introverted than 'only' and later-born boys; there is no difference in the levels of introversion between the latter two groups.

2. *Girls:*
   Table 3 shows the I-scores for the girls.

TABLE 3

	I (First-born)	II (Only children)	III (Later-born)
N	81	89	123
M	6·358	5·865	5·56
σ^2	7·733	7·456	5·61

Test of differences:
I–III: t = 1·983 (df = 202) significant
I–II: t = 1·613 (df = 168) not significant
II–III: t = 0·359 (df = 210) not significant

The only significant difference—at the 5 per cent level—is between first-born and later-born girls, the former being more introverted.

3. *Boys and Girls Compared*

When the means of the three groups of boys are compared with those of the three groups of girls, no significant differences emerge. The variances of the groups are also not significantly different from each other.

4. *The Whole Sample*

Table 4 shows the I scores for the combined groups.

TABLE 4

	I (First-born)	II (Only children)	III (Later-born)
N	166	163	258
M	6·536	5·712	5·376
σ^2	7·64	7·565	6·95

Tests of differences:
    I–III: t = 4·311 (df = 422) significant
    I–II: t = 2·711 (df = 327) significant
    II–III: t = 1·230 (df = 419) not significant

The following conclusions can be drawn for the whole group of 587 children: First-born children are significantly more introverted than 'only' and later-born children; there are only chance differences between 'only' and later-born children.

SECONDARY INVESTIGATION

1. *Degree of introversion and family composition*

Table 5 shows the I scores for families with just male (m) or female (f) siblings.

TABLE 5

	m	f
N	136	176
M	5·61	6·27
σ^2	7·8	8·13

A t-value of 2·031 (df = 310), significant at the 5 per cent level, is obtained for the differences between the means of the two groups, suggesting that families with exclusively female siblings tend to be more introverted.

Similar comparisons were made with groups I and III, as well as for boys and girls taken separately; all the t-values for these comparisons were not significant.

2. *Degree of introversion and mother's age at child's birth*
   The relationship between degree of introversion of the children—analysed as a total group and separately in boys' and girls' groups—and their mothers' age (classified here as under or over 30 years) at children's birth was investigated. No significant relationship was found.

3. *Degree of introversion and child's attendance at kindergarten*
   For the whole group of 587 children it was found that those who have attended a kindergarten are less introverted than those who have not (t = 2·843, df —585). Similar significant differences were found for: group III boys, all the boys, and all later-born children.

4. *Degree of introversion and child's age*
   Children in two age groups—11 to 12 and 13 to 14—were compared within the three boys' and girls' group, on the I-scores; there were no significant differences. From this it may be assumed that the significant differences reported earlier were not determined by age.

SUMMARY

The hypothesis, based on every-day experience, was tested that first-born children are more introverted than those born later. A number of parents rated their own children (a total of 587) of 11 to 14 years on 15 items of the extraversion-introversion scale of Mitteneker & Toman (C-score of the P-I test) (Ref. 4). Prior to this an analysis based on 30 extreme extra-verted and 30 extreme introverted children had shown the test to be valid. Results of the main investigation were: (1) first-born children were more introverted than later-born and 'only' children; (2) there were no sex differences in introversion between first-born, later-born and 'only' boys and girls; (3) children who had sisters only were more introverted than those who had brothers only. No marked relationship was found between mother's age at child birth and introversion, nor between the age range studied and introversion.

REFERENCES

1. HEGNAUER, H., Zur Bedeutung nichtgenetischer pränataler Faktoren für die Entwicklung intellektueller Begabung. *Geburtsh. u Frauenheilk.* **14**, 6, 1954.
2. HILLINGER, F., Extra-und Introversion und Stellung in der Geschwisterveihe. Dissertation, University of Vienna, 1957.
3. JUDA, A., *Hochstbegabung*, Vienna: Urban & Schwarzenberg, 1953.
4. MITTENEKER, E. & TOMAN, W., Der P-I Test—*Beih. l z. Wr. Zschr. Phil. Psychol. Päd*, Vienna, **20**, 1950.
5. NAVRATIL, L., Alkoholismus und Geburtennummer *Wr. klin. Wochschr.*, **68**, 158–160, 1956.
6. RUDIN, E., *Zschr. menschl. Vererb. u Konstitl.*, **30**, 166, 1951.
7. VOGEL, E., Inaugural Dissertation. Munich, 1953.

28

A New Scale for Personality Measurements in Children

SYBIL B. G. EYSENCK

First published in
British Journal of Educational Psychology, **35**, 362–367, 1965

A BRIEF description is given in this chapter of the Junior E.P.I.: a questionnaire for use with children from the ages of 7 to 16. The questionnaire was developed by extensive factor analyses carried out separately for the various age groups considered and detailed norms are available for boys and girls separately at each age. The questionnaire contains scales for the measurement of neuroticism or emotionality, extraversion-introversion, and a lie scale. The intercorrelations of these scales are given and there is a discussion of the relations observed between the temperamental traits measured on the one hand and sex and age on the other.

INTRODUCTION

Teachers and educational psychologists have, in the past, concentrated their efforts almost exclusively on the cognitive field, at least in as far as normal children are concerned; even when children are sent to a child guidance clinic, intelligence tests figure more prominently in the investigation conducted by the educational or clinical psychologist than do measures of personality. One of the reasons for this state of affairs has possibly been the absence of properly developed questionnaires in this field and the known lack of reliability and validity of projective techniques. Two questionnaires for children are in use at present, but there are objections to both. One is the Cattell IPAT scale (Ref. 9), the other the Junior M.P.I. (Ref. 5). In both cases it should be noted that there have never been conducted proper item analyses and factor analyses for all the questions used and for the various age groups separately; it is suggested that such analyses are a requisite minimum qualification for a properly constructed scale. Furthermore, both scales are afflicted with American-type wording (the Junior M.P.I. was adapted from the Pintner Scale which, like the Cattell scale, was made and standardized

M

in America). For these reasons it was considered desirable to create a new personality scale for children, which was named the Junior E.P.I. to denote its derivation from and resemblance to the Eysenck Personality Inventory, which is an improved version of the M.P.I. (Ref. 1).

The scale was designed to measure the two major personality variables of neuroticism (stability-emotionality) and extraversion-introversion. The inventory also contains a lie scale for the detection of faking. The construction of the 108-item scale was begun by carefully selecting, adapting or rewriting items contained in the adult version of the E.P.I. and adding further items. These scales were administered to school children, mostly from the Rotherham area but also from various London schools. Their ages ranged from 7 to 16, inclusive, and both boys and girls were tested. It should be noted that the older children, i.e., those in the 15 to 16-year age groups are not as good a sample of the general population as are the younger children because some children in these age groups elect to leave school, so that those who remain are self-selected. We made up the numbers by including 16-year-olds from youth clubs and some apprentices in industry who had left school. Since the 16-year-old group is, by necessity, so heterogeneous it may be as well to interpret results from this age with some caution.

These 108 items were then intercorrelated separately for each age group so that in all nine correlation matrices were computed. The total number of children involved in this part of the work was 6,760. Factor analyses were carried out on all the matrices, except those of the 16-year-old children where the number was too small to make this worth while. The method of principal components was used and in each case the first two factors extracted contributed much the greatest part of the variance and in addition could readily be identified as neuroticism and extraversion, respectively, by reference to those items known from previous work to measure these two dimensions. Table 1 gives the latent roots for the various groups of the N and E factors. It will be seen that there is no systematic change with age as far as the N factor is concerned but that there is a fairly steady increase in the size of the latent roots with age as far as E is concerned, with the 7 to 8-year-olds having relatively low latent roots, the 13, 14 and 15-year-olds having relatively high latent roots and with the other groups intermediate. These results suggest that neuroticism can be measured adequately at all these age levels but that as far as extraversion is concerned either this is a personality dimension which is not clearly emerging until the age of 9 or 10, or its measurement by means of questionnaires presents unusual difficulty with the youngest age groups.

TABLE 1

LATENT ROOTS

n	Age	N	E	L
491	7	9·615	3·573	2·718
580	8	9·320	3·560	3·023
761	9	8·447	3·834	3·340
844	10	8·684	3·919	3·300
989	11	9·596	4·188	3·140
747	12	9·617	4·295	3·681
804	13	9·209	5·453	2·974
786	14	8·309	4·927	3·077
527	15	8·914	6·615	4·188

A lie scale of sixteen items was constructed by again adapting and rewriting items from the senior E.P.I. and adding others; this scale was given to a further set of school children not previously tested, amounting in all to 2,777. Intercorrelations were computed between these items for all age groups separately and nine factor analyses carried out, again omitting the 16-year-old groups. One factor only was extracted, loading on all the items and contributing latent roots which are indicated in Table 1. There appears to be a slight increase in the size of the latent roots with age but this is probably too small to be of any great significance.

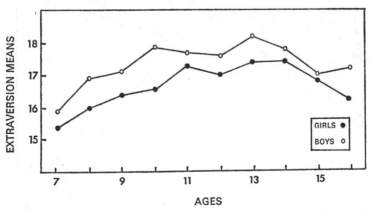

Figure 11

On the basis of these factor analyses, 60 suitable items were chosen for the final inventory of which 24 measured E, 24 N and 12 constituted the L scale. The choice was based on the loadings of the items for their respective factors, and their lack of loading on other factors. The correlations between the E and N scales for the different age groups are given in the Manual (Ref. 3); they are positive in three cases, negative in the rest, and on the whole the figures suggest a slight negative correlation between neuroticism and extraversion which, however, is too small to be of any practical importance.

Standardization data are also given in the Manual. They show certain interesting changes in scores on both extraversion and neuroticism with age, and also some interesting sex differences. Figure 11 gives the scores for extraversion. The trends shown in this Figure, i.e., the regular increase for both sexes up to the age of 14 or so, and a higher mean score at all levels for boys, were shown by analysis of variance to be significant beyond the 0·001 level. The sex difference observed here confirms similar findings with adult populations where also males tend to obtain higher scores than females.

Figure 12 gives a similar picture for neuroticism scores. It will be seen that while both groups start out on roughly the same level, girls show a consistent increase, boys, if anything, a slight decline. Analysis of variance demonstrated that sex, age and the sex by age interaction were

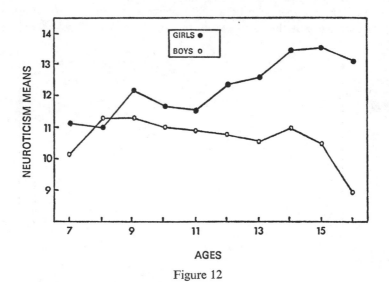

Figure 12

all significant beyond the 0·001 level. It thus appears to be a fact that girls become more emotionally unstable with increasing age, whereas boys remain at much the same level, or even become somewhat more stable. (It is assumed, of course, that the questionnaire scores are indicative of true life behaviour.)

As regards the lie scale there is a marked shift from high scores in the younger children to low scores in the older children. This shift is quite monotonic and is best shown in Figure 13 which gives lie scores in percentages for the oldest and the youngest groups tested, respectively. This finding is in good agreement with the known lying behaviour of children (Ref. 8).

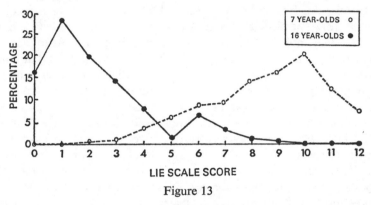

Figure 13

The split-half reliabilities of the scales indicate that they are reasonable for group comparisons at the younger ages, and possibly for individual testing at the older ages. For neuroticism the values range between 0·8 and 0·9, and there is no detectable change with age. For E there is an increase with age from values around 0·65 for the youngest groups to values approaching 0·9 for the oldest groups. The lie scale, as might have been expected from the fact that it is rather short, shows the lowest reliabilities ranging from 0·41 for the youngest groups to 0·78 for the older ones.

Test/retest reliabilities are available for additional samples of 1,056 boys and 1,074 girls. Typically these range between 0·7 and 0·8, with isolated values up to above 0·9. There is a tendency for test/retest reliabilities to increase with age for the E scale and to a slight extent for the N scale as well; there seems to be no such tendency for the L scale. Altogether test/retest reliabilities are somewhat lower than split-half reliabilities.

It has already been mentioned that correlations between E and N are rather slight, averaging above -0.15; this does not appear to vary very much with age or sex, and is, of course, too small to be of any practical importance. There is a slight negative correlation for the older children between E and L of approximately the same size, which is in good conformity with data found in adults. Correlations between N and L are rather larger, averaging above -0.3 and in some cases exceeding -0.4. The size of the correlation appears to be largely independent of age and the data suggest that children with high lie scores will tend to have low neuroticism scores, possibly due to conscious attempts at faking. There is too little direct evidence as yet to establish the usefulness of attempts to control for this by any known statistical procedure, but further experimental work, particularly using criterion groups of known neurotic children, may indicate optimal ways of controlling attempts to fake.

The personality theory on which this test is based suggests that E and N are independent of intelligence, and work with adults has usually substantiated this hypothesis. It seemed desirable to obtain additional information for children, and data were obtained on 373 girls and 334 boys in all. The children had been given the Junior E.P.I. as well as two verbal intelligence tests; ages represented were from 11 to 16, but the number of cases in the 16-year-old group was too small to give reliable data. The data show no evidence of any correlation between E and I.Q.; they show a slight tendency for N to be negatively correlated with I.Q., but the numerical values of the coefficients are small and not always in the same direction. There is a definite tendency for lie scale scores to be negatively correlated with intelligence although here again an overall value of the correlation is only between 0.2 and 0.3. It had already been found in some unpublished work with an E.P.I. scale specially prepared for subnormal subjects that these give much higher lie scores than normal subjects so that this association must be regarded as being very likely a true picture of the situation.

Too little is known as yet about the validity of the Junior E.P.I. to make any claims for its use, other than as an instrument for experimentation. 229 child guidance clinic subjects have been tested and rated with respect to the extraverted or introverted nature of their symptoms. It was found that the group as a whole was very significantly above the standardization group with respect to neuroticism and that there was a very significant difference with respect to E between children showing extraverted symptoms and those showing introverted symptoms. It seems probable, therefore, that the scale may have some validity in

connection with clinical investigations and it seems not unreasona[ble to]
expect that a similar validity will attend measurements in n[ormal]
children.

We may perhaps end by pointing out some of the areas of research
where this scale may be most useful.

(1) It has been demonstrated that intelligence test scores may show a
curvilinear relationship to neuroticism and may, therefore, require
correction to give optimal forecasting efficiency as far as school achievement and other criteria are concerned (Ref. 7). This is an important area
of research in view of the importance which intelligence tests and other
anxiety-producing examinations have in the life of children. Indeed, the
whole structure of intellect may be different in persons of different
personality (Ref. 2).

(2) School and university achievement has been found to be related
to introversion and neuroticism, as well as to intelligence, and much
further work is needed to put these findings on a secure basis and dis-
entangle the causal effects which may be responsible (Ref. 4).

(3) Experiments in educational psychology have usually consigned
personality differences to the error variance rather than investigate them
directly. This seems a strategic error which may have far-reaching consequences. To quote but one example, Thompson & Hunnicutt have shown
that the work of introverts improves with praise, that of extraverts with
blame (Ref. 10). If they had simply treated these personality differences
as part of the error variance they would have come to quite erroneous
conclusions and would have missed a finding which may be of crucial
significance for teachers and educationalists alike.

(4) Among the many investigations which may benefit from closer
attention to personality variables are studies using teaching machines.
It is unlikely that the conclusions usually drawn in published papers
applied equally to all children; it may be suggested with diffidence that
extraverted and introverted children, or stable and unstable children,
may show quite different and even contradictory reactions to identical
conditions of testing.

(5) The same may be said of experimental variants in classroom
procedure. There is already evidence that extraverted children accumulate
reactive inhibition much more quickly than do introverted children and
would, therefore, benefit from repeated rest pauses, which are unneces-
sary for the introverts (Ref. 6). Theory suggests many other ways in
which individual differences between children may cause them to
respond differently to different classroom arrangements, but enough

has been said already to indicate that few educational experiments can satisfactorily be designed without taking into account individual differences in personality. It is in this field rather than in the clinic that we believe the major importance and usefulness of the Junior E.P.I. to lie.

REFERENCES

1. EYSENCK, H. J. & EYSENCK, S. B. G., *The Eysenck Personality Inventory*. London: Univ. of London Press, 1964.
2. —— & WHITE, P. O., Personality and the measurement of intelligence. *Brit. J. educ. Psychol.*, **34**, 197–202, 1964.
3. EYSENCK, S. B. G., *The Junior Eysenck Personality Inventory*. London: Univ. of London Press, 1965.
4. FURNEAUX, W. D., The psychologist and the university. *Universities Quarterly*, **17**, 33–47, 1962.
5. —— & GIBSON, H. B., A children's personality inventory designed to measure neuroticism and extraversion. *Brit. J. educ. Psychol.*, **31**, 204–207, 1961.
6. GRASSI, J., Experimental Investigation of Cortical Inhibition in Children. London: Unpublished Ph.D. thesis, 1964.
7. LYNN, R. & GORDON, I. E., The relation of neuroticism and extraversion to intelligence and educational attainment. *Brit. J. educ. Psychol.*, **31**, 194–203, 1961.
8. McFARLANE, J., ALLEN, L. & HONZIK, M., *A Developmental Study of the Behavior Problems of Normal Children*. Calif.: Univ. Calif. Publ. in Child Developm. Vol. 2. Univ. of Calif. Press, 1954.
9. PORTER, R. B. & CATTELL, R. B., *The IPAT Children's Personality Questionnaire*. Champaign, Ill.: Inst. Person. & Abil. Testing, 1960.
10. THOMPSON, G. G. & HUNNICUTT, C. W., The effect of repeated praise or blame on the work achievement of 'introverts' and 'extraverts'. *J. educ. Psychol.*, **35**, 257–266, 1944.

29

College Students' Personality Correlates of Early Parent-Child Relationships[1]

MARVIN SIEGELMAN

First published in *Journal of Consulting Psychology*, **29**, 558–564, 1965

INTROVERSION-EXTRAVERSION and anxiety characteristics reported by 54 male and 97 female undergraduate college students were compared to their recollections of loving-rejecting and casual-demanding parental behaviours. The Cattell 16 PF and a questionnaire concerning parental behaviour were the principal instruments employed. Anxious and introverted males reported rejecting fathers and mothers. Extraverted females noted loving fathers. Socioeconomic background and tendencies to agree and give socially desirable responses were considered. Implications of results for reinforcement and modelling aspects of social-learning theory were also suggested.

INTRODUCTION

Several prolific factor analytically oriented researchers, such as Cattell and Eysenck, working with different methods and tests, have reported conceptual frameworks of personality that are quite similar (Refs. 5 and 13). Two fundamental or closely related personality dimensions reported by these and other authors are introversion-extraversion and anxiety (Refs. 2 and 5). Most of these frameworks were empirically or inductively derived from extensive observation and testing. In the area of child-rearing practices, the attempt has also been made to develop a taxonomy or conceptual framework of parental behaviour. Although this classification may appear premature at this time, Schaefer, Roe & Siegelman and Maccoby report strikingly similar dimensions of parental behaviour presented by several investigators using diverse methodologies (Refs.

[1] Appreciation is expressed to Charles DeCarlo and John J. Stifel of IBM for their contribution of free 7090 computer time. Daniel Prior spent many hours scoring and key punching test data, for which the author is grateful. The study was supported by a grant from the Alumni Association of The City College of New York.

17, 22 and 25). Studies which describe parents' accounts of how they treat their children (Ref. 25), parents' attitudes about child-rearing practices (Refs. 8, 18 and 24), direct observation of parent-child interactions (Ref. 1) and adult retrospective memories of how their parents treated them when they were growing up (Ref. 22) all suggest the parental behaviour factors of love-reject and casual-demand [i.e., autonomy-control). Here again, the logic or technique used by these investigators was that of factor analysis. Using factor analytically derived dimensions and scales, the major purpose of this paper is to examine the relationship between a subject's personality structure (i.e., introversion-extraversion and anxiety) and his parents' behaviour toward him when he was growing up (i.e., loving-rejecting and casual-demanding).

This investigation is, in part, a replication of one major aspect of the Origin of Interests (OI) study conducted by Roe & Siegelman (Ref. 23). The Harvard senior sample of the OI study will be compared with the college group evaluated here. In addition, the present investigation evaluates female as well as male undergraduate students whose socio-economic backgrounds, religious affiliations, academic achievements and college majors differ from the Harvard seniors used in the OI research. The dependent personality variable of anxiety is examined along with the OI introversion-extraversion dimension. The design of the present study is simpler than the one used in the OI research in that it employs only one instrument to measure parental behaviour and one technique for assessing personality structure. The major independent parent-child relationship variables and dependent personality variables considered in the OI approach, however, are also considered here.

The principal hypothesis of the OI study was that toward-person or extraversion tendencies were associated with recalled loving behaviour of parents, while introverted orientations were related to recollections of rejecting parental behaviour. It was only hypothesized in the OI research that casual-demanding parental characteristics were not related to extraversion-introversion tendencies. These predictions were derived from a theory formulated by Roe (Ref. 21). The above hypotheses were generally supported in the OI study. Investigations by Bayley & Schaefer, Becker, and Peterson, Becker, Shoemaker, Luria & Hellmer also suggest that loving and casual parents have children who are less anxious than rejecting and demanding parents (Refs. 3, 4 and 20). Based on the above reports, the specific hypotheses tested in the present study are the following:

1. Subjects with extraversion tendencies recall their parents as loving when they were growing up, while subjects with introversion inclinations remember their parents as rejecting.

2. There is no significant association between extraversion-introversion tendencies and recalled casual-demanding parental behaviour during their childhood.[1]

3. Subjects scoring low on anxiety recollect their parents as loving when they were growing up, while subjects scoring high on anxiety report their parents as rejecting.

4. Subjects scoring low on anxiety describe their parents as casual during their upbringing, whereas subjects scoring high on anxiety depict their parents as demanding.

METHOD

Subjects

Two sample groups included 57 males and 97 females, mainly sophomores and juniors, comprising the total enrolment in six sections of a child-development course at the City College of New York (CCNY). The mean age was 22 for males and 20 for females. For males, the religious preferences were 51 per cent Jewish, 21 per cent Catholic, 7 per cent Protestant and 21 per cent noting no religious affiliation. For females, the choices were 70 per cent Jewish, 13 per cent Catholic, 3 per cent Protestant and 14 per cent none. Most of the subjects came from upper-lower class or middle-class socioeconomic backgrounds. For both male and female students, the average parental education completed was 12th grade. All students were interested in teaching by virtue of their being in a course that is part of an education sequence required for teacher licensing in New York City. The range of college majors for both males and females, however, was quite wide and included almost all areas of concentration.

Instruments

Socioeconomic Index (SI). The socioeconomic measure used to categorize the CCNY samples was a composite score based on father's education and occupation, plus the subject's response to a biographical

---

[1] The prediction made here is that the results will not permit the conclusion that a nonzero correlation exists in the population. This hypothesis will also be evaluated in terms of the magnitude of error involved in concluding that the population correlation is 'trivial', here defined as 0·20 or less (Ref. 9).

question concerning his family's financial position when he was growing up. Father's education score was based on a 7-point scale ranging from 'Less than seven years of school' to 'Graduate professional training' devised by Hollingshead & Redlich (Ref. 15). The grouping of father's occupation followed the procedure outlined by Hamburger (Ref. 14), which is a modification of the Warner, Meeker & Ellis revision of the Edwards Classification (Ref. 30). The Hamburger scale includes seven socioeconomic class levels.

The biographical questionnaire item used was the following:

What was your family's financial position while you were growing up?

1. Wealthy

2. Above average; no worries

3. About average; careful management was necessary

4. Below average; money was a chronic strain

5. Very poor; outside help was often needed

Twice as much weight was given to the father's occupation as was given to the father's education and to the biographical questionnaire item. In other words, the score for father's occupation was multiplied by 2, while the score for father's education and the score on the above question were used as they were. This weighting was roughly equivalent to the weights assigned by Hollingshead & Redlich for father's education and occupation, which they derived by multiple-regression techniques using expert opinion of social status as the criterion (Ref. 16). The range of the SI is 4–26, the low scores indicating high socioeconomic status.

Parent-Child Relations Questionnaire (PCR). The relationship of early parent-child interactions and personality development has been approached mainly through the study of young children and their parents (Ref. 15). One reason why few studies have been reported of early parent-child relations associated with adult personality structure is that few reliable instruments are available for measuring adult retrospective reports of early parental behaviour (Ref. 15). The Roe-Siegelman PCR (Ref. 21) was developed to meet this need. The PCR consists of 130 questions for father and, except for 11 items, the same set of questions for mother. It purports to measure 10 parental behaviours: protecting, rejecting, casual, demanding, loving, neglecting, symbolic-love punishment and direct-object reward. Subjects are asked to recall the behaviour of their parents toward them when they were 12 years old or younger.

TABLE 1

ROTATED FACTOR LOADINGS, COMMUNALITIES, PERCENTAGE OF VARIANCE AND RELIABILITIES

PCR variable	Male father[a] (N = 54)				Male mother (N = 57)				Female father (N = 96)				Female mother (N = 97)			
	I^b	II^c	h^{2d}	r_{tt}^e	I	II	h^2	r_{tt}	I	II	h^2	r_{tt}	I	II	h^2	r_{tt}
Loving	0·91	0·11	0·84	0·88	0·93	0·11	0·88	0·90	0·82	0·21	0·72	0·92	0·88	0·12	0·70	0·88
Rejecting	−0·90	−0·20	0·85	0·87	−0·88	−0·28	0·85	0·83	−0·88	−0·26	0·83	0·88	−0·88	−0·25	0·83	0·80
Neglecting	−0·89	0·35	0·90	0·86	−0·93	0·17	0·89	0·81	−0·92	0·14	0·86	0·86	−0·88	0·12	0·79	0·78
Casual	−0·06	0·96	0·92	0·84	−0·01	0·91	0·83	0·83	−0·08	0·92	0·85	0·83	−0·11	0·93	0·87	0·83
Demanding	−0·21	−0·68	0·51	0·82	−0·12	−0·89	0·81	0·85	−0·35	−0·85	0·85	0·88	−0·38	−0·78	0·76	0·71
Protecting	0·07	−0·10	0·02	0·82	−0·09	−0·02	0·01	0·68	0·32	0·08	0·12	0·86	0·17	−0·03	0·03	0·79
% Common variance	0·61	0·39			0·59	0·41			0·60	0·40			0·62	0·38		
% Total variance	0·41	0·26			0·42	0·29			0·42	0·28			0·42	0·26		

a Male student responses about his father
b Factor love-reject
c Factor casual-demand
d Communalities
e Generalized Kuder-Richardson Formula 20 reliabilities

Specific parental behaviours rather than attitudes are referred to throughout in order to increase the objectivity of results. In the present study, only the first six areas are evaluated as they are most directly related to the hypotheses considered. In addition, there is much greater clarity in defining and interpreting the factors derived from the first six PCR variables in contrast to all 10 dimensions.

Generalized Kuder-Richardson Formula 20 reliabilities (Ref. 29), rotated factor loadings, communalities and percentage of the variance are presented in Table 1.[1] For male CCNY subjects, reliability estimates for the father PCR ranged from 0·82 to 0·88 and 0·68 to 0·90 for mother. Reliabilities for female students ranged from 0·83 to 0·92 for father and 0·71 to 0·88 for mother. The findings of the OI study for the Harvard seniors, which generally upheld the hypotheses derived from Roe's (Ref. 23) theory, supported the construct validity of the PCR. Principal-component factor analysis, using unity communality estimates and subsequent varimax rotation of the CCNY data, yielded two orthogonal factors labelled I: Love-Reject (LR); and II: Casual-demand (CD) for male father, male mother, female father and female mother. These factors, which were essentially the same as those found for the Harvard sample, accounted for the major part of the total variance. Factor scores for the LR and CD dimensions were calculated for a given subject by finding the sum of the standard PCR scores for each of the six variables multiplied by the obtained rotated factor loadings.

Cattell Sixteen Personality Factor Questionnaire (16 PF). The factors included in Cattell's second-order factor of anxiety are calm-emotional, trustful-suspecting, confident-insecure, controlled-lax and composed-tense. Comprising the second-order factor of extraversion-introversion are the dimensions of warm-aloof, enthusiastic-glum, adventurous-shy, conventional-bohemian and dependent-self-sufficient. A detailed account of the development, reliability, validity and research using the 16 PF can be found in Refs. 5 and 6.

The PCR and 16 PF were administered on separate days in group form to an entire class. The 16 PF was given one week after the PCR. A few days later, a one-page biographical questionnaire (BQ) was completed

---

[1] Complete data for all 57 males and 97 females were not available for certain analyses relating to father behaviour. Three males and one female were unable to complete the father PCR because divorce or death caused his absence when the subjects were very young. In Tables 1 and 2, therefore, there is a reduced sample for the analyses concerning fathers of male and female subjects. In Table 2 there is an additional reduction of three female subjects who refused to complete the 16 PF.

by the students concerning educational and vocational objectives, parental education and vocation, religious affiliation, etc.

RESULTS

Table 2 includes the product-moment correlations between the PCR and 16 PF factors. As was predicted in Hypothesis 2, the casual-demand parental factor was not significantly associated with extraversion-introversion tendencies for both males and females.[1] Contrary to expectations noted in Hypothesis 4, the casual-demand dimension was also not related to anxiety. The findings partially supported Hypotheses 1 and 3 in that extraverted and low-anxious male students reported more loving fathers and mothers, while introverted and high-anxious male students depicted their fathers and mothers as more rejecting. In addition extraverted females indicated more loving fathers, whereas introverted females remembered their fathers as more rejecting. For females, however, Hypotheses 1 and 3 were not supported by the associations between the LR father and mother factors with anxiety and the LR mother factor with extraversion-introversion. Of 12 positively predicted associations, therefore, 5 were supported—4 for males and 1 for females.

Although the hypotheses of this paper are concerned with dimensions derived through factor analysis, it is informative to consider some of the associations among those variables from which the factors were derived. For illustrative purposes, the significant correlations between the six PCR traits and the 16 PF dimensions will be noted.

Males who described their fathers as rejecting were glum, timid, suspicious, insecure and tense. Parents reported to be loving had sons who were warm, enthusiastic, conscientious, adventurous, dependent and composed. Aloof, nonpersistent, self-sufficient and tense males recalled neglecting fathers. An over-protective father was associated with low ego strength in the son, a casual father with responsiveness in the son, and a demanding father with shyness and exacting tendencies in the son. Rejecting mothers were noted by aloof, timid, insecure and

---

[1] One does not have high confidence, however, in concluding that the population correlation is trivial (0·20 or less) as the beta error involved in detecting such a true correlation is 0·69 for the 54 males and 0·50 for the 93 females (Ref. 10). In the Harvard sample of 142, where results concerning Hypothesis 2 agreed with the results of this study, the beta error was 0·34 for detecting a true 0·20 correlation. Because of relatively low power, therefore, larger sample results must be analysed to conclude with reasonable confidence (power $\geq 0·80$, or $N \geq 200$) that the population correlation is trivial. Such a study is currently being conducted by this investigator.

TABLE 2

CORRELATIONS BETWEEN PCR AND 16 PF FACTORS

| | 16 PF factors | | | |
| | Males (N = 54) | | Females (N = 93) | |
PCR factors	Anxiety	Extraversion-Introversion	Anxiety	Extraversion-Introversion
Father				
Love-reject	0·28[1]	0·42[2]	0.17	0·22[1]
Casual-demand	0·01	0·13	0·14	0·00
Mother				
Love-reject	0·32[2]	0·34[1]	0·13	0·03
Casual-demand	0·13	0·08	−0·19	0·12

[1] $p < 0·05$
[2] $p < 0·01$

tense males. Loving mothers had sons who were sociable, conventional, confident and composed. Serious, retiring, unconventional, anxious and excitable males depicted a neglecting mother. A demanding mother was associated with a suspicious son. Of the 96 correlations computed between the 6 father PCR variables and the 16 Cattell traits for the 54 males, 19 proved to be significant. Between the mother PCR and the 16 PF there were 14 significant associations.

Females who were emotional or not mature described their fathers as rejecting, neglecting and low on loving. Rejecting fathers were also associated with self-sufficient daughters and neglecting fathers with lax, rather than exacting, daughters. Sociable females noted protecting fathers and trustful females reported demanding fathers. Females who were emotional, dominant and critical recalled neglecting mothers. Rejecting mothers were also reported by emotional females. Casual mothers had self-sufficient daughters. For the 96 correlations between the father PCR and the 16 PF variables for the 93 females, seven were significant. Only five significant relationships were found between the mother PCR and the 16 PF dimensions for the females.

For males there were 33 significant correlations between the PCR and the 16 PF attributes, while for females only 12 significant relationships were found. For both males and females there were more significant associations between PCR father and 16 PF than between PCR mother and 16 PF characteristics.

There were no significant correlations between the SI and the 16 PF variables for the male sample. For females, SI was not significantly associated with anxiety or extraversion-introversion but it was related to the 16 PF properties of dull-bright, emotional-calm and submissive-dominant. Girls from higher socioeconomic backgrounds tended to be brighter, emotional and dominant.

With one exception, SI was not significantly associated with the father and mother PCR factors and separate variables for both male and female students. The exception indicated that males with rejecting mothers tended to come from higher socioeconomic backgrounds.

DISCUSSION

The significant positive association between extraversion-introversion tendencies and loving versus rejecting mothers for the CCNY males agrees with the OI study results concerning 142 Harvard seniors (Ref. 23) as well as other investigations (Refs. 3, 4 and 28). The above relationship was significant for the fathers of male CCNY students, but not for the fathers of the Harvard sample. The further correlations for males between anxiety and LR father and mother and for females between LR father and extraversion-introversion in the present study supports the significant role of the father, as well as the mother, in their child's personality development. The recent trend to intensively evaluate paternal, as well as maternal, influences on children's personality structure (Refs. 4 and 20) is justified by the present data.

The observation that significant correlations between PCR and 16 PF dimensions were more numerous for males than for females was also indicated in the OI study when male engineers and social workers were compared to female engineers and social workers. In the longitudinal research of Bayley & Schaefer (Ref. 3), however, there was considerable variation in the degree of relationship between maternal behaviour and the personality of boys versus girls, depending upon the age of the child. If future studies reveal a consistent tendency for parental behaviour to be frequently associated with certain male, rather than female, personality characteristics, one might consider some interesting speculations. Is parental behaviour toward girls more uniform than toward boys? Is heredity a more important determinant of female personality structure? Does similarity between a mother's and a father's behaviour differentially affect a child's personality development?

In the Harvard study and in the Bayley & Schaefer (Ref. 3) paper, subjects from higher socioeconomic backgrounds had more loving fathers and mothers. In the present investigation, the opposite relationship was found for mothers of male students. Part of the OI data was in accord with this later finding also. The general ambiguity of findings in this area (Ref. 15) and the relatively weak association reflected in the present research probably suggest that one can consider the independent variable of parental behaviour without being overly concerned with socioeconomic background as seriously confounding.

The important factor of response-set tendency (Ref. 7), especially for the PCR data, was not evaluated for the samples reported upon above. Two response-set tendency questionnaires, however, were recently administered to a group of CCNY students (20 males and 35 females) enrolled in a child-development course, along with the PCR. Out of 40 correlations, 20 for male and 20 for female, no significant associations were found between the Marlowe-Crowne Social Desirability Scale (Ref. 12) and the PCR responses for mother and father. Of 40 correlations derived from pupil reactions to the Couch & Keniston Agreeing Response Scale (Ref. 11) and the PCR, one correlation was significant at the 5 per cent level of confidence. Correlations between the 16 PF and the response-set tendency data yielded results similar to those found for the PCR. Although there may be some contamination of the PCR and 16 PF due to the tendency to agree or to give socially desirable responses, the effect is not pervasive or strong (Ref. 27).

The social learning theory of Bandura & Walters (Ref. 2) appears relevant to some of the hypotheses derived from Roe's theory (Ref. 2) and evaluated in the current study. Bandura & Walters give particular emphasis to imitation and direct reinforcement learning principles as they operate in a social context. Loving parental behaviour, for example, may represent an extraverted model for the child and it is probable that a loving parent, more than a rejecting parent, would reward the extraverted behaviour of his child. Similarly, using the principles of imitation and reinforcement, it is not likely that the casual versus demanding behaviour of parents would be specifically associated with extraverted or introverted tendencies in their children. The use of the Bandura & Walters social learning theory in conjunction with Roe's theoretical orientation may prove useful for future research.

The results reported in the present paper are tentative in so far as all data were collected from the same subjects. A more precise study should include independent measures of parental behaviour and personality structure. The knotty problem of causality concerning a parent's behaviour and his child's personality (Ref. 28) is another major limitation of the present study.

REFERENCES

1. BALDWIN, A. L., KALHORN, J. & BRESSE, F. H., The appraisal of parent behaviour. *Psychological Monographs*, **63** (4, Whole No. 299), 1949.
2. BANDURA, A. & WALTERS, R. H., *Social Learning and Personality Development*. New York: Holt, 1963.
3. BAYLEY, NANCY & SCHAEFER, E. S., Maternal behaviour and personality development data from the Berkeley growth study. *Psychiat. Res. Rep.*, **13**, 155–173, 1960.
4. BECKER, W. C. The relationship of factors in parental ratings of self and each other to the behaviour of kindergarten children as rated by mothers, fathers and teacher. *J. consult. Psychol.*, **24**, 507–527, 1960.
5. CATTELL, R. B., *Personality and Motivation Structure and Measurement*. New York: World Book, 1957.
6. ——, SAUNDERS, D. R. & STICE, G., *Handbook for the Sixteen Personality Factor Questionnaire*. Champaign, Ill.: Institute for Personality and Ability Testing, 1957.
7. CHRISTIE, R. & LINDAUER, FLORENCE, Personality structure. Pp. 201–230 in P. R. Farnsworth (ed.), *Annual review of Psychology*. Palo Alto, Calif.: Annual Reviews, 1963.
8. CLINE, V. B., RICHARDS, J. M. Jr. & NEEDHAM, W. E., A factor analytic study of the father form of the Parent Attitude Research Instrument. *Psychol. Rec.*, **13**, 65–72, 1963.
9. COHEN, J., The statistical power of abnormal-social psychological research: a review. *J. abnorm. soc. Psychol.*, **65**, 145–153, 1962.
10. ——, Some statistical issues in psychological research. In B. B. Wolman (ed.) *Handbook of Clinical Psychology*. New York: McGraw-Hill, 1965.
11. COUCH, A. & KENISTON, K., Yeasayers and naysayers: agreeing response set as a personality variable. *J. abnorm. soc. Psychol.*, **LX**, 151–174, 1960.
12. CROWNE, D. P. & MARLOWE, D., A new scale of social desirability independent of psychopathology. *J. consult. Psychol.*, **24**, 349–354, 1960.

13. EYSENCK, H. J., *The Scientific Study of Personality*. London: Routledge & Kegan Paul, 1952.

14. HAMBURGER, M., Realism and Consistency in Early Adolescent Aspirations and Expectations. Unpublished doctoral dissertation: Columbia University, 1958.

15. HOFFMAN, LOUIS W. & LIPPITT, R., The measurement of family life variables. Pp. 945–1013 in P. H. Mussen (ed.), *Handbook of Research Methods in Child Development*. New York: Wiley, 1960.

16. HOLLINGSHEAD, A. B. & REDLICH, F. C., *Social Class and Mental Illness: A Community Study*. New York: Wiley, 1958.

17. MACCOBY, ELEANOR, E., Developmental psychology. Pp. 203–250 in P. R. Farnsworth (ed.), *Annual review of Psychology*. Palo Alto, Calif.: Annual Reviews, 1964.

18. NICHOLS, R. C., A factor analysis of parental attitudes of fathers. *Child Development*, **33**, 791–802, 1962.

19. PETERSON, D. R., BECKER, W. C., HELLMER, L. A., SHOEMAKER, D. J. & QUAY, H. C., Parental attitudes and child adjustment. *Child Development*, **30**, 119–130, 1959.

20. PETERSON, D. R., BECKER, W. C., SHOEMAKER, D. J., LURIA, ZELLA & HELLMER, L. A., Child behaviour problems and parental attitudes. *Child Development*, **32**, 151–162, 1961.

21. ROE, ANNE, Early determinants of vocational choice. *J. consult. Psychol.*, **4**, 212–217, 1957.

22. —— & SIEGELMAN, M., A parent-child relations questionnaire. *Child Development*, **34**, 355–369, 1963.

23. —— & ——, The origin of interests. *Amer. Pers. Guid. Ass. Inquiry Stud.*, **1**, 1–98, 1964.

24. SCHAEFER, E. S., A circumplex model for maternal behaviour. *J. abnorm. soc. Psychol.*, **59**, 226–235, 1959.

25. ——, Converging conceptual models for maternal behaviour and for child behaviour. Pp. 124–146 in J. C. Glidewell (ed.), *Parental Attitudes and Child Behavior*. Springfield, Ill.: Charles C. Thomas, 1961.

26. SEARS, R. R., MACCOBY, ELEANOR, E. & LEVIN, H., *Patterns of Child Rearing*. Evanston, Ill.: Row Peterson, 1957.

27. SILLER, J. & CHIPMAN, A., Response set paralysis: implications for measurement and control. *J. consult. Psychol.*, **27**, 432–438, 1963.

28. SLATER, P. E., Parental behaviour and the personality of the child. *J. genet. Psychol.*, **101**, 53–68, 1962.

29. TRYON, R. C., Reliability and behaviour domain validity: reformulation and historical critique. *Psychol. Bull.*, **54**, 229–249, 1957.
30. WARNER, W. LLOYD, MEEKER, M. & ELLIS, K., *Social Class in America: A Manual of Procedure for the Measurement of Social Status*. Chicago: Science Research Associates, 1949.

30

Loving and Punishing Parental Behaviour and Introversion Tendencies in Sons[1]

MARVIN SIEGELMAN

First published in *Child Development*, **37**, 985–992, 1966

THE HYPOTHESES that introversion in children was related to punishing and low loving parental behaviour were supported by data from sociometric measures of introversion and fourth-, fifth- and sixth-graders' current descriptions of their parents. The findings concurred with previously collected data based on adult recollections of parent treatment and self-report personality information. Reinforcement and modelling learning principles served as underlying assumptions for the hypotheses.

INTRODUCTION

From a theory concerning the early determinants of vocational choice (Ref. 12) presented by Roe, the hypothesis was derived that personal orientation or extraversion in later life is associated with loving attention received from parents during childhood and that introversion is associated with rejecting parents (Refs. 14 and 18). An underlying assumption of the Roe theory is that because the child finds loving parental behaviour satisfying, he is motivated to interact with people in anticipation of similar pleasurable experiences. Unpleasant experiences for the child, on the other hand, resulting from rejecting parental behaviour might produce anxiety about, and a need to escape from, interpersonal contacts as he grows older. Loving parents may also present extraverted behaviour models which increase their child's extraversion inclinations via parental identification (Ref. 1). Rejecting

[1] This study was made possible by a grant from the City College Research Foundation and free 7090 computer facilities generously made available by the IBM Data Processing Centre in New York City. Part of the study was presented at the September, 1965, meeting of the A.P.A. The author is grateful to Ruth Obrien and David Fromm for data collection. The data reported here were selected from a larger project co-directed by Sam Meer, Burt Kauffman and Marvin Siegelman.

parents perhaps display more of an introverted model to their children. Finally, a loving parent may be more inclined to reward extraverted rather than introverted behaviour in his child. An additional expectation is that casual versus demanding parental reactions are not related to extraversion or introversion traits in offspring.

Support for the above hypotheses was obtained through questionnaire studies of 142 Harvard Seniors (Ref. 14) and for 54 male and 93 female City College of New York (CCNY) students (Ref. 18). These results were based upon college students' retrospective recollections of how their parents treated them when they were growing up (Ref. 13) and self-report personality data, mainly of the type found in the Cattell *Sixteen Personality Factor Scale* (Ref. 2). The present study re-examined the relation between loving, punishing and demanding parents and introversion tendencies in their sons, using as subjects children rather than adults and using different instruments for measuring parental behaviour and personality traits of sons.

METHOD

Subjects

Fourth-, fifth- and sixth-grade males (N = 106) served as subjects. The elementary school they attended is located in the Bronx, New York. The religious background of the sample was predominantly Jewish. The socioeconomic background of the boys appeared to be middle class, with most of the working parents employed in white collar or professional vocational areas. In order to evaluate the relations among parental behaviour, personality of sons and socioeconomic background, a socioeconomic index (SI) was constructed. This index was based on father's occupation (Ref. 5) and father's education (Ref. 8) and was identical, with the exception of a biographical questionnaire item concerning financial position, to the SI scale fully described by Siegelman (Ref. 18).

Parent Behaviour Questionnaire

The children described how their parents treated them at the time of testing by responding to the Bronfenbrenner Parent Behaviour Questionnaire (BPB) (Ref. 19). The child's immediate perceptions of his parents were recorded with the BPB, whereas adult retrospective recollections were relied upon in earlier studies using the Parent-Child Relations

TABLE 1

Rotated Factor Loadings, Communalities, Percentage of Variance and Reliabilities

BPB Scale	Male father[a] (N = 110)					Male mother (N = 113)					Female father (N = 116)					Female mother (N = 120)				
	I	II	III	h^2	r_{tt}[b]	I	II	III	h^2	r_{tt}	I	II	III	h^2	r_{tt}	I	II	III	h^2	r_{tt}
Nurturance	0·81	−0·14	0·16	0·69	0·70	0·72	−0·34	0·15	0·66	0·74	0·88	0·08	0·04	0·78	0·73	0·79	−0·01	−0·08	0·63	0·74
Affective Reward	0·81	−0·17	0·14	0·70	0·60	0·67	−0·32	0·21	0·60	0·56	0·77	−0·16	0·12	0·64	0·60	0·83	−0·12	0·03	0·70	0·69
Instrumental Companionship	0·75	0·12	0·18	0·61	0·70	0·76	−0·08	0·03	0·58	0·66	0·69	−0·06	0·10	0·49	0·75	0·70	0·13	−0·13	0·53	0·80
Affiliative Companionship	0·82	0·02	0·03	0·68	0·60	0·80	−0·12	0·10	0·67	0·60	0·81	0·03	−0·08	0·66	0·54	0·83	−0·04	0·01	0·70	0·62
Prescriptive	0·26	0·08	0·54	0·36	0·61	0·56	0·45	−0·04	0·52	0·50	0·22	0·50	−0·17	0·33	0·30	0·43	−0·03	0·70	0·68	0·50
Social Isolation	0·00	0·73	0·35	0·66	0·60	−0·12	0·67	0·35	0·58	0·65	−0·07	0·76	0·23	0·63	0·52	−0·13	0·58	0·26	0·41	0·64
Expressive Rejection	−0·17	0·75	0·07	0·60	0·60	−0·20	0·76	0·09	0·62	0·60	−0·35	0·49	0·45	0·57	0·61	−0·51	0·47	0·35	0·61	0·68
Physical Punishment	−0·09	0·83	−0·08	0·70	0·77	−0·23	0·72	0·21	0·62	0·97	−0·18	0·65	0·31	0·56	0·78	−0·39	0·49	0·49	0·63	0·81
Deprivation Privileges	−0·06	0·84	0·24	0·77	0·72	−0·13	0·69	0·25	0·56	0·80	−0·01	0·73	0·29	0·62	0·59	−0·12	0·68	−0·12	0·49	0·79
Protectiveness	0·20	−0·03	0·68	0·50	0·51	0·11	0·02	0·75	0·57	0·66	0·30	−0·04	0·72	0·61	0·50	0·21	0·58	−0·14	0·40	0·41
Power	−0·06	0·12	0·80	0·66	0·70	0·14	0·13	0·75	0·60	0·62	0·31	0·41	0·48	0·50	0·62	0·04	0·62	−0·14	0·41	0·56
Achievement Demands	0·29	0·10	0·53	0·37	0·33	0·21	0·29	0·46	0·34	0·45	0·27	0·31	0·50	0·43	0·45	0·02	0·59	−0·01	0·35	0·51
Affective Punishment	−0·03	0·22	0·59	0·40	0·27	0·02	0·04	0·75	0·56	0·49	−0·32	0·14	0·70	0·61	0·54	−0·22	0·40	0·44	0·40	0·46
Principled Discipline	0·55	−0·23	0·35	0·48	0·63	0·63	−0·39	0·13	0·57	0·64	0·63	−0·04	0·04	0·40	0·60	0·70	−0·05	−0·15	0·52	0·66
Indulgence	0·36	−0·23	−0·04	0·18	0·59	0·11	−0·48	0·14	0·27	0·65	0·30	−0·60	0·35	0·58	0·63	0·28	0·06	−0·55	0·38	0·61
% Common variance	0·38	0·33	0·29			0·38	0·27	0·35			0·42	0·33	0·25			0·48	0·32	0·20		
% Total variance	0·21	0·18	0·16			0·21	0·15	0·20			0·24	0·18	0·14			0·25	0·17	0·10		
Combined scale reliability[b]	0·83	0·83	0·81			0·80	0·77	0·73			0·82	0·73	0·63			0·79	0·75	0·36		

[a] Male child responses about his father
[b] Generalized Kuder-Richardson Formula 20 reliability

Questionnaire (PCR) (Refs. 14 and 18). The BPB consists of 45 items and purportedly measures 15 types of parental activity, three items covering each category. The BPB may also be utilized by computing factor scores from groups of variables derived from a factor analysis of the 15 scales. Table 1 depicts the rotated BPB factors derived from principal component factor analysis and subsequent varimax rotations (Ref. 6). Three major factors can be described for both father and mother as I, loving; II, punishing; III, demanding; with the loving and punishing factors accounting for approximately 39 per cent of the total and 73 per cent of the common variances. The BPB scales comprising a given factor are designated in Table 1 by italicized factor loadings. The male father factor II, punishment, for example, includes social isolation, expressive rejection, physical punishment and deprivation of privileges. Although the current study is concerned with male pupils, the BPB data for both males and females are presented in Table 1 for comparison with previously reported BPB results (Ref. 19). The BPB factor reliabilities range from 0·73 to 0·83 for males and from 0·36 to 0·82 for females. These findings are similar to the BPB data reported for a low socioeconomic sample of fourth-, fifth- and sixth-graders (Ref. 19). Several differences between the low socioeconomic sample and the current middle socioeconomic group can be noted. For the present sample, the following BPB characteristics were found: the indulgence variable for male mother and female father was negatively loaded on factor II, punishment; principled discipline loads high on factor I for all four parent-child combinations; for female mother, factor II includes demanding variables; factor III appears to be completely different for the female mother combination than for the other three combinations. In eight independent factor analyses with blind rotation of axes, for the low socioeconomic sample and for the present middle-class Jewish sample, the only 'factor failure' was for the current female mother combination. For attitudinal data, the factor structure is quite stable. Factorial validity and construct validity of the BPB were indicated in the recent study by Siegelman (Ref. 19).

Sociometric Personality Ratings

Whereas self-report personality type questionnaires were used with the college-student samples previously studied (Refs. 14 and 18), the present investigation examined sociometrically derived personality variables. Each boy and girl in a given class responded to the Wiggins & Winder Peer Nomination Inventory (PNI) (Ref. 22) by rating all the boys in their class on 62 items. Wiggins & Winder reported that the PNI standardization sample included 710 boys from a middle-class suburban community comprising all available fourth-, fifth- and sixth-grade classes in nine different schools. They indicated satisfactory internal scale consistencies ranging from 0·76 to 0·95 and concurrent validities based on teacher and peer ratings ranging from 0·33 to 0·69. The five major dimensions purportedly tapped by the PNI and their generalized Kuder-Richardson reliabilities (Refs. 4 and 21) for the present sample are aggression (0·87), dependency (0·93), withdrawal (0·96), depression (0·82) and likeability (0·95). The correlations between the boys' ratings of the boys and the girls' ratings of the boys also indicated high PNI reliabilities (aggression = 0·90, dependency = 0·92, withdrawal = 0·95, depression = 0·90, likeability = 0·71). A high score on the withdrawal factor indicated that 'the boy, by implication or act, minimizes interaction with others. Thus, he characteristically does not respond to situations which would stimulate participation in most boys. He tends to be described by others as quiet, non-aggressive, shy (shies away from), non-participating etc., (Ref. 22, p. 650). Low scores on the withdrawal factor may reflect extraverted tendencies, but this has not been empirically tested. The PNI concept of withdrawal is similar to Cattell's Sixteen Personality Factor Questionnaire (Ref. 2) extraversion-introversion factor defined, in part, as socially outgoing and uninhibited versus shy, aloof, quiet.

RESULTS AND DISCUSSION

Table 2 indicates that sons who report their parents to be punishing are rated by their male classmates as withdrawn, and that sons who perceive their parents as loving are seen by their male peers as not withdrawn. In addition, no significant associations were found between demanding parents and withdrawal symptoms in their sons. These data support the major hypotheses of this study and are generally consistent with the Harvard results (Ref. 14) and the CCNY (Ref. 18) results as far as male pupils' introversion tendencies are concerned.

Only introversion, ranging from low introversion to high introversion scores, was examined in the present investigation. The bipolar extraversion versus introversion dimension used in the Harvard and CCNY studies was not utilized. In the Harvard and CCNY researches, the PCR data yielded the bipolar factors of loving versus rejecting and casual versus demanding. The college students saw their parents as either loving

Table 2

CORRELATIONS BETWEEN BPB AND PNI VARIABLES

PNI Factors	BPB Factors						r_{tt}[a]	SI
	Father (N = 102)			Mother (N = 106)				(N = 37)
Male Rate Male	Love	Punish	Demand	Love	Punish	Demand		
Aggression	0·08	0·20[1]	0·10	−0·08	0·13	0·09	0·87	−0·03
Dependency	−0·02	0·25[1]	−0·01	−0·22[1]	0·21[1]	0·08	0·93	−0·12
Withdrawal	−0·38[3]	0·24[1]	−0·17	−0·48[3]	0·25[2]	0·16	0·96	0·08
Depression	−0·17	0·21[1]	−0·02	−0·29[2]	0·13	0·19[1]	0·82	−0·01
Likeability	−0·01	−0·06	−0·18	−0·07	0·05	−0·25[1]	0·95	0·01
SI (N = 37)	−0·20	0·19	0·05	−0·08	0·23	0·24		

[a] Generalized Kuder-Richardson Formula 20 reliabilities
[1] $p < 0.05$
[2] $p < 0.01$
[3] $p < 0.001$

or rejecting, casual or demanding and themselves as extraverted or introverted. If they were extraverted, they usually described loving mothers and fathers. If they were introverted, they more often depicted rejecting parents. The elementary school pupils of the current study described their parents in three independent unipolar ways: loving to not loving, punishing to not punishing, demanding to not demanding. These children were in turn rated by their classmates as having different degrees of withdrawal behaviour. Also, rejection, as measured by the PCR, is not directly covered in the BPB punishment factor, but it is strongly suggested. Although the Harvard and CCNY studies are not exactly comparable to the present project, the similarity appears great enough to consider the current data to be a positive replication.

All correlations between the SI, BPB and PNI dimensions shown in Table 2 are not significant. Because the correlations between the SI and BPB factors are modest in size and based on a small number of cases, the possibility of population correlations of modest size (i.e., between $+0 \cdot 25$ and $-0 \cdot 25$) cannot be ruled out. The extremely low correlations between the SI and PNI factors, however, do rule out the possibility of explaining the BIB-PNI correlations as resulting from their common associations with SI.

It can also be seen in Table 2 that for both mother and father the BPB love factor is more strongly associated with the PNI withdrawal tendency than is the BPB punishment factor.[1] This finding is similar to the conclusion reached in the Sears, Maccoby & Levin study that a mother's warmth and rewarding orientation, in contrast to a punishing tendency, is more effective in bringing about changes in their children's dependency, aggression and conscience characteristics (Ref. 17). In the Sears *et al.* research, the mother's warmth versus punishment was examined in terms of the direct conscious attempt by the mother to increase or decrease aggression, dependency, or conscience (Ref. 17). In the present approach, extraversion was assumed to result from satisfying social experiences with loving parents who acted as social models and rewarded extraverted behaviour in their children.

---

[1] Using a two-tailed test for correlated coefficients of correlation (Refs. 4 and 9), the difference between the correlation for PNI withdrawal and BPB male father love factors ($r = 0 \cdot 38$) and the correlation for PNI withdrawal and BPB male father punishment factors ($r = 0 \cdot 24$) was not significant. The difference between the correlation for PNI withdrawal and BPB male mother love factors ($r = -0 \cdot 48$) and the correlation for PNI withdrawal and BPB male mother punishment factors ($r = 0 \cdot 25$) was significant at the $0 \cdot 05$ level.

For general interest and comparison with previous studies, the PNI aggression, dependency, depression and likeability variables are compared to the BPB dimensions in Table 2. The frequently found association between rejecting parents and aggressive children (Refs. 1 and 7) is again seen for fathers but not for mothers. The lack of a significant association between punishing mothers and aggressive sons is not in accord with the conclusions of Sears *et al.* who evaluated 5-year-old children (Ref. 17). Fathers and mothers of dependent children were described as punishing, which supports the findings of Sears *et al.*, Smith and Wittenborn (Refs. 17, 20 and 23). Depression in boys, which includes being overly moralistic and excessively self-critical, was more typically found in punishing, demanding and nonloving mothers and fathers. Previous investigations (Ref. 10) have generally been in accord with such findings.

The findings of this paper in no way deny the probable contributions of such factors as heredity (Refs. 3, 11 and 16) and sibling position (Ref. 15) to extraversion-introversion development. The unaccounted-for variance in the correlations reported above must be sought in such variables as these.

REFERENCES

1. BANDURA, A. & WALTERS, R. H., *Social Learning and Personality Development*. New York: Holt, Rinehart & Winston, 1963.
2. CATTELL, R. B. & STICE, G. F., *Handbook for the Sixteen Personality Factor Questionnaire*. Champaign, Ill.: Institute for Personality and Ability Testing, 1957.
3. GOTTESMAN, I. I., Heritability of personality: a demonstration. *Psychological Monographs*, **77**, No. 9 (Whole No. 572), 1963.
4. GUILFORD, J. P., *Fundamental Statistics in Psychology and Education*. (4th ed.) New York: McGraw-Hill, 1965.
5. HAMBURGER, M., Realism and Consistency in Early Adolescent Aspirations and Expectations. Unpublished doctoral dissertation, Columbia Univ., 1958.
6. HARMAN, H. H., *Modern Factor Analysis*. Chicago: Univ. of Chicago Press, 1960.
7. HOFFMAN, M. L. & HOFFMAN, LOIS, W. (eds.), *Child Development Research*. New York: Russell Sage Foundation, 1964.
8. HOLLINGSHEAD, A. B. & REDLICH, F. C., *Social Class and Mental Illness: a Community Study*. New York: Wiley, 1958.

9. HOTELLING, H., The selection of variates for use in prediction, with some comments on the general problem of nuisance parameters. *Ann. math. Statist.*, **11**, 271–283, 1940.
10. KOHLBERG, L. Moral development and identification. In H. W. Stevenson (ed.), Child psychology. *Yearb. nat. Soc. Stud. Educ.*, **62**, Part 1, 277–332, 1963.
11. LINDZEY, G., WINSTON, H. D. & ROBERTS, L. E., Sociability, fearfulness and genetic variation in the mouse. *J. Pers. soc. Psychol.*, **1**, 642–645, 1965.
12. ROE, ANNE, Early determinants of vocational choice. *J. counsel. Psychol.*, **4**, 212–217, 1957.
13. —— & SIEGELMAN, M., A parent-child relations questionnaire. *Child Development*, **34**, 355–369, 1963.
14. —— & ——, A study of the origin of interests. *Amer. Personnel Guid. Ass. Inquiry Stud.*, **1**, 1–98, 1964.
15. SAMPSON, E. E., The Study of Ordinal Position: Antecedents and Outcomes. Unpublished manuscript, Univ. of Calif., Berkeley, 1964.
16. SCARR, SANDRA, The inheritance of sociability. *Amer. Psychologist*, **20**, 524 (Abstract), 1965.
17. SEARS, R. R., MACCOBY, ELEANOR E. & LEVIN, H., *Patterns of Child Rearing.* Evanston, Ill.: Row Peterson, 1957.
18. SIEGELMAN, M., College student personality correlates of early parent-child relationships. *J. consult. Psychol.*, **29**, 558–564, 1965.
19. ——, Evaluation of Bronfenbrenner's questionnaire for children concerning parental behaviour. *Child Development*, **36**, 163–174, 1965.
20. SMITH, H. T., A comparison of interview and observation measures of mother behaviour. *J. abnorm. soc. Psychol.*, **57**, 278–282, 1958.
21. TRYON, R. C., Reliability and behaviour domain validity: reformulation and historical critique. *Psychol. Bull.*, **54**, 229–249, 1957.
22. WIGGINS, J. S. & WINDER, C. L., The Peer Nomination Inventory: an empirically derived sociometric measure of adjustment in preadolescent boys. *Psychol. Rep.*, **9**, 643–677, 1961.
23. WITTENBORN, J. R., A study of adoptive children: III. Relationship between some aspects of development and some aspects of environment for adoptive children. *Psychological Monographs*, **1, 2, 3** (Whole Nos. 408, 409, 410), 1956.

Follow-up Studies of Shy, Withdrawn Children
II: Relative Incidence of Schizophrenia

CARMEN MILLER MICHAEL, DON P. MORRIS
& ELEANOR SOROKER[1]

First published in
American Journal of Orthopsychiatry, **27**, 331–337, 1957

IN PSYCHIATRIC literature the idea has prevailed that the majority of schizophrenic patients have had so-called introversive prepsychotic personalities. Certainly, many patients who are diagnosed as having schizophrenia manifest introversive personality characteristics. In fact the diagnosis itself is often based upon evidence of 'withdrawal from the outside world'. The correlation between schizophrenia and introversion is therefore predetermined to a large degree by definition. Furthermore, when there are problems of differential diagnosis, and when social histories are available on the patient, the diagnosis is also often influenced by descriptions of the prepsychotic personality. When there is evidence of schizoid (introversive) psychotic trends, the balance is usually tilted in favour of a diagnosis of schizophrenia.

It should not be surprising, then, that studies on the social histories of schizophrenic patients have frequently indicated that their prepsychotic personalities could often be described as shy, shut-in, lacking in outside interests, etc.

On the other hand, there is no preponderance of evidence that schizophrenic patients do not also manifest concomitant characteristics which could be called extraversive, nor is there convincing evidence that a great many schizophrenic patients did not have prepsychotic personalities which were predominantly extraversive. Bellak & Parcell (Ref. 1), for example, studied the prepsychotic personalities of 100 cases diagnosed dementia praecox. They found that '35 had distinctly

[1] The authors wish to acknowledge the assistance of the Hogg Foundation, the Board for Texas State Hospitals and Special Schools, the Dallas Child Guidance Clinic, the V. A. Centre at Waco, and all the other institutions and individuals, too numerous to mention here, who helped make this study possible.

extravert prepsychotic personalities, 28 had distinctly introvert prepsychotic personalities and 37 had to be considered as ambivert, or a mixture between extraversion and introversion'. They concluded, therefore, that 'the conventional conception, that a majority of schizophrenics have typical prepsychotic introverted personalities, does not hold true'. Suffice it to say, then, that there are frank inconsistencies and points of disagreement in the literature on the relationship between schizophrenia and introversion in the prepsychotic personality.

A disadvantage of most, if not all, studies on this problem has been that the social histories have been taken in retrospect. That is to say, the patient's social history has usually been compiled by interviewing relatives and acquaintances and exploring other sources of information after the patient has become psychotic. This is a disadvantage in that reliable informants may often be difficult or impossible to find, facts become changed or distorted with the passage of time and informants may be influenced in their opinions by what they have heard about mental illnesses and by their possible knowledge that the person in question is in the care of a psychiatrist.

In a previous study by Morris, Soroker & Burruss (Ref. 4), an evaluation was made of the current adjustment of 54 individuals who were seen as shy, withdrawn children 16 to 27 years previously in the Dallas Child Guidance Clinic. While the authors had expected to find a relatively high incidence of mental illness, especially schizophrenia, in such a group, it was found that the subjects 'were relatively free of overt mental or emotional illness and getting along quite well'.

The present study was undertaken in order to pursue this topic further and to contribute further evidence toward answering the question of the correlation between schizophrenia and introversion in the prepsychotic personality. Furthermore, it was our intention to approach the problem in a way which would not include the disadvantages of the usual procedure of relying upon anamnestic information.

Subjects

Subjects were selected from the files of the Dallas Child Guidance Clinic. All cases were white males seen at the clinic from 14 to 29 years prior to the present study. The age range of the subjects when they were seen at the clinic was 2 to 18 years; and at the time of follow-up (1952), 24 to 47 years. The average subject was seen at the clinic 26 years prior to follow-up. He was 9 years old when seen at the clinic, and 35 at the time of follow-up. All subjects had a record in the clinic of a comprehensive social history, one or more psychological examinations, including the Stanford-Binet Intelligence Scale, and a psychiatric interview. Cases with physical conditions which might obscure the clinical picture (with reference to the child's behaviour) were not included. Most of the cases had been classified as diagnostic or consultation cases and recommendations and advice had been given; but there was no continuous treatment by the clinic staff. The IQ ranged from 80 to 155 and the mean was 101.

Each case was also classified independently by each of us according to three categories: Internal Reactors (introverts), External Reactors (extraverts) and Mixed Reactors (ambiverts). Only those cases were used in which the opinions of the three judges were unanimous.

PROCEDURE

The list of 606 subjects was checked against the files of all the Texas state mental institutions: the Veterans' Administration Hospital and Regional Office in Waco, Texas; the Dallas County Court (records of lunacy hearings); the Dallas City-County Hospital (Parkland Hospital); and the V.A. Hospital near Dallas. Summaries were obtained from these institutions of all cases found in their files.

Further statistical analysis of subjects. On the average, the introverts were 8 years 3 months of age when seen at the clinic, the extraverts were 10 years 6 months, and the ambiverts were 8 years 6 months. The differences in age between the introverts and extraverts and between the ambiverts and extraverts are significant at the 0·01 level. The difference in age between the introverts and ambiverts is not significant even at the 0·10 level. These results are incidental to the purpose of the study, but are noteworthy in that they may suggest that children of the acting-out, destructive, or delinquent type come to the Child Guidance clinic at a later age than the others. There are many possible reasons for such later referral and the present study does not provide more than a stimulus for speculations. It may be, for example, that such symptoms do not typically appear until a later age, or that parents of delinquent-type children are, for various reasons, less likely to take them to a Child Guidance Clinic at an early age.

The age of the subjects at the time of follow-up was also computed. The mean ages were: introverts, 34 years 4 months; extraverts, 37 years; and ambiverts, 33 years 7 months. The differences between the introverts and extraverts and between the ambiverts and extraverts are significant

N

at the 0·01 level. The difference in age between the introverts and ambiverts is not significant even at the 0·10 level. This means that the extraverts at time of follow-up were about three years older than the subgroups and therefore had three more years to become known to various institutions. The possible effect of this age difference on the results of the study will be considered in the discussion of results.

One further difference between subgroups is apparent in their mean IQs. The mean IQ of the introverts, when tested at the clinic, was 105; of the extraverts, 97; and of the ambiverts, 102. The differences between the introverts and extraverts and between the ambiverts and extraverts are significant at the 0·01 level of confidence. The difference between the introverts and ambiverts is significant at the 0·10 level. All subgroups have mean IQs which are average, and the few points of difference would not seem to be of great significance in the interpretation of results of the study. However, it is of incidental interest that the children who presented introversive symptoms had higher IQs than the children with symptoms of an extraversive type, and that the children with mixed symptoms had IQs in between the others. There are many possible reasons for such IQ differences and, again, the present study does not provide more than a stimulus for speculations. For example, it may be that all the subgroups actually possess the same basic intellectual endowment, but that, for various possible reasons, the extraverts are not able to score as high when tested; or it may be that, because of basic differences in intelligence, the children developed different modes of behaviour.

Results of follow-up. Of the 606 cases, 10 (1 introvert, 3 extraverts, and 6 ambiverts) were found to have had a diagnosis of schizophrenia or dementia praecox at some time according to the records of one or more of the institutions whose files were checked. See Table 1. Two of the 10,

TABLE 1

RESULTS OF FOLLOW-UP: INCIDENCE OF MENTAL ILLNESS

Group	N	Incidence of Schizophrenia	Incidence of Other Mental Ilness	Total Incidence
Introverts	164	1	0	1
Ambiverts	174	6	6	12
Extraverts	268	3	8	11
Total	606	10	14	24

both extraverts, had been classified with other diagnoses at times. Both had been given the diagnosis of psychopathic personality (with criminal tendencies) with psychosis, and one of the two subjects had also been diagnosed at one time as having a manic-depressive psychosis, manic type. All 10 subjects were between the ages of 20 and 28 when they were first diagnosed as schizophrenic.

Fourteen additional cases (8 extraverts and 6 ambiverts) had various neuropsychiatric diagnoses, but were at no time diagnosed as having schizophrenia.

One more case (ambivert) was listed in the County Court files as having been committed to a hospital, but there was no other information in the files and the hospital had no record of this patient.

DISCUSSION

The results of this study do not lend support to the assertion that children who might be classified as introverts are more likely to develop schizophrenia than children who are extraverts or ambiverts.

However, because the population for this study consisted only of individuals who had been referred to the clinic, one might raise the question of whether such a population might be atypical or not cross-sectional to such an extent that generalizations are unwarranted. We can only state that the clinic served a wide variety of clients from all socio-economic groups, that the types of problems which the children presented were manifold, and that referrals came from a wide variety of sources. It is interesting to speculate, however, as to whether there may be a higher incidence of schizophrenia among disturbed children whose parents are not concerned about or aware of the problem to the extent that they consult the Child Guidance Clinic. Of particular consequence in this study is the question of whether unequal proportions of introverts, extraverts and ambiverts have parents who are unconcerned or unaware. It is possible, for example, that ambivert and extravert children have some symptoms which, in contrast to the introverts, more obviously annoy other people and call attention and awareness to the problem. If this were true, then it could also be true that the introvert group in this study was composed of children whose parents were unusually well informed and aware, and that there might have been a large group of introverted children, possibly with a more pathogenic family environment, who were not seen by the clinic. Therefore, it might also follow that the introverted children most likely to develop schizophrenia were not seen at the clinic. However, in the absence of evidence that unequal proportions of the introverts, extraverts and ambiverts actually do have unaware parents, we assume that the three subgroups are comparable in this study.

The results of this study are not meant to be comparable with national trends of incidence of schizophrenia or other mental illness. They are not comparable primarily because there is no estimate of the number of the 606 subjects who might have moved to another state or might have received private psychiatric care. On the other hand, the incidence of schizophrenia in the three subgroups of subjects (introverts, extraverts, ambiverts) is comparable statistically because each subject had an equal opportunity to be located in the institutional files. It should be mentioned, however, that there may have been migratory differences between the subgroups; and it is not inconceivable that one subgroup may be more unstable geographically and therefore cannot be located as often in the same state in a long-term follow-up study. Or, it could also be hypothesized that one subgroup may have come from a higher socio-economic group and therefore tended more than the other groups to seek private rather than institutional care. Although these factors of mobility and socioeconomic status were not given special attention in the present study, we are not acquainted with any evidence which would indicate that such factors might have caused any distortion of the results of the study.

The matter of the differing ages of the subgroups at time of follow-up should also be considered. Since the extraverts were approximately three years older than the other two groups, the question arises as to whether a smaller proportion of schizophrenic extraverts would have been located (in the institutional files) if they had been three years younger. This possibility seems less likely in view of the fact that although the mean ages of the extraverts, introverts, and ambiverts were 37, 34 years 4 months, and 33 years 7 months, respectively, none of the ones found to be schizophrenic was over 28 years of age at the time his name was first entered in any of the hospital records. Moreover, although the ambiverts had the lowest mean age, the proportion of schizophrenics among that group was the greatest. It would appear, therefore, that the fact of older age of the extraverts at the time of follow-up does not tend to invalidate the conclusion that the evidence does not justify the belief that introverted children are more likely than others to develop schizophrenia.

The results of this study not only suggest very strongly that introverted children are not especially likely to develop schizophrenia later on, but also suggest that those children are less likely to develop it than ambiverted children, and also may possibly even be less likely to develop it than extraverted children. Furthermore, the 14 additional (non-schizophrenic) cases who had been given neuropsychiatric diagnoses did not include a single case from the introvert group. This result strongly suggests that the introverted children may be least likely to develop neuropsychiatric disorders, at least of a type which would require hospitalization.

Actually, the ambivert group appears to be the group most likely to develop psychiatric disorders severe enough to warrant hospitalization. This study does not answer the question of why this should be true. However, we might speculate that the children whose problems are expressed in both introverted and extraverted behaviour are the ones who have the most unstable, unpredictable, and inconsistent patterns of dealing with themselves and their environments. They may be less able to build up and use stable and adequate defences, and such individuals may be more likely to suffer from various personality maladjustments.

In psychiatric literature it has been common to use the terms 'introverted' and 'schizoid' interchangeably. If the terms are synonymous, then the present study tends to contradict the common assumption that schizoid children are likely to become schizophrenic adults. However, there may well be some justification for maintaining this assumption if the term 'schizoid' is defined, as in studies by Jenkins & Glickman (Ref. 2) and Lorr & Jenkins (Ref. 3), as a syndrome which is separable from what they call the 'pattern of internal conflict'. This latter pattern is most like that of the introverted child in the present study. On the other hand, the schizoid syndrome, as defined by Jenkins and associates, is most like the pattern of the ambiverted child in the present study. This syndrome tended to overlap with the 'pattern of internal conflict' or 'overinhibited syndrome', but it also tended to overlap with a pattern called the 'unsocialized aggressive syndrome'. If Jenkins and his associates meant to assume that the schizoid children were more likely than the others to become schizophrenic adults, the assumption would find some substantiation in the present study in that those schizoid children would correspond most closely to the ambiverted rather than the introverted children in the present study.

SUMMARY AND CONCLUSIONS

This study was undertaken in order to investigate, by means of a long-term follow-up study of male children seen in a child guidance clinic, the

374   *Theoretical and Methodological Issues*

likelihood of a correlation between schizophrenia and introversion in the prepsychotic personality. The subjects were seen at the Dallas Child Guidance Clinic an average of 26 years prior to the follow-up. On the basis of their clinic histories, they were classified as introverts (of whom there were 164), extraverts (268) and ambiverts (174).

The list of 606 subjects was checked against the files of Texas state mental institutions and various other institutions. Ten subjects were found to have had a diagnosis of schizophrenia. Only one had been classified as an introvert, 3 were extraverts, and 6 were ambiverts. The results point to the conclusion that there is not adequate justification for the assertion that children who might be classified as introverts are more likely to develop schizophrenia (than children who are extraverts or ambiverts) or that a large proportion of schizophrenics have introverted prepsychotic personalities.

There were 14 additional cases who had various neuropsychiatric diagnoses, but who were at no time diagnosed as having schizophrenia. Of these, eight were extraverts and six were ambiverts. Not one was an introvert. This result points to the additional conclusion that the introverted children may be least likely to develop neuropsychiatric disorders of various types, at least of types which would require hospitalization.

A statistical analysis of the differences between the IQs of the introverts, extraverts and ambiverts, at the time they were seen at the clinic, and also of differences between the groups in age at time of referral to the clinic, revealed some significant differences. These results were incidental to the purpose of the study, but provide a further stimulus to speculation concerning differences between the three groups.

REFERENCES

1. BELLAK, L. & PARCELL, BLANCHE, The pre-psychotic personality in dementia praecox. *Psychiat. Quart.*, **20**, 627–637, 1946.
2. JENKINS, R. L. & GLICKMAN, SYLVIA, Common syndromes in child psychiatry. I: deviant behaviour traits. II: the schizoid child. *Amer. J. Orthopsychiat.*, **16**, 244–261, 1946.
3. LORR, M. & JENKINS, R. L., Patterns of maladjustment in children. *J. clin. Psychol.*, **9**, 16–19, 1953.
4. MORRIS, D. P., SOROKER, ELEANOR & BURRUSS, GENETTE, Follow-up studies of shy, withdrawn children. I. evaluation of later adjustment. *Amer. J. Orthopsychiat.*, **24**, 743–754, 1954.

32

Follow-up Studies of Introverted Children
III: Relative Incidence of Criminal Behaviour

CARMEN MILLER MICHAEL

First published in
Journal of Criminal Law and Criminology, **47**, 414–422, 1956

INTRODUCTION

MUCH has been written concerning personality characteristics of individuals who come to be classified as delinquent[1] or criminal[2] in their behaviour. Although there has been some difference of opinion, most criminologists have not only suggested that there are recognizable personality differences between criminals and non-criminals, but they also suggest that personality differences between the two groups are present and may be recognized even before the one group really manifests delinquent or criminal behaviour. Actually, the factors which are usually believed to contribute toward delinquency are not simply described as personality factors, but are thought to represent a complex interplay of many forces: somatic, temperamental, intellectual, sociocultural, etc. Various writers have concentrated on one or another of these forces and have ordinarily concluded that in predicting crime and delinquency, one must somehow take into consideration more than one or two factors— that one must take a multidimensional approach.

In their study, *Unravelling Juvenile Delinquency* (Ref. 2), the Gluecks have taken such an approach. It is beyond the scope of the present paper to review their findings. However, one finding is of special relevance to this paper, which is one of a series of follow-up studies of introverted children. Namely, the Gluecks found that their group of delinquent boys were distinguishable temperamentally from their non-delinquents in that a larger proportion of the former were likely to be extraverted.

---

[1] The term 'delinquency' is used in this paper to refer to the type of acts recognized by the law as juvenile delinquency.

[2] The term 'crime' is used in this paper to refer to acts prohibited by the penal law which are committed by individuals over the statutory age for specialized treatment of juveniles.

The delinquents were also secondarily more likely than the others to show a mixture of extraversive-introversive trends; and they were less likely than the non-delinquents to manifest introversive trends.

In their series *Follow-up Studies of Shy, Withdrawn Children* (Refs. 3 and 4), the authors began by attempting to evaluate the later adjustment of introverted children. Since in the first study it was found that the subjects appeared to be surprisingly well adjusted in adult life, the authors decided to study the incidence of mental hospital admissions in the introverted group relative to extraverted and ambiverted groups. In that study, the introverted group turned out to have the lowest incidence of mental hospital admissions. Now, in this third study, the groups are compared with each other with regard to the relative incidence of delinquent and criminal behaviour. It was thought that such a study would be of particular interest in the light of the above-reported findings of Sheldon and Eleanor Glueck (Ref. 2). The present approach also has a particular advantage of being a true long-term follow-up study rather than a retrospective or cross-sectional study.

ORIGINAL GROUP OF SUBJECTS

Subjects were selected from the files of the Dallas Child Guidance Clinic. There was a total of 600 subjects, all white males. The subjects were seen at the Clinic from 16 to 31 years prior to the present study and ranged from 2 to 18 years of age at the time they were seen at the Clinic. At the time of follow-up (1954), subjects ranged from 26 to 49 years of age. The average subject was seen at the Clinic 28 years prior to follow-up. He was nine years old when first seen at the Clinic and 37 years old at the time of follow-up. All subjects had a record in the Clinic of a comprehensive social history, one or more psychological examinations (including the Stanford-Binet Intelligence Scale), and a psychiatric interview. All subjects had a Binet IQ of 80 or above and cases with physical conditions which might obscure the clinical picture (with reference to the child's behaviour) were not included. Most of the cases had been classified as diagnostic or consultation cases and recommendations and advice had been given; but there was no continuous treatment by the Clinic staff. The IQs ranged from 80 to 155 and the mean was 102.

Each case was also classified independently by three judges (Ref. 3) according to three categories: introverts, extraverts, and ambiverts (mixed).[1] Only those cases were used in which the opinions of the three judges were unanimous.

PROCEDURE

The list of 600 subjects was checked against the files of the Dallas County Juvenile Department; the Dallas City County Boys Industrial School at Hutchins, Texas; the Gatesville (Texas) State School for Boys; the Police Department of the City of Dallas; the Sheriff's Office of the County of Dallas; and the Texas Prison System at Huntsville, Texas. Summaries were obtained from these institutions of all cases found in their files.

FINAL GROUP OF SUBJECTS

It was found, in checking the files of the various penal and correctional institutions, that out of the list of 600 cases, one of the introverts, 42 of the extraverts, and six of the ambiverts had already had some record of delinquency before the time they were seen at the Child Guidance Clinic. Since the presence of aggressive, destructive behaviour was used by the judges as part of the criteria for classifying the subjects into the three categories, it seemed to beg the question to some extent if the subjects who had already manifested some delinquency were included in the follow-up statistics. As a result, it was necessary to exclude subjects who came to the attention of legal authorities before having been seen at the Clinic.

The total number of subjects was therefore reduced to 551. The number of introverts was 165; there were 224 extraverts; and there were 162 ambiverts.

RESULTS OF FOLLOW-UP

Out of the list of 551 cases, 5 per cent of the introverts, 11 per cent of the ambiverts and 25 per cent of the extraverts were found to have had a record of delinquent and/or criminal behaviour at some time in the files

---

[1] Introverts were those children showing predominantly shy, withdrawn, anxious or fearful behaviour, those who were tending to develop neuroses, or those who were bothering themselves rather than others. Extraverts were those showing behaviour problems, those who were acting out their difficulties, or those who were bothering other people. Ambiverts were those showing some characteristics of each of the above groups.

TABLE 1

RESULTS OF FOLLOW-UP: INCIDENCE OF DELINQUENCY AND CRIME

Group	N	Incidence of delinquency and/or crime		Incidence of delinquency		Incidence of crime		Incidence of delinquency only		Incidence of crime only	
		N	per cent	N	per cent	N	per cent	N	per cent	N	per cent
Introverts	165	8	4·84	4	2·42	5	3·03	3	1·82	4	2·42
Extraverts	224	57	25·44	50	22·32	22	9·82	35	15·63	7	3·13
Ambiverts	162	18	11·11	14	8·64	8	4·94	10	6·17	4	3·47
Total	551	83	15·06	68	12·34	35	6·35	48	8·71	15	2·72

Follow-up Studies of Introverted Children   379

of one or more of the institutions whose records were checked. These figures are shown in Table 1. The difference in incidence of such behaviour between the extraverts and the two other groups is significant in both cases at better than the 0·01 level of confidence. The difference between the introverts and ambiverts is significant at the 0·05 level.

There were 68 subjects who were found to have had a record of juvenile delinquency. Two per cent of the introverts, 22 per cent of the extraverts, and 9 per cent of the ambiverts became delinquent. The difference between any two of these percentages is significant at the 0·01 level.

A total of 35 subjects (3 per cent of the introverts, 10 per cent of the extraverts, and 5 per cent of the ambiverts) were found to have committed crimes in adult life. The difference between the introverts and extraverts is significant at the 0·01 level. The difference between the ambiverts and extraverts is significant at the 0·05 level in the stated direction. And the difference between the introverts and ambiverts is not significant even at the 0·10 level.

TABLE 2

RESULTS OF FOLLOW-UP: INCIDENCE OF CRIME AMONG DELINQUENTS AND NON-DELINQUENTS

Group	N	Delinquents Incidence of Crime		N	Non-Delinquents Incidence of Crime	
		N	per cent		N	per cent
Introverts	4	1	25·00	161	4	2·48
Extraverts	50	15	30·00	174	7	4·02
Ambiverts	14	4	28·57	148	4	2·70
Total	68	20	29·41	483	15	3·12

As can be seen in Table 2, there were 483 subjects who were not found to be delinquent. Of these, however, there were 15 subjects (2·5 per cent of the non-delinquent introverts, 4 per cent of the non-delinquent extraverts and 2·7 per cent of the non-delinquent ambiverts) who committed offences in adult life. There were no significant differences between these three groups in the percentages who first came to the attention of legal authorities in adult life.

Of the 68 cases found to have been juvenile delinquents, 20 (25 per cent of the delinquent introverts, 30 per cent of the delinquent extraverts, and 29 per cent of the delinquent ambiverts) were found to have continued to commit crimes in adult life. There were no significant differences between the percentages of introverted, ambiverted, and extraverted juvenile delinquents who later committed crimes in adult life.

It should be noticed, then, that although there were no significant differences between the percentages of juvenile delinquent intraverts, ambiverts and extraverts who later committed crimes or between the percentages of non-delinquent introverts, ambiverts and extraverts who later committed crimes, the trend in each case is that the extraverts are most likely and the introverts are least likely to commit crimes in adult life. When the delinquent and non-delinquent groups had been combined (and the N's were larger), the differences between the extraverts and each of the other two groups were significant.

In comparing the delinquents as a group and non-delinquents as a group in incidence of adult crime, the results are more striking. Of 68 delinquents, 20 later committed crimes; but of 483 non-delinquents only 15 later committed crimes. The difference is significant at better than the 0·01 level of confidence.

FURTHER ANALYSIS OF SUBJECTS

On the average, the introverts were 8·2 years of age when first seen at the Child Guidance Clinic, the extraverts were 10·3 years old, and the ambiverts were 8·4 years old. The differences in age between the introverts and extraverts, and between the ambiverts and extraverts are significant at the 0·01 level. The difference in age between the introverts and ambiverts is not significant even at the 0·10 level. These relationships hold true for both the offender (subjects with records of delinquency and/or crime) and the non-offender (subjects with no records of delinquency or crime) groups, though in the non-offender group the differences are significant at only the 0·05 level. Furthermore, the offender extraverts were seen at an older age than the non-offender extraverts (difference significant at 0·01 level). However, there were no significant differences in age of referral between the offenders and non-offenders in either the introvert or ambivert groups. In other words, extroverted children were referred to the Child Guidance Clinic later than the other children, and the extraverted children who were going to become delinquents or criminals were referred even later than the other extraverts. No such patterns were noted in the introvert and ambivert groups. In effect, no relation can be seen between age of referral to the Child Guidance Clinic and later delinquent or criminal behaviour except to the extravert group.

Though there may be many possible reasons for such later referral, the present study does not provide more than a stimulus for speculations. At first glance at the results, one might speculate, for example, that the children who were seen early at the Clinic might have been prevented from developing delinquent or criminal behaviour. But one would also have to assume that some highly effective treatment and prevention must have taken place in the course of only a very few diagnostic interviews and the giving of some direct advice to parents. However, even if such were the case, it would still not be clear why the same pattern would not hold true for the introverts and ambiverts, nor would it be clear why the non-offender extroverts were referred later than the non-offender introverts or ambiverts.

The age of the subjects at the time of follow-up was also computed. Subjects ranged in age from 26 to 49 years. The introverts and ambiverts had a mean age of 36 years at the time of follow-up, and the extraverts had a mean age of 39 years. The difference in age between the extraverts and either of the other two groups is significant at the 0·01 level of confidence. This means that the extraverts at time of follow-up were about three years older than the other subgroups and therefore had three more years to become known as legal offenders.

Since no subject was younger than the age of 26 at time of follow-up, there is no question about the fact that from the age standpoint all subjects had a complete and equal opportunity to become known as juvenile delinquents. However, since at time of follow-up the extraverts were an average of approximately three years older than the other two groups, there is raised the question of whether a larger proportion of introverts and ambiverts would have become known as criminal offenders if they had been an average of three years older. Actually, in comparing the three groups at age of follow-up by a method of cumulative frequency ogives, the groups are found to differ in age not only at the mean; but at any given age from the age of 32 through the age of 45 the cumulative percentage of extraverts is significantly (0·01 level) smaller than that of the other two groups. Although 41 per cent of the subjects were older than 38, no subject committed an adult criminal offence for the first time later than the age of 38. Still, the fact remains that in the age range in which there were differing proportions of introverts and extraverts, some subjects became first offenders. For this reason, there may be doubt whether the differences found between the extraverts and the other two groups in incidence of adult crimes would hold up if the age factor were controlled.

However, since all subjects had reached the age of 26 at the time of follow-up, a calculation was made of the proportions of each of the three groups who committed crimes as adults at or before the age of 26. When the age factor was controlled in this manner, the difference between the percentages of introverts and extraverts who committed crimes as adults was significant at the 0·01 level in the indicated direction; and although the other differences were not statistically significant, the trends were in the expected direction. The results, then, suggest that the extraverts actually are proportionately more likely than the others to commit not only juvenile delinquent acts but also crimes in adult life.

Although among juvenile delinquents there is a trend in favour of the possibility that the introverts would be more likely than the extraverts to 'outgrow' the delinquent pattern of behaviour, it appears that the fact of whether a child is delinquent or not is more predictive of adult crime than his classification as introvert, extravert, or ambivert. In other words, the introverted child who is juvenile delinquent appears to be more likely than the extraverted child who is not delinquent to commit a crime in adult life. One (25 per cent) out of the four delinquent introverts committed a crime in adult life, whereas seven (4 per cent) of the 174 non-delinquent extraverts committed a crime in adult life. In the case of the introverts, the N is too small to allow the differences to be considered statistically significant. But if the ambivert delinquents are compared with the extravert non-delinquents, the N is sufficient to result in a significance of difference in the stated direction at the 0·01 level.

One further difference between subgroups is apparent in their mean IQs. The mean IQ of the introverts, when tested at the Child Guidance Clinic, was 105; the mean of the extraverts was 99; and the mean of the ambiverts was 103. The differences between the extraverts and the other two groups is significant at the 0·01 level. In the indicated direction, the difference between the introverts and ambiverts is significant at the 0·10 level. All subgroups have mean IQs which are average, and the few points differences would not seem to be of great significance in the interpretation of results of the study. However, it is of interest that the children who presented introversive symptoms had higher IQs than the children with symptoms of an extraversive type, and that the children with mixed symptoms had IQs in between the others. These trends hold true for both the offender and non-offender groups, except that the ambiverts in the offender group had a lower mean IQ than the offender extraverts. When the N is broken down this way into offender and non-offender groups, some differences are significant at only the 0·10 level in the indicated direction. Furthermore, it was found that the mean IQ of the non-offender groups as a whole was 103, while the mean IQ of the offender group was 97. This difference is significant at the 0·01 level. There are many possible reasons for such IQ differences and, again, the present study does not provide much more than a stimulus for further study. It may be, for example, that all the subgroups actually possess the same basic intellectual endowment, but that, for various possible reasons, the extraverts are not able to score as high when tested; or, for example, it may be that because of basic differences in intelligence, the children developed different modes of behaviour.

Much has been written about the intelligence of criminals (or delinquents) as compared with non-criminals and varying results have been reported in the literature. Some writers who have found the criminal group to have lower intelligence test scores have proposed that the results may not necessarily mean that legal offenders are less intelligent than law-abiding individuals, but that the results may only mean that the more intelligent offenders have escaped detection. To some extent at least, such an argument is invalidated by the results of the Gluecks' study (Ref. 2). In that study, the non-delinquents were so diagnosed not only because they did not have a court record, but also because a social and psychiatric investigation was made which showed that they were free from delinquent behaviour. When the IQs of the delinquents and non-delinquents were compared, the non-delinquents obtained a significantly higher score (accounted for by a higher verbal score). These results occurred in spite of the fact that the delinquents and non-delinquents were matched as to total IQ (not allowing more than a ten-point difference).

Attention should be drawn to the fact that in the present study subjects were limited to ones with IQs of 80 or above. If subjects with low IQs were included, the absolute means would have been lower. However, there is little reason to assume that the relative standings would have been different.

Summarizing, then, with regard to the differences in IQ between the groups, there were significant differences between the introverts, extraverts and ambiverts; and there was also a significant difference between the offender and the non-offender groups. The order, going from highest to lowest mean IQ, was as follows: non-offender introverts, offender introverts, non-offender ambiverts, non-offender extraverts, offender extraverts and offender ambiverts.

DISCUSSION AND RESULTS

The results of this study tend to corroborate those of some other workers in the field of criminology, notably the Gluecks, who have stated that extraverted children are more likely than introverted children to become juvenile delinquents (Ref. 2).

This study indicates also that ambiverted children are more likely than introverts but less likely than extraverts to become delinquent. This finding, too, corroborates the results reported by the Gluecks.

In the Gluecks' study, as in most other studies, individuals who had already become recognized delinquents were used as subjects. Differences between delinquents and non-delinquents were noted and then these differences were proposed to be predictive of delinquency. It is usually questionable, in such studies, whether the obtained differences between the delinquents and non-delinquents were actually present before one of the groups became delinquent. The present study may contribute towards answering such questions because it is truly a follow-up of children who were not yet recognized as delinquent when first examined.

While the results of the present study indicate that the extraverts are more likely than the other two groups to become juvenile delinquents, there could be some question as to whether the three groups differ in the probability that a larger percentage of one group rather than another will commit crimes in adult life. Although there were no significant differences between the percentages of juvenile delinquent introverts, ambiverts and extraverts who later committed crimes, or between the percentages of non-delinquent introverts, ambiverts and extraverts who later committed crimes, the trend in each case is that the extraverts are most likely and the introverts are least likely to commit crimes in adult life. And when the delinquent and non-delinquent groups had been combined, the differences between the extraverts and each of the other two groups were statistically significant.

It has been estimated by other writers that only about 10 per cent to 20 per cent of young delinquents tend to prolong delinquency into adult years (Ref. 1). In the present study, 29 per cent of the juvenile delinquents went on to commit crimes as adults. The results, however, should be evaluated in the light of the fact that all the subjects were drawn from a child guidance clinic population and that the numbers in the subgroups were not necessarily proportioned to correspond either to the child guidance clinic population or to the population at large.

Actually, however, the figures on the records of incidence of delinquency and crime in these subjects are undoubtedly too low. It is not known how many of the subjects classified as non-delinquent or non-criminal may actually have had criminal records in locations other than those explored in the present study. Primarily for this reason, the results of this study are not meant to be comparable with national trends of incidence of delinquency and crime.

On the other hand, the incidence of delinquency and crime in the three subgroups of subjects (introverts, extraverts, and ambiverts) are comparable statistically because each subject had an equal opportunity to be located in the institutional files. Although it should be mentioned that there may have been migratory differences between the subgroups, the author is not acquainted with any evidence which would indicate that such a factor as geographical mobility might have caused any distortion of the results of the study.

Of the 35 subjects who committed adult crimes, 20 of them, or 57 per cent, had been juvenile delinquents. Although these figures would seem to suggest that a large proportion of adult criminals have been juvenile delinquents, one must again keep in mind the fact that a child guidance population is likely not to be a representative population. Furthermore, and perhaps more important, the subjects in this study were not necessarily drawn to be representative even of the child guidance population.

The results of the present study all point to the likelihood that extraverted boys are more likely than either introverted or ambiverted boys to become delinquent and/or criminal. Perhaps the most frequent pattern of delinquency is one in which the individuals were extraverted children. But if one can speak at all in terms of delinquent personality patterns, it seems likely that there is more than one pattern. Certainly all delinquents are not classified as previously extraverted children. And, of course, not all extraverted children become delinquent. Although some research has been done on the factors which may go together to cause delinquency, further studies along such lines are needed. Forces which may contribute to delinquency among children of a certain temperament, etc., may not do so among other children and what would be prognostic of delinquency in one group may even be prognostic of social adjustment in another.

SUMMARY AND CONCLUSIONS

This study was undertaken in order to investigate, by means of a long-term follow-up study of male children seen in a child guidance clinic, the relative incidence of later delinquent and criminal behaviour among introverted, extraverted and ambiverted children. The subjects were seen at the Dallas Child Guidance Clinic an average of 28 years prior to the follow-up. On the basis of their Clinic histories, subjects were classified as introverts, extraverts, and ambiverts. There were originally 600 subjects.

The list of subjects was checked against the files of various penal and correctional institutions in Texas. It was found that some of the subjects had already had some record of delinquency before the time they were seen at the Child Guidance Clinic. These subjects were excluded from the the study, and the final group consisted of 551 subjects.

The results corroborate those of some other workers in the field of criminology who have stated that extraverted and ambiverted children, in that order, are more likely than introverted children to become juvenile delinquents.

The results also suggest that the extraverts are proportionately more likely than the introverts or ambiverts to commit not only juvenile delinquent acts but also crimes in adult life.

In the present study, the delinquent children were markedly more likely than the non-delinquents to commit crimes in adult life.

Although among juvenile delinquents there is a trend in favour of the possibility that the introverts would be more likely than the extraverts to 'outgrow' the delinquent pattern of behaviour, it appears that whether a boy is delinquent or not may be more predictive of adult crime than his classification as introvert, extravert or ambivert.

A statistical analysis of the differences between the IQs of the introverts, extraverts and ambiverts; between the IQs of the offender and non-offender groups; and between the ages of the introverts, extraverts and ambiverts at time of referral to the Clinic revealed some significant differences. These data were incidental to the purpose of the study, but provide further ideas concerning differences between the groups.

Perhaps the most frequent pattern of delinquency is one in which the individuals were extraverted children. However, all delinquents are not classified as previously extraverted children, and not all extraverted children become delinquent. There is a need for further studies investigating the various factors which may go together to produce delinquency. It is possible that a factor which may be prognostic of delinquency within one constellation of factors may be prognostic of non-delinquency within some other constellation.

REFERENCES

1. BOVET, L., Psychiatric aspects of juvenile delinquency. *W.H.O.: Monograph Series,* **1,** 1951.
2. GLUECK, S. & GLUECK, ELEANOR, *Unravelling Juvenile Delinquency.* Cambridge, Mass.: Harvard University Press, 1950.
3. MILLER, CARMEN, MORRIS, D. P. & SOROKER, ELEANOR, Follow-up studies of shy, withdrawn children. II: relative incidence of schizophrenia. *Amer. J. Orthopsychiat.,* **27,** 331-337, 1957.
4. MORRIS, D. P., SOROKER, ELEANOR & BURRUSS, GENETTE, Follow-up studies of shy, withdrawn children. I: evaluation of later adjustment. *Amer. J. Orthopsychiat.,* **24,** 743-754, 1954.

_e Inheritance of Extraversion-Introversion

H. J. EYSENCK

First published in _Acta Psychologica_, **12**, 95–110, 1956

INTRODUCTION

THE DATA reported in this paper formed part of an investigation conducted under the writer's direction by Dr H. McLeod and Dr D. Blewett from 1951–1953. This investigation was in part made possible by a grant from the Eugenics Society. Some of the results have been reported in Ph.D. theses (Refs. 2 and 16) and in article form (Ref. 3).

The investigation as a whole was designed to answer a number of different questions, only some of which will be discussed in this paper. In essence we shall be concerned with two closely related problems. The first of these is the factorial definition and measurement of the personality dimension or continuum known as extraversion-introversion; the other is the discovery of the degree to which heredity plays a part in determining a person's position on this continuum. Most of the work on extraversion-introversion has been done with adult subjects; in this study we shall be concerned with school children, mostly of an age between 145 and 185 months.

A number of questions arose in the course of the investigation, or were from the outset considered to determine the design of the experiment. These additional questions, such as, for instance, the relationship between extraversion-introversion and Rorschach's concept of the extratensive/introvertive type of personality, will be discussed as they arise in the course of this paper.

THE PROBLEM OF MEASUREMENT

A considerable amount of experimental material relevant to the measurement of extraversion-introversion has been discussed in previous publications by the present writer (Refs. 5, 6 and 10). By and large the results reported there have shown that there is experimental evidence in favour of the existence of some such personality continuum as Jung postulated, at least among adults, that this dimension can be found, both among normal and among neurotic subjects, and that a variety of different tests could be constructed to measure this dimension with different degrees of reliability and validity. It was further found that, as Jung had postulated, extraverted neurotics tended to develop hysterical or psychopathic symptoms, whereas introverted neurotics tended to develop dysthymic symptoms, such as anxiety, reactive depression, or obsessional features. None of the studies carried out in this laboratory, or available in the literature, had concerned themselves with measurement of extraversion-introversion in children. Consequently it appeared worthwhile to test the hypothesis that behavioural relationships similar to those found among adults could also be found among children to define an extravert-introvert continuum.

Among the types of measures used with adults had been objective behaviour tests, ratings and self-ratings and it seemed desirable to include these divergent types of measures in the children's study also. In addition, however, it was decided to include a rather different type of test, namely, the Rorschach. Although the writer has been somewhat critical of its use as a 'global' measure of personality, some attempts made by members of the department had indicated that when scores on this test are used in the usual psychometric manner, meaningful relations can be established, although (or possibly because) the test thus loses its subjective and interpretive character (Ref. 4). The main reason for introducing the Rorschach into the experiment was, of course, the fact that Rorschach's theory contains the concept of the opposed types of the 'extratensive' and the 'introvertive' person. Although Rorschach workers often deny that these terms are co-extensive with Jung's typology, nevertheless it seemed a reasonable hypothesis to expect a considerable degree of similarity. Curiously enough no test of this hypothesis had ever been carried out previously to our knowledge and consequently a number of Rorschach scores were included in our battery.

In addition to the variables discussed so far, we also included a battery of intelligence tests and a battery of autonomic measures. There are two main reasons for the inclusion of the battery of intelligence tests. In the first place, some at least of the tests used for the measurement of extraversion were known to be also measures of intelligence. Without the inclusion of reliable and valid measures of intelligence, therefore, contamination between the effects of extraversion and those of intelligence might easily have taken place. This is particularly obvious in the case of some of the Rorschach variables. Thus, for instance, a high movement score on the Rorschach, according to Klopfer, indicates high intelligence. It also, however, indicates introversion. Assuming, for the moment, both these hypotheses to be true, before using the M per cent score as a measure of extraversion, we would have to partial out that part of the variance assignable to intelligence.

The second reason for including tests of intelligence in our battery was as follows. Most of the work on the inheritance of intelligence has made use of a single test. This does not seem permissible as Eysenck & Prell have argued in a recent paper (Ref. 11), because the fact that the score on a given test has a high h^2 when a comparison is made between the scores of identical and fraternal twins is indeterminate as long as we have no way of assigning the hereditary component indicated in this way to a specific part of the factor variance.[1] Thus, for example, if the Binet test were found to give much higher intra-class correlations for identical than for fraternal twins, we would still not know whether the hereditary influences thus indicated affected the general intellectual ability measured by the test, or the verbal ability also measured, or the numerical ability, or any of the other factors contributing to the total variance. The conclusion reached by Eysenck & Prell was that it is not test scores which should be submitted to such analysis but factor scores and accordingly a number of intelligence tests were included here to make possible such an analysis of factor scores (Ref. 11).

Also included were a number of autonomic measures, such as systolic and diastolic blood pressure, pulse rate in the resting state and under stress, sub-lingual and finger temperature, and dermographic latency. The main reason for the inclusion of these measures was as follows. In *The Structure of Human Personality* (Ref. 8) a number of studies have been summarized suggesting that autonomic lability may be related to neuroticism. If this were true, then it should follow that autonomic measures of this type should correlate with measures known to be good indicators of neuroticism, such as, for instance, body sway suggestibility. Thus, if autonomic measures and a few known tests of neuroticism were included, and if the theory were to be substantiated by our research, then we would expect, in addition to a factor of extraversion-introversion and a factor of intelligence, also to find a factor of neuroticism containing some, if not all, of these autonomic tests. In this way it was hoped to extend the work begun by Eysenck & Prell in 1951 (Ref. 11).

[1] h^2 is the symbol used by Holzinger to denote a statistic proposed by him as a measure of the degree of hereditary determination of a given trait or ability. For a critical discussion of it, cf. May (Ref. 17).

The actual tests and measures included in this study will be described briefly in the third section; a much longer description will be found in the theses by McLeod & Blewett (Refs. 16 and 2). In most cases the rationale for including a test has not been given here because considerations of space make this impracticable. A thorough documentation can be found in the writer's previous summaries of work done on these problems. Quite generally it may be said that a test was included as a possible measure of introversion-extraversion when it either had in the past been found in factorial analyses to have significant projections on this factor among adults, or when it had in the past been found to differentiate significantly between hysterics, the neurotic prototype of the extravert, and dysthymics, the neurotic prototype of the introvert. This would, of course, be reasonable only on the assumption that the behaviour of children and their responses to the test situation are similar to those of adults. This assumption appears to be reasonable and, as will be seen in the section on Results, is, in fact, borne out.

THE SAMPLE STUDIED

Little need be said here as in all essentials this study is a duplication of the Eysenck-Prell study. We have relied again on the differences found between identical and fraternal twins to give us evidence regarding the hereditary determination of any particular test score or factor score used in the investigation. The general theory is too well-known to be discussed in any detail; it depends on the fact that differences between identical twins must be due to environment; differences between fraternal twins may be due to either environment or heredity. If, therefore, differences between identical twins and differences between fraternal twins are equal in size, the total variance of the particular test under investigation can be ascribed to environmental influences. The greater the similarity of identical twins as compared with fraternal twins, the greater will be the amount of hereditary influence it is necessary to postulate. A convenient formula to assess the amount of hereditary influence has been given by Holzinger. His statistic, which he calls h^2, has frequently been criticized. A general discussion of the twin method, the difficulties which it gives rise to, and possible criticisms of it is given elsewhere (Ref. 11) and a discussion of Holzinger's h^2 statistic will be found in Ref. 17.

The exact details of the population of children used in the present study have been published by Blewett (Ref. 3). Here it is merely necessary to summarize the main points. Our sample was drawn from four metropolitan boroughs in South London. Our thanks here are due to the co-operation of the London County Council who wrote to headmasters of all the L.C.C. secondary schools in the boroughs of Camberwell, Southwark, Lambeth and Lewisham, requesting a report on any twins on their registers. 102 pairs of twins were located, of whom 56 pairs were subsequently tested. Four of these were later dropped on a random basis to equate numbers of pairs in the four groups: male identical, female identical, male fraternal, and female fraternal, retaining 13 pairs in each group. A thorough check was carried out to avoid various well-known sources of error in the selection of the sample; these are discussed in detail by Blewett.

The criteria used in this study were practically identical with those used by Eysenck & Prell, including rating scales for closeness of similarity of facial features, general habitus, hair colour and distribution, iris pigmentation, shape of ears, and teeth. Height and weight were measured and the ability of the subjects to taste phenyl-thio-carbamide was established. In addition, blood groupings and fingerprints were taken into account. Again, details are given by Blewett (Ref. 3) and there is little doubt that the final decision regarding the zygoticity of the twin pairs arrived at on the basis of all these criteria is essentially correct. The mean age of the children tested was 166 months, with a standard deviation of 11 months. Age was partialled out from the intercorrelations in the factor analysis as it seemed essential to have data not contaminated by this variable.

TESTS USED

The tests used in this investigation will now be briefly described. In connection with each will be given an index which will enable the reader to identify it in the factor analysis. The first two variables included in the factor analysis are zygoticity (index number 1) and sex (index number 2); these are not exactly tests in any sense of the word, but are referred to here, nevertheless, in order to keep all the index numbers together. The scoring in these cases was as follows: zygoticity $-M = 1$, $D = 2$; sex $-M = 1$, $F = 0$.

Next we have the set of intelligence tests included in this investigation. Most of these were taken from Thurstone's tests of primary mental abilities for ages 11–17. These are so widely used that it would serve no useful purpose to describe them in detail. The directions given in the Revised Manual (1949) were followed in the administration, and Thurstone's scoring methods were used throughout. The particular tests used were the verbal scale (index number 8), the numbers scale (index number 9), the space scale (index number 16), the reasoning scale (index number 17), the fluency scale (index number 18) and the total score (index number 19), calculated according to Thurstone's formula: $V+S+2N+2R+W$.

In addition, we used the Furneaux level and speed tests. These are described in some detail by Eysenck and by Blewett (Refs. 7 and 3).

Our next set of scores is derived from the Rorschach test. Standard methods of administration, enquiry, and testing the limits were employed. We followed the method outlined by Klopfer & Kelly (Ref. 15). The following scores were used: Popular responses (index number 28), average response time (index number 29), D (index number 31), To÷de $(H+A÷Hd+Ad)$ (index number 32), FM÷M (index number 33), F per cent (index number 34), M per cent (index number 36), FM+m $-Fc+c+C$ (index number 37), range of response times (index number 13) and lastly a composite score of pathological indicators devised by Blewett and given in detail in his thesis (index number 30). Most of these variables had odd and abnormal distributions and had to be transformed in various ways, usually by a logarithmic transformation.

Also included with the Rorschach group might be another test, the Rosenzweig Picture Frustration test, as this too is often considered as a projective technique. The only score used here was the extrapunitive one (index number 35).

The autonomic tests employed were as follows: Systolic blood pressure (index number 39) and diastolic blood pressure (index number 40). (Room temperature and humidity were measured at the time this and the other autonomic tests were administered, and wherever a significant relationship was found, temperature and humidity were partialled out.) The other measures used were pulse rate after stress (the stress consisted of pulling a hand dynamometer ten times, as hard as possible) and pulse rate after resting (index numbers 41 and 42). Sub-lingual temperature (index number 43) and finger temperature (index number 44) were also taken. Lastly, dermographic latency (index number 35) was determined using Wenger's method (Ref. 23).

The next set of variables consisted of ratings and sociometric measures. Questionnaire scales were used, both in the form of self-assessments and teachers' assessments. The scales used were adaptations of Guilford's C and R scales, which have been shown to be good measures of neuroticism and extraversion respectively (Ref. 8). The detailed scales employed are given in the theses by Blewett and McLeod respectively (Refs. 2 and 16). Based on these scales, then, we have a teacher's rating of extraversion (index number 4), a teacher's rating of neuroticism (index number 15), self-ratings of extraversion (index number 5) and self-ratings of neuroticism (index number 7). A lie scale based on the well-known MMPI—but adapted for use with children—was also employed (index number 6).

Two sociability scores were obtained, both derived from a sociometric examination. The subjects were asked simply to write down names of their choice to a series of questions. These questions were of the following kind: 'Whom would you like to sit by during class?', 'Who do you think would choose you to sit beside them in class?', 'Whom would you like to be with after school?' and so forth. The two scores were the total number of names given (index number 53) and the total number of different names given (index number 54). The hypothesis underlying this test was, of course, that extraverts, being more sociable, would give a larger number of names in both categories.

The last set of tests to be considered consists of objective behaviour tests. The first of these is the body sway test of suggestibility (index number 11); the second, the finger dexterity test (index number 14). Both these tests are described fully in *The Scientific Study of Personality* (Ref. 6). Next, we have three tests or rigidity taken from the work of Ferguson and his colleagues (Ref. 20). These are the opposites test (index number 22), the alphabet test (index number 23), and the arithmetic test (index number 24). These tests are based on the interfering effects of highly habituated culturally induced behaviour patterns in tasks involving largely cognitive processes. Another index of rigidity, called the index of flexibility, is a measure of the amount of change in level of aspiration by actual performance (index number 25). It is taken from a test using the so-called triple tester described in *The Scientific Study of Personality* (Ref. 6), as is the affective discrepancy score (index number 50) which is the sum of the goal discrepancy and the judgment discrepancy scores. The rationale and meaning of these scores are discussed in *Dimensions of Personality* (Ref. 5).

Two tests of persistence were included, namely, the leg persistence test (index number 26) and the dynamometer persistence test (index number 27). Both tests have been described in previous publications. As a test of expressive movement two of Mira's tasks were used, namely, the drawing of sagittal lines and the drawing of vertical lines (Ref. 19). The score on this test was the total area covered by the lines (index number 38). Two tests of humour were included, one of orectic (index number 46) and one of cognitive (index number 47) humour. The test consisted of 30 cartoons which had to be rated with respect to the amusement derived from them; the rationale for this test is given in *Dimensions of Personality* (Ref. 5).

The Porteus Maze test was also given to the children. As Hildebrand and Foulds have shown (Refs. 13 and 12), certain qualitative performances differentiate hysterics from dysthymics. Included in our study, therefore, were scores 'wrong directions' (index number 48) and 'lifted pencils' (index number 49). Two scores were also taken from the track tracer described in *Dimensions of Personality* (Ref. 5). One of these is an accuracy score, the other one a speed score (index number 51 and 52).

Last of all, a score was included consisting of the level-speed discrepancy on the Furneaux test (index number 21). Here a high score indicates a lack of such discrepancy; in view of results reported by Eysenck (Ref. 7), this may be regarded as evidence of normality.

RESULTS

Variables indexed in the section above were intercorrelated, the effect of age was partialled out from the intercorrelations and a factorial analysis undertaken of the resulting matrix. In order to avoid subjective determination of axis rotations by the writer, the rotations were carried out in the statistical section of the writer's department under the direction of Mr A. E. Maxwell. The results are therefore not influenced by the writer's own conceptions, although this may, of course, intrude in the interpretation of the results given later on. However, the reader will be able to check these interpretations against the figures. Table 1 gives the factor saturations for the 52 variables on the 6 factors extracted, as well as the communalities. The peculiar constitution of the sample, i.e. the fact that it is composed of closely related subjects, makes it impossible to apply any known tests of significance to the residuals and we have probably erred in taking out more factors than is warranted. However, no interpretation is here attempted of the last three factors and those with which we shall be concerned are indubitably both significant and meaningful.

The main loadings on factors I and II have been plotted in Fig. 14 and it will be seen that we are dealing essentially with the factors of intelligence and extraversion-introversion. The identification of the intelligence factor leaves very little room for doubt. The Thurstone total score has a loading of 0·947. All the other Thurstone scores have appropriately high loadings (verbal = 0·695; number = 0·569; space = 0·635; reasoning = 0·821; frequency = 0·629). The two Furneaux scores had loadings of 0·529 and 0·677. Finger dexterity, as is reasonable with children, has a loading of 0·389. Two of the rigidity tests have high loadings; the opposites test 0·579 and the alphabet test 0·656. The nature of the material used makes these high correlations intelligible and suggests that these tests cannot properly be used with children. It is not unexpected to find that the Mazes 'wrong direction' score has a high negative correlation with intelligence (−0·448) or that inaccuracy on the track tracer has a somewhat slighter negative correlation (−0·389). It may be surprising and is certainly interesting that the more intelligent apparently give more truthful self-ratings; the correlation between truthfulness on the lie scale and the intelligence factor is 0·374.

TABLE 1

Variable	I	II	III	IV	V	VI	h²
22	0·579	−0·103	−0·055	0·091	0·019	−0·034	0·359
14	0·389	0·012	−0·215	0·037	0·099	−0·016	0·209
8	0·695	−0·016	0·014	−0·181	−0·050	0·062	0·523
11	0·258	0·090	0·061	−0·162	−0·062	−0·025	0·109
20	0·529	−0·006	−0·041	−0·293	−0·092	−0·042	0·378
16	0·635	0·105	−0·066	0·106	0·037	−0·033	0·432
19	0·947	0·075	0·124	0·036	−0·015	0·075	0·925
10	0·677	−0·019	0·291	0·285	0·101	−0·086	0·624
18	0·629	−0·071	0·225	−0·057	−0·048	0·092	0·465
9	0·569	0·096	0·200	0·047	0·025	0·162	0·402
40	0·232	−0·230	0·452	0·015	−0·014	−0·046	0·314
17	0·821	0·095	0·123	0·198	0·040	−0·021	0·739
23	0·656	0·151	0·264	0·197	−0·011	0·038	0·563
6	0·374	0·200	0·109	−0·301	−0·046	−0·015	0·285
34	−0·296	0·286	0·095	0·089	−0·124	−0·067	0·206
24	−0·161	−0·106	0·219	−0·140	−0·010	−0·099	0·115
48	−0·448	0·013	0·110	−0·231	−0·021	0·071	0·272
51	−0·389	0·162	0·041	−0·016	0·006	−0·098	0·189
15	−0·159	0·165	−0·177	0·084	0·021	0·005	0·091
44	0·031	0·300	−0·181	−0·066	0·056	−0·023	0·132
33	−0·090	0·501	−0·292	0·137	−0·013	−0·046	0·365
1	0·167	0·217	−0·166	−0·226	0·057	−0·010	0·157
46	−0·149	0·162	−0·026	−0·358	−0·077	−0·002	0·183
28	0·095	0·242	0·107	−0·227	0·023	0·106	0·142
31	0·164	0·510	0·106	−0·192	0·047	0·077	0·343
26	−0·004	0·229	0·129	−0·087	0·050	0·167	0·107
53	0·073	0·632	−0·017	0·061	0·011	−0·067	0·413
54	0·121	0·574	−0·094	0·094	0·029	−0·083	0·370
43	−0·121	0·200	0·620	0·034	0·011	0·096	0·450

TABLE 1 *continued*

Variable	I	II	III	IV	V	VI	h²
36	0·191	−0·626	0·175	−0·084	−0·030	0·014	0·467
52	−0·098	−0·378	−0·047	−0·171	0·050	0·115	0·200
30	0·013	−0·396	−0·022	−0·272	0·096	−0·078	0·247
32	0·112	−0·189	−0·191	−0·264	−0·013	0·050	0·157
38	−0·045	0·027	0·184	−0·215	0·051	−0·087	0·088
49	−0·148	−0·111	0·177	−0·250	−0·092	−0·049	0·137
42	0·076	−0·066	0·913	0·148	0·006	−0·026	0·894
2	0·065	−0·057	0·855	0·122	−0·054	−0·025	0·781
29	−0·079	0·032	0·162	0·594	−0·126	−0·016	0·402
5	−0·104	−0·091	−0·282	−0·030	−0·135	0·011	0·118
27	−0·020	0·013	−0·197	0·141	−0·037	0·127	0·077
50	0·124	0·007	−0·447	0·123	−0·164	0·009	0·257
21	−0·136	−0·015	−0·240	−0·466	−0·172	0·035	0·324
45	0·193	−0·002	−0·216	−0·233	0·023	−0·049	0·141
47	−0·096	−0·056	−0·192	−0·406	0·001	−0·096	0·223
13	−0·006	−0·100	0·109	0·530	−0·118	−0·024	0·317
7	0·076	0·095	0·140	−0·350	−0·073	−0·023	0·163
4	0·042	0·176	−0·042	−0·326	0·073	−0·045	0·148
35	0·096	0·119	0·103	−0·228	0·021	0·024	0·087
25	0·032	−0·009	0·062	−0·197	−0·048	0·082	0·053
39	−0·019	−0·132	0·389	0·063	0·066	0·037	0·179
41	0·108	−0·123	0·839	0·115	−0·002	−0·013	0·744
37	0·065	−0·121	0·290	−0·059	−0·027	−0·011	0·107

An interesting feature of this study is the complete failure of the Rorschach scores to correlate with intelligence. The only one to achieve even the very modest correlation of −0·296 is the Rorschach F per cent. This, in spite of the fact that of all the scores included, the F per cent score is one of the few that is in general considered not to be a measure of intelligence. M, which is usually taken as a good index of intelligence, only achieves a correlation of 0·191. It is difficult not to conclude that the Rorschach scores which we have used here, and for many of which extravagant claims have been made as measures of ability, fail to measure intelligence to any significant extent.

We now come to the second factor which has been identified as extraversion. Before discussing this interpretation it will be necessary to present some details regarding the method followed in interpreting the Rorschach scores. While there is a good deal of agreement among Rorschach writers in the interpretation of certain scores, this agreement

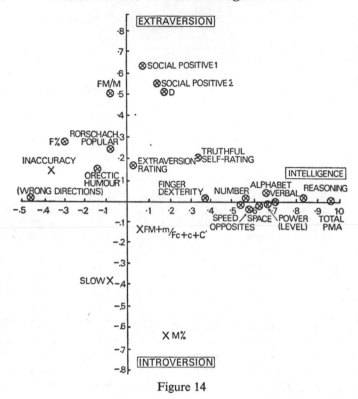

Figure 14

is far from perfect and it would be possible in a posteriori fashion to explain away discordant findings by referring to some obscure authority as having interpreted this particular score in the manner required to substantiate one's own hypothesis. To avoid this danger, the following method was followed. The scores used were communicated to an expert who had been using the Rorschach clinically and teaching it to students for a number of years. He was requested to write down in detail the relevance of each of the scores to the three variables of intelligence, extraversion-introversion, and neuroticism. He was to base himself entirely on the agreed interpretations of the most widely accepted Rorschach authorities, and on independent factual research evidence. His decisions were written down and implicitly followed in our inter-pretation; wherever necessary they will be quoted in full. This, of course, does not ensure that other Rorschach experts will necessarily agree; it does ensure that our interpretation of the results is not falsified by an attempt to justify observed findings in the manner outlined at the beginning of this paragraph.

Let us now look at the variables defining the two poles of the factor which we have identified as one of extraversion-introversion. The variable having the highest saturation on the introverted side is M per cent (−0·626). According to the expert, 'a high M suggests introversion, a low M extraversion'. This interpretation has found a good deal of factual support, such as, for instance, a recent study by Barron (Ref. 1) who has attempted to devise a psychometric measure of M by means of a series of specially constructed blots and who found considerable correlations between movement scores and introverted personality traits. The other introversion score is indicative of slow and accurate work on the track tracer (−0·378); this Himmelweit (Ref. 14) and Eysenck (Ref. 5) have found indicative of introversion.

On the extraverted side, the two scores having the highest saturations are the two sociometric scores indicative of social popularity and general social liking (0·632 and 0·574). This relationship between extraversion and positive social relationships is, of course, in line with our hypothesis. Only slightly less highly correlated with extraversion is the Rorschach D score (0·510). This is what our authority has to say about a high D score: 'A high D is said to indicate a "practical" man, a down to earth extravert; a low D is said to indicate a "theoretical" man, a "theorizer". A high D is associated with hysteria, a low D with dysthymia'. The interpretation is thus in accord with our hypothesis. Almost equally high as the D score is the FM ÷ M score (0·501). This score, of course, is not independent of the M score we have already considered, and can therefore not be used to add very much to our interpretation of the latter. However, for what it is worth, our authority summarizes the literature by saying that a high FM ÷ M ratio 'may indicate extraversion', a low FM ÷ M ratio 'may indicate normality, but also introversion and intelligence'.

The F per cent score has a correlation with the extraversion factor of 0·286. The interpretation of this score appears excessively difficult. Our authority says that 'a high F per cent is found in the records of psychopaths; a high F per cent is found in the records of many hysterics ("flat hysterics")'. This would suggest that a high F per cent is indicative of extraversion. Against this hypothesis speaks the fact that 'a high F per cent indicates "over-control" which could characterize an introverted neurotic'. Altogether, 'experts seem in some disagreement' so that we cannot really interpret this particular score. The next Rorschach score, the number of popular replies, has a factor of 0·242. According to our expert, 'a large number of popular responses suggests a dull extraverted person or hysteric'. Apparently 'a small number of popular responses suggests a person out of contact with his environment, or may be due to a perfectionist attitude exhibited by obsessive, compulsive neurotics'. In all, he concludes that 'a high number of popular responses might, therefore, suggest extraversion, a low number, introversion'.[1]

Three more scores are to be considered and lend weight to this interpretation. Inaccurate work on the track tracer has a loading of 0·162 which, although low, is in the right direction. Orectic humour also has a loading of 0·162 which is also low, but again in the right direction. Truthful self-ratings, with a loading of 0·200, is slightly higher and also in line with previous work which has shown a slight tendency for extraverts to obtain more truthful scores on the lie scale. With the possible exception of the F per cent score, we can therefore say that all the scores considered support the interpretation of this factor as one of extraversion-introversion.

A number of items have moderately high correlations with the factor but have not been considered in this connection because they neither argue for nor against our interpretation and may be chance projections on this factor. Among these scores are, for instance, item 44, high finger temperature, which has a correlation of 0·300, and item 40, high diastolic blood pressure, which has a correlation of −0·230. Our data are not sufficient to make it possible for us to say whether these additional items, which the reader may like to study intensively in Table 1, throw any additional light on either the identification of the factor or its measurement. The work of Theron and of Van der Merwe (Refs. 21 and 22), as summarized in *The Structure of Human Personality* (Ref. 8), has opened up the possibility that extraversion-introversion may be related to certain autonomic measures, and certainly this line of enquiry is promising and deserves to be followed up. It cannot, however, be

---

[1] Score 37, the Rorschach FM+m÷Fc+c+C has a loading of −0·121 and should therefore be a measure of introversion. According to our authority 'high FM+m is probably introverted, high Fc+c+C probably extraverted by majority opinion'. This is in line with our hypothesis, but the correlation is much too small to carry any weight. It may, however, serve to counterbalance item 32, the Rorschach To÷de where 'a high score is indicative of an uncritical attitude, perhaps suggesting abnormal extraversion'. Here also the correlation (−0·189) is too small to carry much weight. Ratios, in view of their well-known statistical unreliability, should never be used in work of this kind, particularly when the scores entering into the ratios are themselves not very reliable (Ref. 18).

maintained that at the present moment our results throw any further light on this problem.

A few words may be said about the third factor. This, quite clearly, is an autonomic one, having very high saturations indeed on pulse rate resting (0·913), pulse rate stressed (0·839), systolic and diastolic blood pressure (0·389 and 0·452) and on sub-lingual temperature (0·620). Finger temperature is rather out of line (−0·181), but this may be due to difficulties and inaccuracies of measurement. Dermographic latency has a relatively low loading of −0·216. The interpretation of this factor as an autonomic one appears somewhat invalidated, however, by the fact that item 2 (sex) has a very high loading of 0·855. This suggests that quite possibly the correlations observed are produced very largely by sex differences, and are therefore of less interest than they might otherwise be. No further analysis or discussion of this factor will be given here as it does not seem relevant to our main purpose. The same may be said of the remaining three factors, which do not lend themselves to any obvious interpretation and will therefore not be considered any further.

Factor scores were estimated for the first three factors. For the extraversion-introversion factors, the following items were used: 53, 54, 31, 33, 28, 4, 6, 46, 52, 36. For the intelligence factor, the following items were used: 17, 10, 16, 18, 8, 9, 20, 14, 48. For the autonomic factors, the following items were used: 39, 40, 41, 42, 43, 44, 45. Thus, each one of our subjects obtained scores on the three factors of intelligence, extraversion, and autonomic activity.

TABLE 2

	Intelligence	Extraversion	Autonomic
Intelligence	—	0·030	−0·103
Extraversion	0·155	—	−0·018
Autonomic	−0·074	0·001	—

Intercorrelations of factor scores for identical twins (below leading diagonal) and for fraternal twins (above leading diagonal).

Intercorrelations of factor scores were calculated for fraternal twins and identical twins separately, and are given in Table 2. It will be seen that there are no significant relationships between the factors. Next, intra-class correlations were run for the three factors between the identical and also between the fraternal sets of twins. These correlations, as well as the h^2 values calculated from them, are given in Table 3. A test

o

was made of the significance of the differences between the intraclass correlations. For the intelligence factor, $t = 2.13$; for the extraversion factor, $t = 2.43$; for the autonomic factor, $t = 2.09$. The t values for the intelligence and autonomic factors are significant at the 5 per cent level; the t value for extraversion is significant at the 2 per cent level. We may, therefore, conclude with some statistical justification that the differences observed between identical and fraternal twins are unlikely to have been caused by chance factors and would be found again if the study were duplicated. From this it may be concluded that heredity plays a significant part in the causation of all three factors.

TABLE 3

	Identical:	Fraternal:	h^2
Intelligence	0·820	0·376	0·712
Extraversion	0·499	−0·331	(0·624)
Autonomic	0·929	0·718	0·748

Intraclass correlations for identical and fraternal twins, on three factor scores.

One feature in Table 3 requires discussion. It will be seen that the intra-class correlation for the fraternal twins on the extraversion factor has a negative sign. This is an extremely unlikely occurrence on any reasonable hypothesis, but a thorough checking of the figures failed to reveal any errors in calculation. It seems likely that this value represents a chance deviation from a true correlation of zero, or of some slight positive value, an assumption strengthened by the fact that a correlation of the observed size is not statistically significant. Under the circumstances, however, we cannot regard the h^2 statistic derived for the factor of extraversion as having very much meaning, and it has therefore been put in brackets in Table 3 to indicate its extremely doubtful status. Much more reliance, fortunately, can be placed on the significance of the differences between identical and fraternal twins for this factor which, as has been shown above, is fully significant.

SUMMARY AND CONCLUSIONS

In this study an effort has been made to provide evidence for the existence of a factor of extraversion-introversion among children, similar to that found among adults and to measure this factor. By and large, this attempt has been successful and the factorial analysis reported in this paper gives clear evidence of a strong factor of extraversion-introversion.

It was hypothesized that the concept of extraversion-introversion, as operationally defined in the writer's previous work, would be closely parallel to Rorschach's concept of extratensive-introvertive personality. The inclusion of a number of R scores in the factor analysis made it possible to test this hypothesis and the results on the whole favoured acceptance of this theory.

Two further factors were isolated in the analysis, namely, one of intelligence and one of autonomic activity. These additional factors were found to be independent of each other and also to be independent of extraversion-introversion. Factor scores were calculated for all three factors for the members of the experimental populations.

As the major aim of the investigation was to study the effects of heredity on extraversion-introversion, the subjects of the investigation were 13 pairs of male identical twins, 13 pairs of female identical twins, 13 pairs of male fraternal twins, and 13 pairs of female fraternal twins. By using standard methods of intra-class correlation for different types of twins, it was shown that for all three factors, identical twins resembled each other significantly more closely than did fraternal twins. This was regarded as proof that heredity played an important part in the determination of intelligence, extraversion, and autonomic reactivity.

REFERENCES

1. BARRON, F., Threshold for the perception of human movement in inkblots. *J. consult. Psychol.*, **19**, 33–38, 1955.
2. BLEWETT, D. B., An Experimental Study of the Inheritance of Neuroticism and Intelligence. Unpublished Ph.D. thesis, University of London Library, 1953.
3. ——, An experimental study of the inheritance of intelligence. *J. ment. Sci.*, **100**, 922–933, 1954.
4. COX, S, M., A factorial study of the Rorschach response of normal and maladjusted boys. *J. genet. Psychol.*, **79**, 95–115, 1951.
5. EYSENCK, H. J., *Dimensions of Personality*. London: Routledge & Kegan Paul, 1947.
6. ——, *The Scientific Study of Personality*. London: Routledge & Kegan Paul, 1952.

7. ——, La rapidité du Fonctionnement mental comme Mesure de l'Anomalie mentale. *Rev. Psychol. Appl.*, **3**, 367–377, 1953.

8. ——, *The Structure of Human Personality*. London: Methuen, 1953.

9. ——, *The Psychology of Politics*. London: Routledge & Kegan Paul, 1954.

10. ——, A dynamic theory of anxiety and hysteria. *J. ment. Sci.*, **101**, 28–51, 1955.

11. —— & PRELL, D. B., The inheritance of neuroticism: an experimental study. *J. ment. Sci.*, **97**, 441–465, 1951.

12. FOULDS, G. A., Temperamental differences in maze performance. Part 1. characteristic differences among psychoneurotics. *Brit. J. Psychol.*, **42**, 209–218, 1951.

13. HILDEBRAND, H. P., A Factorial Study of Introversion-Extraversion by Means of Objective Tests. Unpublished Ph.D. Thesis, University of London Library, 1953.

14. HIMMELWEIT, H. T., Speed and accuracy of work as related to temperament. *Brit. J. Psychol.*, **36**, 132–144, 1946.

15. KLOPFER, B. & KELLY, D., *The Rorschach Technique*. London: Harrap, 1952.

16. McLEOD, H., An Experimental Study of the Inheritance of Introversion-Extraversion. Unpublished Ph.D. Thesis, University of London Library, 1953.

17. MAY, J., Note on the assumption underlying Holzinger's h^2 statistic. *J. ment. Sci.*, **97**, 466–467, 1951.

18. MEADOWS, A. W., A Factorial Study of Projection Test Responses of Normal, Psychotic and Neurotic Subjects. Unpublished Ph.D. Thesis, University of London Library, 1951.

19. MIRA, E., Myokinetic psychodiagnosis: a new technique of exploring the conative trends of personality. *Proc. R. Soc. Med.*, **33**, 9–30, 1940.

20. OLIVER, J. A. & FERGUSON, G. A., A factorial study of tests of rigidity. *Can. J. Psychol.*, **5**, 49–59, 1951.

21. THERON, P. A., Peripheral vasomotor reactions as indices of basic emotional tension and lability. *Psychosom. Med.*, **10**, 335–346, 1948.

22. VAN DER MERWE, A. B., The diagnostic value of peripheral vasomotor reactions in the psychoneuroses. *Psychosom. Med.*, **10**, 347–354, 1948.

23. WENGER, M. A., Studies of autonomic balance in army air forces personnel. *Comp. Psychol. Monog.*, **19**, 1–111, 1948.

NAME INDEX

SUBJECT INDEX

Activity factor, 160–165
Aggressive-inhibitive factor, 131
Aitken's Pivotal Condensation Method,
  Ledermann's modification, 138
Allport-Vernon-Lindzey Study of Values
  test, 297–305
Alphabet test, 394, 396
Annoyances Questionnaire, 135
Anxiety (see Neuroticism)
Anxiety factor, 180, 181, 184–187, 189–190
Anxiety states, 140
Arithmetic test, 394
Arousal, 49–77
Autonomic measures, 389–390, 401–403

Belmont Hospital, 133
Bernreuter Personality Inventory, 31, 32
Bronfenbrenner Parent Behaviour Ques-
  tionnaire, 359–361, 363–365
Byrne Repression-Sensitization Scale,
  252–258

California Psychological Inventory, Soci-
  ability and Self-Control Scales, 146,
  147, 150
Cattell's IPAT scale, 337
Cattell's 16 P.T. test, 180–192, 345–353,
  359
Character, 18
Children's personalities perceived by
  teachers, 158–168
Cognitive humour test, 394
Colgate Mental Hygiene Inventory C2,
  31, 32
Colgate Personal Inventory C2, 30
Conditionability (see Dynamism), 52
Construct validity, 125
Cool Rationality-Pathemia factor, 180,
  188, 190
Couch-Keniston Agreeing Response
  Scale, 354
Cultured tact-spontaneity factor, 180,
  189

Dermographic latency, 390, 393, 401
Desirability response set in children, 238–
  244
Developmental studies, 309
Diastolic blood pressure, 390, 393, 400,
  401
Discriminant function analysis, 41, 42, 43
Disposition, 18
Dominance factor, 195
Duncan's Range test, 300
Dynamism of nervous system, 52–77
Dynamometer persistence test, 394
Dysthymia, 130
Dysthymics, 140, 265

Edwards Social Desirability Scale, 209,
  217–221
Embedded figures test, 259
Emotional stability factor, 166
Emotionality (see Neuroticism)
Expansiveness (sociability) scale, 226
Expressive movements tests, 394
Extraversion-introversion
  and acquiescence response set, 213–215
  and after-images, 39, 40
  and age differences, 155–156
  and alcohol consumption, 260
  and alcohol effects, 24–25
  and arousal, 49–77
  and autonomic vs. central nervous
    system, 29
  and blame, 343
  and birth order, 329–336
  and body build, 11
  and central nervous system, 150
  in children, 159
  and child's age, 335
  and child's attendance at kindergarten,
    335
  and cigarette consumption, 260
  and 'classics' and 'romantics', 19
  and conditionability, 39, 40, 44, 49–77,
    125